The West Midlands from AD 1000

Regional History of England

General Editors: Barry Cunliffe and David Hey

For full details of the series, see pp. xiv–xv

The West Midlands
from AD 1000

Marie B. Rowlands

Longman
London and New York

Longman Group UK Limited
Longman House, Burnt Mill, Harlow
Essex CM20 2JE, England
Associated companies throughout the world

Published in the United States of America
by Longman Inc., New York

First published 1987

British Library Cataloguing in Publication Data

Rowlands, Marie B.
  The West Midlands from AD 1000. – (Regional
  history of England)
  1. Midlands (England) – History
  I. Title   II. Series
  942.4   DA670.M64

ISBN 0-582-49215-7 CSD
ISBN 0-582-49216-5 PPR

Library of Congress Cataloging-in-Publication Data

Rowlands, Marie B., 1932–
  The West Midlands from AD 1000.

  (Regional history of England)
  Half title: The West Midlands from AD 1000.
  Bibliography: p.
  Includes index.
  1. West Midlands (England) – History.   2. West
Midlands (England) – Economic conditions.   3. West
Midlands (England) – Social conditions.   I. Title.
II. Title: West Midlands from AD 1000.   III. Series.
DA670.W495R68   1986   942.4′9   85–19872
ISBN 0–582–49215–7
ISBN 0–582–49216–5 (pbk.)

Set in Linotron 202 10/12pt Sabon Roman
Produced by Longman Singapore Publishers (Pte) Ltd.
Printed in Singapore.

Contents

Part two:
The Later Middle Ages

Part three:
Adjusting to changing conditions

List of plates

List of figures

List of tables

Note: Unprinted primary sources have been listed separately from printed primary and secondary sources in the Bibliography. Documents in the list of unprinted sources are identified by (U) in the text.

General Preface

England cannot be divided satisfactorily into recognisable regions based on former kingdoms or principalities in the manner of France, Germany or Italy. Few of the Anglo-Saxon tribal divisions had much meaning in later times and from the eleventh century onwards England was a united country. English regional identities are imprecise and no firm boundaries can be drawn. In planning this series we have recognised that any attempt to define a region must be somewhat arbitrary, particularly in the Midlands, and that boundaries must be flexible. Even the South-West, which is surrounded on three sides by the sea, has no agreed border on the remaining side and in many ways, historically and culturally, the River Tamar divides the area into two. Likewise, the Pennines present a formidable barrier between the eastern and western counties on the Northern Borders; contrasts as much as similarities need to be emphasised here.

The concept of a region does not imply that the inhabitants had a similar experience of life, nor that they were all inward-looking. A Hull merchant might have more in common with his Dutch trading partner than with his fellow Yorkshireman who farmed a Pennine smallholding: a Roman soldier stationed for years on Hadrian's Wall probably had very different ethnic origins from a native farmer living on the Durham boulder clay. To differing degrees, everyone moved in an international climate of belief and opinion with common working practices and standards of living.

Yet regional differences were nonetheless real; even today a Yorkshireman may be readily distinguished from someone from the South East. Life in Lancashire and Cheshire has always been different from life in the Thames Valley. Even the East Midlands has a character that is subtly different from that of the West Midlands. People still feel that they belong to a particular region within England as a whole.

In writing these histories we have become aware how much regional identities may vary over time; moreover how a farming region, say, may not coincide with a region defined by its building styles or its dialect. We have dwelt upon the diversity that can be found within a region as well as upon common characteristics in order to illustrate the local peculiarities of provincial life. Yet despite all these problems of definition, we feel that the time is ripe to attempt an ambitious scheme outlining the history of England's regions in 21 volumes. London has not been included – except for demonstrating the many ways in which it has influenced the provinces – for its history has been very different from that of the towns and rural parishes that are our principal concern.

In recent years an enormous amount of local research both historical and archaeological has deepened our understanding of the former concerns of ordinary men and women and has altered our perception of everyday life in the past in many significant ways, yet the results of this work are not widely known even within the regions themselves.

This series offers a synthesis of this new work from authors who have themselves been actively involved in local research and who are present or former residents of the regions they describe.

Each region will be covered in two linked but independent volumes, the first covering the period up to AD 1000 and necessarily relying heavily on archaeological data, and the second bringing the story up to the present day. Only by taking a wide time-span and by studying continuity and change over many centuries do distinctive regional characteristics become clear.

This series portrays life as it was experienced by the great majority of the people of South Britain or England as it was to become. The 21 volumes will – it is hoped – substantially enrich our understanding of English history.

Barry Cunliffe
David Hey

Regional History of England

General Editors: Barry Cunliffe (to AD 1000) and David Hey (from AD 1000)

The regionalisation used in this series is illustrated on the map opposite.

*already published

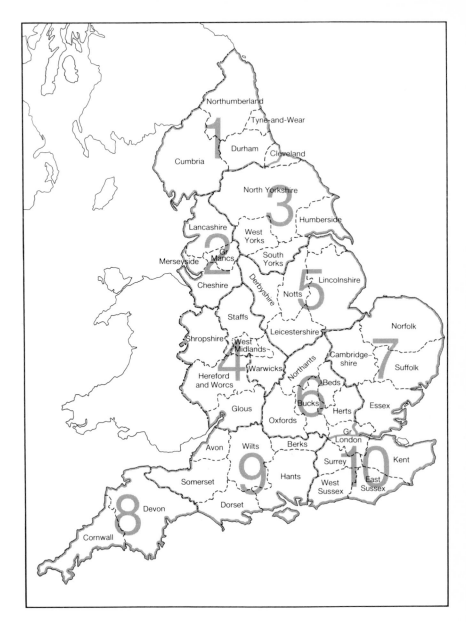

1. The Northern Counties
2. The Lancashire/Cheshire Region
3. Yorkshire
4. The Severn Valley and West Midlands
5. The East Midlands
6. The South Midlands and the Upper Thames
7. The Eastern Counties
8. The South West
9. Wessex
10. The South East

Glossary

agister   A Royal Forest official who received payment for the tenants' beasts pastured in the forest by the tenants.

assart   an intake of land from the waste or forest.

boonworks   A day's work performed for the lord by a tenant on special occasions or at particular seasons.

bordars   One of the lowest ranks in feudal society. A bordar was allocated some land for subsistence and performed menial work for the lord.

brazier   One who works in brass.

breviary   A book containing the prayers, readings and other texts for the daily recitation of the divine office required of all persons in holy orders.

burgage   A land or tenement held in a town and subject to the customs of the town.

chandler   One who made and sold candles.

chape   The iron spike of a buckle.

coneygre   Rabbit warren.

dassels   Pack saddles for a pack horse.

enches   Customary tenants working full-time for the lord of the manor.

escheat   The reversion to the lord or the crown of an estate.

famuli   Full time workers for the lord of the manor.

feet of fines   Copies of judgments concerning the legal use of specified land after real or fictitious disputes at law.

ferretts   Silk tape.

firma burgi   Payment to the Crown by a town.

foreign   Land surrounding a town and associated with it.

foro   A market.

frankpledge (view of)   The inhabitants of each vill were bound to stand security for each other's good behaviour. They were grouped in tithings, and the tithings were reviewed by the sheriff or by the court leet. The inspection was called the view of frankpledge.

frankpledge   In Saxon times certain villagers were bound to stand security for the good behaviour of the village. The view of frankpledge ensured that the system was maintained. In practice the manorial court leet usually took over the responsibility from the sheriff.

fuller (fulling mills)   One who thickens cloth with fuller's earth or hydrous silicate of alumina. The process of beating the cloth was performed by water power in fulling mills.

hays   An enclosure in woodland for the management of animals.

xvi

heriot   Payments made by the heir of a deceased tenant on entering the holding; heriots usually included the best beast and other goods.

hide   An ancient measure of land for assessment varying in area with soil quality. It could be as little as 60 acres or as much as 180 acres but is often taken to be a notional 120 acres.

inkles   Narrow decorative tapes.

inquisitiones post mortem (IPM)   Inquiry to establish the date of death of a tenant-in-chief of the King, the age of the heir, and the lands held, together with the rents and dues payable by his tenants.

leet   Court (yearly or half yearly) or record held by lords of the manor.

litharge   Monoxide of lead.

lorimer (lorrimer)   One who makes the metal parts for horse harness, e.g. spurs, bits, buckles etc.

malster   One who makes and sells malt.

mandrel   A miner's pick.

mercer   A retailer of cloth and other commodities.

merchet   Payment to the lord on the occasion of the marriage of the daughter of an unfree tenant.

missal   A book containing prayers and readings for masses.

nativii   Unfree tenants.

nuncupatory will   A will which was spoken or dictated, not written.

opus dei (Divine Office)   The 'work of God', i.e. the regular sequence of prayers at fixed intervals through the day by priests, members of religious orders and some lay men and women. Also known as the 'hours'.

ordines romanae   The official liturgy of the Roman Church.

pannage   A payment made by tenants to their lord for the right to pasture pigs in the lord's waste or woodland.

Paraphrases   The *Paraphrases* or commentary on Holy Scriptures written by Erasmus, and ordered to be placed in all churches in 1552.

pinder   The parish official responsible for the pound or pinfold where stray beasts were kept.

portmoot   A town court.

psalter   Book containing the psalms.

radman   A man who gave service to his lord on horseback.

regarder.   A forest official.

shearman   One who finished woollen cloth by shaving the nap.

strike   A measure of grain usually equal to a bushel, 4 pecks or 8 gallons.

subinfeudated   The regranting of land by a tenant-in-chief of the King to an inferior on the same terms as he held it from his superior.

tallage   Tax taken by the lord from his unfree tenants. Tallage was also taken by the King from tenants in towns and boroughs of ancient demesne.

treen ware   Wooden ware.

verderer   An officer responsible for the presentation of offenders against forest law.

vill   Feudal township.

villeins   An unfree tenant. In return for his holding he was required to perform services and pay fines and other customary payments. His holding was at the will of the lord.

virgate   A variable measure of land. It could be as little as 15 acres or as much as 60 acres, but was normally about 30 acres. Also known as a yardland.

woodwards   Officers in a royal forest.

Acknowledgements

I am grateful to many friends and colleagues for help in the making of this book. In particular I should like to thank Dr David Hey, Dr Christopher Dyer, Professor David Palliser, Dr Bill Wardle, Dr Peter Coss and Dr Peter Challinor who all read early drafts of the book and substantially improved it by their comments, corrections and suggestions. I would also like to thank Dr Stanley Ellis, lately of Leeds University, who most generously made available to me an account of midland dialect based upon his lifetime of study of regional speech. I would like to thank Mr Paul Bradley and Mr Paul Beattie who prepared the maps and photographs, Mrs Rose and Miss Cleveland who not only typed the whole manuscript twice but made so many valuable suggestions, and Hazel Clawley who prepared the index. Above all I would like to thank Mrs G. M. Rowlands who read and improved every successive version, who visited with me almost every parish in Staffordshire and Warwickshire, and without whose encouragement the book could never have been completed.

The publishers wish to acknowledge the following for their specific permission to reproduce plates in the text: (3.2, 3.3, 3.4 and 3.5) by permission of the British Library; (2.2, 2.4, 5.2, 5.9, 5.10 and 6.5) Coventry City Libraries; (4.1, 4.2, 4.5, 5.4, 5.5 and 6.4) University of Reading, Institute of Agricultural History and Museum of English Rural Life; (1.1, 1.2, 4.9, 4.11, 5.1, 5.3, 5.6, 5.7, 5.8, 6.1, 6.2 and 6.3) reproduced by permission of the Reference Library Department, Birmingham Public Libraries; (2.3) by courtesy of the Vicar, Burton Dassett Parish Church; and (2.1, 3.1, 4.3, 4.4, 4.6, 4.7, 4.8, 5.11 and 6.6) William Salt Library. We have unsuccessfully attempted to trace the copyright holder of plate 4.10, and would appreciate any information that would enable us to do so.

M. B. Rowlands
Newman College
Birmingham
July 1986

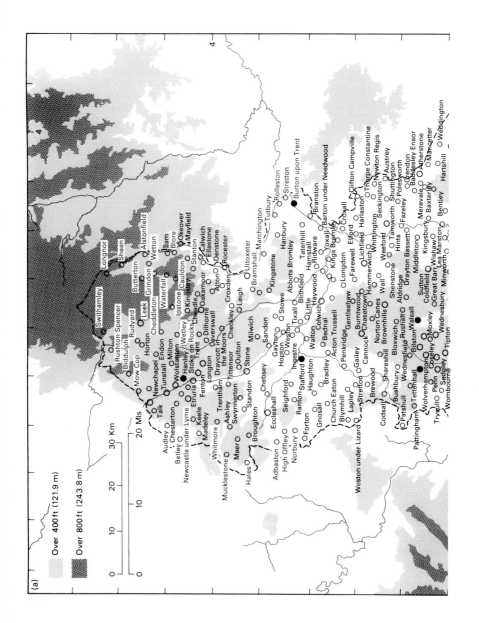

(b)

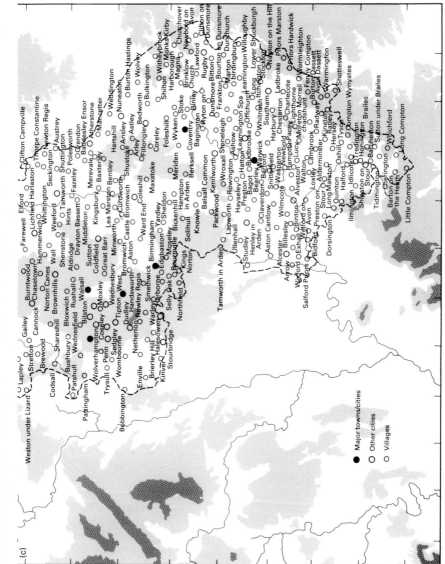

Figure 1.1 ((a), (b) and (c))   Villages and towns of Staffordshire and Warwickshire (based on Mee 1936–7)

Introduction

The area to be studied is that which was from 1974 to 1986 defined for administrative purposes as the counties of Staffordshire, Warwickshire, and the metropolitan county of the West Midlands, an area some 70–80 miles from south to north and 30–40 miles from east to west. At Long Compton, Cherington and Brailes in the southernmost part of Warwickshire the eastern Cotswolds meet the Oxfordshire plain. The oldest buildings in these places are of warm yellow oolite limestone, and manor house, church, inn and market place lie close together surrounded by fields sleek in summer sunshine. Only 80 miles further north on the millstone grit of the Pennines is the hamlet of Flash: at 1,518 ft, claiming to be the highest in England. Hereabouts families work through bitter spring days and cold summers on the moors, and live in isolated greystone farms miles from church, shop or neighbour.

The feature which most quickly identifies someone belonging to the Midlands is their manner of speaking, the combination of pronunciation and word usage which even today can be readily linked with a particular district. Characteristically the midland language is itself mixed and variable from north to south and east to west, for it still reflects variations within the area of settlement contacts and environment which will be the constant frame of reference for much of this study.

Stanley Ellis of Leeds University characterises midland speakers as follows:

> The whole of Staffordshire and the western part of Warwickshire are traditionally in the west Midland dialect area. Certain features that we can still hear today from old people, such as the pronunciation of '–an' and '–am' in words like 'man', 'bank' and 'hammer' as 'mon', 'bonk' and 'hommer', are observable in fourteenth-century spellings where 'o' is used. This feature is not heard in east Warwickshire dialect and so those who use pronunciations like 'mon' must be from west Warwickshire or Staffordshire.
>
> On the other hand, north Warwickshire and Staffordshire

1

speakers do not lengthen the 'a' sound in words like 'last' and 'bath' as south Warwickshire folk do. In Staffordshire and north Warwickshire too the tendency is to pronounce a 'g' at the end of words like 'long' and 'tongue', in central and north Staffordshire the tendency is to make the words rhyme, using an 'o' vowel. North Staffordshire is perhaps most famous for its conversion of the standard 'ee' vowel in words like 'cheese' into an 'ey' pronunciation, and words with 'a' or 'ai' like 'came' and 'drain' come out as 'keem' and 'dreen'.

Another feature of north and central Staffordshire not heard elsewhere in the area is the use of the old negative –ne tacked on to a word instead of the later form 'not'. These various specialities manage to produce catchphrases for north Staffordshire such as 'I munne see I conne say it', a totally inadequate rendering on paper of the local 'I mustn't say I can't see it'.

In north Staffordshire and Warwickshire they always used to 'keep chicken', but in south Staffordshire and Warwickshire they would 'keep fowl'. In north Staffordshire they said 'jed' for 'dead', and 'shulling' for 'shelling' peas. However, we must not always think of north Staffordshire as the odd one out, for the local pronunciation of words like 'flies' and 'sky' with a kind of 'oi' sound is one that the whole county traditionally shares with Warwickshire.

One noticeable feature in Warwickshire south of Birmingham that still remains in rural speech is the traditional 'r' sound after a vowel in words such as 'turn' and 'heard'. In the speech of the north and east of England this ancient sound has disappeared, though still left in the spelling.

Speech such as this is generally heard from older people who have lived in the smaller towns in Staffordshire and Warwickshire and in the villages. The city of Birmingham, growing fast in the nineteenth century, produced an identifiable speech of its own, partaking of many of the local region's features but developing a distinctive local flavour, and that speech in turn 'split off' into varieties in the suburbs to the north and south. 'Brummy' speech is recognisable as distinct from north Staffordshire, but recently an identifiable city speech from Birmingham has spread out towards Dudley and Stratford.

(Ellis 1984)

These variations are the product of centuries of conversations with family, with neighbours and with strangers, and reflect a sense of community derived not only from language, but from common experience of getting a living, of nurture, of local government and of ideas. Many influences combine to create this sense of a particular local identity and of these the most basic is the nature of the land itself.

The mid land is crossed by two important rivers, the Trent and the Avon.

The Trent rises at 800 ft on Biddulph Moor, bisects Staffordshire and flows slowly in a south-easterly direction before turning north to pass through Derbyshire and Nottinghamshire to join the Humber and enter the North Sea. Further south the Avon flows south-west, bisecting Warwickshire and Gloucestershire before meeting the Severn and passing into the Atlantic. Both rivers acted to some extent as natural boundaries in the early Middle Ages. To the south of the Avon lay agricultural land known as the Feldon and to the north of the river the pastoral woodland called the Arden, a distinction noted by all topographers writing about Warwickshire from Camden onwards, and rightly so for it underlies much of the history of the county. The river Trent was also a boundary dividing civilised Roman Britain from military Roman Britain, Anglo-Saxon Mercia from the Pennine British and the Cornovii, and later English Wessex from the Danelaw. The landforms of the Midlands range from alluvial lowlands less than 100 ft above sea-level to moorlands above 1,000 ft, and the variations of geology relief and climate produce many different environments for man. It is convenient to divide the two counties into nine districts to indicate the broad differences in topography, resources and accessibility within the Midlands.

A broad swathe of land on either side of the *river Avon* is composed of a series of river terraces, and their level surfaces and light well-drained soils make them particularly suitable for cultivation. They attracted settlement from very early times, and by 1086 cultivation probably occupied much of the valley space. The Avon basin ranges from 250 to 100 ft in height. It is overlooked to the south by *the Feldon*, a low, gently undulating plateau about 300–400 ft in height, rising in the south to the ridge of Edge Hill (700 ft) and to the scarp foot of the Cotswolds. The Lower Lias clay and limestone produce calcareous clays which were very heavy and tended to become either water-logged or hard but which were nevertheless cleared and cultivated from an early period. North of the Avon was the area known as *the Arden* which was composed of Keuper marl and upper carboniferous rocks which provided a medium loam soil and probably remained well-wooded until the eleventh century (Thorpe 1971:32). The land lies at about 200–400 ft above sea-level and is gently undulating in character and merges in the north into the basin of the Tame, Blythe and Cole rivers. To the east lies the east Warwickshire coalfield with its heavy loam and clay soils. In the north-east of Warwickshire the soils are sandy and pebbly.

To the north-west of Warwickshire lies the Birmingham plateau and the *south Staffordshire coalfield*. Here the land rises to 400–800 ft and its highest point at Walton Hill to 1,000 ft. The clay soils are heavy to work but at the heart of the plateau the 10-yard seam of coal outcrops providing some of the most accessible coal in England. The area also contains iron ore and limestone and an extrusion of basalt. To the west of the boundary fault of the coalfield the land changes abruptly and in the *valleys of the Stour and Smestow* the land is free-draining, easy to work and the climate is slightly milder than other parts of the Midlands. It was an area of early settlement with links with the Severn valley further west. A little further north *central Staffordshire* is open undulating land under 400 ft, drained by the rivers Sow and Penk where the Keuper marl weathers to produce good agricultural loam soils. Western and eastern Staffordshire were divided by the ridge of Cannock Chase, an area of dry stony soils at about 600–700 ft which looked south to the Cannock coalfield and north to the upper Trent. *Eastern and south-eastern Staffordshire* provided some of the best agricultural land in the area. The broad open valleys of the slow-moving Trent and Tame rivers and their tributaries are subject to floods and provide good alluvial soils. Rising above the flood plain is a low, wide gravel terrace which afforded dry settlement sites. *North-western Staffordshire* and the upper reaches of the Trent valley had upland characteristics. The land lies at between 450 and 600 ft and under the heavy clays lay the north Staffordshire coalfield. On the north-western boundary of Staffordshire is a small fertile area adjoining the Cheshire plain. *North-east Staffordshire* lies on the southernmost end of the Pennine chain, a mountainous land rising to over 1,000 ft, with little cultivatable soil and much moorland. To the east the hills are composed of a carboniferous limestone plateau deeply notched with the narrow, steep, sided valleys of the rivers Dove, Manifold and Hamps. The western hills are composed of millstone grit with three grit scarps called 'edges' with few streams or trees, where the water lies on the surface to create acid peaty soils. The hills contain seams of coal and of copper and lead ore (Kinvig 1967: 265–89).

The area presented some obstacles to early travellers but in general was not difficult of access. The rivers were not navigable but the valleys provided routes into the area and enabled settlers to penetrate the higher lands. From at least the Iron Age a long-distance route passed through Warwickshire by which salt was carried from Droitwich to the east Midlands, and a north–south route crossed the Avon continuing north-west to the river Severn. The Romans, when they pushed their attack westward to Wales, built a supply line (later called Watling Street) from London which turned directly west just south of Cannock. When they had consolidated their first advance pausing along the river Trent, a new road, the Fosse Way, was built from north-eastern England to the south-west providing another highway through the Midlands. Later a second crossroute was built further west: Ryknield Street from the south-west through Alcester and Metchley crossing the Watling Street at Letocetum. Another major road linked this with Droitwich and the salt ways. In the north a road from the saltworks of Middlewich crossed Staffordshire leaving the county at Rocester, going towards Littlechester near Derby. From this road a branch went north through the high moors to Buxton. By the eleventh century these roads were already a thousand years old and between them there was a multiplicity of trackways and crossroads recorded in charters and in connection with land disputes. A number of such roads focused on Wolverhampton – for example, Penwie, Alde Street, Port Street and Beorgythes Street (Hooke 1983: 47). The routes of early roads were often determined by the places at which the many rivers of the area could be forded. The road that was to develop into the main London–Carlisle road, for example, crossed Weeford, Meaford, Strongford and Hanford, and the traveller from Stone to Rugeley crossed Shallowford, Bridgford, Stafford, Radford and Milford (SHC 1934: 17–21).

The Midlands was also an area of debatable land frequently subject to competing powers, especially between English and Dane in the tenth century when Edward of Wessex recovered the area and guarded it with fortifications at Tamworth and Stafford. It was during this period that the administrative units of shire and hundred began to be recorded. The boundaries of Staffordshire and of Warwickshire were defined at a late stage of the evolution of settlement and are influenced by other and earlier divisions. The rivers Dove and Trent form part of the north-east boundary of Staffordshire, and Watling Street provided part of the boundary of eastern Warwickshire. The boundary between south Staffordshire and north Worcestershire followed older diocesan boundaries and in south-west Warwickshire the boundary was influenced by the antecedent boundaries of the bishop's lands. In general however the boundaries of both counties were administrative demarcations superimposed on more ancient and natural groupings of people.

The shires were divided into units of administration and finance known as hundreds which also dated from at least the tenth century. Staffordshire had five hundreds each fairly compact in shape. They all derived their names from ancient topographical landmarks. Totmanslow and Offlow were burial mounds, Cuttlestone was at the junction of the Penk and the Sow, and Pirehill was called after a small hill. The changes in hundred boundaries in Staffordshire from the Middle Ages were very slight (Pinnock 1971: 34). The pattern of shire and hundreds was less clear in Warwickshire and took longer to become permanent. Almost the whole of Warwickshire north of the river Avon was originally included in the hundred of Coleshill which later came to be known as Hemlingford Hundred, from the court meeting at Hemlingford Green near the river Tame. The rest of Warwickshire was divided into nine hundreds, all small areas with irregular boundaries, namely Ferncombe, Pathlow, Brinklow, Marton, Stoneleigh, Hunsbury, Tremlow, Foxhole and Barcheston. The boundaries were complicated by detached portions and further by the independent hundred of Pathlow which was a franchise of the Bishop of Worcester for his estates. In the twelfth century the ten royal hundreds were reduced to four – Hemlingford, Knightlow, Barlichway and Kineton (also known as Kington). The episcopal hundred retained some independence as a subsection of Barlichway known as the liberty of Pathlow. The smallest unit of organisation was the township or vill, a group of families living in some sense as a community, with some degree of common concern for the management of resources and the maintenance of order. It is probable that many of the villages recorded in the Domesday account of Staffordshire and north Warwickshire were derived from groups of such small townships and

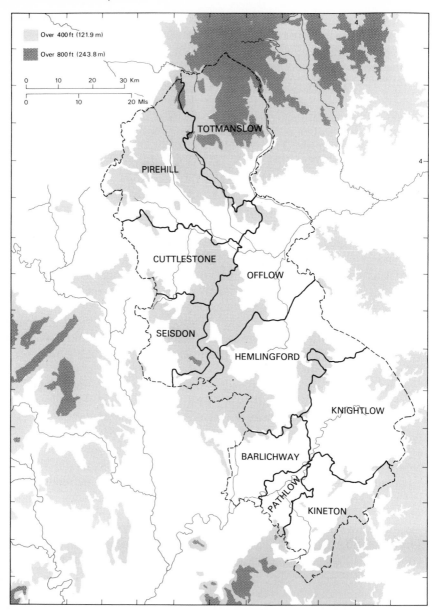

Figure 1.2 The hundreds of Staffordshire and Warwickshire (based on Darby and Terrett 1971)

that the nucleated village was a comparatively late development in the settlement pattern of the woodland and upland areas (Hooke 1981: 34–7; Hooke 1983: 49–51). It certainly cannot be assumed that the village of the eleventh century lay immediately below the village of later times. The layout of individual villages could change greatly even when habitation was continuous and can only be rediscovered by the most microscopic attention to local evidence and topography.

Meanwhile the Church had established its own units of jurisdiction and administration. The bishopric of Lichfield was originally based upon the kingdom of Mercia and had emerged as a recognisable unit by the seventh century (Wise 1950: 109). The cult and relics of St Chad (d. AD 672) lent prestige to Lichfield, but in 1075, ten years before the Domesday enquiry, the see had been transferred to Chester on the grounds that Lichfield was too small to support the dignity of a cathedral. The diocese at this date comprised Staffordshire, Cheshire, Derbyshire, northern Warwickshire, part of Shropshire and Lancashire (Barlow 1979: 218).

The diocese of Worcester had been formed for the old kingdom of the Hwicce about AD 680 and comprised the populous arable lands of Gloucestershire, Worcestershire and south-west Warwickshire. The Warwickshire boundary of the diocese, and also that of the ancient kingdom, ran across the middle Avon from Tamworth by Warwick to Kineton and Whichford (Sawyer 1979: 146). The bishops were elected by the Benedictine monks of Worcester Abbey. Worcester could not boast the relics of a founder saint but Bishop Wulfstan II (1062–95) was a potent leader who supported William at the Conquest, retained his see, and was later canonised (Barlow 1979: 226–7). By the eleventh century there were in addition to the dioceses other subordinate ecclesiastical units. In the Midlands the old form of minster organisation was still in evidence at Wolverhampton, Penkridge, Wootton Wawen, Stratford and other places, where a central minster church with a number of clergy was endowed with lands spreading over a wide area. Parish organisation came into existence in general in the later Anglo-Saxon period as landowners endowed priests, and as churches were built to serve more localised communities. Some parishes in the Midlands were created to serve several pre-existent townships (Hooke 1981: 103), others for single large estates and communities. Brailes in south Warwickshire was already the mother church of three dependent chapels (Sawyer 1979: 155). New chapels continued to be established in the twelfth and thirteenth centuries and although the parish boundaries were for the most part defined by the eleventh century there remained many extra parochial places on heaths and moorlands, and many anomalies created by competing jurisdictions or changes in landholding.

The establishment of boundaries is essential in all matters concerning landholding, jurisdiction, taxation and accountability, and in all generations such boundaries have been carefully recorded and jealously guarded. In other areas of experience boundaries are constantly crossed or ignored. In making a living, in gaining ideas and insights, in family relationships, in trading and travelling, men and women create their own horizons, and these horizons are continually shifting, expanding and contracting. For many in the Middle Ages death was no more than a horizon, yet for many in the twentieth century it is the ultimate boundary. In attempting to co-ordinate what we know of Warwickshire and Staffordshire from the eleventh to the twentieth century, the importance and the unimportance of boundaries will both have to be taken into account.

Part one

The Middle Ages: Communities old and new in Staffordshire and Warwickshire, 1000–1300

Chapter 1

The lords and the tillers of the lands

In 1066 the most powerful lay lord in the Midlands was Edwin of Mercia. Cnut had appointed Leofwyne as Earl of Mercia and after him his son Leofric of Mercia, who died in 1057 and was succeeded by Alfgar. Edwin was the son of Alfgar and became Earl in 1062. As the Normans prepared for conquest Edwin was in a key position. However, the Vikings invaded the Humber estuary and Edwin went north, only to be heavily defeated at the battle of Fulford Gate in Yorkshire and so did not assist Harold at the battle of Hastings. Two years later he was in revolt against William and, when he died in 1071, his lands were confiscated by the Crown and the earldom abolished. The King took the major share of his midland estates and the remainder went to form the earldoms of Shrewsbury and Chester. In the aftermath of the rebellion the King's armies marched through Staffordshire after harrying Yorkshire, Cheshire and Derbyshire, and punished the Mercian revolts by devastation of the countryside. Warwickshire does not appear to have suffered in the same way, but a royal army passed along the Fosse way, and at Harbury in 1086 the commissioners reported '*vasta est per exercitum regis*' ('it is laid waste by the army of the king').

This was fifteen years later when information was being gathered for the Domesday Survey which the King had ordered at his crownwearing at Gloucester at Christmas, 1085. The King's commissioners surveying Staffordshire and Warwickshire collected details from 334 Staffordshire villages and 279 Warwickshire villages. There were few answers from the mountainous north, where the hills rose to over 800 ft, nor from the mid-Staffordshire areas, later part of Cannock and Needwood forests, nor from the heavily wooded area between Kineton and Berkswell and the river Alne in mid-Warwickshire. With these exceptions the coverage of the area was good, although the detail of some of the entries, especially those for north Staffordshire, was meagre (Darby 1971: 174).

In the first twenty years of William's reign the process of the taking and redistribution of manors in the Midlands had proceeded gradually and in a piecemeal fashion. In 1086 the King still had in his own hand sixty-four places in Staffordshire. These included some of the few estates that Edward the Confessor had possessed in the Midlands. William also retained some of the villages that formerly belonged to Earl Leofric of Mercia (d. 1057) and his family. Nevertheless, the King did not establish a territorial base in Staffordshire. Thirty-two of his villages in Staffordshire were recorded as waste, his castle at Stafford, built about 1070, was in ruins by 1086 and thirteen of the forty houses he held in the town were deserted (VCH Staffs IV: 37).

In Warwickshire the King held only nine manors, but he maintained a strong presence in the shire town. In Warwick he had 113 houses and in 1068 had cleared a site of 4 houses in order to build a royal castle on a strong rock high over the river Avon. He had had comparatively little difficulty in subduing Warwickshire, and had been able to rely upon the support of the Bishop of Worcester, Alwin the sheriff of Warwickshire and Alwin's son Thorkell.

The Bishop of Lichfield, more properly known in 1086 as the Bishop of Chester, and the Bishop of Worcester were both influential landholders in the Midlands, and held some of the earliest settled land. The Bishop of Chester's entire holding included six manors in Shropshire, two in Derbyshire, three in Warwickshire and twelve in Staffordshire, together with burgess tenements in Chester, Shrewsbury and Warwick. His Staffordshire lands centred on ancient Christian communities at Eccleshall and Lichfield. Lichfield lay just above the river Trent, near to the old Roman road and a former Roman town. The Bishop's patrimony included Lichfield itself and twenty-one dependent settlements strung out along the river valley. In addition, he held a number of woodland manors a mile or so to the north-west and south-east, on the gentle slopes of the river valley, for example at Yoxall, Weeford and Hixon. Further up the Trent river valley, the Bishop held a similar cluster of estates at Eccleshall with its thirty dependent villages and hamlets. On the western side of the Cannock hills, the Bishop had another group of manors at Brewood, Acton Trussel and Baswich, on the edge of the forest, and three manors in Warwickshire. As a royal servant and administrator, Bishop Robert de Limesi must have looked to his estates to produce revenue rather than food. Twenty-five of his forty-six Staffordshire estates were in the hands of undertenants by 1086 – some of them Englishmen and some newcomers from the Continent (VCH Staffs IV: 1–37; VCH Warks I: 269–96; Plaister 1976).

The Bishop of Worcester had nine manors in Worcestershire, three in Warwickshire and five in Gloucestershire. They lay in the valleys of the river Stour (the southern Warwickshire Stour) and the river Severn. $241\frac{3}{4}$ hides were held in the Bishop's own management and of the remainder, $79\frac{1}{4}$ hides were held by the monks of Worcester and $259\frac{1}{2}$ by thirty-six named lay tenants, only eight of whom bore English names. The lay tenants usually held the outlying and less profitable hamlets and other subsidiary settlements. This estate was 'large, populous and highly organised, yet there may have been room for growth' and it was already the result of four hundred years of acquisition, accretion, loss and gain (Dyer C. 1980: 36–8).

The estates of the two Bishops present obvious contrasts. The Bishop of Chester's lands were more scattered, less valuable, and more difficult to manage, while the estates of the Bishop of Worcester were richer and more compact. However, both holdings were derived from the early pattern of settlement, from the oldest Christian centres and the grants of the rulers of the Old English kingdoms. Their territorial lordship supported a prestige which was already ancient in 1086.

Staffordshire and Warwickshire did not attract many large Benedictine foundations. Only two important foundations had been made by 1086, the Abbey of Burton on Trent and Coventry Priory. This was in marked contrast to the richer agricultural lands not far to the south-west in south Worcestershire and Gloucestershire where great abbeys dominated the landscape and held the lands. Burton Abbey was founded about AD 1000 by Wulfric Spot and held lands in Burton, Abbots Bromley, Darlaston by Stone, Okeover, Whiston and Bedington. The Abbey had more recently acquired Austrey in Warwickshire from Leofric and Branston from Godiva. All the manors were well sited in or near the Trent valley and had large demesnes and only four were granted to subtenants. Coventry Priory had been founded in 1043 by Leofric of Mercia and his wife Godiva and held twenty manors in the south and central areas of Warwickshire, comprising some of the original endowment and some more recently acquired. The manors were mainly in the better agricultural areas and supported large populations of villagers.

By far the greater part of both Staffordshire and Warwickshire was in the hands of great lay lords with estates in many shires, and in many cases their main interests lay outside the region. There were 8 such lords. In Staffordshire 8 great lay lords held 117 manors, and another 6 lay lords held 205 manors in Warwickshire. Several of the most powerful lords were men of the royal family circle who had played leading political and military roles in the Conquest. The greatest landowner in Warwickshire was Robert of Beaumont, Count of Meulan, who held 62 manors in the county, 43 of which were granted to tenants. He had fought at Hastings and was one of the most important lay Councillors of both King William I and William II. His brother Henry had been keeper of the royal castle of Warwick since 1068 and was created Earl of Warwick by William II. In about 1100 seventy estates were transferred to Henry from Thorkell of Arden to supplement the Earldom and a few years later Henry also acquired the sixteen estates in Warwickshire of Hugh de Grantmesnil and also succeeded to the Warwickshire estates of his brother Robert. The combination of the estates of Robert and Henry, of the Count of Meulan, of Thorkell of Arden and of Hugh de Granmesnil meant that Henry, Earl of Warwick, before he died in 1123, was lord of something like three-quarters of Warwickshire.

There was no comparable territory in Staffordshire; nevertheless there were three landowners whose Domesday territories were to prove to be the basis of long-lasting power. William Fitzansculf held 104 manors in ten counties, including 31 in Staffordshire, 14 in Worcestershire and 5 in Warwickshire. These midland manors all lay within a day's journey of Dudley, where he had established the centre of his barony and built a castle on the limestone ridge of the south Staffordshire plateau. Here a compact block of territory had been created from the lands formerly held by many Englishmen. By 1086, many of the manors were in the hands of undertenants most of whom had Norman names. Henry Ferrers had a similar substantial block of territory in south Derbyshire and ten holdings in the adjoining part of Staffordshire, an estate built up from those of several previous English owners. He built a castle at Tutbury overlooking the rich pasture lands of the Dove valley to consolidate his power. In 1086 Robert de Stafford was the largest landholder in Staffordshire with twenty-eight estates and he held other estates in Warwickshire, Leicestershire and Oxfordshire. His lands lay scattered throughout the region, but they were mainly concentrated in and near Stafford, from which town he took his name. Robert de Stafford and his descendants were to continue to play a leading role in the county for four centuries. By 1086 most of his lands were subinfeudated to tenants, two-thirds of whom had Norman names, who also established enduring dynasties in the district. Members of the families of Bagot, Harvey, Stretton and de Gresley were to be prominent among the knightly class until well into modern times. Only one Englishman had a large holding – Thorkell of Arden who held seventy manors in 1086. His father had been an English sheriff of Warwickshire, but only five of his estates came to him from his father, the rest had been acquired in the interim and although he was called 'of Arden', his lands were scattered throughout Warwickshire. His manors soon passed to Henry Earl of Warwick.

In the immediate aftermath of the Conquest, the larger landowners took possession of their estates and reinforced their authority by building ring works and motte and bailey castles. The Ferrers built a motte and bailey at Tutbury and at Chartley, Fitzansculf erected a castle at Dudley and the Count of Meulan fortified Seckington. In all, about twenty private fortresses were erected by the Normans in the Midlands, some of which fell into decay as the country became more settled, while others were ordered to be destroyed by Henry II. However the foundations, once built, were indestructible and became the bases of stone castles built in the twelfth and thirteenth centuries (Cantor 1966: 38–46).

Thus while a great take-over had been accomplished in twenty years by a small number of lay lords from the Continent, much remained the same. The Church, despite changes in the occupiers of ecclesiastical office, exercised power and held property derived from older territorial organisations and from four hundred years of accumulated grants and acquisitions. Both secular and religious lords were dependent upon the people whose labour made the estates profitable, and for them the daily struggle for survival had been little changed by the Conquest.

The great majority of these people remained anonymous, recorded only as component individuals in numbers of villeins, bordars and serfs. Nearly three thousand were recorded in Staffordshire and seven thousand in Warwickshire.

A tabulation of the distribution of the recorded population in the two shires brings out the contrast between north Staffordshire and south Warwickshire.

North Staffordshire under	0.0–2.5 per square mile
South Staffordshire	2.5–5.0 per square mile
Mid-Warwickshire	5.0–10.0 per square mile
South Warwickshire	10.0–15.0 per square mile

The northern part of our region was comparable with Cheshire and Lancashire, but south Warwickshire compared in population with East Anglia, East Kent and the Thames valley (Darby and Terrett 1971: 46). The largest settlements were the towns of Stafford and Lichfield (Pinnock 1971: 60–1). In Warwickshire the largest community was Warwick which probably had a total population at this time of over 1,000 (Slater 1981: 35). Most other large settlements were in the Avon valley, in the southern lands bordering on Oxfordshire, and in the river valleys of the Dove, Trent and Lower Tame. Brewood in central Staffordshire and Tutbury Rolleston and Clifton Campville in the east were also sizeable communities.

The categorisation of the land workers in the Staffordshire and Warwickshire folios of the Domesday Survey is even more simplistic than in other shires and gives little indication of the nature of midland society.

Table 1. Categories of tenants in each county as a percentage of the total recorded population.

	Warwickshire	*Staffordshire*	*National*
Villeins	55%	58%	51%
Bordars	28%	31%	32%
Serfs	13%	8%	10%
Other	4%	3%	17%

(Source: Darby 1971: 290).

Freemen were scarcely mentioned as such but serfs were almost always included where there was demesne, for example under Mitton the clerk wrote, 'In the demesne there is one plough and two serfs.' In the Midlands it seems the commissioners were content to record only the most obvious and familiar categories. Surveys of Burton estate in 1114 reveal that there was an important group of semi-free rent paying villeins called '*censarii*' and these are also

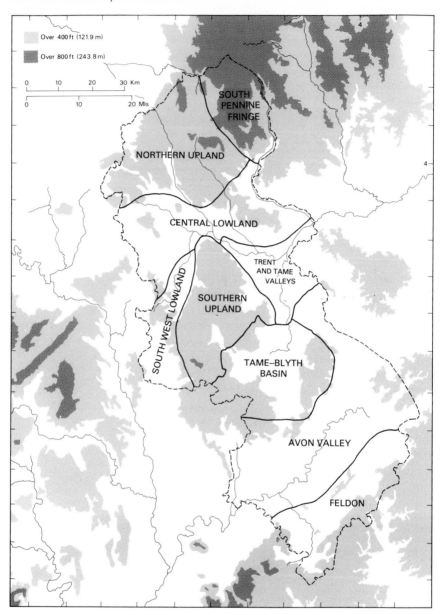

Figure 1.3 Regions within the Midlands (based on Darby and Terrett 1971)

recorded on the Bishop of Worcester's manors (Dyer 1980: 74). It has been suggested that they represented some 30 per cent of the tenants and that they had also existed in 1086, only thirty years before, but had been omitted from the Domesday record (Walmsley 1968: 73–80). If a similar degree of under-recording obtains elsewhere, the general picture must be altered considerably.

For the ten thousand or more families who had to support the Bishops, the lay lords and themselves by daily work on the land, the question of who held the land was only one of the influences shaping their lives. The soil they cultivated, the natural resources of their area, the lie of their land and its altitude, local weather and communications were all at least as important. Each village and hamlet had its peculiar combination of resources and difficulties and every community evolved its own particular variant of social organisation to deal with them. Staffordshire and Warwickshire manifested great variations within a few miles, for the great variety of soil types produced a very complex pattern of land use.

In the valley of the river Avon favourable conditions had encouraged the growth of large river villages which supported considerable numbers of people. There was plenty of meadow for hay and early pasture, and water corn mills were numerous. One of the largest of the valley communities was Stoneleigh, situated near the junction of the rivers Avon and Leam, which had 72 recorded tenants, 2 mills, 20 acres of meadow and woodland, and pasture for 2,000 pigs. To the north of the river was Coventry, recorded as having 64 tenants. Nothing in the Domesday Survey suggests that it was at this stage other than a large agricultural community in the King's hand, and it is a matter of debate whether there was an existing urban community omitted from the record. To the south of the river Avon lay the Feldon, through which four rivers ran northwards to join the Avon. By 1086 this area too had long been cleared and intensively cultivated. The largest community in the Feldon was Upper and Lower Brailes, supporting a hundred villeins, thirty bordars and thirteen serfs on the demesne. Dugdale in the seventeenth century first noticed that this large community included outlying lands in the forest, 20 miles to the north at Tanworth in Arden, and modern historians have not only accepted this suggestion, but made similar links between Packworth and Wasperton, Stratford upon Avon and Bushwood Shottery and Nuthurst. In these and other cases a populous, mainly arable community had pasture rights in woodland places at a distance (Ford 1979: 4–50). There were numerous water corn mills in the Feldon and much meadow. Wormleighton had 45 acres of meadow, sufficient for considerable numbers of livestock. In summer they could have grazed on the pasture of the higher lands to the east (Thorpe 1965: 38–9). It is possible that livestock may have been moved regularly to summer pastures at a distance, with several Feldon and Arden communities intercommoning in the woodlands near the headwaters of the rivers Alne and Arrow (Ford 1979: 150).

In the northern half of Warwickshire, traditionally known as Arden, the older settlements were widely scattered, often established on the gravel terraces and southward facing slopes. In the tenth and eleventh centuries the people of these villages were branching out into many subsidiary settlements on the heavier soils, clearing woodland and moving on to higher ground. The frequency of place names with 'green', 'ley', 'wood' and 'hurst' terminations give evidence of the process. Thus Yardley families established new settlements at Tyseley and Greet. The population density of this area was low and there were few mills, for this was a wood-pasture area rather than a corn-growing district. Here and there were larger communities – Aston, for example, had forty-four recorded villeins and, a little further south, Hampton in Arden had sixty-nine recorded people.

In south Staffordshire, the upland characteristics became more pronounced. Most of the settlements lay either on the edges of the plateau where water was available or on hill sites, and much of the area was scarcely settled at all. Wednesbury, an old settlement on a hill, had outliers at Shelfield and Bloxwich, and recorded what was for the area the large number of twenty-eight people.

In south-west Staffordshire the lower contours, gravelly lighter soils and warmer air provided a much more favourable environment for the villages of the valleys of the Stour, Penk and Smestow rivers. Halesowen by the river Stour was a large manor of 11 hamlets in a sheltered valley. There were only 4 ploughteams on the demesne, but the 36 villeins, 18 bordars and 4 radmen had between them $41\frac{1}{2}$ ploughs. There was much woodland but little meadow for the sandy soils were too dry, and between the settlements there were undulating moors and uncultivated heaths, rising in the Clent and Lickey hills to 1000 ft. Further north, Staffordshire was bisected by the river Trent which ran in a south-westerly direction through a wide shallow valley for most of its course. The older communities in the valley were putting out subsidiary settlements over a considerable area. Burton on Trent and Abbots Bromley each had detached dependent hamlets in the woodlands and in the upland. Some of the villagers of Tattenhill had spread down-river to Barton under Needwood and Newbold. The area was rich in meadow and well provided with mills, and most of the manors in the Trent valley from Wolstanton in the north to Alrewas in the east were assigned a high value.

Up-river, the Sow and the Penk flowed through undulating fertile clay land into the Trent in *central Staffordshire*, and on their banks too were substantial villages almost as large as those downstream. The land was bounded to the north-east by the heavily wooded slopes of Needwood and to the south-west by the Cannock ridge where there was little settlement, and much of the land was in the process of being reserved as Royal Forest.

In north-west Staffordshire villages were small and scattered, some scarcely more than single households. Thus Gamel held Balterley, where there was no demesne, only one villein and three bordars with half a team and half an acre of meadow. The *north-east* was even more mountainous, the rainfall was heavy and the land boggy with peat and heather. The average number of ploughteams in this area was less than 0.2 per square mile and the population only one per square mile. However, not all the north-east presented such a grim aspect. Where the limestone valleys widened out there was excellent meadow and pasture land. Rocester had 20 acres of meadow and land, which supported 2 ploughs in demesne, while 8 villein families and 10 cottage families had 9 ploughs and, further down-river, Uttoxeter recorded 2 ploughs in demesne, 24 villeins and 11 cottages with 11 ploughs. Rocester, Uttoxeter, Rolleston and Elford and Clifton Campville in the valleys of the Dove and Mease rivers all had values of over £10, which was high for Staffordshire (Pinnock 1971: 71–2).

Sixty-two Staffordshire villages were described as waste – *vasta est* – by the commissioners. Traditionally this devastation was attributed to the punitive raids of William the Conqueror or even Danish ravages in 1016. However, fifteen of the settlements so described were high up in the northern valleys – over 600 ft. It seems probable that the more difficult higher ground had been deserted rather than devastated, the population moving downhill to occupy better sites (Palliser 1976: 58). The King himself held thirty-two of the waste estates. There were only eight waste estates in Warwickshire, mostly in the south near the Fosseway.

Much of Staffordshire was evidently poor: two-thirds of its manors were valued at under £2 and three-quarters of its few cornmills were located in the river valleys of central Staffordshire. Arden was broadly similar in its apparent poverty. In contrast the Feldon and the valleys of Trent and Tame in Staffordshire seem to have been much more prosperous, with many corn mills and large meadows. In terms of population, ploughteams and tax assessment they compared well with some of the most developed parts of southern England. However the Domesday commissioners were less interested in pasture than in arable assets and it is probable that the evidence they obtained exaggerated the contrast between the wealth of the arable south and the pastoral north (Pinnock 1971: 87). Nevertheless the contrast in soils and settlements did exist and continued to exercise a significant influence, not only upon the economy and structure of the communities but also upon their cultural evolution.

Chapter 2

A living from the land: 1100–1300

Between 1086 and 1300 it is probable that the population of England trebled and the indications are that the population of Staffordshire and Warwickshire was growing at least as rapidly. At Rugeley in mid-Staffordshire the Bishop had 90 tenants by 1298, at Cannock another 90, and at Brewood 147. At King's Bromley further east there were 80 tenants in 1300 and well over 100 at Barton under Needwood in 1327. At Alstonfield in north Staffordshire there were 70 tenants in 1308 (VCH Staffs V1: 6–7). The existence of large populations in forest areas and in the uplands is evidence of increasing numbers of people spreading into the less attractive areas. In the south Warwickshire Feldon the population was also growing but more slowly (Harley 1960: 86–91). At Long Itchington near Southam the population in 1086 has been estimated as 400 and that of 1327 as 500 (Wilson 1979–80: 4). At Tredington the Bishop of Worcester had 48 tenants in 1170 and 63 in 1229 (Dyer 1980: 85). Nevertheless the villages of the south were still larger than those of the Arden. The hundred rolls for Stoneleigh and Kineton (1279–80) show that in these two hundreds 45 per cent of the villages had between 150 and 300 people, and 10 per cent had more than 300 inhabitants, most of them in Kineton Hundred (Hilton 1966: 91).

The subsidy rolls of 1327 provide an opportunity to survey the whole of Staffordshire and Warwickshire at a critical time, both in terms of the names and numbers of taxpayers and of the amounts they were expected to pay. The returns are subject to all the uncertainties of tax lists – they were reduced by evasions, under-assessment and the omissions of individuals or corporate bodies such as the Church. However, the picture which emerges is consonant with that derived from other sources. From the subsidy lists for Warwickshire a median has been calculated of 11.3 taxpayers for each 1,000 acres. Most of the places with large numbers were in the south of the county and to the north-east between Coventry and Watling Street. In Arden the numbers of taxpayers were notably less, and only 15 places rose above the median (Stanley 1982: 242–3).

For Staffordshire the pattern was less sharply differentiated. In general, the more numerous groups of taxpayers lived in the western lowlands from south to north, although there were also large lists from some townships in the valleys of the Trent, Mease and Dove, and some limestone parishes in the north-east. The millstone grit parishes of the north, the Cannock area and the coalfield parishes of central and south Staffordshire still made a comparatively poor showing (Pinnock 1971: 94–102).

The total number of taxpayers listed for Staffordshire was 4,400 and for Warwickshire about 6,000. The relationship between the numbers of taxpayers and the numbers of people must remain unknown, for although an estimate has been made for Warwickshire that the taxpayers represent 30 per cent of the population (Stanley 1982: 240) it must be said that the ratio would vary in different communities, depending on the economy of the particular township. In Staffordshire some of the highest assessments were from places in the east of the county in the valley of the river Dove and near Needwood Forest. Rocester, Denstone and Waterfall, cow pasture parishes, had 43 taxpayers who paid 96s. between them. At Butterton, with Sheen and Caldon, 26 taxpayers paid 54s. 8d.

The most usual individual assessment was 2s. and only 165 people in Staffordshire and 284 in Warwickshire paid 5s. or over. The highest individual assessments were upon six townsmen of Coventry assessed at £1 or over and two burgesses of Stafford, who were expected to pay 40s. each. Outside the towns, the highest individual assessment in Warwickshire was that of Thomas West of Snitterfield, who was assessed at 26s. 8d. In Staffordshire the larger taxpayers were men bearing familiar names such as Giffard, Meynell, Trussel, Bagot and Chetwynd (Bickley 1902 & H.C. 1886 and 1887).

As the population grew, the process of creating new subsidiary settlements continued. Fenton in north Staffordshire was probably a single vill in 1086, but by 1300 there were also Fenton Vivian and Fenton Culvert. Clayton near Newcastle under Lyme had become Clayton Culvert and Clayton Griffin (Palliser 1976: 71–3). At Stoneleigh in the Avon valley, where the population increased fourfold, new outlying hamlets were established at Stareton, a mile to the south-east; at Canley, a mile north-east; Cryfield, three miles north-west, and at Fletchampstead, north-west of Cryfield. In 1308 139 tenants were paying tallage. The growth of the community probably owed something not only to the good riverside soil and plentiful land, but also to the immediate neighbourhood of the new town of Coventry and the foundations of the priory of Kenilworth (1122) and of Stoneleigh Abbey (1154) (Hilton 1960: xlvii).

In the woodland areas by the thirteenth century numerous single houses surrounded by a moat were being built. The remains of at least 200 of these have been identified in Warwickshire and at least another 108 in Staffordshire (Emery 1962: 378–88). Many were manor houses or farmsteads of prosperous families. Aston, Wednesfield, Sutton Coldfield and Walsall all have examples which have been excavated. It is believed they were always single dwellings, and that the purpose of the moat was to keep out deer and other woodland

21

animals, and to ensure a dry site on heavy clay soils, rather than to protect the inhabitants against human enemies. However, a number of them do show signs of having their defences strengthened in the disturbed period of the Barons' Wars of 1250–80 (Roberts 1965: 26–37).

In Staffordshire and in Arden the increase in population was being accommodated from at least the twelfth century by taking in assarts. Forty-five of the two hundred families at Eccleshall were recorded as holding assarts – one of them, Roger de Broughton, to the amount of 88 acres (Spufford 1964: 16). At Stoneleigh on the upper Avon individual tenants of the Abbey made assarts to the north and south of the river (Hilton 1960: xlvii–xlix), and in the Lichfield and Cannock area in 1155 the King granted the Bishop 1,500 acres of assarts made in the previous twenty years. Additional land was also brought into cultivation by draining. In about 1180, for instance, the Canons of St Thomas drained land in Eccleshall manor and place names suggest drainage works at Throwley, Pipe, Ridware and Silkmere (Palliser 1976: 71). Assarting and colonisation on this scale required labour and capital, and were carried out by lords and the more substantial tenants. However men of modest means also cleared assarts of 5 acres or less. At Alvechurch in north Worcestershire, in 1299, there were eighteen tenants of established holdings, who also held assarts and new land, eight of them men who held half or whole yardlands (15 or 30 acres). The other ten were small holders, and there were also thirteen tenants who had no lands, other than small assarts (Dyer 1980: 91).

Between 1180 and 1250 the lord of the manor of Tanworth in Arden, the Earl of Warwick, made many grants of land away from the old field. Some were small holdings of 2–15 acres, leased out at a regular rate of 2*d.* an acre, spreading northward from the settlement on to heath land. Others were larger grants of land, 15–60 acres, probably in regular rectangular parcels and adjacent to each other, limited by neighbouring hedges. The Earl also granted newly cleared land to his officials, of whom the most notable were the Archer family. In due course individual homesteads were built on these enclosed lands and, by buying and selling, freemen and the richer tenants consolidated their holdings in the thirteenth century and a few, after a further period of growth and accumulation, established sub-manors with their own courts (Roberts 1968: 101–4).

Both freemen and villeins not infrequently left their manor to live elsewhere. Movements of individuals can be deduced from surnames formed from place names. In the manorial surveys of the Bishop of Worcester (1299), the surnames suggest that people moved from about a 15 mile radius, although two incomers into Alvechurch had come from further afield – one from Oxfordshire and one from Wiltshire (Dyer 1980: 86). Halesowen, a mile or so further into the woodlands from Alvechurch, had a surplus population by the end of the thirteenth century and 67 men and women of unfree status left the manor between 1270 and 1348. Those whose new home is recorded in the rolls did not go very far – to King's Norton, Northfield, Birmingham, Aston,

Smethwick and Dudley, all nearby. Some were attracted to the towns of Warwick and Coventry (Razi 1980: 30–1).

Close study of a number of early village plans in the Midlands has shown that they changed considerably in layout and appearance in the early medieval period. Traces of long vanished settlements lie beneath the field land of later villages in south Warwickshire (Ford 1976: 286), and in the Feldon the colonisation of the thirteenth century may have overtaken earlier villages. Villages such as Claverdon, Shrewley and Shelfield township in Aston Cantelow may have begun as scattered farmsteads which later developed into villages with church, manor house and houses close together. At Lillington it has been suggested that there was a 'radical reorganisation' of the village in about 1120 involving building over earlier fields (Roberts 1982: 125–47). Villages were usually irregular in shape, growing with the needs of the community and according to the lie of the land, the access to water and to adjacent communities. Each house included barns, stables, outbuildings and sheds, yards, muckheap and storage as well as trees and patches of cultivated land (Hilton 1966: 92–4).

The Midlands had a plentiful supply of building materials. In the north the houses were built of local stone with roofs of stone flags, and in the south of Warwickshire on the Cotswold fringe the local limestones provided good building stone. In the river valleys and plateau areas the predominant mode of building over a long period was the timber frame house. The earliest surviving houses are cruck-framed with pairs of beams split from a single log placed at intervals of about 16 ft apart and rising to a height of about 18–20 ft. The crucks were connected by cross beams and the roof rested on this frame. Such a construction was described as a bay of building and larger houses consisted of two, two and a half or more bays forming a rectangular plan. Lower Farm at Bloxwich was built in about 1330 and had an internal height of 21 ft and a width of 17 ft 6 in, and many others which have been studied have similar construction and dimensions (Penn 1963–4: 69). All of these houses were open to the rafters and had a central hearth with a roof opening for the smoke. The houses had two windows to a bay and a floor of earth. Mancetter manor house, built about 1330, had a screened passage between back and front doors and a separate office wing (Pevsner 1966: 347; Alcock 1973). West Bromwich manor house had two main bays and a service bay separated from the main living space by screens (Jones 1975–6: 1–65). In some cases the larger houses had a separate solar but this was without a hearth (Hilton 1960: 96–9).

The stone houses of the north and south were probably rectangular in plan, with the farm buildings occupying some two-thirds of the space of narrow buildings which were up to 100 ft long.

From the twelfth century onwards evidence of cultivation is available for individual communities. All generalisations are necessarily drawn from the specific experience of a few individual villages, and for every generalisation there can be found many exceptions. However, some attempts to aggregate the evidence concerning the organisation of cultivation have been made. Harley in his study of Warwickshire field systems came to the conclusion that villages with two fields divided into strips were common in the Feldon of Warwickshire, especially in the older settled areas. Individual families held strips in both fields and a pattern of distribution can be discerned. In the older settled lands of the Avon valley, moreover, there was evidence of three-field and early multiple-field groupings – for example, at Snitterfield and Aston Cantlow (Harley 1960: 211–14).

In Arden and in Staffordshire there seems to be more evidence for three-field systems and of three-course rotations of cultivation. Court rolls in the early fourteenth century record the communal management of fences and pasturing upon the arable. At Tanworth there was an area of strip fields from at least 1200 (Roberts 1968: 103). At West Bromwich in 1300 there was a three-course rotation of rye, oats and fallow, and at Madeley in 1337 in the north of the county the arable demesne had 180 acres sown with grain and 60 acres fallow (SHC 1913: 612). At Elford in 1332 there was common pasture for two years after the corn had been harvested and in the third year pasture on the fallow for the whole year. Pasture in the woodland of Elford was also organised on a three-yearly cycle (SHC: 20–1). Birrell was prepared to state that 'three fields were general in central and south east Staffordshire' (VCH Staffs VI: 13). More recently Yates in a careful summary of known evidence for two and three field systems and for two and three shift rotations of crops comes to broadly the same conclusion. Most of the evidence for three shift rotations comes from mid-Staffordshire on the better lands but there is also evidence from Bentley of three-shift cultivation on poor soils. The evidence for two-shift rotations is much more meagre and equivocal. It is clear however that in many places where open fields and rotation were organised it was frequently only one element in the village economy. Some assarts were cultivated as separate individual holdings, others were included in the shifting of rotation of crops. Rotation might operate separately on demesne or within the bounds of large single fields as on the Cistercian Granges. The individual holdings in open fields were not necessarily distributed evenly in the open fields, and at Brewood, Stretton and elsewhere up to nine fields were grouped and subject to rotation. Some of the villages on the poorer soils never organised even a two-yearly cropping system. At Baswich, Clifton Campville and Wednesfield it seems probable that a variation of the infield–outfield system was practised. Some land was manured and cultivated intensively to provide additional arable for a few years before it became exhausted and was allowed to return to the heath (Yates 1975: 196–218).

In many parishes of Staffordshire, Arden and north Worcestershire the dispersal and arrangement of the fields were very irregular. Halesowen had twelve rural settlements in the area of the manor, of which Oldbury in the north and Romsley in the south with about thirty families, were the largest. Oldbury had five big open fields and Romsley had three (Razi 1980: 6–7).

Fields in woodland areas were small in area and very irregular. At Field in the upper Blythe valley strips were dispersed in fields which were simply irregular blocks of land taken in from the moors (Palliser 1975: 76–7). At Stoneleigh Abbey there was no regular division into common fields and tenants' holdings were unevenly distributed and widely scattered (Hilton 1960: 147–52). At Church Bickenhill in north Warwickshire there was a great assortment of small open fields, roughly organised into six or seven groups. Tenants held different acreages in different fields. Although these were 'open fields' there is no evidence of crop rotation on a communal basis (Skipp 1963: 15–18).

Under the pressure of growing population in the late thirteenth century, land was made into open arable fields in the high valleys and also along the river Dove. The limestone soil of this area was more suitable to pasture than arable and it was later converted back to pasture for dairying (Palliser 1983: 61–70).

A wide range of crops were grown on the varied soils of the region. The Bishop of Lichfield grew wheat, rye, oats and barley on his Warwickshire manor, but at Haywood, Baswich, Brewood and Eccleshall in Staffordshire, oats predominated. At Longden in mid-Staffordshire in 1304 mixtum (wheat and rye) was planted in autumn and barley in spring. At Tredington in south Warwickshire wheat, barley, peas, beans and oats were grown. One-fifth of the harvest was retained for seed, one-fifth was sold and the remainder consumed by the manorial workers, their animals and the Bishop's household (Dyer 1980: 69). Villagers' crops were similar to those grown on the demesne. On their holdings in the arable fields the peasants grew all four main cereals, wheat, rye, barley and oats, often mixing wheat and rye as maslin, and barley and oats as drage. In the high lands of the north at Wetton and Alton rents were paid in oats and even in less adverse circumstances there seems to have been some predominance of oats (Birrell 1962: 15).

Arable lands were improved not only by the dung of the animals pastured upon them, but also by the use of marl. Men were fined for the digging of marl to the inconvenience of others and a poor man at Yardley, John of Seek, died when the sides of a marl pit in which he was working collapsed upon him (Skipp 1970: 47).

At Tutbury the cultivation of 120 acres of arable on the demesne required the full-time work of four paid ploughmen and a carter. They were paid in a combination of money and allowances of oats, rye and peas. Two horses and twenty-one oxen were used and fed on oats and hay. The seed corn was drawn from the crop, but some additional seed peas were brought in (Birrell 1962: 40).

The tools available for cultivation were the oxdrawn plough, harrows, spades, mattocks, reaping sickles, hooks and scythes. Peasants as well as lords might possess a plough and sometimes a cart with ironbound wheels. For the most part, however, the work was accomplished by sheer human toil, and physical strength was at a premium. The majority of the tasks involved the co-operation of several individuals and a sufficient number of able bodied men. Co-operation and communal organisation was not merely an economic system, but an ineluctable condition of daily survival.

Over much of the Midlands while arable farming supplied food for consumption, pastoral farming produced money income (Harley 1960: 205). The religious houses kept large flocks of sheep, the largest probably being Croxden with over 7,000, judging from wool sales. The Bishop of Lichfield kept about 2,300 sheep by the early fourteenth century (VCH Staffs VI: 10). Almost every village had some sheep, and the aggregate number must have been considerable. At Alrewas, in the Trent valley, individuals had flocks of 80, 100 or even 160 sheep. Sheep were kept mainly for wool production. On large estates they were transferred from manor to manor for grazing, and occasionally brought from distant places to improve the stock from time to time. The fleeces were collected at Haywood from the Staffordshire and Shropshire manors of the Bishop of Lichfield and there sold to merchants. At Tredington the sheep were moved from upland in summer to lowland in winter (Dyer 1980: 70). The Tutbury shepherds tried to strengthen the lambs by feeding them with oats, a little wheat, milk and ale. They applied grease and verdigris against disease, but little could be done to combat the high mortality and the low lambing rate. At Tutbury the shepherd earned $5\frac{1}{2}$–6d. a week and additional labour was paid $1\frac{1}{2}d$. per twenty sheep washed and sheared (Birrell 1962: 158).

Many herds of cattle grazed in central Staffordshire and in the valleys of the rivers Dove and Trent. Burton Abbey had a herd of 26 at Leigh, 39 at Branston, 36 at Weston and 28 at Burton, while Sir Robert de Holland, lord of Yoxall, kept 40 dairy cows at Needwood. Villagers also kept one or two cattle and a tenant at Alrewas had six. Oxen were the principal draught animals and some may have been reared for sale, judging from the court case of 1320 recording the sale of forty oxen at Ombersley, Worcestershire, belonging to John of Trysull (VCH VI: 10). Riding horses were also reared at Tutbury where as many as 120 were recorded in 1313. In summer they were taken to graze at Needwood and Kenilworth and to Duffield over the Derbyshire border (Birrell 1962: 167–70). Except in north-east Staffordshire meadowland was in short supply and there were many disputes in villages about the alleged destruction of mowing grass, and about pasture rights over fallow, waste and woodland (Birrell 1962: 182).

Evidence concerning land tenure is rather more abundant and less equivocal than that concerning the cultivation of the land. The demesne lands of the lord, whether resident or not, can usually be clearly identified. The arable land of the lord's demesne was sometimes dispersed in open fields intermixed with those of the tenants. In Wednesbury, in 1315, Juliana Heronville was assigned as part of her jointure 145 strips or selions of arable land in the three common fields, Monway Field, Church Field and Hall Field. At his death her husband had held 120 acres of arable land in demesne, also in the open fields, and 10 acres in the common meadow. In other places the demesne was consolidated and separate from the tenants' land. At Keele the two types were combined in that the lord in 1331 had 120 acres of arable demesne in severalty and 120 acres in strips in the common fields. The Earl of Lancaster's demesnes at Uttoxeter comprised 420 acres and at Tutbury 334 acres (Birrell 1962: 14). The serfs who had been so closely associated with the demesnes in 1086 were by 1170 described as *bovarii*. These men held very small scraps of land and were virtually full-time workers on the demesne. At Hampton Lucy in 1270 they all lived together in a '*domus bovarium*' (Dyer 1980: 97).

By 1300 a great number of tenant families held freeholdings, especially in Staffordshire and the Arden (Harley 1960: 96). Free tenure was sought after, because it enabled the tenant to sell his holding and move freely. The hundred rolls (1279) for Stoneleigh (Arden) and Kineton (Feldon) Hundreds in War-wickshire show that in Stoneleigh 50 per cent of the tenants were freeholders, whereas only 30 per cent were freeholders in Kineton (Harley 1960: 196). In Staffordshire, among 95 villages for which information is available 40 per cent were free tenants. At Church Eaton (1315), Wiggington (1315) and Henley in Arden, all the recorded villagers were freemen. Although free tenants might have felt superior in legal and perhaps social status they were by no means all superior in assets and resources. At Stoneleigh three-quarters of the freeholders had 15 acres or less (Harley 1960: 209). Some free tenants at Audley in north Staffordshire and at Barton under Needwood, in the east, held only 6 acres, others even less. On the Bishop of Worcester's estates while 21 per cent of the 422 free tenants held 30 acres or more, 27 per cent held 14 acres or less.

In contrast customary tenants were burdened with labour services, paid higher money rents and were liable to a range of fines and occasional payments. John of Turlshill in Sedgley, an upland manor in south Staffordshire belonging to the de Somerys, was required to plough the lord's arable every Monday from February to Easter (festivals and weather permitting), to reap the lord's corn, mow the lord's meadow and carry hay from Overton, in Warwickshire, to the lord's castle at Dudley. At Christmastime he had to collect and deliver nuts and fuel to the castle. There were in all about fifty customary tenants on the manor performing similar works (SHC 1888: 32–3).

On many manors the greater part of the weekly work upon the demesne was performed by full-time workers (the '*famuli*'). At Tredington, in south Warwickshire, the daily work on the arable demesne was performed by eight famuli and six men called 'enches' who had the status of customary tenants, but worked full-time for the lord (Dyer 1980: 72). The extent to which tenants were required to perform labour services varied from holding to holding, from manor to manor and over time. There were manors in both Staffordshire and north Warwickshire which had no demesne at all, as at Audley and at Tysoe, and others where the proportion of arable demesne to tenant land was small. Such manors had little need for labour services on the demesne. In contrast it is possible to find manors, especially in south Warwickshire, with large demesnes where some work was demanded from the wealthier peasants every other day. At Bishops Itchington the demesne of between 50 and 60 acres was worked by 65 tenants who worked three days a week and also did some seasonal work, and 10 more who did seasonal work only.

The fact that a lord held demesne in a manor did not, of course, imply that he and his household lived there. Only 9 of 75 villages in Staffordshire had a resident lord, but in Kineton Hundred in the Feldon, on the other hand, three-quarters of the villages had a resident lord. On ecclesiastical estates there were, on the whole, more mouths to be fed than on secular estates and at least some of the household of abbey, bishop or preceptory would always be resident. The position was even more complicated in the many villages which had more than one lord. In 1280 in the village of Harbury in south-east Warwickshire there were nine manorial lords – five religious and four laymen. There were six separate demesnes each possessing its own peculiar tenurial relationship with its customary tenants (Hilton 1966: 125–6).

In south Warwickshire Hilton found that 10 of 48 manors in Kineton hundred had no labour services at all, and there were 8 in which he characterised the labour services as light. There were 22 where they were 'seasonal', that is to say where tenants were required to work on the lord's land 20–30 days a year, and, on the remaining, eight week work was required: that is, work for a fixed number of days throughout the year. In Stoneleigh Hundred, north of the Avon, he found that 18 of 45 manors had no labour services and there were 12 in which there were only light labour services. On only 13 were there 'seasonal' labour services and only 2 demanded week work. In Arden work was often only required for 10–30 days in the year and in Staffordshire services were generally light. They contrasted favourably in this respect with manors to the south-west in Gloucestershire and south Worcestershire, but were comparable with other woodland areas, such as the Forest of Dean (Hilton 1950: 16–18).

Seigneurial policies with regard to the balance of labour services and money rents were changed through the period in response to the changing price of grain and the varied needs of the lord's household. In the twelfth century some changes from labour services to fixed rents were recorded. Cash payments in lieu of services which he did not need also gave the lord a flexibility which he could 'manage' to his benefit. However, the price of grain rose in the latter part of the thirteenth century and many lords again found it more profitable to cultivate the demesne (Harley 1960: 199). The ploughs on the Bishop of Lichfield's estates increased from 10 to 18, and on Burton Abbey from 4 to 16, while the Bishops of Worcester took their demesnes back into cultivation and appointed bailiffs and reeves to run them. Consequently the demands for tenant labour increased. Though on the whole traditional week work remained the same, by 1299 the tenant was supposed to provide more men. Carrying services were increased and the occasional works were made more onerous. Villeinage was in general more strictly defined and associated more clearly with labour services. A number of groups of tenants on Midland manors tried to claim free status in the courts, indicating that the distinction between unfree and free carried real day-to-day economic penalties as well as theoretical disabilities.

However important labour services were on many manors in the region, the income which the lord derived from money rents and from the profits of lordship were even more significant. In 1313 the Earls of Lancaster received 11 per cent of their income from the demesne, 50 per cent from rents and 39 per cent from court fees, fines and perquisites. The Bishop of Lichfield, in 1291, received 15 per cent of his income from demesnes, 47 per cent from rents and 38 per cent from lordship. In the north-east the Verdun family of Staffordshire received 26 per cent from demesne, 55 per cent from rents and 19 per cent from lordship (Hilton 1970: 1–20).

The moneys derived from the exercise of lordship were very varied and were not always demanded. They included amercement for manorial offences, trespass by animals, failure to attend court, and breach of the assize of ale. Sums of 2s., 3s. or 4s. were charged for marriages within the manor and more for marriages outside it. Permission for a man to leave the manor could cost as much as 5s. The payment of tallage and pannage could be onerous, thus tallages levied by the Bishop of Lichfield provided 4 per cent of his total manorial income and the incidence was arbitrary (Hilton 1970: 234–5).

The payment of a heriot, upon the death of the tenant, represented an increasingly severe tax upon the tenant family's resources. Heriots at Barton under Needwood were: the best beast, brass dishes, ironbound carts and wains, all beehives, uncut cloth, horses, foals, pigs, sides of bacon and cash. Payment of heriot was a comparatively recent obligation in the thirteenth century and was a levy on goods that the tenants had accumulated. Evidence of the actual payment of heavy heriots comes from manors of many kinds – lay and ecclesiastical, large and small.

Burton Abbey had large demesnes and looked for heavy labour services. By 1280 all the Burton tenants were called *nativii* (unfree tenants) and they were paying both money and labour services. In 1228 the tenants were already in dispute with their lord concerning his encroachments on the common pasture. The dispute was extended to become a direct challenge to the lord's 'new' demands for labour services and the whole issue of villein status was raised. The Abbot retaliated by confiscating 506 sheep belonging to the tenants, a number which indicates their acute need for pasture. Walmsley shows that the dispute took place against a background of an increase not only in labour services, but also in money rents, reaping and harvest services, entry fines and heriots. There was a cottage and an acre in Burton for which the Abbot charged 6s. entry fine, 2s. per annum and 15 days' work on the demesne. Meanwhile the increase in population meant that the size of tenants' holdings was decreasing. Whereas three-quarters of the holdings in the twelfth century had been of full virgate size, i.e. about 30 acres, by 1280 only a quarter of the holdings were full virgates and even small holdings were subdivided (Walmsley 1972: 12–47).

Many conflicts over status and dues are recorded – for example, at Wolverhampton the Dean tried to prove his tenants were of unfree status and at John Perton's manor at Tettenhall in 1282 (Hilton 1975: 238–9), at Rolleston in 1320, and in other places, there were conflicts between tenants and lords in which the villeins claimed that the lord's exercise of lordship was increasingly oppressive (VCH Staffs VI: 60).

At Halesowen the arrival of the canons in 1215 led to a long and bitter dispute between the Abbey and the tenants concerning boonworks, entry fines, corn mills and tallage. The tenants put up a vigorous resistance and the disputes lasted for forty years (Razi 1980: 9; Hilton 1966: 158–60). The property had formerly been a 'royal manor' or ancient demesne and the tenants claimed this gave them certain rights. At the same time the same issues were being contested only 5 miles away on the manor of Wednesbury which had also been a royal manor until 1164. John de Heronville inherited as a minor and came of age in 1265 but seven years later he was sued in the court of King's Bench by 25 of his tenants who claimed that he had exacted from them 'other customs and services than they used to render when the manor was in the hands of the ancestors of the King' (i.e. a hundred years before). Judgment was delayed for eight years, but pending a decision John de Heronville was ordered to restore his tenants' goods. This he failed to do and moreover interfered with their cultivation, thus placing himself in contempt of court and was accordingly prosecuted by the Crown. In 1307 an inquisition reported on Heronville's levy of tallage and upon his appropriation of common woodland. In 1310 the tenants set out what they believed to be the proper customs of the manor 'of ancient demesne', namely that they should pay 5s. per year for every virgate, attend court only twice a year and pay tallage only when the King also collected tallage. They claimed that Heronville had demanded suit of court every three weeks, had tallaged them high and low, had demanded merchet and other villein services and customs which they had not been accustomed to perform. The claims set out by Heronville's attorney were not only more onerous in themselves, but involved the confirmation of villein status. He claimed that they could be tallaged to any amount, that they should perform a few days' labour services – ploughing, mowing and reaping – and that they must pay a penny to brew beer, pay pannage of pigs, pay 2s. merchet within the manor and 3s. out of it, and heriots of half the deceased tenant's pigs, his boar, all his male colts, a cart bound with iron, uncut cloth and whole hams. The decision of the Court is not known and there is no certainty that the statements of either side bear detailed relation to reality, but it is at any rate clear that the issue of villein status was vigorously contested by the tenants for over thirty years (Ede 1962: 42–6; Hilton 1975: 238–9). The tenants' leaders in these legal battles were men who had both resources and self-confidence.

On many manors there were some families of rising status who could secure and exploit an advantage, and who were able to hold large amounts of land and be in a position to accumulate more. On Halesowen manor the 'rich peasants' were sharply differentiated from the 'poor peasants'. 'Rich peasants' held 25–30 acres of arable land and acquired in addition assarts and patches of land in severalty. They had rights of fallow pasture and rough grazing and some enclosed pastures. They had access to what little meadow there was. On this basis they could keep more livestock and produce and gain a cash surplus. They brewed ale for sale. They acquired leases of demesne land when it became available, and they lent money to other peasants. They could sustain cases in the public law courts and they held village office. The average tenant family was four to five – they tended to exceed this average. They further added to their workforce by employing cottagers and labourers.

The 'poor peasants' on the other hand had 7 acres or less of arable. They kept pigs, a few sheep and a cow or two, but rarely had draught animals or breeding stock. They borrowed but did not lend and were never elected to village office. They were constantly in trouble with the manor court, especially for scrounging food and fuel from the hedges, fields and commons. They were most affected by disease, dearth and accident, and they had smaller families. Their daughters were three times as likely to be fined for fornication as the daughters of rich peasants (Razi 1980: 139–50). In the Avon valley manors the 'rich peasants' comprised only slightly more than half of all the tenants, for example 53 per cent at Hampton on Avon and 51 per cent at Stratford, and the remainder were smallholders (Dyer 1980: 90).

In most parts of the Midlands the proportion of smallholders was much higher. At Stoneleigh 62 per cent of the tenants had under 7 acres. Everywhere the number of smallholders would be seen to be even greater if we had information about subletting by the richer tenants (Hilton 1960: xli–xlii). Tenants who had 14 acres and less could not fulfil their needs from the cultivation of the land alone, and they survived by working for others, by gathering and by craftwork if the opportunity offered. But with all this there must have been a constant struggle for survival, intensified by population pressure by the beginning of the fourteenth century (Titow 1969: 78–93; Dyer 1980: 108–12).

By the reign of Henry II about one-third of the realm was subject to Forest Law. Three Royal Forests were already in existence in Staffordshire by 1200 – Cannock, Kinver and Brewood. A 'New' forest was probably made about 1170 in the upper Trent, but it has a short and largely unrecorded existence. Needwood was a district of fertile woods and grassland which before 1285 was administered as a Chase by the Ferrers and after 1285 under Forest Law by the Earls of Lancaster (Cantor 1968: 39–53). Warwickshire Arden was never royal forest – the name denotes a district not a jurisdiction. However, the Royal Forests of Feckenham (mainly in Worcestershire) and of Kinver were partly in Warwickshire.

Within the Royal Forest were enclosures for the management of deer

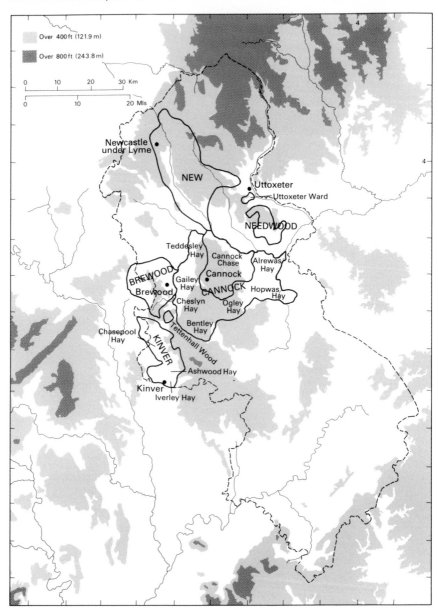

Figure 1.4   Medieval forests of the Midlands (based on VCH Staffs II: 336)

known as hays – for example, Chacepool Hay and Ivetsey in Kinver Forest. In Cannock Forest the names Alrewas Hay, Ogley Hay and others came to apply to a subdivision of the Forest Jurisdiction. There were villages on forest land – Upper Penn, Orton and Trysull in Kinver Forest, for example – and the villagers who lived in or near the forest were able to carry on cultivation and had rights of pasture, but they were subject to the overriding jurisdiction of Forest Law which ensured the preservation of large and small game. The Royal Forest was controlled by a staff of officers, the verderers and regarders, the agisters and the woodwards. Offences against Forest Law were heard by the Court of Attachment which met every forty days and then more serious offences by the Swanimote. Every four years or so the Justices of the Forest would arrive in the area to survey the forests and to fix fines and punishments for a backlog of cases. The verderers and jurors were often members of local families of landholders while the regarders, agisters and woodwards were paid servants (SHC 1907: pt. 1). Lords of lands followed the example of the King, and also conserved forest areas for hunting red and fallow deer. The Earl of Warwick was granted 2,500 acres in Sutton Coldfield to make a great Chase and the Bishop of Coventry and Lichfield was granted a portion of Cannock Forest as a Chase in return for donations to the crusade of Richard I. The Lords of Dudley maintained Pensnett Chase and Baggeridge.

Other landowners created their own deer parks usually on demesne land. In 1311 the Dean of Wolverhampton was licensed to take in 240 acres in Prestwood and 160 acres in Blakesley, to enclose it with a ditch and reserve it as a deer park. Chartley Park was separated from Needwood as a deer park from at least 1279. About 100 such parks have been identified in medieval Stafford-shire, the earliest at Stretton in 1175. Lord Stafford's great park in Madeley was in use throughout the Middle Ages (Cantor 1968: 39–54). The parks, like the larger areas of forest and chase, needed constant management and the lords employed park keepers to carry out hedging, culling and feeding of the animals.

The forests, chases and parks provided pasture for red and fallow deer and for dairy cows, pigs, and oxen, but not for sheep which would have destroyed the pasture of the deer (Gould 1965–6: 28–9). Regular supplies of venison, of fish from the fish ponds and hart and hawks were sent from the royal forests to the court. The King made gifts of oak and timber to his supporters for building castles, abbeys and churches. The grant of forest office was an opportunity to exercise patronage and the Forest Courts provided an important source of income (VCH Staffs II: 335–57). The cases heard by the justices reveal two main groups of offenders poaching in the Royal Forests.

The first category were groups of gentlemen who appear to have made it a regular part of social life to sally forth into the forest in parties and carry off one or two deer for sport rather than for food. These attacks took place in the daytime and often appear to have been undertaken almost at the whim of the moment. In 1286 the court heard that Roger de Somery, while hunting in his chase of Baggeridge, put up a stag with his dogs which fled towards the Forest of Kinver where one of his servants shot it with bow and arrows and took the dead beast to Roger's house.

The second category were the poor people who took game at night, using traps and snares taking the animals for food not sport (Birrell 1982: 19–22). Many of the villagers living on the edge of the forests were also prosecuted for taking assarts of forest land and were fined sums from 12*d.* to half a mark each, but they were not removed from their assarts and the fine thus stood as a form of rent (SHC 1884b: 144–5, 160–1; Birrell 1982: 9–23). Many places claimed disafforestation and by 1300 so many claims had been admitted that the forest was much reduced and limited to the Hays. By the fourteenth century even the reduced areas of the Hays were being disafforested and cultivated. At an inquisition before the Chief Forester of Cannock Forest in 1311, the officials were condemned for impeding cultivation in an area between Sutton Chase and Cannock Chase and Sutton Forest. Although remnants of ancient rights and laws lingered on in some of the Hays until the seventeenth century, Forest Law had long since ceased to have any effective influence (Gould 1965–6: 38–9). However the chases and lords' deer parks remained and 'the royal claim to sole control of deer in the forest was replaced by private persons' claim to control all game on their own lands, a development which gave poaching a new and a different significance' (Birrell 1982: 23).

Chapter 3

Towns old and new: 1086–1300

There had been relatively little urban development in the region in Anglo-Saxon times. Only 4 of the 112 English towns recorded in Domesday Book lay in Staffordshire and Warwickshire. Only the 2 shire towns, and the old royal burgh of Tamworth, can be traced back with certainty to the tenth century. Stafford seems to have been in a poor way in 1086 for 51 of the 128 recorded houses were waste and the castle that had been erected in about 1070 was in decay. All the principal Staffordshire landowners, the King, the Bishop of Chester (Lichfield) and five leading lay lords had houses in the town, and the ancient chapel of St Bertelin had been converted into the well-endowed College of St Mary, but the town remained small and insignificant. It was not on any main route and its river was merely a small tributary of the Trent (VCH Staffs III: 303; VI: 201–5). In contrast Warwick was already in the tenth century a substantial town with a large population, diversified economy and important administrative and market functions (Slater 1983: 10–11). In 1086 the King had 113 houses and another 127 other houses were recorded, divided between 27 lords; 19 free burgesses lived within the walls; and 100 bordars had small plots beyond the walls. A castle had been built in 1068, and the town was surrounded by a defensive ditch and already had north, east and west gates (Cronne 1951: 8–9; Klingelhöfer 1975: 1–11).

Tamworth in the fertile valley of the river Tame had been a burgh with earth and wood fortifications and a royal mint town in Mercian times (Slater 1982a: 179). It had developed on both sides of the river Tame which was the county boundary at this point, so that there was a Staffordshire half and a Warwickshire half of Tamworth. Tamworth Castle was built within the borough defences and granted to Robert Despenser, but he did not hold the town of Tamworth (Gould 1971–2: 18–19). Tutbury had a market and a castle built by Henry de Ferrers, and Domesday recorded 42 men who lived by trading only and paid with the market (*foro*) £4 10s.

Between 1086 and 1300 the economic and administrative status of these older towns remained modest. Earl Roger built a new castle outside Stafford at Castle Church, but there is little evidence of an interest of the family in the shire town at this period. It was, of course, the centre of royal administration, but even this was of little significance since the sheriffdom of Stafford was usually combined with that of Shropshire and the courts were held at Bridgnorth on the river Severn, while the Royal Justices in Eyre at this period held court at Lichfield on the main road north rather than at Stafford. The town obtained a grant in 1206 from King John of free borough status and paid 5 marks in tax directly to the crown, and by 1315 a new charter permitted them to elect their own coroner. They had had two officials called reeves since the 1150s, but the qualification for burgess status and the extent of the activity of the reeves remains uncertain (VCH Staffs VI: 200–1, 220–2).

Both halves of the royal town of Tamworth continued to be held by the Crown, taxed as royal demesne and administered as part of the royal manor of Wiggington. The town was visited by kings, used for royal prisoners and one Tamworth man at least became a king's clerk. As burgesses on royal demesnes the men paid their own *firma burgi* of 46s. 10d., held their own view of frankpledge, elected their own bailiffs, and collected their own tolls and rents. They held a three-weekly court called the Portman Moot, and kept records which are extant from 1280. However, the succession to the castle of the powerful Philip Marmion soon demonstrated that even royal burgesses could feel the heavy hand of seigneurial power. After he had assisted the King at Evesham, Marmion was granted for life the two halves of Tamworth and the manor of Wiggington to add to the castle and its liberty. He had a record of causing violent disturbances, and the burgesses now claimed that he had taken the land of some of their number, seized the horses of persons lodging in the town, interfered with their freedoms and required them to grind corn at his mill. The burgesses maintained their position in the courts until, at the death of Marmion, the Staffordshire half reverted to the Hastings family and the Warwickshire half to the Crown (Gould 1971–2: 21–4).

Warwick became more and more dependent upon the patronage and power of the Earls of Warwick. At first two manor courts were held, one for the shire town itself and one at the castle gate, but gradually the castle increased its authority over the town and Warwick was granted to the Earl in 1198. All Saints Church was originally the church within the gates of the castle and in the town itself there were seven parish churches. By another extension of castle influence Earl Roger de Beauchamp in 1123 transformed the principal parish church of St Mary's into a well-endowed college and all the other seven town churches, including All Saints, were in some degree combined with it, though they kept their own rectors.

Newcastle under Lyme although royal in origin soon came permanently under seigneurial influence. It was mentioned as a royal borough in the Pipe Roll of 1172–3 and was a foundation which consolidated royal control of the increasingly important route through Staffordshire to Chester and north Wales. By 1212 there were 160 burgesses in the town. However in 1267

Newcastle was granted to Edmund, Earl of Lancaster, who asserted his authority over the new borough and in 1293 obtained from the mayor and community a renunciation of their rights in his favour. They resumed them after his death, but Thomas his successor raised the borough rent to £40 a year (Birrell 1962: 17).

No less than 40 of the 140 new towns established in England between 1100 and 1300 were in Staffordshire, Warwickshire and north Worcestershire. It has been suggested that this abundance of foundations was due to the 'frontier' within this region between the predominantly arable economy of the 'lowland zone' and the predominantly pastoral economy of the 'highland zone'. Other factors could include the relative ease of communications in the area, and the prevalence of free tenure (Palliser 1963: 12–72). One of the earliest and most successful initiatives was that of the Bishop of Worcester, John of Coutances, who about 1200 planned the new town of Stratford on Avon, in the parish of Stratford, with six streets laid out on a grid plan on a 70 acre site near the river Avon. The burgages of $3\frac{1}{2}$ perches by 12 perches of land were offered at 1s. a year. The burgesses were granted freeman status, freedom to alienate land, and freedom from manorial dues. The burgage plots were taken up quickly and by 1252 there were 300 burgage tenements, 14 shops, 10 stalls, 2 ovens and 2 dye vats. Stratford soon had a flourishing market and by 1332 it had more taxpayers than Warwick (Carus Wilson 1965: 46–63) while many of the original buyers' plots had been divided into thirds or halves (Slater 1983: 212).

The Bishop of Lichfield was encouraging the development of burgess plots at Lichfield on the other side of the water from the Cathedral close. By 1130 the town had a ditch and bargates and was served by a new church, St Mary's, built and endowed for the town in addition to the old pilgrim church of St Chad and the Cathedral. In the later thirteenth century the town acquired a conduit of water, some of the streets were paved and a fourth church, St Michael's, was built for the people living beyond the town in the suburbs. Lichfield lay on the London to Chester road and was able to profit from long-distance travellers and also attracted pilgrims to the Shrine of St Chad (Taylor 1968–9: 43; Thorpe 1954: 150–62). The Abbots of Burton obtained a licence in 1200 to make a borough at Burton and at Abbots Bromley, the Dean of Wolverhampton granted the burgesses on his manor of Wolverhampton the 'liberties of Stafford' (1253), Halesowen Abbey made Halesowen a town of burgesses in 1272, and the Abbot of Dieulacres laid out building plots at Leek.

Lay lords were as active as the clergy. At Tutbury the Ferrers set aside two acres as burgess plots. There were over 200 burgesses' plots by 1300 and the town was worth nearly £40 to the Earl of Derby in 1313–14 (Birrell 1962: 19–20). The Ferrers also started a new town by the woodland village of Agardsley, in about 1101, which soon became Newborough with 101 burgesses each paying 1s. 6d. a year. Further up the Dove Valley the Ferrers founded Uttoxeter in 1252, which soon had 145 burgesses and 32 stalls in the market.

Most of the midland townsmen were acquiring some 'urban liberties', but how much real power and independence they exercised depended on circumstances. There was usually a powerful lord to be reckoned with, who saw profit and value in encouraging urban development for their mutual benefit, but who was reluctant to relinquish the manorial dues, profits and jurisdiction.

From 1197 to 1247 the lord of the manor of Walsall was William Ruffus and at some point during his long tenure of power he granted the townsmen freedom of all services in return for 12 marks of silver. The burgage rent was the usual 12*d.* a year and the townsmen paid a fine for breaches of the brewing and baking regulations. The charter did not mention officials, markets or courts, but it was clearly a negotiated agreement between townsmen and lord. In 1309 the two joint lords of the manor were Roger Morteyn and Thomas Ruffus, and together they made a further grant to the Walsall burgesses. The burgesses were freed from payment for pannage and tallage and the fines for brewing and baking were reduced from 6*d.* to 1*d.* and were completely suspended between 25 December and 2 February. The new charter explicitly extended the burgesses' field of self-government. From thence forward they could only be impleaded in the borough court and were therefore freed from suit at the separate manorial court. In cases of damage for trespass on the lord's crops an arbitration panel consisting of two burgesses, two foreign tenants and the lord's bailiff was to adjudicate. Thus the duality of town and foreign, or of town and manor, first received documentary expression. Finally, and most importantly, the charter granted to burgesses complete responsibility for determining the admission of new burgesses. The charter was witnessed by the lords of surrounding manors and provided the basis for the future development of the town (Brown 1975–6: 65–75).

The growth of Coventry from the manor of 1086 to a great town of about 4,000 inhabitants by 1280 is as clearly evident as the process of that growth is obscure and controversial (Harley 1960: 98–104). It is probable, although not proven, that the entry in Domesday concerning the manor of Coventry conceals by omission the existence of a pre-Conquest town. The manor was granted after 1086 to Earl Ranulph of Chester by the King. Coventry's pre-Conquest Benedictine Abbey by 1086 held twenty-six manors, and when Bishop Robert de Limesi transferred the see from Chester to Coventry, he made the Abbey into a Priory and himself titular Abbot and claimed rights in the town, rights which continued to be asserted by the Priors after Limesi's death (Poole 1869: 6). By 1280 there were 257 burgages and 105 cottages in the 'Earl's Half' and 93 burgages and 247 cottages in the 'Prior's Half'. The problem lies in determining to what extent and at what period these two 'halves' really divided the town, and how far the community of the town developed as a whole (Davis 1976: 1–19) or in two separate halves which subsequently came together (Harris 1898: 56).

Ranulph, Earl of Chester, made a grant to 'his burgesses' at some unknown date between 1129 and 1153, confirming burgess tenure and granting them the 'laws and customs of Lincoln', a portmoot and an elected justice (Gooder 1981: 2). The date of this grant is known only from the confirmation in 1182 obtained at a cost of 20 marks, and by four further charters of confirmation in the ensuing hundred years. Meanwhile the Prior too was increasing his power. In 1250 the Prior purchased from Ranulph's heirs, the Montalts, the 'Earl's Half of Coventry' although they retained the rest of the manor. For a time the Prior appears to have exercised manorial jurisdiction, including a fortnightly court, for the tenants of the whole town (Coss 1974: 137–51).

The 'Earl's Half' contained the most numerous taxpayers and some of the most wealthy merchants. The market, however, was in the 'Prior's Half'. In 1309 the Prior sued sixty-seven of the townsmen – all but two of them being merchants living in the Earl's half – for trading in the Earl's Half in Earl Street on market days. This he claimed infringed his rights in the market in Prior's Half. His opponents counterclaimed that his jurisdiction extended to his own Half only. The dispute became more and more aggravated with claims and counterclaims supported by forged charters. By 1321 a sworn conspiracy had been formed against the Prior and the Priory was besieged for six days. This led to prosecutions in the Court of Common Pleas. In 1322 to 1323 the case took an even more dramatic turn when a prosecution was undertaken in the Court of King's Bench against twenty-seven Coventry men – among whom were named eleven of the Prior's enemies in the former disputes. Two years later Pope John XXII was moved to institute an enquiry and the townsmen were accused of employing a necromancer to bring about the deaths of the King, the Prior and others (Gooder 1981: 13–16).

This episode in Coventry has been seen as a precursor to similar events at St Albans and Bury St Edmunds in 1327, when there was widespread resistance by townsmen to ecclesiastical control. There was increasing tension between the commercial and urban liberties of the townsmen and the manorial context. The men of Coventry were not without resources and raised very considerable sums to prosecute their cases or to pay for charters or grants of liberties. They acted sometimes in opposition to the lords and sometimes in co-operation with them, and when possible they sought and obtained royal support. The process was one of a shifting balance of influence in which a position of advantage was gradually established. The legal formulae of charters grossly oversimplify the daily realities. Indeed in many cases the charters themselves were a codification of practice and a summary of the position reached rather than a grant of new privileges.

One sign of the separate identity of the town was its encircling wall or ditch. At Stafford there had been an enclosure by 1086 and walls were built in

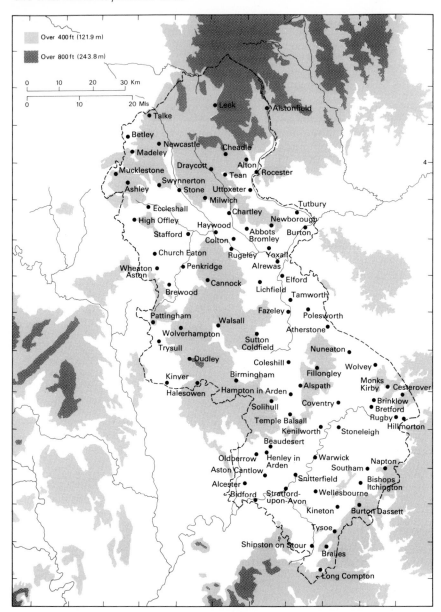

Figure 1.5 Midland markets in the Middle Ages (based on Palliser and Pinnock 1970–1: 70; and Slater 1981: 60)

1220–40 and at Warwick in 1280, Tamworth had a ditch, bank and palisade, and Coventry also had an early defensive ditch. Wolverhampton and Birmingham had remnants of 'town ditches' recorded by later antiquarians.

40

On the other hand Newcastle and Stratford did not embark on the expense of wall building and Coventry's very elaborate walls were started only at the end of the fourteenth century.

Outside many midland towns lay an area known as 'foreign'. Dudley, Walsall, Wolverhampton, Birmingham, Halesowen and Warwick all had a 'foreign' and at Coventry the manor of Cheyslmore stood in the same relation to the town. These areas were derived from the antecedent manorial jurisdictions, but at a later date were to come under the influence and often the control of the emergent towns.

The growth and intensification of exchange was marked and encouraged by the very numerous grants of market charters. In England as a whole some 1,200 charters were granted in the period 1227–1350, many of them to communities which were to remain villages. Nearly fifty villages in Staffordshire and Warwickshire had market charters. Nevertheless, the grant of market rights was an important, indeed essential, contribution to urban development. The charters entitled the lord or the townsfolk or both to take tolls of persons coming into market and usually included a clause permitting townsfolk to trade in other markets. Thus burgesses of Dudley were freed of tolls in Birmingham and Wolverhampton and the burgesses of the royal town of Newcastle under Lyme were free of tolls throughout England. The market places might be separate triangular or rectangular areas in front of the parish church as at Tamworth, Birmingham and Alcester or wide high streets as at Henley and Dudley (Slater 1982b: 189).

Tamworth market was held on Saturday, with stalls in both halves of the town. Some houses had upright posts fixed permanently outside to use for supporting stalls. Goods on sale included the usual country products, eggs, butter, hens, grain, fresh and salted fish, and salt. Bread, ale and meal were made and sold in considerable quantities, and candles at one penny a pound. Butchers slaughtered bulls after they had been baited, and other cattle, sheep and oxen meats were immediately salted or sold, women sold the entrails, and skinners, tanners and horners made good use of the remainder. Although Tamworth market was predominantly a local market, the larger towns attracted merchants from a distance (Palliser and Pinnock 1970–1: 50–63).

The occupations of the townspeople before 1350 have to be deduced from surnames and from references in deeds. The occupations of 305 Coventry traders and craftsmen, so collected, comprised 68 persons in the wool and cloth trades, 58 concerned with the production and purveying of food and drink, 46 in the leather and fur trades, 42 in the metal-working trades, 32 merchants and mercers, 21 in the building trades and 38 others. The largest group, probably because more likely to be documented, were the merchants and mercers who lived mainly in Much Park Street, Earl Street and Gosford Street. Weavers and dyers were well represented, but so also were tanners and saddlers. The metalwares produced included edge tools, girdles, mirrors and needles, and there were eight mentions of goldsmiths (VCH Warks VIII: 153).

In Coventry, a very mixed economy clearly prevailed. If the merchants of cloth dominated the long-distance trade, this did not exclude a lively development of other manufactures locally. In the smaller towns a similar mixture of trades prevailed. Stratford had rope makers, coopers, mercers, tanners making a living alongside tailors and butchers and at Lichfield there were textile workers, tanners and metal workers, but also goldsmiths, bellfounders, a number of masons and some parchment makers (Thorpe 1954: 166–7).

The numbers of taxpayers assessed for subsidy in 1332–3 provide some indication of the relative size of midland towns. Both the older boroughs of royal foundation, and the seigneurial towns had already become sizable communities. Birmingham and Nuneaton both had more taxpayers than Lichfield and Stafford. No overall estimate of the size of the towns can be made since the proportion of taxpayers and the area within which they lived in each case must remain uncertain (see Table 2).

Table 2   Numbers of taxpayers, 1332–3

Coventry	135	Abbots Bromley	38
Warwick	92	Southam	35
Birmingham	69	Sutton Coldfield	34
Nuneaton	66	Uttoxeter	31 (plus 32 *cum membris*)
Stratford	66 (est.)	Coleshill	30
Tamworth	62	Wolverhampton	30 (plus 80 *cum membris*)
Lichfield	57	Kenilworth	26
Stafford	56	Himley	25
Newcastle	55	Tutbury	25
Alcester	49	Walsall	25
Burton on Trent	40	Audley	25
Rugeley	41		

Other places with burgesses all returned fewer than 25 taxpayers.

(Sources: SHC 1889; Carter 1965)

Some light is shed on migration into the towns in the fourteenth century by the surnames in subsidy and poll tax lists. Of the names of poll tax payers in Lichfield, in 1377, 71 per cent came from villages within a radius of 15 miles from the city (Thorpe 1954: 168). In Warwick 127 of 500, or one-third of the whole list, had surnames derived from places outside the town. Stratford taxpayers had names derived from villages within a radius of 15 miles mainly from south Warwickshire (Carus Wilson 1965: 46–63). In 1332 one-third of the taxpayers of Coventry had surnames suggesting that they originally came from villages and towns elsewhere (Fowler-Carter and Wellstood 1926).

Migration into towns is also indicated by the subletting of burgage plots. In Coventry of 260 burgage plots 60 had been subdivided and sublet. The most extreme example was one burgage which had been divided and sublet as 30 cottages and 16 curtilages (Hilton 1966: 185).

It is not clear how far the burgesses had organised themselves into merchant or craft gilds by 1320. Stafford had a Skinners Gild in the thirteenth century and Newcastle a Merchant Gild from 1235. At Coventry where it might be expected that gilds would develop early, there are no gild records before the late fourteenth century and the presumption that they existed depends upon analogy with Leicester and other textile towns.

Of course, some seigneurial enterprises failed to take off into permanent towns. Bretford in Brandon was sited where the Fosseway crossed the Avon and, on the face of it, should have been a good site for development. The de Verdons of Brandon Castle established 19 burgesses in 1280 and obtained a market charter in 1307. By then there were 23 burgages and 24 'places', but although the burgage rent was only 6*d*. per burgage the town failed to attract settlers (Hilton 1966: 192). Atherstone, Talk, Kinver, Coleshill, Penkridge, Betley, Brewood, Alrewas and Nuneaton all saw attempts to establish burgesses at various times, but experienced little or no further growth of urban status in the Middle Ages. Other places such as Long Compton and Burton Dasset were granted market charters but remained villages. Nevertheless by 1340 there was a town to every 34,000 acres in the Midlands, and only the wealthy and prosperous West Country counties of Devon, Gloucestershire, Wiltshire and Somerset had a greater number.

Chapter 4

Dioceses, parishes and religious communities

By the eleventh century, parishes, boundaries and organisation linked to manorial centres had been established in the older areas of settlement. In the less settled areas the parishes were still developing, reflecting in their topography and organisation the gradual extension of subsidiary settlements and the colonisation of remoter areas (Fisher 1968: 54–70). In the Feldon the parishes tended to be small and compact, usually of about 11 square miles. Further north the parishes contained numerous small hamlets. Stoke on Trent was a parish of 12,406 acres which comprised six upland hamlets, all of which eventually acquired their own chapels. Traces of the older minster type of ecclesiastical organisation remained. The church of Penkridge was the headquarters of a parish with subsidiary chapels at Cannock, Copenhall, Shareshill and Stretton. In Warwickshire Leek Wootton continued as the mother church of Leamington, Lillington, Milverton and Ashaw and may have been another early minster church (Slater 1983: 9).

Seventy-one priests appear in the Domesday record for Warwickshire, but only thirty-four for Staffordshire, five of them canons at Lichfield. Churches are only referred to twice for Staffordshire of a probable total of forty, and none for Warwickshire. While this is clearly an omission, traces of Saxon churches in the counties are scant. There was, however, much building and rebuilding of churches in the twelfth and thirteenth centuries. Solihull, Berkswell, Wootton Wawen, Wolverhampton, Stafford (St Mary's) and many others were built in the grand manner. Indeed almost every parish church was rebuilt during the Norman period (Jeavons 1962–3; 8–9). The size and style reflected the glory of God and the economic status of the benefactors rather than the practical needs of the parish. By 1291 the taxation list made for Pope Nicholas, though notoriously incomplete, recorded 84 parish churches in Staffordshire, 153 in Warwickshire (SHC 1915: xxx, xxxii). Many new parishes and parish churches were being established, especially in the towns and areas of new settlement.

The parish churches, whether simple or elaborate, provided for most people the one large building which they felt was their own. It was the one place where there were a few items of beauty, dignity and mystery. However crude and inadequate the parish church, it was the place where men and women sought to come to terms with good and evil and with life and death.

Attendance at Mass in the parish church every Sunday and on the feast-days of the year was a canonical duty enjoined on every individual of every degree throughout his or her life. Servile work could not be required upon those days. The Sunday mass at this period was usually at 9 a.m. The gathering together of the whole parish Sunday after Sunday, year in year out, strongly reinforced the sense of community and in the large scattered upland parishes brought together people who might see little of each other during the week. It was an opportunity for trade and social gathering as well as for worship. Sunday markets were held in Wolverhampton, Lichfield, Eccleshall, Halesowen, Newcastle, and no doubt elsewhere until they were transferred to a weekday in the reign of King John.

Within the church the trend was towards more defined and organised forms of worship. The mass of the *Ordines Romanae* was becoming the norm. The missal provided a settled and universal form of worship in place of the earlier collection of antiphonaries, lectionaries and sacramentaries. During this period the sacraments were established as seven and the pattern of the church's year, which had been evolving slowly since earliest times, became more or less fixed. Bishop Giffard of Worcester was insisting that every parish should have a Sarum Missal, antiphonaries, two propers, and two graduals.

The clergy who served these parishes were the base of the ecclesiastical hierarchy and the key figures in the day-to-day relations between the people and the church. At the end of the Middle Ages Warwickshire contained 94 rectories and 47 vicarages (Bill 1967: 5) and Staffordshire contained 41 rectories and 38 vicarages (*Valor Ecclesiasticus* 1810–35 iii: 99–150). The rectors of parishes were the more educated and more mobile of the clergy. In Warwickshire they found it easier to get licences to leave their parishes for study or other purposes. Their income, averaging about £10 a year, was derived from endowments, glebe lands and tithes. The vicars were more likely to be resident in their parishes. Their income averaged about £4–8 and was derived from a stipend and allowance (Bill 1967: 5).

In order to be ordained a priest, a man had to be twenty-three years of age, literate and legitimate. Dispensations could be obtained if any of these conditions were not fulfilled, but not without investigation. Henry of Warwick, clerk, was not born in wedlock and sought a dispensation to proceed to Holy Orders in 1307. He had to apply to the papal nuncio in London, who then authorised the Prior of Worcester to investigate and to award the dispensation if he thought fit. The Prior passed on the enquiry to the Archdeacon's official and a series of ten questions concerning the applicant's parentage and his own character were put to persons who had known him and his family. It emerged that he was, in fact, illegitimate but that no danger of his

Plate 1.1 The Abbess of Polesworth. An effigy in St Editha's Church, Polesworth, Warwickshire. A Benedictine house of nuns was established at Polesworth in the tenth century and re-established in the eleventh century. The effigy dates from about 1200.

Plate 1.2 Hugh the deacon. An effigy in St John the Baptist's church, Avon Dasset, Warwickshire. Date about 1200.

encouraging laxity was apprehended since he himself was chaste, docile and of honest conversation. A dispensation was granted by the Prior on the authority of the papal legate (WHS 1893–7: 258).

The ordinands were expected to have secured a benefice before proceeding to priest's orders. Of eighty-five men presenting themselves for ordination by Bishop Reynolds (1308–13) only forty-six were in fact beneficed. Many of the ordinands were members of religious orders. Bishop Giffard (1268–1302) ordained 1,629 men to all grades in five years and of these 1,540 were regulars (WHS 1898–1902 and 1907–29). By this time not only monks but also priests were expected to be celibate and the midland bishops, like their colleagues elsewhere, ensured that hearth companions (or more unkindly concubines) were put away. The Bishops of Worcester also made some effort to ensure that the priests were literate, and they were expected to possess, in addition to the liturgical books, the episcopal constitutions and the Bishop's tract on penance. They were to bring them to deanery meetings, and could be called on at random to read aloud.

In 1094 the see of Lichfield was transferred, from Chester to Coventry, where Bishop Limesi obtained a papal grant vesting him with the title of Abbot of Coventry and thus appropriating the wealth of the Abbey. Limesi's four successors were elected at Coventry, but the canons of Lichfield and of Chester did not relinquish their rights. The three competing bodies pursued their battles with a bitterness which precipitated the intervention of kings, archbishops of Canterbury and eventually of papal legates. In 1228 Pope Gregory IX negotiated a kind of peace, and it was decreed that the monks at Coventry and the canons of Lichfield should elect alternately. Needless to say the bitter disputes continued and ended only when the process of election itself ceased to have much meaning in the late fourteenth century (VCH Staffs III: 7–14).

The chapter of Canons of the cathedral church at Lichfield was reconstituted in 1130. They had parish incomes assigned to them, but no parochial duties. Instead they were expected to attend the cathedral, for which they received 4*d.* a day on ferias, 6*d.* for feast-days and 1*s.* on the solemn festivals. At Christmas, Easter and on the Feasts of St Chad and the Assumption (15 August) they received a special bonus of 5*s.* They had to be in residence three months in the year and attend Chapter on Fridays. They were organised as a community with their own dean, precentor, treasurer and chancellor, each with their own additional endowments. This left plenty of time for a career in the royal service and in the thirteenth century many of the canons were non-resident. Therefore they presented vicars to deputise for their cathedral duties, and the vicars in their turn were provided with endowments of houses and lands (VCH Staffs III: 140–5).

The old Saxon church was rebuilt; the work was commenced under Robert Peche (1121–6) and was completed by Roger de Clinton (1129–48). In the thirteenth century there were additions including the Lady altar. The work is not well documented, but the sequence derived from studies of the building itself suggest that by 1150 the church consisted of a nave and a large apse. To this were added transepts and a chapter and a new choir and a chapel of St Chad for the increasing pilgrimage traffic. The tower and the west front were probably built at the turn of the fourteenth century and the west spires *c*. 1320–30, by which time the basic layout and construction was complete (VCH Staffs III: 141–4).

The central authority of the bishop was imposed on the diocese, not only through the church courts, but also through the traditional process of visitations. The thirteenth- and fourteenth-century bishops of Worcester travelled through the diocese with a suite of clerks and packhorses carrying records, visiting the religious houses, hearing complaints and making adjudications. The secular clergy were required to attend at a central church of the deanery. Bishop Bransford visited the Worcester archdeaconry, which included Warwickshire, during October 1390. In seventeen days he personally visited four deaneries, two hospitals and four other religious houses, covering 120 miles. After a rest, he resumed his journey visiting in the next sixteen days, four deaneries, the episcopal churches of Stratford and Hampton Lucy, and nine religious houses. Earlier in the year in February and March he had covered 150 miles and in thirty-six days had slept at twenty-nine different places (Haines 1965: 158–60).

Although much of the bishop's judicial and administrative work was delegated to subordinate officials, certain pastoral duties appertained to him alone, in virtue of his consecration. Only a bishop could ordain; regular records of ordinations begin in both dioceses from the thirteenth century. They were held in various centres in the diocese, as the bishops moved from one manor or palace to another. Bishop Gainsborough held 17 ordinations in 4 years, Bishop Cobham 10 in 37 years. The industrious Bishop Bransford ordained 757 acolytes, 681 subdeacons, 713 deacons and 680 priests from 1339 to 1349. It appears that the majority of those who received the lesser orders did, in due course, go on to take priests' orders (Haines 1965: 164–71.

Between 1100 and 1380 the Midlands felt the influence of the foundation movement which was spreading rapidly in Europe as a whole. In Staffordshire two new Benedictine houses for men were started at Canwell and Sandwell and two for women at Brewood and Farewell. The Ferrers family established a Benedictine house at Tutbury. In Warwickshire also there were two new Benedictine houses for men and two for women. At Nuneaton there was a filiation from Foutrevault in Normandy, founded as a double monastery for men and women, but whereas the women's community grew rapidly to ninety-three nuns by 1234, the men's side never developed, and the endowment was eventually used by a community of secular priests.

Several Cistercian houses for men were founded. Merevale was founded in 1148 in Arden and this was soon followed by Coombe and Stoneleigh in

Warwickshire, and Croxden (1179), Dieulacres (1214) and Hulton in north Staffordshire, and there was also a Cistercian house for women at Pinley. True to their rule these houses were established in underdeveloped areas, which nevertheless had economic potential.

The Benedictine and Cistercian houses in Staffordshire and Warwickshire were small compared with the great houses of Gloucestershire and Worcestershire. Perhaps the most successful religious order in the area was that of the Augustinian canons. They founded a total of six houses in Staffordshire, five in Warwickshire and two in north Worcestershire. The earliest and most important of their houses was Kenilworth, founded by Geoffrey de Clinton in 1122, and all the others (St Thomas, Rocester, Trentham, Stone, Colwich, Dudley, Studley, Warwick, Halesowen) were founded by the end of the twelfth century, except for Maxstoke, a belated foundation of 1336.

The Augustinian canons were not monks but groups of priests living a common life of prayer, yet aiming at a revitalisation of the work of the priest among the people. They worked in the towns and larger villages and also engaged in agriculture. The prior was required to live in common with the canons and accounts were to be rendered annually. The founder at Maxstoke laid down that the prior and canons must wear a black cloak and cowl when out of doors, and that they should be good, honest and sufficiently learned, with a voice good enough to sing the office. They were to attend every day the Lady Mass, the Chapter Mass, and worship at the canonical hours. They were to pray for the soul of the founder saying an additional *Ave* at the end of every service. At least nine of the canons were to be ordained priests (Dugdale 1730: 524–6).

The communities were part of movements of thought and spiritual initiative in the church in Europe as a whole. While their influence was entirely local they nevertheless provided a link with the wider world of western Christendom.

The founders of midland houses included some local landowners. Dudley Priory, a Cluniac cell of Much Wenlock, was founded by Gervase Pagnel of Dudley Castle about 1160. In his charter of foundation he recites how his father, Ralph, had planned the work and how he for his own soul and for the souls of his wife and son had granted to the monks serving God in Dudley the profits of various parish churches, land in Churchill and Dudley, and renders of fuel, bread and venison, and fish. He permitted them to take stone for their buildings from his land under the supervision of his steward. The tiny monastery, which probably never had more than three or four monks, was built within sight of the castle at the foot of Castle Hill, and had a stone chapel and wooden domestic buildings, which were later replaced with limestone buildings. It was always closely linked with the castle (Radford 1940: 449–59).

Other midland foundations were made by royal officials and bishops,

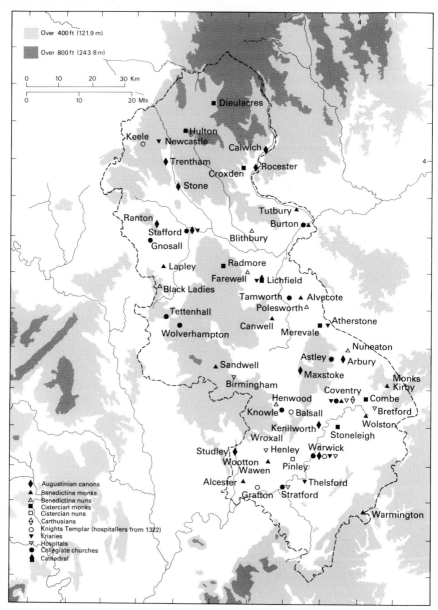

Figure 1.6 Midland religious houses in the Middle Ages (based on Greenslade and Stuart 1965: 24; and Slater 1981: 44)

notably Roger, William and Guy de Clinton. In making these foundations the founders sought to achieve a whole range of interconnected objectives. Religion was to be given a visible and permanent embodiment, the leadership of the patron's family was reinforced, economic advantages would accrue, and provision was made for a variety of contingencies to be anticipated in this world and, more important still, in the next. Dependants could be provided for, the weak and poor looked after vicariously, prayers and masses could be commanded and a perpetual name achieved. The investment of time and money was expected to bring a great variety of long-term blessings.

The revenue of the religious houses was drawn from the foundation endowment, later gifts and endowments, and also from the 'spiritualities', that is regular income in return for providing spiritual services. This raised some very fundamental problems in the Middle Ages which were never fully resolved. Some preached that for a priest to derive any sort of income at all from administering the sacraments was to commit the sin of simony. This stance, though impressive, was entirely unrealistic in the context of feudal society. The priest's spiritual powers were derived from his ordination by the bishop, but the bishop could not maintain him. It was the feudal lord and the land which provided him with an income. The bishop was required only to ordain those who had a title to a benefice and he was supposed to establish this before ordaining a man to the subdiaconate. The title to the benefice was conferred by the owner of the land or benefice.

Increasingly in the thirteenth century, religious houses provided the spiritual services in a parish and in return they were licensed to appropriate or take over the profits of the benefice. They employed a vicar or appointed one of the community to carry out the parish duties. By 1330 about two-thirds of the Warwickshire benefices were in the gift of ecclesiastical patrons and one-third in the hands of lay men. Kenilworth Priory accumulated fifteen benefices, Coventry seven, the collegiate church of St Mary's, Warwick, two (Proudfoot 1982: 208).

Such ponderous machinery for establishing the work of God inevitably aroused criticism and consequently the direct simplicities of the orders of preaching friars had great appeal in the Midlands as elsewhere.

During the thirteenth century the main orders of preaching friars were all speedily established in the west Midlands. As early as 1230 the Franciscans or Greyfriars were provided with a foundation in Coventry by Ranulf, Earl of Chester. Their church was an important stone building in the town and the friars, although they received some support from royalty, were also supported by many small bequests from the citizens of Coventry.

The other principal order of friars, the Preaching Friars or Dominicans (1170–1221), was equally quickly established in midland towns. At Newcastle there were twenty Dominicans by 1227 and thirty at Warwick by 1263, although these large numbers were not maintained. The Austin friars also had a house at Warwick and another at Stafford. A Carmelite house of friars was also established at Coventry in 1343, and the Theatines had a house at Thelsford near Atherstone. Essentially all these orders had the same purpose – to minister and to preach to townspeople and the poor. Among the services they undertook at Coventry, not the least was the burial of plague victims.

Much remains obscure about the Church in the Midlands in the early Middle Ages, and it is particularly difficult to evaluate the response of the people to the moral demands made upon them. This was a period of regulation, when organised institutions were being elaborated. The Church was becoming more hierarchical, more feudal, more clerical, more and more enmeshed in property and perpetual rights. While the Midlands shared fully in the general developments in western Christendom, including the foundation movement, the region appears to have contributed little to the wider Church in the way of leadership or initiatives. The clergy were becoming more and more an order apart and although as a body they were recruited from a broad social band, leadership in the Church lay with those of noble family and patronage. The ordinary laymen and women on the other hand were in this, as in every other aspect of life, required to support by their labour and devotion an increasingly elaborate and complex structure.

Chapter 5

Order, power and politics: 1100–1377

Peace and order in the provinces depended on the uncertain and shifting balance of power between kings and magnates. The principal royal official was the sheriff. The shrievalty of Staffordshire was combined with that of Shropshire, and that of Warwickshire was combined with Leicestershire. Nevertheless the separate identity of the shires was maintained, they were separately administered and accounted separately to the exchequer. Neither sheriff had a castle as was customary elsewhere but the Sheriff of Staffordshire usually made his headquarters at Bridgnorth on the Severn in Shropshire and the Sheriff of Warwickshire carried on his Warwickshire business from the Common Hall in Warwick where his clerks worked, and the sheriff's court met. There were sheriffs' jails at Stafford and at Warwick. Before the reign of Henry III the sheriffs were often noblemen carrying out their duties through agents and subordinates, but from the mid-thirteenth century they were usually professional royal servants, men such as Walter de Cantilupe and Ralph Fitznicholas who had experience of royal administration in more than one area of England and whose power depended upon the support of the king.

Royal justices perambulated the shires from 1166, arriving about every seven years. In Warwickshire they held their sessions at Warwick in the Common Hall and occasionally at Coventry, and in Staffordshire at Lichfield. They audited royal revenues, heard crown pleas and inspected the general administration of the county. In each county royal coroners were appointed usually four to each shire who were responsible for making preliminary enquiries and recording accusations. By the thirteenth century they were also responsible for holding enquiries into cases of sudden death. By the time the justices arrived there were large backlogs of cases and many of the felons had already made themselves scarce. In 1306 in Warwickshire ninety-one of those presented for murder and thirty-four presented for other killings had already fled (Hilton 1966: 259).

The manor courts not only organised the economic life of the community but also absorbed much of the work of keeping the peace between neighbours, dealing with disruptive persons and disputes between the villagers and the lords. Much of the business properly belonging to the village and hundred courts had by custom and convenience passed into the manor court. This process of absorption was legitimated by grants of 'sac and soc, toll and team and infangthief' which, if fully exploited, empowered a lord to erect gallows for the execution of thieves caught redhanded (Hilton 1966: 230)

By the early fourteenth century the wealthiest magnate in Staffordshire was the Earl of Lancaster. This great family of blood royal had land in twenty-two counties. In Staffordshire they held Tutbury Newcastle under Lyme and the manors of Rolleston Marchington and Barton under Needwood (Hilton 1969: 221). The estate had formerly belonged to the Ferrers family who had been established at Tutbury since 1107 and had built up a great honour in Staffordshire and Derbyshire of 200 manors and in 1232 they had acquired from the Earls of Chester the castle of Chartley.

Meanwhile the heirs of Roger de Teoni were quietly building up their power and estates by shrewd marriages. The first of the Stafford family to be ennobled was Edmund Lord Stafford who died in 1308. In the ensuing fifty years the family was enriched by the estates of the Bohun and Clare families. Ralph became the first Earl in 1350 and a great castle was built on a hill about a mile from Stafford with commanding views to north and south. It was a large rectangular building with five towers and walls 7 ft thick at their base.

In Warwickshire the only real magnate family were the Earls of Warwick. The earldom had been held by the Newburgh family from 1088 to 1263 when on the intervention of Henry III the heiress was married to John de Plessis, a royal servant. From them the estate passed to the Maudit family and in 1298 through the marriage of Isabella Maudit to William Beauchamp of Elmley Lovett, Worcestershire. Warwick Castle became the main residence of the family and was extended and rebuilt. Guy Earl of Warwick who died in 1315 was a close associate of Edward I, held many royal offices, and was the first to bring the family into national politics. At his death he held land in eight counties including ten estates in Warwick and had a clear income of about £700 (Mason 1975: 67–77).

In addition to the aristocratic and ecclesiastical lords there were several families of 'lesser magnates' in the area. In 1301 thirty Staffordshire tenants held land worth £40 a year and over (Birrell 1962: 9). Dudley Castle passed from the Fitzansculfs to the Paganels and then to the de Someries who in 1264 fortified a derelict Norman castle. In 1322 the great estates were divided between co-heiresses and the de Sutton family from Malpas made Dudley their principal residence. The de Someries and the de Suttons exercised great local influence in south Staffordshire and north Worcestershire. The Audley family were of similar rank. Their castle was at Heighly in north-west Staffordshire and they had manors in six neighbouring villages, five in Shropshire and one in Cheshire. Not all influential families were tenants in chief. The de Bermingham family held nine fees in Warwickshire and Staffordshire of the Lords of Dudley and also acquired wide lands by marriage in Cheshire, Northamptonshire, Buckinghamshire and Leicestershire (Watts 1979–80: 5–10).

The majority of landowning families in Staffordshire and Warwickshire were men of very much more modest wealth and status. There were perhaps about 150 families in the two counties who held one or two manors and some other parcels of land and who exercised influence mainly over their manorial tenants. By the thirteenth century about sixty in Warwickshire and about thirty-five in Staffordshire were knights, by this period a social rather than a military status, although there was no close correlation between wealth and knighthood. They varied from families assessed for taxation in 1337 as having an income of £20 or £30 a year, families such as Pype Legh and Wasteney in Staffordshire, to those with only £5 a year, a group which included Coyne of Weston and Hughford (Hilton 1970: 216–18). Men of these families filled many important roles in local society. They were called upon to act as members of special commissions, as keepers of the peace, as assessors and as commissioners of array for the crown. They frequently acted as jurors, brought many cases to the courts and were frequently themselves involved in disputes as defendants (Hilton 1969: 225). They attached themselves to the greater magnates, witnessed charters and indentures, joined the magnates' retinues on state occasions, acted as their agents and receivers, supported the magnate in peace and war in return for a variety of favours and opportunities. In their younger days they went in the armies of the magnates or of the crown to fight in Scotland, Wales, Ireland, Gascony and France and sometimes returned enriched with ransoms and loot, sometimes suffered sickness or wounds.

In the course of the long-drawn-out struggles for power between the magnates and the Crown, midland families were from time to time drawn into the contests at court, the *coups d'état* and the civil wars. There was much fighting in the Midlands during the wars of Stephen and Matilda (1135–54) (Crouch 1982). Ranulf Earl of Chester built up enormous independent power and played a major political and military role. His town of Coventry was besieged in 1143. Henry II gained control of the Midlands early in his reign, but the rebellion of the third Earl of Derby in 1175 involved many midland families and when the King recovered his authority the castles of his opponents including Tutbury and Dudley were demolished. During the reign of John both the Earl of Warwick and the Earl of Ferrers supported the King but in the last years of that reign and the early years of Henry III there was much disruption of administration in the Midlands and when in 1227 Henry III declared himself of full age and sought to assert his power he was opposed by both the Duke of Lancaster and the Earl of Warwick. Later in the reign the King's chief opponent Simon de Montfort had many allies in the Midlands and Midlanders were taken in the retinues of the great lords to fight at Lewes. After the defeat and death of Simon de Montfort in 1265, more than thirty Warwickshire families had their estates surveyed by the crown with a view to confiscation (Hilton 1950: 119). Robert Ferrers Earl of Derby lost five Staffordshire manors and eighteen manors elsewhere and many of his midland estates including Tutbury Castle passed to the Earl of Lancaster. The Ferrers kept diminished state at Chartley. The reign of Edward I saw royal officials and magnates in unusual harmony struggling with some success to restore order and regular government at least until 1294. In the last years of the reign of Edward I good relations began to deteriorate under the pressure of the King's money-raising activities.

During the reign of Edward II, Guy Earl of Warwick played a leading part in the opposition to Piers Gaveston and to the King, and it was he who eventually seized Gaveston in 1312, held him prisoner at Warwick Castle and had him summarily beheaded at Blacklow Hill near Kenilworth. Six years later it was the rise of the Despenser family which revived the opposition of the magnates to the Crown and on this occasion it was Thomas Earl of Lancaster who was the most conspicuous leader of the opposition holding conference with others at Leek in 1318 to agree on a scheme to control the King. Thomas was a national not a local figure, holding the earldoms not only of Lancaster but also of Leicester, Derby, Lincoln and Salisbury and lands in many counties. Nevertheless the King was able to gain the upper hand and the Earl was defeated at the battle of Boroughbridge in Yorkshire and beheaded. The aggregation of a great baronial power was interrupted and royal control was reasserted. The Midlands continued to be the scene of disturbances, culminating in 1326 when Edward II was brought prisoner to Kenilworth and forced to abdicate before being taken to Berkeley Castle where he died. By 1330 Edward III was able to secure royal control and if men of the Midlands went to war, it was in France.

In all these episodes the younger men of baronial, knightly and gentry families were called upon to fight in distant places and for those who remained at home there was from time to time fighting, bloodshed and taxation. On the whole however it is the continuity through these excitements which is remarkable. The lesser landowners and the local families retained their estates, and even when lands were forfeited they were often recovered by the heirs. Neither the Stafford nor the Warwick families ceased to add to their wealth despite fluctuations of power, and already patterns of leadership and affinity were beginning to be established which were to persist.

Part two

The Later Middle Ages

Chapter 6

Population and housing: 1300–1530

Well before 1300 there were signs in many places that most of the land suitable for agriculture was occupied and that soils producing grain crops would soon become exhausted. Long Itchington, Wormleighton and other populous manors of south Warwickshire had already reached and passed the peak of optimum growth before 1300 (Thorpe 1965: 41).

In the late thirteenth century there had been a series of bad harvest failures and in 1315–17 all northern Europe was hit by a great famine. Croxden Abbey chronicle lamented a year of high prices, famine, disease and death (VCH Staffs VI: 36). The position was made worse by sheep murrain (1317–19), and cattle plague (1319–21). Severe drought followed in 1325–6. There was famine in Halesowen as early as 1293 (Razi 1980: 38), and in the decades between 1310–20 many manorial records speak of deaths and surrenders of holdings, of holdings kept in the lord's hand for want of tenants and of crops untended (VCH Staffs VI: 37).

The Black Death reached the Midlands in the spring of 1349. No overall judgement can be made on its severity in the Midlands as compared with other areas, but it had a catastrophic effect on particular groups and communities. About 40 per cent of the clergy of both dioceses died; and also, in June, July and August of 1349, fifty-three clergy of Worcester diocese died, well over twice the normal number for such a period. In 76 out of 175 parishes of Warwickshire new presentations had to be made because of the death of the incumbent, and in some parishes two or three incumbents followed each other in one year. The Bishop ordered the clergy to remain at their posts, celebrate mass faithfully, and hold public prayers of intercession on Wednesdays and Fridays (VCH Warks II: 17–18).

At Stoneleigh whole families were wiped out (Hilton 1969: xxxix), and at Halesowen 40 per cent of adult males died and child mortality was also high (Razi 1980: 106–8). At Alrewas on the Trent, mortality seems to have been particularly severe. Sixty died in May 1349, seventy in June and fifty in July, compared with the usual two or three deaths a month. One-third of those who died were landless, many of them cottagers (VCH Staffs VI: 37–8).

Plate 2.1   Brass memorial of John Egerton esquire of Wrinehill, who died in 1518, and of his wife Elizabeth. The memorial is in Madeley parish church, Staffordshire.

Holdings had been falling vacant on some manors for fifty years or so before the plague, even while assarting still continued on other manors. Nevertheless, the number of vacant holdings in 1348–50 does provide some indication of the impact of the plague. At Keresley there were twenty-eight holdings vacant, but only twenty-two new tenants to undertake them, and the windmill and the horse mill were out of use. The bailiffs of the Bishop of Worcester reported that the customary tenants had died of deadly pestilence; mills and forges were vacant, pigeon houses empty and tithes unpaid (VCH Warks II: 18).

In other places vacant holdings, though numerous, were quickly taken up. Newcomers and existing tenants were available to take on the vacated holdings at Erdington, Wootton Wawen, Yardley, Hanbury and other places in Arden and Staffordshire. However, the plague and other epidemics persisted with further major outbreaks in 1361–2, 1368 and 1374–5, and it was this repeated mortality, rather than the initial onslaught which in the long run depleted the population. Decay of rents and abandonment of holdings attributable to pestilence can be traced in the later fourteenth century at many manors, among them Stafford, Madeley, Branston, Tittensor, Stone and Norton in the Moors (VCH Staffs VI: 38–9).

For a century and a half after 1350 population at best replaced itself and there is little evidence of growth in particular communities in the Midlands. Records of the poll tax of 1377 (paid supposedly by all persons over fourteen) are extant for Stoneleigh and Kineton Hundreds of Warwickshire and for Staffordshire. The Staffordshire lists suggest an average of about 20 persons per square mile and in Warwickshire 20 to 29 per square mile. This compared with an average of 30 and over in East Anglia and a populous belt stretching from Devon in the south-west to Yorkshire in the north-east. In Staffordshire the larger groups were still to be found in the west and in the valley of the Trent, but there is also evidence of some growth in the parishes of the eastern river valleys of the Dove, the Trent, the Tame and the Mease. There was also apparently some growth of population in the northern communities such as Leek, Sheen and Grindon, and on the south Staffordshire plateau especially around Walsall. The numbers of taxpayers were more evenly distributed, and it does appear that the effects of the Great Famine and the Black Death, however severe in the short term, did not change the profile of the relative sizes of particular communities to any great extent (Pinnock 1971: 34). It seems probable that some towns were able to continue to grow in size even during the fifteenth century. This was certainly the case at Coventry, Birmingham and Walsall (Pinnock 1971: 134).

The subsidy of 1523 provides the next opportunity to survey the comparative size and wealth of particular communities, for it was based on a new assessment on land, goods and wages. It seems that there had been a marked shift in the distribution of both taxpayers and their wealth during the fifteenth century. The north-eastern moorlands of Staffordshire still had less than four people per square mile and in this they may be compared with the hill and moorland country of much of northern England. The rest of Staffordshire and all of Warwickshire was more comparable with southern and central England, the average number of taxpayers per square mile was in the 5–9 category, bringing the greater part of the area into the 'lowland zone'. Secondly there was considerable growth in the Needwood Forest area, and although the western communities had not declined they were no longer preponderant. The numbers of taxpayers in Hemlingford Hundred in north Warwickshire had increased from 20 per cent of the whole county in 1327 to 31 per cent in 1523. The great majority of the places with more than average numbers of taxpayers were in the north and north-east of Warwickshire, and in the south only Stratford had increased in numbers.

In Staffordshire 42 per cent of the 316 communities had less than 10 taxpayers and in Warwickshire 35 per cent of the 273 communities. In the woodpasture region of south Staffordshire and Arden there were more taxpayers but they were diffused through several linked hamlets. In this area there were 43 villages out of 52 with more than 10 taxpayers. Seisdon Hundred had 25 places with over 30 taxpayers and Hemlingford had 25. Individual villages that listed over 60 taxpayers, included Knowle (64), Berkswell (68) and Fillongley (68), and the riverside village of Alrewas with its outlying hamlets returned 96 taxpayers.

The trends in the amounts of tax paid reinforce those indicated by the distribution of the numbers of taxpayers. Coventry had 6 per cent of the taxable wealth of the county in 1325 but had 37 per cent by 1523, even though it had already passed the peak of its growth. The citizens paid an average of about 12s. per head (Stanley 1982: 248) and yielded more in taxation than any other city except London, Norwich and Bristol (Hoskins 1976: 13). The richer agricultural regions of the Trent, Dove and Avon paid amounts of tax averaging 21s. a square mile and in Warwickshire the highest average apart from the towns was in Kineton Hundred where the taxpayers paid about 4s. per head.

South Staffordshire and Arden were becoming more prosperous as well as more populous if the amount of tax they paid can be used as an indicator – the average for this area was 14–18s. a square mile. There already appears to be some correlation between prosperity and areas where pastoral and woodland conditions offered opportunities supplementary to those of husbandry (Sheaill 1968: 306–12; Pinnock 1971: 173–4).

It is clear that there continued to be a good deal of movement of people in and out of manors; a turnover of between 30 per cent and 80 per cent has been shown for some midland manors in the fifteenth century. In the later Middle Ages families could seek to enhance their status and improve their living, by moving into towns or alternatively by moving into other manors. It has been suggested that some, at least, of the increased proportion of population in Arden and the forest areas was probably due to migration from the Feldon.

When villagers moved from one manor to another such evidence as there is suggests that they usually did so with specific and planned purpose. They moved when they inherited land in the new manor, or to marry a bride. In Halesowen after the Black Death many of the people moving into the manor were able to secure a title to land immediately and many already had relatives who lived in Halesowen (Razi 1981: 120–4). The incomers came from surrounding parishes for the most part but a few had arrived from as far away as Herefordshire and Derbyshire.

A few Staffordshire villagers are known to have moved into small towns such as Kidderminster, Droitwich and Bridgnorth and even to have gone further afield to Stamford, Leicester and Lincoln (VCH Staffs VI: 42). However during the later Middle Ages it is probable that there was much less immigration into towns, and that movement into other villages was a more attractive economic prospect (Field 1983: 4–43).

In England as a whole the pressures of subsistence, the plagues and the famines, the successive waves of various epidemic diseases combined to reduce the population to an estimated 2,100,000 by the generations of 1400–30 and the evidence of the early sixteenth century suggests that recovery had scarcely begun. In general this was probably true also of the Midlands, but the detailed studies of Pinnock and Stanley suggest that in some parts of Arden and the valleys of the Trent and Tame there were communities which by the late fifteenth century were already experiencing some quickening of growth.

Even a stagnant population needed to be rehoused from generation to generation and the more prosperous Midlanders were building themselves houses of greater comfort and dignity. Cruck-framed houses continued to be built in Staffordshire and most of Warwickshire, but the post-and-truss construction also began to be employed. The main posts were of heavy oak with large panels of wattle of hazel twigs and daub of the abundant clay to fill in the spaces between the timbers. The houses of the gentry in the late Middle Ages had two floors and a stairway leading from the cross passage. At Kinvaston Hall, West Bromwich Manor House and other places, the main hall building was flanked by two cross wings, one at each end. One cross wing formed a service wing and the other contained a solar and chamber overhead. In these houses the chimney was now an integral part of the building. In many smaller houses in the Midlands the stone chimney was a self-standing structure of stone which survived several rebuildings of the timber-framed house adjoining.

By the late fifteenth century the house wrights were using greater numbers of smaller beams, and 'close studding' became a characteristic local feature by the sixteenth century. The windows were protected with wooden screens sliding in wooden grooves and there was some moulding of the beams and the door frames. However in general there was little decoration on midland houses. The space upstairs was divided into two or three chambers. The roofs were either thatched or more usually made of stone flags. At West

Bromwich (*c*. 1450), Pillaton Hall (1488) and other gentlemen's houses of the period the cross wing contained a separate chapel with gallery for the family. At Weoley Manor the chapel was a separate stone building with a lead roof. In 1424 there was also at Weoley a great hall, chambers, nursery, pantry, buttery, kitchen, a stable of eleven bays, and bakehouses and brewhouses, all situated inside the great moat. The moat was crossed by an elaborate drawbridge with a gate house, and there was a stable by the outer gate for strangers' horses.

In towns houses were built upwards rather than outwards, confined on their burgess plots of 30 ft width. They were often aligned sideways to the street and the workshop was at the front with a living room behind and chambers above. The hearth was an integral part of the building and the upper storey jettied out to give protection. Roofing materials varied according to local materials. In many parts of Staffordshire heavy flat stone tiles cut from sandstone were used but in southern Warwickshire where there was more corn grown thatch was the standard form of roof, in both country and town. In Stratford, despite the obvious dangers, most town houses were thatched in the Middle Ages. Only the largest and most important buildings had glazed windows or tiled floors, but by the fifteenth century most of the houses had some lead roof drainage.

The timber frames were fashioned by the carpenters who assembled the frame on the site, but another group of workmen, the wallers, filled in the spaces in the frame with wattle and daub and if required covered the wall with lime and plaster of Paris. The workmen were not organised in a gild and often came from the surrounding villages to work in the towns. The carpenters in the fourteenth century earned 4*d*. a day which rose in the second and third decades of the fifteenth century to 5*d*. and 6*d*. a day. The assistants and labourers were earning 4*d*. a day by the end of the fifteenth century. Building was a slow operation; the building of the Angel, a tavern in Henley Street, Stratford, took six years to complete (Lloyd 1961: 13–25).

Meanwhile the castles of the great magnates were extended with great halls and solars built within the older fortifications. About 1390 a magnificent great Hall was built at Kenilworth Castle for John, Duke of Lancaster, second only to Westminster Hall in its size and grandeur. It was 90 ft long and 45 ft wide with large windows to the courtyard and to the outer bailey, a spacious bay window on each side and at the lower end an adjoining tower containing buttery, pantry and other service rooms. The Hall was approached by a grand outer staircase and a magnificent porch. Other large living rooms were added on both ground and upper floors to the south of the castle. In the grounds Henry V ordered the building of a gracious 'Pleasaunce', a dining hall of timber on the edge of the great lake.

More and more the emphasis was on comfort, dignity and some degree of privacy for those who could afford it. In the mid-fifteenth century John Brome and his son Nicholas were responsible for building Baddesley Clinton Hall, a beautiful moderately sized home with large windows, moulded beams and large chimneys. There was a moat, and a gateway and porch with arrowslits, but the military is visibly subordinate to the domestic use of the building.

At Coughton the Throckmortons publicised their rising prestige by undertaking an extensive rebuilding of their home from about 1500 to 1510. The gatehouse was large and impressive, built of stone with a great four-centred vaulted archway and symmetrical windows on either side. Within the archway was the courtyard with timber-framed range of buildings on either side. By the time they came to decorate the dining room in 1530 the Renaissance had crept in, bringing foliage and medallions (Pevsner 1966) and suggesting that for a minority, despite the difficulties of plague, famine and civil wars, there was a margin of wealth to purchase comfort and adornment to make life more gracious.

Chapter 7

Adaptation and change in agriculture: 1300–1530

The fourteenth and fifteenth centuries saw major adjustments in the patterns of farming, in land management, and in social organisation. Shortage of manpower was one, but only one, of the factors involved. Others included changing economic opportunities, the intensification of exchange, the growth of the non-agricultural sector of the economy, and perhaps even changing climatic conditions. Change was cumulative rather than catastrophic. On the Staffordshire estates of the Duchy of Lancaster, after the Black Death the vacant holdings were re-leased and the rent rolls of the 1370s were only 10 per cent lower than in 1313 (VCH Staffs VI: 42). Evidence from many estates in the Midlands and other areas suggests that price and rents did not fall dramatically in the fourteenth century. For some fifty years or so after the Black Death some lords and tenants were able to find ways of making some profits despite the troubles.

In the immediate aftermath of the crisis some lords sought to compel the remaining tenants to carry out more services. Others, including the Bishop of Worcester, tried to attract tenants to take up vacant holdings by reducing entry fines and moderating payments. Whatever the short-term reaction, in the longer term the trend was to payment of rents in cash. The decline in labour services was already a marked feature before 1300, and by the fifteenth century they had become an anachronism (Dyer, C. 1981: 9). Prices for agricultural work rose considerably in the late fourteenth century but nevertheless lords continued by and large to use full-time labour and casual-paid labour, and to balance this by concentrating on the more profitable and less labour-intensive forms of farming.

From the 1390s the Bishops of Worcester used their arable lands only for food required for consumption and employed wage labour to cultivate them. On many manors labour services disappeared by agreement and by the negotiation of money rents. However, the manorial courts were frequently required to deal with groups of tenants who were actively resisting demands for labour services. The troubled history of Halesowen manor entered a new phase in 1379 when the tenants in the hamlet of Romsley refused to perform services for a year. At Farewell, Kinver, Burton and Walsall and other places in the Midlands the tenants refused customary services. The objection was not only to the remnants of week work, but also boon works for haymaking, harvesting and ploughing. At Romsley, the discontent developed into full-scale rebellion, when the bondmen declared themselves free. The dispute was so prolonged and bitter that the ringleader was put in prison and died there.

Some tenants of the Bishop of Worcester at that date were refusing to pay tallages, recognitions and fines, which they asserted were servile or unfair. At Lighthorne rents were reduced because the tenants declared that otherwise they would be forced to quit the manor to earn a living (Hilton 1975: 63–7).

As work payments declined, so rents became more and more important. The Bishop of Worcester was collecting £400 and £500 at a time in rents, but on the whole rents were falling by the fifteenth century to about two-thirds of what they had been in the thirteenth century. At Tutbury for example the demesne was leased at 1s. an acre in 1313. A hundred years later 100 acres of it was leased at 10d. and the remaining 140 acres at 6d. an acre or less. At Uttoxeter rent of demesne land fell from 10d. an acre in 1313 to 6d. an acre by 1414 (VCH Staffs VI: 39).

Rural lords had probably reached a peak of prosperity in the early fifteenth century, and by the mid-fifteenth century, many of them were in some difficulty. There were rent strikes in the 1430s when peasants refused to pay at Southam and Brockhampton as in many other parts of the country (Dyer 1968: 11–33). The difficulties of the lord are illustrated by the accounts of the Duke of Clarence in 1480. The demesne was leased out, but the rents were reduced and so were the rents for fisheries on the Avon. No one could be found to lease the demesne of Sutton Coldfield and even the dovecote was in ruins (Hilton 1952: 85–6). Faced with difficult and possibly deteriorating situations, lords of manors tried many expedients to restore profits, among them the leasing of demesne, concentration on sheep farming, or changing organisation of rents and services (Birrell 1962: 213–16).

The decline of serfdom and the disappearance of week work corresponded with the decline on many estates of direct cultivation of the demesne. The Bishop of Worcester had leased out his demesne by 1392, and the Priors of Coventry by 1411. The Beauchamps leased out seven of their eleven demesnes by 1390 and three more by 1403 (Dyer, C. 1981: 4). The demesnes of the Duke of Lancaster were leased at Agardsley, Barton, Marchington and Uttoxeter (VCH Staffs: 42–3). The Lucys on the other hand continued to manage their demesnes themselves and the Catesbys kept one manor in hand until the 1470s while leasing out the rest (Dyer, C. 1981: 4).

The terms of the leases were very diverse even within one estate. At Sutton Coldfield there were 30 leases, one-third for life, the rest for terms from 20 to 100 years. During the fifteenth century leases tended to get longer – terms of 40, 60 and 99 years are noticed. The lessees came from many different social groups. Of 75 demesnes leased in Warwickshire (1375–1511) 18 were taken by gentlemen, 4 by clergymen, 3 by townspeople and 19 by peasants while the remainder could not be identified. Gentlemen such as the Harewells of Stratford, the Throckmortons of Coughton and the Catesbys of Radbourne leased demesnes near their own manorial base. As they consolidated and extended their landed wealth so they also took on local office, and gained access to the networks of power and influence and through land and patronage, raising their social status (Dyer, C. 1981: 4). Similarly, wealthy freemen worked their way to gentry status, as did the Boughtons who were stewards of the Cistercian Abbey of Pipewell (Northamptonshire) (John 1970: 21–9). Lessees often acted in groups. For example, in Barton under Needwood in 1410 Richard Holland, John Pennyfather, John London and John Hopkinson, together took a ten-year lease of 40 acres of demesne, meadow and a sheepfold (VCH Staffs VI: 43). Demesne leasing gave opportunities to tenants to extend the farms and gradually made landholding accessible to a wider social group. The terms were the result of negotiation and bargaining and closely related to economic realities for both lord and tenant (Dyer, C. 1981: 5).

As labour services gradually disappeared customary tenure slowly came to depend upon a written copy of the court roll and the custom of the manor. Copyhold tenure was protected by the courts in practice, and copyholders could pass their land to their heirs after a token surrender to the lord. At Erdington in the fifteenth century there was an unbroken succession of family holdings, a small heriot was paid, but no surrender took place and there was no entry fine.

On some manors heriots and entry fines remained burdensome and indeed became even heavier, including not only beasts but carts, brass, pigs, bees and many other items. Entry fines could still be very high, as much as £6–15 (Hilton 1975: 234–5). Rents, dues and taxes in the west Midlands were mainly paid in money which was raised by buying and selling animals and foodstuffs in the local markets and, where opportunity offered, using local materials to make saleable manufactured articles.

The broad tendency of the fifteenth century was for individual holdings to become larger, and for the land to be concentrated in the hands of fewer families. Thus at Ladbrook the 58 holdings of 1389, had been reduced to 37 by 1457. At Keresley there had been 28 holdings in 1389 but 22 in 1457, and Alveston had 85 in 1389 but only 32 by 1502. The 'normal' size of holding or arable land tended to increase, ranging from 30 to 90 acres on manors in both the north and south of the region (Dyer, C. 1981: 7–8).

Despite the trends to pastoral farming and leasing by individuals, communal mixed farming was the basis of economic life in the majority of villages, and the management of some open arable fields was a central feature, albeit as part of a complex and varied whole. Many central Staffordshire manors in the fourteenth century provide evidence of three-field organisation and three-course rotation, and this was also the case in Arden and the upper Avon valley. In the Feldon, however, there are suggestions that the older two field rotations were developing into four or more fields. Older two field organisation was reorganised to three field at Long Lawford, Southam and other south Warwickshire parishes.

Wheat prices offered no incentive to develop specialist arable farms, but grain and peas and beans had to be grown to feed the farmers themselves, the numerous townsfolk, and also their animals. Wheat and maslin or mixtum (wheat and rye mixed) continued to be sown before winter and barley and oats in the spring. In the Feldon drage was grown (barley and oats mixed) and winter wheat and rye. Oats were little grown in the Feldon, but continued to be important in Arden and north Staffordshire. Smallholders and cottagers grew vegetables, had orchards and small hemplecks where flax or hemp was grown (VCH Staffs VI: 30–5).

In much of Warwickshire and parts of Staffordshire there was a marked movement from arable to pasture farming in the late Middle Ages. This was partly due to conversion of arable to pasture and partly to extension of the existing grazing lands (Dyer, C. 1981: 9–10). At Hatton on Avon (near Hampton) and at Walton Deyville all the former open fields were converted to pasture. In other villages new pasture was contrived within the existing structure, unwanted arable being temporarily converted to grass 'leys'. At Long Itchington and Lower Shuckborough headlands were used as grassland and grass strips maintained among the corn. By the end of the fifteenth century such 'leys' had become an integral part of the management of the land at Alveston and Tachbrook (Dyer, C. 1981: 12).

Many of the demesne farmers carried on little or no arable farming. The Lucys built up sheep pastures in a five-mile radius around Stratford on Avon on the sites of six deserted villages, where in 1519 they kept 2,676 sheep, about 100 cattle, 16 pigs and 11 horses. The Catesbys held the whole of Radbourne as a 1,000 acre pasture on which, in 1476, they had 2,742 sheep, 54 cows and 129 other cattle, 9 horses and hundreds of rabbits (Dyer, C. 1981: 19). However it was mainly the gentry and leaseholders who specialised in sheep farming, together with some town-based graziers. Such were Benedict Lee of Warwick, Thomas Hawkes of West Bromwich and Thomas Lench of Birmingham (Dyer, C. 1981: 16–18). Large peasant flocks were mentioned incidentally in law suits from time to time – as when 300 sheep and 60 lambs were stolen from a peasant's close in Streethay in 1398 (VCH Staffs VI: 46).

The Spencers provide a notable example of specialisation in sheep farming. As freemen they rented then bought abandoned arable land, pasture and meadow around Wormleighton in the late fourteenth century. By the end of the fifteenth century they had leases of pasture lands at Napton, Lower Shuckburgh, Burton Dassett, Ascote, Wormleighton and Stretton under Fosse. By 1520 this land was enclosed with great hedges and ditches. The hedges were double-planted with oak trees at intervals, and sluices and channels provided water for the animals. Much of the output was sold direct to London (Thorpe 1965).

Not all conversion to pasture was for sheep farming. John Brome built up a specialist cattle farm at Baddesley Clinton in the 1450s, which included enclosed grassland and woodland. He bought about seventy cattle a year and sold them after two years, mainly to butchers in Coventry and Warwick. He occasionally supplied beef to the royal household (Dyer 1972: 1–14). Many of the cattle that grazed in Warwickshire and Staffordshire were brought in from Wales by drovers. After being fattened during the summer they were sold as beef in Coventry, Birmingham, Worcester, Banbury and sometimes London (Dyer, C. 1981: 20). Wolverhampton churchwardens added an honest penny to church funds by hiring out fields overnight to the drovers as they passed through the town ((U) WLS Churchwardens' Accounts).

Leases were made to freeholders and copyholders of herds as well as of land. Individuals hired animals to each other, or combined in twos and threes to trade in cattle. Thirty-seven cattle were stolen at Uttoxeter, 40 at Church Eaton and 24 at Mancetter, each herd belonging to an individual tenant. Agistment was paid for 81 cattle, 68 horses and 784 pigs by tenants in Needwood Forest. In villages where pasture was limited the increased stock put pressure on the available pasture. Overcharging was recorded on many manors, including Madeley, Horton, Cannock and Rugeley (VCH Staffs VI: 46–7).

Changing patterns of farming induced landholders at many different levels of society and for many different reasons to enclose land formerly open. On the whole the late settled areas of Arden and Staffordshire tended to be enclosed earlier and with less disturbance than elsewhere in the region. The old open-field village of the river valleys and the Feldon could be enclosed only at the cost of greater social tension. By the end of the fifteenth century many villages had a highly complex combination of open and enclosed land, the product of five hundred years of adaptation and change. By 1408 Knowle had 70 fields and by 1463 Erdington had 87, 51 of them held in severalty (separately). The market town of Birmingham had 36 several-arable fields, 36 several-pasture closes, and a miscellany of gardens, tofts and crofts. At Bordesley there were 143 free tenements in the hands of 54 tenants, 10 acres of demesne leased out and 234 enclosed crofts (Hilton 1975: 134–6).

Permanent hedges and fences tended to interfere with traditional rights. Manor court rolls show presentments of individuals fined for arable land enclosed in severalty 'which ought to lie fallow' at Aston, Temple Balsall, Erdington, Middleton, Kenilworth and Sutton Coldfield. Neighbours disputed about newly erected fences and words often lead to direct action – for example, fences were thrown down at Kingswood in 1512. Despite such excitements, much enclosure took place by agreement. Some lords accepted a fee for a licence to enclose. At Sambourne between 1445 and 1472 about 240 acres were enclosed by agreement of sixteen 'half-yardlanders'. They consolidated their strips, built hedges and kept the gates in repair. This was in addition to other enclosures going on at the same time in the 2,000 acre parish (Dyer, C. 1981: 27).

Substantial depopulation occurred in at least 120 settlements in Warwickshire, 70 of them in the Feldon, and a possible further 50 wholly or partly depopulated in Staffordshire. Among the villages which disappeared in eastern Staffordshire were Syerscote, Croxall, Chartley and Blore (Bate and Palliser 1970–1: 31–6). Most of these villages were in the river valleys and clay plains while comparatively few woodland villages were depopulated. The majority of the cases, known or suspected, date from between the early thirteenth century and the mid-fifteenth century.

The reasons for the disappearance of villages were always various and usually particular to the circumstances of each community. Some villages had grown up in the period of population expansion on marginal lands. Now the population had declined, poorer sites were abandoned in favour of better. Such was the case at Broughton, Dorusley and Eccleshall in the fifteenth century. Small settlements with an inadequate number of able-bodied men soon became non-viable (Bond 1982: 149). Depopulation was usually gradual rather than catastrophic, and evidence of holdings not being taken up, of unbalance between small and large holders, and the reorganisation of holdings preceded the decline of population (Dyer, C. 1982: 24).

Long Itchington parish comprised in the thirteenth century a large village in the valley of the river Itchen, a hamlet called Bascote, and a number of dispersed farmsteads. The population of Long Itchington reached its peak in the mid-fourteenth century, but some desertion of crofts is identified from archaeological evidence from the end of the thirteenth century. The village was shrinking at both the eastern and the western end. The adjoining hamlet of Bascote also shrank considerably, probably in the fifteenth century (Wilson 1979–80: 120–32). Conversion to sheep pasture certainly accelerated the process of depopulation but at Wormleighton, Weston juxta Cherington and Hatton, in Hampton Lucy, conversion was the result rather than the cause of depopulation, when lords faced with dwindling rent rolls removed the remaining tenants to create enclosed pastures (Dyer, C. 1982: 29).

By the beginning of the sixteenth century the midland landscape presented an extraordinary variety of open fields, closes, great pasture ranches and single subsistence farms. Almost every kind of economic organisation of agriculture can be found somewhere in the two counties, and each was itself the outcome of many factors. Soils, markets and price changes were certainly important influences upon the outcome, but so were the reactions of individuals and of groups of people to the challenges they presented.

Chapter 8

Burgesses and citizens

After 1315 the founding of new towns came to a halt, but many of the existing towns not only survived, but were able to grow and develop in the changed economic and social context, on a basis of diversified commercial activity.

Coventry grew rapidly in population so that in 1377, 4,817 people in the town and its suburbs paid poll tax, as many as at Norwich and Bristol. Indeed only York and London had more taxpayers. The population continued to grow to a peak of about 10,000 by 1430. No other midland town came near Coventry in size, for Lichfield with 367 poll-tax payers was the next largest.

The towns characteristically comprised men and women of varied occupations. Even in towns such as Coventry, Warwick and Lichfield where the wool cloth trades were the principal source of wealth, there were significant numbers of metalworkers and leatherworkers, and individuals in these groups were among the wealthiest townsmen. Butchers and other food sellers were numerous and there were in each town one or two important innkeepers as well as many alesellers. By the early sixteenth century these merchants, craftsmen and retailers lived and worked in solid, well-furnished, timber-frame houses around the market place, like James Leveson's 'High House' in the High Green at Wolverhampton.

During the fourteenth century some midland towns gradually assumed a greater degree of control over their own affairs and over the relations between their town and other authorities.

In Coventry the drama of the transition from the disarray of 1322 to the power of 1377 began in 1327 when Queen Isabella, widow of Edward II, purchased from the Montalts the manor of Cheylesmore and the Earl's 'Half' of Coventry. The prior was now faced with a formidable adversary and the merchants had a powerful ally. Between 1332 and 1345 the prior found it increasingly difficult to exercise jurisdiction over the whole town and his 'half' was gradually reduced by pressure and attrition (Gooder 1981: 14–16).

Meanwhile, the wealthy and powerful merchants formed gilds. In 1340 they were able to find £1,000, no less, to secure a royal licence for the merchant gild of St Mary. In 1343 the religious gild of St John the Baptist was chartered and that of St Katherine. In the year of the Black Death when the cult of the Blessed Sacrament was being invoked all over Europe, the Coventry Corpus Christi gild was established and in 1364 the Holy Trinity Gild. The rapid succession of grants and charters is an indication of the wealth and cohesiveness of the merchants and their access to royal favour. During the 1360s an informal union developed between the gilds and this was made official in 1392; the composite fraternity was known as the Trinity Gild and dominated the town.

In 1345 the Crown granted to Isabella, and through her to her tenants in Coventry, the right to corporate status with mayor and bailiffs. This was the first such grant to be made in England. They could maintain their own treasury and lease out town lands. The first mayor and bailiffs were appointed in 1348 and the council functioned from at least 1375, controlling the market and paying their own fee farm of £50. The charter implied government of the whole town but there remained the problem of the prior's jurisdiction. Against so powerful a combination the prior could only submit and the outcome was the 'tripartite indenture' of 1355, an agreement between Isabella, the priors and the commonalty that the mayors and bailiffs should exercise their corporate rights throughout the city and that the old portmanmoot (which seems to have been temporarily overridden during the prior's ascendancy) should hear small pleas for the whole town (Gooder 1981: 1–39). The process of independence was carried further in 1375 when Coventry was made independent of the county sheriff and in 1377 when it had a recorder or chief justice of its own and by 1398 the mayor, the recorder and four townsmen were empowered to act as magistrates. After a visit to the town in 1451, Henry VI made Coventry a city and county exercising jurisdiction over the nineteen suburban villages of Cheylesmore manor. Thus Coventry achieved the same status as York and Norwich.

Furthermore, the twenty-four who met daily to supervise officials and conduct town business were themselves the elite of the Trinity Gild and Corpus Christi Gild. The complex interrelationship between the two separate, but closely intertwined bodies – the Gilds and the Corporation – has been analysed in depth. The craft gilds provided the entry at the lowest level into the hierarchy of civic power. A young man on election to the craft gild became a freeman of the town, entitled to practise his trade. The masters and officials of the craft gilds could be elected to the junior Corpus Christi Gild, and office holders in the Corpus Christi Gild could be elected mayor. After holding this dignity and being by this time of mature years they were to be found as members of the Trinity Gild, senior in wealth, worship and authority. The masters of the Trinity Gild were also the aldermen and sheriffs of the city.

All these offices of dignity and seniority were represented to the whole community by the rank and precedence and due order kept on all public occasions, but most especially in the public processions. For the officials concerned the processions were onerous and expensive. They wore rich robes

Plate 2.2   Saint Mary's Hall Coventry, built in 1342 for the Gild of Merchants.

of office, according to their degree, and were expected to provide lavish hospitality on particular occasions and to support all the public expenses of the city. No man worth less than £300 was considered suitable. The prestige of office and the responsibility of authority were brought home to the officials themselves and to the community by the elaborate series of oath-taking ceremonies and the rituals and customs which accompanied them. The holders of office were expected to be worthy and respectable and this in the fifteenth century involved full and frequent participation in religious rituals and acts of worship. The mayor and the council were expected to begin every day's business with public and ceremonial attendance at mass (Phythian-Adams 1972).

Town government in some other midland towns proceeded on broadly similar lines, though on a smaller scale and with less pomp and circumstance. At Newcastle under Lyme, for example, the mayors were members of the *'prima duodena'* (or first council of twelve) and *'secunda duodena'* (second council) of the gild. During their actual year of office they withdrew from the gild council, but returned to it afterwards. As in Coventry there was a regular hierarchy of civic office to be served lasting a minimum of five years and a maximum of ten years before a man might become mayor. The daily decision-making of the town was carried out by a small group known as the mayor and his brethren – that is the aldermen.

On taking up the more important offices a burgess was required to take his corporal oath. Persons refusing to serve were disenfranchised, as were those who disobeyed the mayor. They were readmitted by the mayor on making a penitential payment to the church (e.g. 2 lbs of wax, or a thousand shingles for the church roof) and on promising formally during service time due obedience to the mayor in future (Pape 1928: 186–7).

There were always close links between the ruling urban elite and the most prestigious of the gilds, similar to those at Stratford on Avon where the Gild of the Holy Cross 'acted as a sort of shadow government additional to the official borough court' (Hilton 1982: 6–7).

While Coventry, Walsall, Newcastle and Tamworth established town councils with real power and independence, many of the seigneurial boroughs founded in the twelfth century acquired only rudimentary elements of urban organisation. Nuneaton burgesses elected bailiffs and goodmen, and at Halesowen, Birmingham and Burton on Trent they elected a high bailiff and low bailiff, with some assistant officers. Warwick, although a royal borough and shire town which sent burgesses to Parliament, nevertheless continued to be dominated by the Castle. The Earl's officers held court for the town, appointed the bailiff and the rent collector, and the only officials were four constables, two aletasters and four pinders – little more than could have been found in any village. The Earl remained responsible for the market and received about £21 yearly in tolls and tallage. In 1383 a group of the wealthier citizens formed the Gild of the Holy Trinity and St Mary which in addition to its religious functions came to be responsible for the bridge over the Avon. A second gild of St George was formed, but neither body at this stage took responsibility for the government of the town.

The success in economic and constitutional terms of some towns contrasts with the decline of other hopeful initiatives of the thirteenth century. Poleshill, Chipping Basset, Eccleshall, Talk and Kinver were amongst the places with burgesses and markets which nevertheless remained in essence manorial villages. Perhaps half of the markets chartered in the thirteenth century had ceased trading by 1500; adverse circumstances included the stagnation of population for most of the period, the recurrence of disease especially in towns, bad harvests and high food prices and the better opportunities for some in the villages. Even established towns were suffering from decay and distress. Lichfield and Warwick both sought relief from taxation on this ground and the decline of Coventry from its peak in about 1450 has been analysed in detail. The city slipped from the rank of third to ninth largest provincial town, as it was subjected to severe epidemics, high grain prices, stagnation in the textile industry and difficulties in obtaining raw materials. There was some recovery in the last years of the fifteenth century, but decline continued in the early sixteenth century. More people preferred to live and trade in rural areas and there were fewer employers in the city. By 1520 some 500 habitations within the walls were in decay. The dignity and grandeur expressed in civic and religious ritual in Coventry contrasted with the administration of the city which was often acrimonious, turbulent and pettyfogging. The fifteenth century saw a series of bitter disputes which were often carried on for years.

The decline of Coventry, already well advanced by 1515 was turned into a crisis between 1518 and 1525 by a local slump, high food prices, a national trade depression and very heavy taxation. Between 1522 and 1525 Coventry contributed in all £2,044 to the Treasury leading to a local shortage of coin.

These troubles coming together have been vividly described as 'desolation of a city', and by the early sixteenth century they were having long-term effects upon the city's social and economic life, and were beginning to undermine its dominance of the region (Phythian-Adams 1979: 33–51).

The balance of population and taxable wealth, as we have seen, was already shifting to the Arden and coal-field parishes of north Warwickshire and south Staffordshire and the market towns in this area with their rural industrial hinterlands were showing signs of prosperity in marked contrast to the decay of Coventry. The rebuilding of Dudley church, St Edmunds, possibly after a fire in 1475, was on a considerable scale. Wolverhampton church was almost entirely reconstructed beginning in 1439 when members of the leading town families, Leveson, Hampton and Swynnerton, obtained the stone on favourable terms and the work continued at intervals until 1520. During this period a clerestory and transepts were added, the walls were raised and battlemented, and a new central tower completed. The money and the initiative for the rich furnishing of the church in the early sixteenth century came substantially from the townspeople, not from the Dean.

Systematic studies are as yet wanting, but there seems to be *prima facie* evidence that Walsall, Wolverhampton and Birmingham, at least, were maintaining their prosperity during what were nonetheless difficult times. The numbers of taxpayers listed in 1525 provide some support for this suggestion. Coventry now had only 713 but, in contrast, many smaller towns had increased their numbers of taxpayers. Stafford, Burton, Walsall, Coleshill and Tamworth, all now had over a hundred, Wolverhampton, with its outlying villages, had 168 and Birmingham, in a much smaller geographical area, had 153. The amounts assessed in each town also support in general terms the suggestion that some towns were becoming more prosperous while Coventry declined. Birmingham, a town with only a very small area of 'foreign', was required to produce £23, that is, one-tenth of the assessment for the whole of Hemlingford Hundred, and Solihull, Coleshill, Burton on Trent, Uttoxeter and Tamworth were all assessed at sums of about £10. Moreover these market towns were beginning to establish links with London and with Bristol on their own account, and to show signs, however modest, of independent economic growth.

Chapter 9

Travel, commerce and industry

It is easy to underestimate the number of roads in the Middle Ages since most of them are known to us only through incidental references in deeds and disputes. The great artery of the region was now the London to Chester road, passing through Hill Morton, Southam, Coventry, Coleshill, Lichfield, Stone and Newcastle under Lyme. This was crossed at Lichfield by the principal Bristol to Doncaster road, passing through Birmingham and Sutton Coldfield (Darby 1973: 175).

From the principal towns main roads led off in every direction, from Stratford to Alcester, Birmingham, Evesham and Oxford; from Birmingham to Alcester, Stratford, Warwick, Shrewsbury and Lichfield; from Walsall to Wolverhampton, Lichfield and Sutton Coldfield, and from Coventry to Leicester and Warwick. Even the small market towns were the centre of four or five lanes leading to neighbouring towns and to the highways. There was much movement along the roads of the medieval midlands. The great lords moved from estate to estate, bishops, archdeacons and deans with their retinues made visitations, carters brought specialised materials into the towns, Welsh drovers moved slowly through the region with their herds. Most important, however, was the constant movement of goods to and from market. All buying and selling theoretically took place in the public markets at the official hours marked by the ringing of the market bell and in the customary market place. The bellman's duties included prevention of nuisances, maintenance of the legal rules of trading, supervision of weights and measures, control of standards and, above all, collection of tolls. The market officials licensed stall-holders – at Tamworth twenty-two were licensed in 1422 and forty in 1455.

Almost every market town and some market villages had a market cross which could be a building of some elaboration with a room above. By the end of the fifteenth century there was usually also the shambles and the town clock, and permanent shops and stalls were becoming a feature of houses fronting the market places (Slater 1982b: 190).

The goods brought into the markets were for the most part foodstuffs drawn from the immediate area and raw materials in small quantities for the use of local craftsmen. Goods entering Lichfield market in 1299 included vegetables, livestock and wine, a wide range of textiles, broadcloth, worsted canvas and even silks, and alum for the fullers. There was also coal, salt and millstones, and metals including iron, lead, brass, tin, copper and small steel bars (Thorpe 1954: 140–61).

Corn merchants sometimes travelled considerable distances from market to market, and grain merchants became the target of attack in years of high corn prices. In August 1401 the Birmingham, Stratford and Alcester roads were dangerous for corn merchants travelling to the markets of Coleshill, Birmingham, Walsall and Dudley. They were attacked by groups of men lying in wait and their horses put to flight, so that the women and children riding on the horses with sacks filled with corn fell off and some died. The sacks were cut and the corn scattered along the roads (Cal Pat Rolls 1399–1400: 552–3).

Among the people using Tamworth market were individuals from Coleshill, Hopwas, Doddington, Drayton Overton and Rushall, all local villages and small towns; and occasionally a trader from Derby, Lincoln or Leicester. Early sixteenth-century recognisances for debt recorded at Coventry show that Coventry's customers were coming from further afield, including other parts of Warwickshire and the western villages of Northamptonshire. Individual merchants came from Leicester, Banbury and Birmingham, from Shrewsbury, Stratford and Warwick, and twelve came from London.

By 1500 there had been about eighty grants of fairs in Staffordshire and Warwickshire. These attracted merchants from wider distances and a more varied range of merchandise. At St Giles Fair at Alcester there were sales of iron goods, pottery, baskets, tinware, salt and spices. At Coventry Fair the wealthy could buy imported aniseed, almonds, sugar, white soap, prunes and oranges, pomegranates, liquorice and white paper. Lichfield and Birmingham Fairs provided similar commodities. The Willoughbys of Wollaton Hall near Nottingham did much of their household purchasing at fairs and made use of Birmingham, Lichfield and Penkridge, as well as fairs in Derbyshire and Nottinghamshire (Phythian-Adams 1979: p. 29).

Coventry was the centre of much long-distance trade. Carters carried goods regularly from and to Chester which linked the city with Ireland. Dublin merchants belonged to the Trinity gild in the fifteenth century and the Corpus Christi gild in the sixteenth. There were regular contacts with Bristol, and French wines were imported. There were also regular carriers to and from Southampton and it was from that port that Coventry obtained woad for its Coventry blues. Wool convoys went to and from King's Lynn and Boston, and returned with imported goods from the Baltic. Coventry cloth went to London and to York. There was trade with all the larger commercial towns of England, and Coventry made formal trading agreements with Southampton and Bristol. Such connections were not confined to Coventry. Birmingham merchants traded with King's Lynn and with Bristol and sixty-four Birmingham men took out the freedom of Bristol (Toulmin-Smith 1871).

In the Midlands as elsewhere an important commodity of trade was wool and the area provided a great variety of types of wool from that of the black-faced sheep of the north moorlands to the Cotswold sheep of the south west. The sales of wool by the religious houses to the Italian merchants give some indication of the significance of the trade. At an estimated 240 fleeces per sack this list alone accounts for the fleeces of over 41,000 sheep. The Cistercian abbeys were producing moderate- to good-quality wool for export. The wool fetched from 16 to 18½ marks per sack on the Flemish market. Croxden wool, however, achieved much higher prices – 21 to 31 marks – and Coombe and Bordesley were obtaining good prices at 19 marks per sack (Hilton 1966: 81–2). However Staffordshire was not a large wool-producing county, the total of sacks being only about one-quarter of that of Lincolnshire or Suffolk (Yates 1974: 5).

It is known that eight Coventry wool merchants were selling wool in Dordrecht in 1343, since they had their merchandise seized there and there were Coventry merchants who had made up a combined cargo of wool which they shipped at Boston in 1400, only to have it confiscated at Stralsund. Margaret Russel, a sister of the Gild of Holy Trinity, had goods to the value of £800 seized by the men of Santander (Harris 1935: xxii). Thirteen merchants from Coventry attended the merchants' assemblies at Westminster in 1340 and 1342, and the York Assembly in 1372 (Pelham 1939a: 43). From 1363 the export of wool was confined to merchants of the Calais Staple and towards the end of the fifteenth century a number of Midlanders became members of that company. James Leveson of Wolverhampton had by the 1520s built up a large fortune in the wool trade and his brother Nicholas, another stapler, became Sheriff of London (Wordie 1982: 10–11). Their fellow townsman, Stephen Jenyns, merchant of the staple, not only became Mayor of London but in 1522 paid £3,500 in tax, the highest assessment in the City (Hoskins 1976: 68).

There were numerous wool merchants at Stafford (VCH Staffs VI: 214), and Lichfield had a wool market, and at Warwick wool merchants headed the list of taxpayers in 1327 and 1332. Such men played a conspicuous part as local benefactors. John Botoner and his brother made major contributions to the rebuilding of St Michael's, Coventry (Harris 1898: 307) and Stephen Jenyings endowed a grammar school at Wolverhampton.

While a few Midlanders became rich by exporting wool, many were becoming involved in the manufacture and sale of woollen cloth at a time when the national export trade was rapidly expanding. There were weavers in most of the towns and many of the villages, and the numerous fulling mills in the Midlands testify to the distribution, wide diffusion and volume of the manu-facture. They were sited near the main commercial centres on narrow streams, easily dammed to provide the modest amount of water power required for fulling cloth. The earliest known mills date from about 1290 and there were at least twenty-six in the two counties by the end of the fifteenth century. There were five in the vicinity of Coventry, one at Stratford, one at Hampton, and six around Birmingham. In Staffordshire there were mills at Burton, Barton under Needwood, Tutbury and Rolleston, Uttoxeter and Rocester in the east, Betley in the north-west and Himley in the south. Not all fulling was done by water power: some fullers lived in the market towns. Stratford on Avon had a street of fullers and Lichfield in 1377 had five fullers, three weavers, two shearmen and a nap raiser who paid poll tax. In 1459 Richard Tyball of Wolverhampton was in trouble with James Leveson for having spoilt cloth entrusted to him. A Wolverhampton fuller, Henry Brice, went to London and became sufficiently wealthy to bequeath to his home parish 20 marks for the church, 20 marks for cloth for the poor and £40 for masses (Mander 1923: 14–16, 169–72).

The dyeing of cloth was an urban specialism, for the town dyers had access to imported woad and madder with which they dyed white cloths received from both town weavers and country weavers. Dyers were working in Burton, Birmingham, Wolverhampton, Stratford and Stafford. Coventry dyers imported dye stuffs in such huge quantities that only London and Salisbury received more and 'Coventry Blue' was especially famous.

The clothiers who collected and marketed the cloths were the key figures upon whom the development and extension of the manufacture depended. Midland merchants were sending cloth overseas by the early-fifteenth century – for example, William Waring of the Lea in Wolverhampton was exporting through London by 1414 and Ralph Spurrier of Birmingham removed to King's Lynn, where he traded with the Baltic. No less than a hundred merchants, including Coventry merchants, had claimed compensation on an earlier occasion when English cloth had been confiscated in the Baltic. The aulnagers accounts of 1397–8, 1400 and 1405–6 for Warwickshire demonstrate the overwhelming predominance of Coventry in the cloth trade in comparison with other Midland centres (Pelham 1945).

Cloth sales in Coventry were supposed to be conducted under regulation at the Drapers Hall, supervised by the Trinity gild and the Common council. In 1355 it was ordained that all that sold cloth on Fridays did so in the Drapery 'unless it be a woman that bringeth a dozen in her arms' (Harris 1898: 100). Sales of cloth from Devon, Cornwall and Ireland were also restricted to the Drapery. Wolverhampton and Dudley also had Drapery Halls in the fifteenth century.

The wool and cloth trades shared in the general depression of the mid-fifteenth century and there are signs that the Midlands were affected by the difficulties. Many of the larger estates, including that of the Earl of Warwick, reduced wool production. Supplies of alum from Genoa and woad from Toulouse were interrupted and the Coventry dyers found it difficult to maintain their monopoly in the face of undercutting and infiltration by hatters and drapers. Trade with the Baltic received a setback in the 1480s, when the merchant adventurers were expelled from Prussia.

One response to the difficulties was to turn to new trades such as capping at Coventry and at Stafford, and hatmaking at Newcastle, Coventry and later Burton. By the end of the fifteenth century the textile industry was ceasing to be the most dynamic sector of trade in the Midlands although it continued to be of considerable importance.

The manufacture which probably ranked next in importance to textiles in the later Middle Ages was leather making and leather working. At Coventry it was the second most important occupation and at Birmingham, Stafford, Stratford and Lichfield some of the wealthiest townsmen were tanners, corvisors and saddlers. Coventry had a Corvisors gild by 1380 and Stafford had a shoe makers gild of six Masters by 1476. Leather workers were important members of the gild of the Holy Cross at Lichfield and the gild of St John Baptist at Walsall.

Commercial metalworking was already of importance in Birmingham, Stratford, Wolverhampton, Coventry and Newcastle under Lyme. Newcastle supplied nails and ironware for the building of the royal castles at Harlech and Conway (Palliser 1974: 24). At Coventry, the association between metalworking and the wool trade encouraged the production of girdle points and woolworkers' cards. There was a Coventry company of smiths, girdlemakers and cardmakers by 1435 regulating the trade, controlling the activities of journeymen and the metals used in the making of girdles. The Coventry girdlers are recorded buying iron from Devon in 1329. However, the company's regulation that the smiths were to shoe strangers' horses on Sundays indicates that even in Coventry the trade was still closely associated with that of the general horse blacksmith. Walsall was a centre for the manufacture of bits, spurs and horse harness. Robert Grubber had a forge in the borough 1362 to 1363 and in 1394 to 1395 Richard Marchall sold nails to the Earl of Warwick's household. Several smithies are recorded both in the town and in the foreign and by the mid-fifteenth century it is clear that metalworking, especially the making of spurs and bits, predominated.

Brass was brought into the towns and braziers and pewterers frequently appeared among urban occupations from the fifteenth century. Thomas Fylkes, pewterer and citizen of London, was living in Walsall before he moved to the capital about 1415. Pewter pots and pans, jugs and drinking vessels were in increasing demand in the later fifteenth century and the pewter industry was one of the few urban industries which were expanding rapidly. There were already links between the midland pewterers and braziers and the city of London. One or two goldsmiths and silversmiths also made a living in each of the principal market towns by the manufacture and repair of domestic and church plate.

While most commercial and much manufacturing activity was concentrated in the towns the extractive industries were of their nature diffused through the countryside and exploitation of mineral resources was managed as an aspect of landholding, within the manorial framework. There was a great variety of stone suitable for many purposes readily available on many manors in the Midlands. In the northern Moorland the Pennine millstone grit was used for millstones, despite the formidable problems of cutting and transporting this heavy and tough stone. Further south sandstone was available in many parts of the region, and the stone for many parish churches was obtained from small local quarries opened for the purpose. At Stratford much of the building stone used came from Warwick and Rowington quarries a few miles away. It was carried in cartloads of half a ton at a cost of $1\frac{1}{2}d$. a mile. Some sandstones were also suitable for grinding and sharpening tools and small quarries in both the north and south of Staffordshire supplied the modest demand. Limestone was used for building stone and fissile limestone was divided to produce stone roof slates at Grafton and Drayton. Limestone was also burnt and ground into powder at Wootton Wawen, Balsall, Wilmecote, Sutton Coldfield, Barr and Cheylesmore. Small quantities of plaster of Paris was available from Welcombe.

The most specialised form of stone working was the cutting and working of the alabaster of the Trent and Dove valleys. From the fourteenth century elaborate funerary monuments began to be erected and the wealthy employed alabaster carvers from Marchington and Burton. The earliest surviving alabaster monument in England is the effigy of John de Hanbury in Hanbury church seven miles west of Burton. Local quarries and workmen became more numerous in the late fourteenth century and specialist carriers of alabaster transported the stone long distances. In 1374 John of Gaunt ordered two large blocks of alabaster to be sent from Tutbury to London for the tomb of his late wife. The craftsmen of Nottingham and of Chellaston just over the county border in Derbyshire were the most famous, but many wealthy painters and workers of alabaster also lived and worked in Burton on Trent. By the early sixteenth century Burton outclassed its rivals and incised slabs, effigies and images were sent all over England (Owen 1978: 170).

There was some mining on all three coalfields of Staffordshire and Warwickshire from at least the thirteenth century. Coal was not really needed as a fuel in a well wooded area, but in some parishes was so easily obtainable that it could be dug out by hand and used when baking, salt making and metalworking. In the north on the manor of Tunstall in 1282 a mine of sea coal was worth 14s. 8d. Coal was worked in Norton-in-the-Moors in 1316, Shelton in 1297 and Keele in 1333. In south Staffordshire coal was worked at Sedgley in 1273, and in Bradley, Bilston, Wednesbury, Amblecote, Kingswinford and Halesowen along the line of the outcrop of the 10 yard seam. The main centre of coal mining was probably Wednesbury where in the late fourteenth century there were protracted disputes between the lord and his tenants, and also among the tenants themselves, concerning the digging of coal in the common fields of the parish. Colliers were sued for breaking down the lord's corn and taking away earth, and some of them were required to enter into a bond of £40 security that they would not dig coal in the manor without a licence from the lord. Henry Hancocks was required to enter into a bond that neither he nor his heirs would dig sea coal

> in a field at Wednesbury called Cock Heath or elsewhere within that town or make any coal mine there without licence . . . nor must the demesne land, meadow or pasture be fouled or trampled to their hurt or prejudice by any mine hereafter made by him or his heirs or by carriage of coal by them dug and by other carried, nor must he enable others to do so without such licence
>
> (Ede 1962: 38)

Lords of the manor and freeholders expected to be able to dig coal on their lands and the right to mine and to license mining was usually reserved to the lord. Copyholders' rights were more uncertain and in a number of south Staffordshire manors, including Sedgley and Darlaston, there were two categories: the 'free copyholders' who had rights to mine, and the 'base copyholders' who had to pay a small fine to do so. There was mining in mid-Staffordshire on the bishop's manor at Longden and in north Staffordshire on Newcastle manor (Birrell 1962: 18). Sea coal was dug on the Warwickshire manors of the prioress of Nuneaton in the 1360s and there was also sporadic activity in Chilvers Coton, Stockingford and Haunchwood. It is probable that the coal so obtained was sold in Coventry, certainly the mayor in 1469 attempted to prevent coal carts entering the city and causing congestion on market days (Grant 1982: 326). All these mines were shallow-surface workings dug for short periods and then abandoned. Indeed, one of the chief causes of their being recorded was when the villagers left open diggings to the annoyance of their neighbours or lords.

Ironstone was also dug in south Staffordshire in the Rushall area, in the foreign of Walsall and in north Staffordshire in the manor of Tunstall. The iron ore was of good quality and was worked mainly by the migrant bloomers, who set up their hearths wherever wood and ironstone were available. There were, however, more permanent forge sites, notably at Sedgley, and forges have also been identified at Cannock, Longden, Rugeley and Kinver (1373) in central Staffordshire and at Madeley (1293) in the north and at Walsall in the south of the county in the thirteenth century, all parishes which were subsequently associated with metalworking. Archaeological evidence has provided details of two water powered forges operating at Rugeley and at Aldridge in about 1480 where the water wheel probably operated the forge hammer.

Quarrying and mining served local consumers and local needs in the late Middle Ages and much of the working was sporadic. The workforce was drawn from the general resources of labour and skill in the local community. The region's mineral industries were as yet very underdeveloped, and still marginal to agriculture and to the manufacture based on wool, wood and leather. In general the scanty records of mediaeval industry suggest that wherever some asset was readily available it was exploited. Manorial organisation in such places adapted itself to exercise supervision of industrial work. If the expectation of profit was sufficiently high the inadequacy of medieval roads and communications did not inhibit the movement either of goods or people.

Chapter 10

Clerics, laymen and reformers

In the later Middle Ages the bishops were more than ever essentially administrators operating in the sphere of central rather than local government. Both their secular and their sacred functions were carried out by an elaborate and permanent body of deputies and subordinates. Their preoccupation with affairs of state and their absence for long periods from their dioceses should not necessarily be characterised as 'neglect' for the life and organisation of the diocese could function smoothly in their absence.

Like all large landholders, the bishops of the Midlands suffered difficulties in the collection of rents during this period of economic adversity. The revenue of the Bishop of Worcester declined from about £1,200 in 1300, then stabilised at about £1,000, and finally rose slightly at the end of the period. At about £700 a year the bishopric of Lichfield was accounted the third poorest diocese in the kingdom. Nevertheless, bishops could supplement their income from lands, from fees, court perquisites and royal generosity. The bishops did, in fact, build up large cash surpluses which they used for church building, endowments of chantries, loans to the Crown and maintenance of large household and lordly lifestyle (Haines 1965: 40).

The real work of pastoral care devolved upon the suffragan bishops who were appointed in unbroken succession from the early fourteenth century. For example John Greene, Bishop of Insulensis, an Augustine canon, was suffragan to Bishop Booth and was responsible for sixteen out of seventeen ordinations taking place in the Coventry and Lichfield diocese. The suffragans also consecrated, dedicated and reconciled churches, conducted episcopal visitations and maintained doctrine and morals (VCH Staffs III: 34–5; VCH Worcs II: 43).

From the fourteenth century there was a vicar general who, when the bishop was away, was the head of episcopal administration. They were mainly concerned with institutions to benefices, elections and appointments. Another

Plate 2.3 Wall painting of a Madonna, discovered *c.* 1966 on the wall of Burton Dassett Parish Church.

high level official with a similar responsibility was the sequestrator general. Booth's Sequestrator was John Redel, who took responsibility for ecclesiastical benefices and administered the revenues of such as were sequestered.

The consistory courts heard a wide range of law suits including matrimonial and financial cases. The courts met at Lichfield or Worcester for a total of 25–32 days a year and litigants and lawyers had to betake themselves to those towns. The archdeacons' courts continued, but lesser cases, including the proving of wills under £5, were carried out by the rural deans. From the fourteenth century onwards priests, among the higher diocesan clergy and from the mendicant orders, were appointed as penitentiaries to supplement the work of the parish priests as experts in moral guidance hearing confessions, granting absolutions, and awarding penances to both laymen and clergy. In the fifteenth century two penitentiaries were appointed for each archdeaconry in Lichfield diocese. The appointees were men who already held important rectories – for example, the rector of Stoke was appointed penitentiary to the archdeaconry of Stafford.

Thus, by the fifteenth century the diocese was not so much a pastoral community, but a huge sophisticated bureaucracy of mandarin-like complexity. Bishops and their officials were for the most part men who had never served a parish or a family, they lived in courts and great communities, travelled constantly, and were surrounded by clerical subordinates. They were enmeshed in an international network of patronage and privilege, and governed by means of a subtle and complex judicial system, with its own esoteric lore of canon and precedent. Between these careerist clergy-administrators and the 'poor parson of a town' there was a social gap as wide as that between a lord and cottager.

By 1533 there were in Staffordshire 41 rectories, 38 vicarages and 18 stipendiary curates and in Warwickshire 83 rectories, 89 vicarages and some stipendiary curates (*Valor Ecclesiasticus*). The incomes of the rectors lay between £5 and £60 a year and the vicars between £2 and £10, and thirty-two incumbents in Staffordshire had income of less than £7. In addition to these there were the ordained priests in religious houses and many clergy employed in gilds, hospitals and colleges and the canons and vicars of the cathedral, so that the proportion of clergy to laymen was probably about one priest to every fifty laymen (Bill 1967: 4).

The majority of the clergy in the fourteenth- and fifteenth-century Midlands were drawn from the families of richer peasants and lesser gentry. About 10 per cent of Warwickshire clergy had a university education – usually at nearby Oxford (Bill 1967: 18). This education was not so much a preparation for clerical life as an extension of it, and many who went to college did so after ordination, on leave of absence (Bill 1976: 19).

There was no systematic preparation for the priesthood. Some ordinands had lived in the bishop's household, or in a monastery, many were themselves members of religious orders. Most of the remainder probably learnt their Latin from a local priest or monk. John of Bredenhill, parish priest of Kingswinford, was a man of a local family who was presented to the parish by the favour of Constance Sutton, lady of the manor of Kingswinford. His living was valued at 24 marks from tithes and dues, and supplemented by 40 acres of church lands. John fell into bitter disputes with his patrons, and complained of them to the court of Chancery, in the course of which he alleged that seventy-nine books had been stolen from him. These included the grammar of Aristotle's physics, twenty-five treatises of logic, music, geometry and science. There was a bible, a sacred history, copies of the *Golden Legend* and the *Pupillae Oculi*, the 'four evangelists glossed', Lombard's *Sentences*, a missal, and breviaries, sermons and poetry. He also had parchment, papers and writing materials, and he may have been teaching or, perhaps, producing books. John de Bredenhill was charged by his enemies with a whole range of crimes of violence including rape and robbery (Guttery 1950). The frequent presence of clerks among the people accused in courts of crimes of violence, assaulting mills, destroying crops and so forth, suggests that they were less law abiding than the laity. However, a detailed study of the 4,000 recorded clergy of Warwickshire, between 1300 and 1500, suggests that the problem was literally more apparent than real. Only about 5 per cent of prosecuted criminals were clerics, including those in minor orders, and the offences were often exaggerated (Bill 1967: 23).

The movement for the foundation of religious houses was spent by the mid-fourteenth century. The last house founded in the west Midlands was the priory of St Anne at Coventry (1385), one of only seven Carthusian houses in England. Carthusian monks lived each in his own cell and little garden, and emerged only once a week for the community mass. They maintained complete silence, and concentrated on solitary prayer, saying the office alone, and meals were provided to each monk separately through a hatch in the door of his cell. The Coventry priory was founded in 1381 by William, Lord Zouch, and its founder monks came from the Charterhouses in London and Nottingham (VCH Warks II: 83). The Coventry house – like other Carthusian houses – was much respected by burgesses and courtiers and maintained its vocation and support. In Coventry, very unusually, the monks educated twelve children.

In general, the foundations made in the early Middle Ages continued without much institutional change. The three houses of the Knights Templar had been granted after sequestration in 1310 to the Knights Hospitallers. In 1377 French monks were expelled from England and only English monks were allowed to join existing houses. Tutbury and Lapley priories were among the 'alien priories' seized by the Crown and farmed out to courtiers and clerics. The property of religious houses was supposedly inalienable in perpetuity, but income could be transferred to other uses. In 1495, the Bishop of Lichfield was able to secure the suppression of the Austin Priory of St John at Lichfield, to provide a site and endowment for a school. In 1526 Wolsey secured the appropriation of twenty-one houses, with a view to their suppression, to provide endowment for the foundation of an Oxford college, among them

St Mary's, Sandwell, and St Giles, Canwell, in Staffordshire. Such suppressions removed only small insignificant houses but they set a precedent for the method to be employed in a wholesale manner in 1536 and 1539 (Hibbert 1910: 20–6).

The old abbeys remained small, Coventry had 20 monks, Kenilworth 18, Burton on Trent 12. Almost all the rest had less than 10. There are reports of too many servants, too many officials, too many non-religious living in the house and too many secular visitors. Abbots absented themselves and quarrels broke out over internal arrangements, and with local lay lords. This picture is one-sided since it is derived from visitations and records made when something was amiss, but it is difficult to find anything to set against the impression of stagnation and lack of positive achievement.

The abbeys certainly supported large numbers of dependants, men and women, the sick and retired, servants and hangers on. The monks kept up the '*opus dei*' and having acquired parishes by appropriation were responsible for the provision of a priest for the parishioners. To the nuns, the bishops wrote in

---

Plate 2.4   St Michael's Parish Church, Coventry. It was erected mainly between 1371 and 1430 at a time when Coventry was growing rapidly in size and status. It was one of the largest parish churches in England and its steeple was almost 300 feet high.

French or English, which suggests that they knew no Latin. This, in itself, is an indication that they were scarcely able to perform the divine office with understanding and skill. At both Brewood and Farewell the nuns seemed to have laboured in the fields themselves.

None of the houses was wealthy and most were outright poor. They found the duties of hospitality to wayfarers, the giving of doles, the support of corrodians and the uninvited guests wished upon them from time to time by bishops and kings, a real strain on their resources.

The grandeur of medieval abbeys such as Tewkesbury and Tintern is so familiar that it is salutary to consider the priory buildings at Sandwell. The church had a chancel of 41 ft and a nave of 57 ft by 18 ft, with an additional south aisle 9 ft wide. There were two chapels and a bell tower. There was a cloister and the priory itself contained three low parlours, three upper chambers and a chimney. A hall was built out from the priory 57 ft by 21 ft and at the far end there was a kitchen, two upper chambers and outhouses. There was a small gatehouse with a chamber over, a large barn, hayhouses, a kiln house, a stable and a water mill of timber and thatch. When surveyed, in 1526, most of the buildings were already ruinous, the moat was dried up and the orchard overgrown (VCH Staffs III: 219).

There was nothing new about individuals praying for the souls of deceased members of their families and making arrangements for masses to be said for them in perpetuity. From the thirteenth century onwards, however, the practice was greatly encouraged. During the troubled and terrifying early fourteenth century the immediacy of an unprovided death must have come home to even the most casual sinner. By the early sixteenth century there were 112 chantries in parish churches in Staffordshire and 39 separate chantry chapels, and Warwickshire had 62 chantries. Only 12 chantries in the two counties were endowed after 1450, although after that time individuals continued to leave money for masses in their wills, to the parish churches and to the cathedral.

Some of the chantry endowments were on a very grand scale. Walter Cook of Lincoln endowed a chantry at Knowle with its own chapel and six priests. Stratford College was originally endowed by the Bishop of Winchester, in 1331, to enable five priests to say masses for him in the parish church of his home town. The chantry attracted further donations and eventually a separate chapel of stone was built in the churchyard together with a house for the priests with separate rooms, but a common hall for meals (VCH Warks II: 123).

Chantries for particular families were expensive and people of more moderate means associated together to found them. Almost every association felt itself responsible for praying for the souls of deceased members and their families, and many of the gilds endowed large chantries of several priests. The interiors of the parish churches were enriched by the building of numerous chantry chapels, often elaborately and expensively decorated as pious layfolk indulged their taste for finery, dressed-up statues, and multiplication of 'lights'.

91

St Michael's parish church at Coventry, had seven chapels endowed by the smiths, the girdlers, the mercers, the cappers and cardmakers, and the dyers. Holy Trinity nearby had chantry chapels belonging to the mercers, the drapers, the butchers, the tanners, the Holy Trinity gild, the Corpus Christi gild, and a chantry chapel dedicated to St Lawrence. Walsall had ten chantries by 1530. They included endowments of masses for the Gild of St John Baptist, a daily mass for the family of Sir Roger Hillary, a daily mass for the royal family and a mass for Walsall men slain at the battle of Shrewsbury (SHC 1915: 301). The chantry priests fulfilled a wide variety of functions. At Coventry they assisted with the relief of paupers and in Birmingham, Stratford and Coventry chantries were used as chapels during time of plague. There were ten chantry schools in Staffordshire and nine in Warwickshire, but the main work of chantry priests was in the parishes. At Birmingham they helped with the 2,000 communicants at Easter and heard confessions in Lent. At Tamworth there were 104 families in a circuit of 20 miles and the chantry priests assisted the vicar. Many of the chantry chapels acted as chapels of ease, especially in winter when, as at Knowle, the people could not get to the parish church (VCH Warks II: 129). At Guy's Cliffe, near Leamington, the chantry provided an income in his old age for John Rous who wrote his *Historia Regnum Anglie*, observed depopulation and practised physics, astronomy, surgery and plainsong.

In every town and some large villages the wealthier and more prestigious men and women combined to form religious gilds. They undertook a variety of social and public responsibilities, but their main purposes were religious and included the endowment of chantries, the maintenance of particular altars and statues, and making contributions to religious dramas and processions.

The Gild of the Holy Cross at Stratford was the result of an amalgamation of three earlier gilds in 1403. Of its thousand or so recorded members over a period of 150 years the occupations of 380 are known. These prove to cover the whole spectrum of elite occupations in the town, merchants, drapers, grocers, bell founders, butchers and smiths. The gild included a few clerics, but it was the established town laymen who dominated the gild (Fox 1953).

The gilds attracted members from outside the community. In the early fourteenth century 30 per cent of the members of the Stratford Gild came from outside Stratford from 300 villages not more than 25 miles from the town and 100 more places further afield. By the end of the century the proportion of outsiders had risen to 70 per cent (Hilton 1975: 94). Among its 3,000 members the Gild of Knowle included men and women, religious and lay, noble and simple, from parishes all over Warwickshire and adjoining counties, especially those to the west of Knowle, notably King's Norton, Yardley and Birmingham (Bloom 1865).

Many of the members from a distance were invited to enhance the prestige of the Gild or because they had connections with the area, the Marquis of Dorset and the Earl of Kent, for example, were enrolled at Knowle in 1506, and so were a number of abbots and other prominent clerics. Coventry gilds attracted merchants from Bristol and Leicester as members and Stratford Gild included two Bristol merchants and three Banbury spicers.

Leadership and organisation of the gilds were entirely in the hands of laymen. They employed the clergy who said the gild masses and obits, they built and decorated their own gild chapels and altars, set up statues, and provided lights, clothes and decorations for them to their own taste. They, rather than the clergy, were responsible for the more ebullient expressions of popular piety. Only the wealthiest of earls could order the Beauchamp chapel and employ the finest artists at a cost of over £2,000. The members of St Katherine's Gild in Wolverhampton, who provided 'Saint Katherine's cote of black velvet, her shoes of silver, a flower with five branches of mastlin weighing 30 lbs and a veil with red crosses' for their gild altar might have had less 'artistic taste' than the Earl, but they expressed the same combination of fear of judgement, desire for prestige in this world, creative enthusiasm and religious piety ((U) WLS Churchwardens' Accounts).

The gilds were gatherings of the wealthy. The entry fine for the Holy Trinity gild at Coventry was £5 and members were expected to provide not only for the objects of the gild, but for its customary banquets and ceremonies and to entertain distinguished visitors. In almost every town where there was any formal structure of local borough government, the gild members dominated its hierarchy and council. Where there was no formal organisation and manorial lordship remained significant the wardens of the gilds and their assistants were nevertheless recognisably the leaders of the local community.

Another form of public endowment characteristic of this period was the hospital. By the fifteenth century sixteen hospitals had been endowed to provide homes and care for various classes of unfortunates – six in Warwickshire and ten in Staffordshire. Provision was made for the sick, the aged, the poor, even for lepers. Hospitals were usually in towns, there were four in Coventry, two in Warwick, Lichfield and Stafford. The oldest in the area were the hospital of St John Baptist at Lichfield, founded about 1140, and St John Baptist at Coventry, founded in 1161, for wayfarers and for the sick and aged poor. The houses continued to attract further donations throughout the late Middle Ages. John Haddon, draper of Coventry, made the very practical gift of 80 yards of frieze for sheets to the Coventry house, which kept twenty beds for wayfarers. Clement Leveson, clerk, and William Waterfall established a small house for six poor people at Wolverhampton. Later, John Pepard of the town gave 'a competent load of coals drawn by five horses' (VCH Staffs III: 296–7).

Each house was intended to be a permanent community with resident warden and staff and a regime of communal prayer, obedience to superiors and often special dress. However, the individual histories of the houses show that most of them went through at least a phase when the appointment of warden had become just another benefice for a non-resident careerist and the numbers of inhabitants dwindled to one or two or even none. St John Baptist, Lichfield, for example, had to be virtually re-established in 1495.

The regulations laid down by those who endowed hospitals and religious gilds provide some indication of what was regarded as the 'best' practice for a family of laymen. Doubtless the founders' instructions represent an ideal rather than a real reflection of a busy Coventry merchant's rule of life. However, the regulations must have borne some relation to the ideals and practices of the pious to which all might aspire even if few actually achieved them. All were required, of course, to attend mass on Sundays and the major feast-days in the parish church. On other days the communities were to attend mass daily in the hospital chapel, and all were also expected to attend matins and evensong daily. The literate (called the learned) were to say the hours and the psalter (i.e. the divine office).

The unlearned were required to repeat the *Pater*, the *Ave* and the *Creed* a given number of times. In the case of Bond's hospital, Coventry (founded 1509) they had to say fifteen *Paters*, fifteen *Aves* and three *Creeds* after supper and kneeling. This type of repetitive prayer was common among layfolk from the twelfth century and was encouraged by the preaching of the Franciscans and Dominicans in the systematic form of the rosary.

The mass itself reflected the stratification of society. The action of the mass was withdrawn behind elaborate rood screens and with the congregation at a distance, stylised gesture, dramatic action and music became more significant, and necessary to communication. In Lichfield and Worcester cathedrals and in the large collegiate churches like Tamworth and Wolverhampton, elaborate music was performed by trained professional singers. At St Mary's, Warwick, there was a school of music and grammar associated with the church since the twelfth century, and by 1409 there were four cantors, a choirmaster and an organist (VCH Warks II: 126). At Lichfield the vicars' choral were examined to make sure that they could chant to an organ, and a vicar who could not sing lost his stall. There were twelve choristers with their own master who was to teach them liturgical music, pricksong and descant, and sometimes to play the organ (VCH Staffs III: 148). At Wolverhampton there were two organs and the organist, Thomas Bradshaw, was also chaplain of the hospital ((U) WLS Churchwardens' Accounts). The vicars' choral at Tamworth were paid £5 a year. They sang the canonical hours and high mass daily and like the vicars of Lichfield were required to live in community, to behave respectably and to keep order among themselves and if they failed to do so they were fined. They had six days' holiday every three months (Johnson 1968–9: 59).

Public religious processions and corporate enactments of the festivals of the Church between Christmas and the Ascension were in some degree common to all parishes and so too were the more secular communal rituals of summer and autumn. However, it was natural that these opportunities for the display of wealth and status reached their most elaborate forms in the larger towns and above all in Coventry where the ceremonies expressed and reinforced the sense of community of the citizens. Coventry had twenty-four gilds, each with their rituals of processions, banquets and gild masses for the dead and in addition there were parish gatherings and public bonfires. The Corpus Christi pageants were recorded from 1407 and on occasions were attended by royalty. The Corpus Christi Gild provided for the processions, the cross, images and canopy, and for the plays, costumes and properties. There were ten wards in Coventry and probably ten religious plays. Each ward was responsible for a particular play and the plays were performed on movable stages or floats of two storeys, paraded about the town (Ingram 198: xvii–xiv).

Coventry town musicians played trumpets, pipes, drums, dulcimer, viols and organs; they wore city livery and played for the town rituals. They also accepted outside engagements and council found it necessary to confine them to a 10 mile radius (Poole 1869: 54–7). Other towns had their religious plays though, doubtless, on a more modest scale. At Wolverhampton the church-wardens kept the costumes and properties and were responsible for spending church rate money on furbishing them. Lichfield had a shepherd play at Christmas and (obscurely) 'the pilgrims' at Easter and the 'nebulae' at Whit.

In contrast with the busy grandeur of the great town churches, mass in the small rural parishes became more modest as a simplified form called 'low mass' became the usual practice. The essentially communal nature of mass could not entirely disappear, but masses for particular intentions and persons became more common, and so did 'private' masses when the priest carried out all the readings and was the only person to receive communion. In order to preach to the people the priest had to descend from the altar to a position part way down the nave and Wolverhampton church was one of many churches which added a specially built pulpit at this time.

By the fifteenth century every parish and abbey church of any pretensions could boast its collection of relics. At Warwick they claimed to possess part of the true cross, parts of the hair, milk and garments of the Blessed Virgin, the assorted bones of thirty saints, the frying pan of St Brendan and more (VCH Warks II: 128). At Wolverhampton they had a silver image with a thorn in it and a cross bound with silver, said to contain part of the holy cross ((U) WLS Churchwardens Accounts). Pilgrimages continued to St Modwena at Burton, and to St Barbara at Halesowen. At Coventry the shrine of the virgin martyr St Osyth drew pilgrims from all over the Midlands and the shrine of Our Lady of the Tower in the Carmelite convent was visited by travellers passing through the city to London. At Lichfield the great shrine of St Chad had cost £2,000 and had been made in Paris, and the pilgrimages brought in £400 a year to the cathedral (Hibbert 1910: 137).

Most large parish churches by the end of the fifteenth century had a parish clerk, a paid assistant, who might be a deacon or a layman. He assisted in the responses, read the epistle at mass, rang the bells and cleaned and prepared the altar, and looked after the church's collection of breviaries, missals and other books. At Tamworth, Wolverhampton and Warwick the clerk or another guardian was required to sleep in the church as security guard, and special rooms with fireplaces were provided. The financial affairs of the parish were looked after by the lay churchwardens who collected church rates. At Halesowen the two churchwardens accounted for the burial fees, the income from parish property and from leasing out the parish cows at 2s. a year. They organised church sales at Christmas, Easter and Whitsun and whenever money was needed for a special purpose. They bought malt and barley at the parish's expense, brewed ale and held a convivial gathering at the home of the churchwarden, and usually raised between £3 and £5 at a time. They expended the income in the maintenance of the church fabric, vestments, altar furniture and mass books. They bought their first printed mass book in 1503 at a cost of 9s., including the expenses of collecting it from Worcester (WHS 1952).

The parish clerks, the churchwardens, the masters of the gilds and chantries and hospitals between them carried a good deal of responsibility for income and expenditure and for the style of building, decoration and para-liturgical ceremonial. Moreover, they made their accounting not to the Church, but to the lay community, whether parish or gild. Not all of them were literate but they had access to those who for a fee could write up their accounts and cast up the totals. Many evidently were able to write their own accounts, make lists, and keep track of parish and gild investments.

In the fifteenth century popular piety grew more and more colourful and sentimental, and the Church tolerated a great deal of superstition and ignorance. Alongside the emotional piety there was also a rising tide of criticism of the clergy as individuals and of the wealth, organisation and even teachings of the Church as an institution.

Lollards were probably never numerous in the Midlands and are recorded mainly in the towns. Nevertheless, they articulated both criticism of the established order and an alternative theology which was probably attractive to more than the committed few who appeared before the Church courts. This wider substratum of criticism can occasionally be heard in the reports of ale house gossip and hot words in market places. The main issues to which the committed Lollards addressed themselves were disendowment of the clergy, redistribution of ecclesiastical property and tithes. Bible study, personal devotion and evangelisation were presented as more important to salvation than the sacraments, indeed they were deeply suspicious of the whole sacramental concept, and most especially the Eucharist.

In 1416 a certain John Grace called a 'false prophet' was wandering about the Midlands preaching. He spoke for three days at Lichfield and also at Birmingham and Coleshill. He spent five days at Coventry where he was tolerated by the town council. Wherever he went he was opposed by the friars (he was himself believed to be a former friar) and debates turned into mob violence against the friars who, it was said, went in fear of their lives. The mayor of Coventry made light of the affair, but the authorities in London called for firm action and John Grace was taken prisoner to the Tower of London and securities were taken from about fifty artisans of Coventry who promised not to maintain heresy and to keep the peace. Already by this time Coventry was one of the provincial strongholds of Lollardy and a few years later in 1431 was marginally involved in planning a Lollard rising. In the aftermath the Duke of Gloucester sent a special commissioner to deal with the heretics in Coventry, where an unknown number were executed, and himself visited the town twice during the suppression of the revolt (Aston 1960: 31–6).

The Warwickshire Lollards continued to evangelise. In 1454 John Woodward of Tanworth denied the sacraments of Eucharist and baptism, and the observance of Lent and had his doubts about the significance of the sacrament of marriage. He was allowed to abjure his errors in Tanworth church, clad in shirt and drawers, bareheaded and barefooted (VCH Warks II: 20–1). On 9 March 1485, John Blumstone, Richard Heigham, Robert Crowther, John Smith, Roger Browne, Thomas Butler, John Falk and Richard Sylvester, all of Coventry, were examined in St Michael's church. In their replies they made it clear that they had been attacking the value of pilgrimages and, in particular, the pilgrimage to the statue of Our Lady of the Tower in Coventry. Crowther denied the virgin birth, Browne spoke of the 'sole efficacy of God's bloodshedding'. The group confessed their guilt, abjured publicly, and for penance were required to go in penitential procession to the cross in the market place bearing bundles of firewood. Afterwards they had to pay due honour to Our Lady of the Tower at the Carmelite friary. On Sunday they had to go together to mass and stand on the altar steps, abjure their heresy again and in English, and listen to a sermon of condemnation (VCH Warks II: 20–1).

In 1511–12 74 persons of Coventry were examined and 45 were eventually charged with heresy, including 15 women who proved particularly voluble and vigorous in resistance. The dissidents were examined first in St Michael's church in Coventry, then they were taken to the bishop's residence at Maxstoke castle and examined again (October to January 1511–12). Their examination reveals that they were a group of tradespeople, self-confident and mutually supportive. Like other Lollards they travelled a good deal in the course of their trades and on their journeys had taken occasion to circulate books, tracts and vernacular scriptures. They had visited each other's houses for reading and discussion and answered with confidence the learned theologians who gathered to examine them; however, they confessed, abjured and did penance, carrying their faggots. Mrs Joan Ward was burned for denying the efficacy of transubstantiation, intercession of images and pilgrimages. This was not the end of the matter, however, for eight years later seven were charged again and were burned on 4 April 1519 to become Foxe's 'seven godly martyrs of Coventrye'. The following year six more people were burned, and in 1521 Robert Silkeb followed them to the stake for denying transubstantiation (Fines 1963: 160–74).

The Coventry dissidents were clearly a cohesive body with many generations of protest behind them. They criticised the miraculous, and attacked the contrast between the simple message of the gospel and the wealth and complexity of the institutionalised Church; they also rejected the subtle intellectualism of the schoolmen in favour of commonsense and practical virtue. In many ways this was a layman's approach to religion, a rejection by these urban weavers, fullers and shoemakers, not only of the Church as an institution, but of the sentimental excesses of popular devotion. It was a religion of the literate artisan, rather than of the mystic or the peasant.

However committed and articulate these men and women might be, their opposition was a small and localised phenomenon compared with the massive institution of the mediaeval Church supported as it was by the state, the system of landownership and the habits and aspirations of the people. Men and women making their wills in the Midlands in the 1520s left money to the cathedral church, to the friars, for masses for their souls and to their parish churches with confidence that their gift was for perpetuity, a confidence which was soon to prove misplaced.

In November 1520 when John Gifford of Chillington and Edward Littleton of Pillaton rode south to represent Staffordshire in what was to become known as the Reformation Parliament, there was little sign of the restructuring of the relations of Church and state which was to ensue. Bishop Blythe of Coventry and Lichfield (1503–33) was active in his diocese and his vicar general, Thomas Fitzherbert, and the suffragan bishops, Wall, Smythe and Sutton maintained the efficient functioning of the diocese (VCH Staffs III: 40–2). In the parish churches the traditional liturgy and customs continued, at Wolverhampton they were building a new high altar costing £95 and at Halesowen they collected money for the candles, altar lights and images. At Barton under Needwood a completely new church was built.

Bishop Blythe died in 1532 and was replaced after a two-year vacancy by Bishop Rowland Lee who had been King's Chaplain and officiated at the marriage of Henry VIII and Anne Boleyn. The Italian cardinal of Worcester was deprived in 1535 and replaced by Hugh Latimer, chaplain to Anne Boleyn. Latimer was already a well-known preacher and professor of theology and had been summoned before Convocation for heresy in 1532. He had been absolved on complete submission, but the following year at Warwick the Abbot of Kenilworth presided over an enquiry investigating the spread of Latimer's words 'that images should be pulled down and that the Ave Maria was no prayer'. Now only two years later the heretical theologian was bishop, and the Abbot of Kenilworth was reading the signs of the times. The dissolutions of 1521 had indicated to local landowners possible opportunity for adding to their lands and their influence. The general dissolution of the monasteries, and later the chantries, gilds and colleges was perceived by Midlanders almost entirely in economic terms. The commissions of local gentlemen who reported on the monasteries in June 1536, before the visitations from central government, were favourable to the religious even while they prepared for the dissolution of their property.

In March 1536 a month before the Act for the dissolution, six small houses were allowed to purchase exemption from the Act, paying sums varying from £20 to £122 6*s*., but the exemption lasted only until the autumn of 1538. By that time the dissolution of the larger monasteries was being prepared by the installation of compliant nominees as abbots at Burton, Coventry and Kenilworth. Of the thirty religious houses only Burton (£267), Merevale (£254), Coventry (£311), Nuneaton (£227), Dieulacres (£227) and Halesowen (£337) had over £200 in income. The distinction between the lesser and the greater dissolutions was blurred since negotiations were going on more or less continuously from 1536 to the completion of the business by early 1540. The smaller monasteries were visited by the royal commissioners, Leigh and Layton, and the monks were required to seal a deed of dissolution in which they acknowledged their evil lives and papistical propensities; in the great majority of cases this was evidently only a formality, although the houses of Lichfield diocese were visited in six weeks (Hibbert 1910: 137). Only about two hundred individuals were involved in Staffordshire and Warwickshire, and almost all were awarded pensions, which varied from £60 to the Abbot of Dieulacres to £1 13*s*. 4*d*. for a nun of Brewood. Most of the monks who were in priests' orders found benefices in the area, many of the women presumably went home (as did Elizabeth Throckmorton to Coughton) and the religious who refused to co-operate were refused pensions (Doyle 1969: 6). The scramble to obtain grants of monastic possessions was at its height in 1538 when Cromwell was besieged with begging letters from Bishop Lee, Lord Stafford, the Earl of Derby, Francis Hastings and Lord Ferrers and many others. Some attempts were made to save certain houses. At Coventry the mayor and corporation sought to prevent the dissolution of Grey Friars and White Friars in 1538 and in the same year obtained the help of the Bishop in trying to save the priory church on the grounds that the Bishop would lose a cathedral and the town would be inconvenienced. Only Burton on Trent survived to be refounded as a collegiate church with the intruded Abbot Eric as Dean, but this new foundation lasted only six years before it too was dissolved (Poole 1869: 11).

The value of the land transferred to the Crown was £3,549 in Warwickshire and £1,874 in Staffordshire. Those who acquired monastic estates greatly enhanced their opportunities for patronage, through presentation to benefices, and also took over rights to tithes. Land was bought at an economic rent of twenty years' purchase and, although many of the initial grants went to lessees and speculators, the local monastic lands eventually became permanently vested in the hands of local gentry and urban families. One of the largest purchasers was James Leveson of Wolverhampton who acquired some 20,000 acres of monastic property that formerly belonged to Trentham, Stone, to Lilleshall and Wombridge Priories (Wordie 1982: 10–11). John Giffard of Chillington, courtier and member of Parliament for Staffordshire, obtained the lands of Sheen, Ronton, Tutbury and Stone and his son acquired the sites of the monasteries of Blackladies and Whiteladies (SHC 1902: 118–20).

The agricultural equipment, beasts, domestic furniture and movable property of the monasteries was immediately disposed of. When the friary at Lichfield was sold up in October 1539, the vestments and the candlesticks were sold first to gentlemen and clergy, and the brick tiles and timber of the buildings, the window glass and the paving stones were bought by local craftsmen, 'the lead cistern at the tenys court end' to Mr Lyttleton and the holy water stoop to a draper. A consortium of gentlemen and townsmen bought the church itself for £46, £23 down and bonds for the remainder, with a view to demolishing it and carrying away the materials (Hibbert 1910: 252–4).

A number of monastic churches were purchased and used as parish churches including Nuneaton, Monks Kirby, Wroxall, Tutbury, Merevale, Polesworth, Stone and Burton on Trent. Many parishes took the opportunity to buy church goods comparatively cheaply. The bells from Wenlock, Shropshire, for instance, were bought for the church at Wolverhampton. There is nothing to suggest that the Midlands were shocked or disturbed by the dissolution of the monasteries and they showed no hesitation in taking advantage of the opportunities to acquire land and goods.

Bishop Lee's injunctions of 1537 to 1538 marked the unobtrusive beginning of liturgical changes in the parish churches. They contained little that was new except the instruction to place in the churches the bible in both Latin and English; churchwardens' accounts show that bibles were duly bought and reading desks provided. The Halesowen churchwardens expended 10*s*. 4*d*. on a bible at Worcester, the pictures on the walls were hidden with whitewash and the candles taken down. At Lichfield Cathedral the shrine of St Chad was dismantled and the reliquary sold for £400, but the bones themselves were taken away the night before by prebendary Arthur Dudley (Hibbert 1910: 159). At Ingestre, Sir William Basset was quick to remove the statue of St Erasmus, and to close the healing shrine where pilgrims had come seeking cures, and pulled down the statues and crutches which some of them had left behind (Stapleton 1892: 133–4). Nevertheless, many traditional practices continued and the forms of worship were little changed even after the introduction of the English litany in 1543. Prayers continued to be said for the dead at Halesowen, a picture of our Lady was set up as late as 1544 and in 1546 the statues were still covered during Lent (WHS 1952).

In the Midlands the changes of the reformation presented themselves not as a radical challenge to established order and custom but as a series of discrete changes in different areas of life, most of which were more or less welcome or at least tolerable and which were carried out by familiar local agencies. The harsh impact of central government initiative was modified and mediated by local influence and local inertia.

Chapter 11

Political rivals and their followers

Both the great midland earldoms became linked to much larger territorial power blocks by the middle of the fifteenth century. The Staffords became dukes of Buckingham in 1444 and made Maxstoke Castle in north Warwickshire their main headquarters. The earldom of Warwick passed in 1449 by marriage to Richard Neville, son of the Earl of Salisbury, creating a massive territorial lordship and making the Earl of Warwick the largest landowner in England. Thus the estates in the Midlands became the resource and supporting base of the great dynastic struggles of the period. The dukes of Buckingham remained loyal to the house of Lancaster but from 1455 the Earl of Warwick associated himself with Richard, Duke of York and supported him in his bid to obtain the regency of the kingdom. By 1455 relations between the Yorkists and the Crown deteriorated to the point of warfare.

By 1460 Richard Neville, Earl of Warwick, had inherited even greater estates and prestige and the main claimant to Henry's crown was Edward, Lord March, son of the dead Richard, Duke of York. Richard, Earl of Warwick put his enormous prestige, experience, armies, estates and power wholly behind Edward's claims, and with the help of Parliament secured the deposition of Henry VI and the coronation of Edward as Edward IV after the battle of Towton. For about three years Richard, Earl of Warwick was effectively ruler of England. He was Lieutenant of Ireland, Constable General of Calais, Captain of Dover, Warden of the western and of the Scottish Marches, Lord Chamberlain and Lord High Steward. His brother was Archbishop of York. Two of his daughters and his sister became royal brides! The continuing struggle for power at Court, to challenge the power of the Earl of Warwick, by the Wydevilles and the revolt of the Nevilles in 1470, the restoration of Henry VI and his final defeat by Edward at the battle of Barnet in 1471, all belong to national rather than to midland history, and the affinity of these midland magnates became a subdivision of the political nation rather than a regional network.

The Earl of Warwick was killed at Barnet in 1471 and his estates passed in 1474 to the Duke of Clarence, who held them for only four years before he died in mysterious circumstances only four years later.

On the death of King Edward IV in 1483 the struggle for power centred on control of Edward's son, Prince Edward. On his journey from Shrewsbury along Watling Street to London he was taken in charge by Richard, Duke of Gloucester and the Duke of Buckingham who supported Richard's appointment as Protector. Buckingham also supported the deposition of Edward V and the coronation of Richard as King Richard III in July 1483. Only four months later however with the support of the Wydevilles, Cardinal Morton and the Courtneys, the Duke of Buckingham raised troops and led a rebellion in favour of Henry Tudor, Earl of Richmond, raising support all over the west and south of England. The Midlands in contrast remained quiet. The rebellion quickly collapsed and the Duke of Buckingham was captured and beheaded at Salisbury. The heirs to the two great midland houses were now Edmund, son of the Duke of Buckingham, aged seven, and Edward, Earl of Warwick, son of the Duke of Clarence, aged nine, so that when Henry Tudor returned leading his own army in August 1485 there were no powerful midland magnates to oppose or to support him. He marched from Shrewsbury to Stafford where he had conferences with the powerful Cheshire Baron Stanley and moved on to Lichfield which Lord Stanley evacuated to enable Henry to be received with kinglike honours. There were more secret meetings at Tamworth, and at Atherstone the powerful brother of the Baron Stanley, Sir William Stanley joined Henry. The Stanleys were a family who had originated in north Staffordshire and, although their great territorial possessions were in Cheshire and Lancashire, there were several important cadet branches in Staffordshire and they were thus not without connections in the Midlands. The Stanleys of Pipe and Elford, the Wrotteseleys and the Egertons came to the camp of the rising star. Richard III had few allies in the Midlands and one of the most important Devereux, Earl Ferrers, died in the battle fought on August 22 near Market Bosworth six miles from Atherstone. The gentry of the shires were all to a greater or lesser extent drawn in to these struggles for power and a few of them fought, were imprisoned or even died in the fighting.

Parliament, during this period, was often the mouthpiece of opposition to the King or of the ruling faction, and was used by contending magnates to articulate demands or to precipitate action. From the mid-thirteenth century knights from the shire were required to attend the King in Parliament from time to time. During the fourteenth century the knights of Staffordshire were in almost every known case heads of local families with a record of service as commissioners, collectors, jurors, escheators and justices. They were men of experience, the average age being forty-six, and of economic security, men with two or three manors. The burgesses sent from the towns of Coventry, Stafford and Warwick and less regularly from Lichfield and Newcastle were usually also men of substance – townsmen resident in the town which sent them, who had served as bailiffs, mayors and wool commissioners. All belonged to the affinities of the great magnates and although their election and the support of their neighbours owed much to the patronage of the magnates, it was also based upon their own standing and experience (SHC 1917: xxxii–xxxv).

In the fifteenth century the role of the House of Commons was of increasing importance in the struggles for power and membership was correspondingly more valued. Members continued to be drawn from the same landowning families, although they were on the whole younger men and there were rather more lawyers amongst them. Some of the members began to build up something of a parliamentary career. Robert Whitgreave of Burton was returned as a member of twenty-four parliaments; John Harpur, chief steward and agent of the Earls of Stafford, was also returned as a member on twenty-four occasions.

From the same families were drawn the responsible executants of order in the provinces. By the reign of Richard II the appointment of keepers or justices of the peace by royal commission had become a regular part of local government. Among the Warwickshire justices were Robert Burgylon, Henry Arden of Curdworth and William Purefoy of Stratford. In Staffordshire Arlbaster, Harpur and Hampton, close associates of Buckingham men were included in the commission of the peace (Rowney 1983: 29–49). Sessions were held in Warwickshire at both Coventry and Warwick to hear presentments from the jurors and constables of the hundreds. They heard cases of felony such as larceny, burglary, arson, trespass and assault, and also lesser matters such as thefts of clothing and cash and breaches of the trading laws, and there were presentments for giving excessive wages (Kimball and Plucknett 1939).

All the justices were associated with the dominant magnates in the shire, and enjoyed the patronage of the Dukes of Buckingham or of the Earls of Warwick, for justices were in a position to speed up or delay litigation to serve the friends and to obstruct the enemies of their lords. The status and cohesion of the gentry as a group was also greatly enhanced, and their own followers protected. If legal measures failed to secure results then the affinity could resort to violence or direct action, protected either by royal pardons or by the political situation.

The legal, social and practical assistance which the gentry could offer each other and their lords were considerably more important than their activity in fighting for the magnates in the battles of the dynastic conflicts. Neither Buckingham nor Warwick found it easy to raise forces even at the heart of their affinity and far more gentlemen were active in securing county office, local alliances and carrying out local government than were willing to answer a call to battle (Rowney 1983: 65–6).

By the early-fifteenth century the long traditions of local patronage and clientage were being reinforced by formal retaining fees paid by the magnates to individuals whom they expected to serve them from time to time. The Stafford family had an affinity of about eighty knights, esquires and yeomen who received sums varying from £10 to £30 a year and twelve men of legal expertise who each received £2 a year. In general retainers could and did receive fees and enter into connections with other lords, but in Staffordshire there were few other great lords to whom they could turn. The knights and esquires formed their own lesser networks of patronage and sustained their position in the shire even when their magnate patrons, more vulnerable because more exposed, fell from power (Rawcliffe 1978: 82). The associations were reinforced by marriage alliances, social gatherings, hunting parties, and mutual favours (Rowney 1983: 82).

The Nevilles as Earls of Warwick in the fifteenth century were less successful in establishing a permanent power base of patronage in Warwickshire perhaps because on the whole their interests were wider-ranging rather than rooted in a long tradition of local association. Their principal ally was Lord Edmund Ferrers of Chartley. In the early-fifteenth century they attempted to detach some of the clients of the Lancastrian Staffords. For a time they were able to gain the adherence of the Wrottesleys of Wrottesley and Astley of Patshull among others (Carpenter 1980: 514) but there was no large-scale shift of allegiance. At local level family quarrels about inheritance and marriages, and long-standing feuds between neighbours became linked through the network of affinity with the dynastic quarrels of the Court. The family of Wrottesley was for Neville while their neighbours and enemies the Levesons were for Lancaster. The Mountford family of Coleshill was one of the wealthiest families in Warwickshire below the rank of baron. They were split by internal feuds and each of the embittered branches of the family sought to strengthen their legal and political power by alliances – on the one side with Buckingham and thus with the house of Lancaster, and on the other with Neville and the house of York. Their political attitudes were rooted in their family quarrels but they nevertheless accepted the responsibility of their commitment to their patrons. Edmund Mountford, for example, followed Henry VI into exile in 1464 and remained there for about ten years before returning to make his peace with the *de facto* monarchy and re-entering politics under the patronage of Buckingham (Griffiths 1979–80: 1–20).

By 1485–1509 the conflicts at both local and national level were played out. The Earl of Warwick was in the Tower and Edmund Duke of Buckingham was living in Gloucestershire as a Renaissance gentleman, building a many-windowed house at Thornbury and establishing a library. However neither could escape the consequences of their blood. Edward was executed in 1497 and the Duke of Buckingham in 1521, both victims to political expediency.

Part three

Adjusting to changing conditions

Chapter 12

Population growth and housing: 1540–1660

From about 1560 the overall size of the population began to grow for the first time since the mid-fourteenth century. The population of England as a whole rose between 1560 and 1640 by about 45 per cent. There was a period of rapid increase between 1576 and 1586, a slackening during the period 1586–1603, then a continuous growth until about 1640 (Wrigley and Schofield 1981). Studies of parish registers of Staffordshire and Warwickshire suggest that in the Midlands the rate of increase was considerably greater than the national average. The middle years of the sixteenth century had been a period of very high mortality. Stratford lost 10 per cent of its inhabitants in 1558–9 and a further 16 per cent in 1564 (Martin 1977b: 11–22). The registers of other towns and villages record very severe mortality in the reign of Mary, and in the first years of Elizabeth (Palliser 1974: 54–9). This, however, gave way in the 1560s to a period of rapid recovery. It has been estimated that the population of Staffordshire rose from about 45,000 to about 90,000 by 1660 (Palliser 1974: 55), and Warwickshire from about 8,000 to 15,600 families, that is an increase of at least 95 per cent (Beier 1969: 79). This is a greater rate of growth than neighbouring Leicestershire, where the increase in the same period was about 60 per cent.

Parish registers in the Midlands as elsewhere show a marked increase between 1560 and 1620 in the numbers of baptisms, and baptisms exceeded burials in almost every one of these years, even in times of dearth and disease. Forty parishes in the east Feldon, nineteen in the Avon valley and five southern parishes all doubled in size. In the woodland area of north Warwickshire the increase was both greater and longer sustained, with thirteen parishes increasing threefold and six rural industrial parishes even more than threefold (Martin 1972: 8). Skipp's detailed study of five Arden parishes shows a growth of 45 per cent between 1570 and 1600, 21 per cent between 1600 and 1625, and 62 per cent between 1625 and 1649 (Skipp 1978: 18). The registers of the southern agricultural parishes of Warwickshire also show a marked natural increase, though it was less than in the northern parishes. At Brailes there was a rapid rise in baptisms sustained until 1594 (Tennant 1977: 14–21).

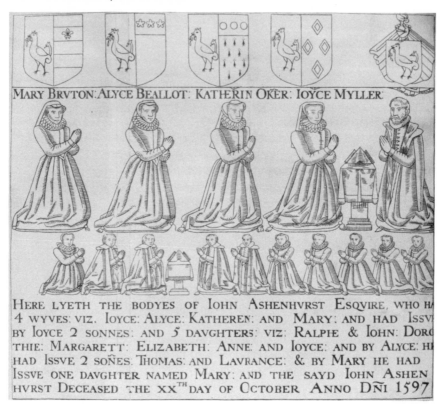

MARY BRVTON: ALYCE BEALLOT: KATHERIN OKER: IOYCE MYLLER:

HERE LYETH THE BODYES OF IOHN ASHENHVRST ESQVIRE, WHO H/
4 WYVES: VIZ. IOYCE: ALYCE: KATHEREN: AND MARY: AND HAD ISSV
BY IOYCE 2 SONNES: AND 5 DAVGHTERS: VIZ: RALPHE & IOHN: DORG
THIE: MARGARETT: ELIZABETH: ANNE: AND IOYCE: AND BY ALYCE: HI
HAD ISSVE 2 SOÑES: THOMAS: AND LAVRANCE: & BY MARY HE HAD
ISSVE ONE DAVGHTER NAMED MARY: AND THE SAYD IOHN ASHEN
HVRST DECEASED THE XXTH DAY OF OCTOBER ANNO DÑI 1597

Plate 3.1 A brass memorial in Leek Parish Church to John Ashenhurst esquire, his four wives and ten children. John Ashenhurst died in 1597.

Here and also at Wellesborne and Alveston nearby the excess of baptisms over burials produced a 25 per cent increase in household numbers. The age of marriage was low, families were large and burial rates for all age groups were low (Martin 1982: 27).

This natural increase of population was interrupted, but not checked, by outbreaks of disease. An epidemic called 'the sweat' following the bad harvests of 1549 to 1550 was noted in the registers of Audley, Bentley, Ellaston and Alstonfield in north Staffordshire and in 1588–9 another epidemic, probably of influenza or typhus, caused the deaths of about 10 per cent of the population.

Plague was almost always recorded in towns rather than in the countryside. There were outbreaks at Dudley in 1563 and at Coventry, Birmingham, Tamworth and Lichfield in 1564. At Stratford plague was blamed for a loss of 16 per cent of the population. High mortality was again evident at Stafford, Lichfield, Audley and Mucklestone in 1587–8. In 1593 six hundred people died of plague at Lichfield and three years later numerous deaths from plague were registered at Walsall, Tipton, Betley and Tamworth. Plague returned in 1603 with serious outbreaks in Lichfield, Eccleshall, Penkridge, Stone, Audley, Wednesbury, Clifton under Dunsmore and Brailes. At Coventry 494 people died – approximately 7 per cent of the population. In the early seventeenth century there was some improvement with only a few 'plague' deaths mentioned in different years, namely, Tamworth in 1602, Wednesbury 1607, Wolverhampton 1613, Dudley 1614, Stratford 1617 and Birmingham 1624. Tamworth suffered again in 1626 and Wolverhampton in 1635 (Palliser 1974: 54–76).

Increasing numbers of people put extra pressure on the available resources of food and the local opportunities for employment. Episodes of high mortality which are thought to be the result of food shortage are recorded throughout the period. Most of these episodes are linked with the bad harvest years, which afflicted not only the Midlands, but the whole of Europe. Bad harvests forced up prices of corn in 1557, 1558, 1586, 1588 and most desperately of all in the period 1591–6, when four bad harvests in succession brought 'savage dearth' to the Midlands as elsewhere (Palliser 1983: 50–1). The 1590s were also a bad time for urban textile workers as the cloth and yarn industries were in decay. At Stratford one-third of the inhabitants received poor relief. At Tamworth the famine brought with it deaths from the 'bloody flux' and the numbers of burials rose suddenly at Alcester and Warwick. Rural parishes were also hard hit and many died, almost certainly from starvation, at Sherborne, Aston Cantelow, Wellesborne, and Snitterfield while at Brailes the number of deaths increased fourfold. Nevertheless, it remains possible that the Midlands suffered less than other regions in these last years of Elizabeth's reign. Food shortages were caused by the failure of harvests and stock, but their incidence in particular places depended upon availability and distribution of supplies.

By 1615 in the Arden parishes of Elmdon, Sheldon, Solihull, Yardley and Bickenhill there was a high rate of mortality, fewer and later marriages, a lower level of conception, and smaller families, more still-born babies and more infant deaths (Skipp 1978: 13–38). These features have also been identified in many other rural Warwickshire parishes for the period 1610–50 (Martin 1972; Martin 1973). The average age of marriage for both men and women rose in parishes as diverse as Audley in north Staffordshire and Birmingham, Alcester, Stratford and Aston Cantelow. The sufferings of poor people are brought vividly to attention by random records of strangers and wanderers dying in winter in church porches and at furnaces. It seems probable that the open upland parishes of the Midlands may have shared with Lancashire and parts of Yorkshire a serious food shortage, leading to increases in the number of burials in the early 1620s.

The 1640s was again a period of severe hardship, exacerbated by the troubles of the civil war. The cost of food and goods continued to rise and harvests were in general deficient, high prices for corn were recorded at

Newcastle, Stafford, Eccleshall and Wolverhampton. There was a severe outbreak of plague at Lichfield in 1647 when the mortality bills which were carefully kept street by street recorded the deaths of 821 persons or about one-third of the whole population (Palliser 1974: 65). Stafford was also hit by plague and 'catastrophic mortality' which, combined with emigration from the town during the war, drastically reduced the total population which did not recover for a generation (Adey 1974: 152–68).

In rural areas the larger communities could not feed their people. At Brailes in south Warwickshire deaths by famine were recorded in the 1630s and emigration exceeded immigration, mortality was high and the total population was declining by 1640. Moreover the age of marriage was still rising, reaching thirty in the period 1645–60. It seems evident that Brailes was a community under economic stress in the first half of the seventeenth century (Tennant 1977), but the Brailes experience was not paralleled in the rural industrial parishes of north-east Warwickshire, south and north Staffordshire. If the 1563 returns of households are compared with the returns of 1662–9 of those paying or exempt from Hearth Tax, it is clear that in these parishes numbers of households increased as much as three or even fourfold.

Martin compared rural and urban communities in Warwickshire and showed that the differences between them were becoming less marked. Although the country was still much healthier than the towns, rural expectation of life was nevertheless declining, child mortality was increasing and completed families were smaller. Although rural communities lived in healthier surroundings they may have suffered more from inflation, malnutrition and in some cases over-population and under-employment (Martin 1973). Towns on the other hand suffered more from disease and from interruptions to trade. They tended to attract the vagrants and poor immigrants. They had higher mortality rates, especially high infant mortality (Dyer, A. 1981: 27). It seems possible that the people of the industrial rural parishes may have had the best of both worlds, living in a healthier environment and having more opportunities to raise cash to cope with seventeenth-century inflation. Certainly such parishes show a remarkable increase in the numbers of households between 1563 and 1666 (Table 3).

In general in the Midlands, although the momentum of growth slowed down, the combined pressures of high populations, bad harvests, inflation, disease and economic trouble were not usually sufficient to lead to an actual decline in the total size of communities let alone a 'crisis of subsistence' (Palliser 1982: 344–8). Specialisation, diversification of the means of support, adaptation and intensification of agriculture enabled many parishes to continue to support a growing population.

A common reaction to difficulties was to move in hope of better things elsewhere, and at least one-third to a half of the people were likely to move at least once in their lifetime. Brailes attracted the poor and landless from the surrounding area, who often stayed only a short time before moving on again,

Table 3   Comparison of households listed in 1563 and in 1666 in some rural industrial parishes

Some rural industrial parishes in Staffordshire and Warwickshire	acres (1801)	1563 Diocesan return households	1666 Hearth Tax	
			assessed	exemp.
N. Staffs				
Stoke on Trent	12,406	83	94	130
Audley	8,727	32	246	
S. Staffs				
West Bromwich	5,851	116	194	117
Sedgley	7,743	126	231	259
Darlaston	800	42	58	87
Kingswinford	7,329	28	283	
N.E. Warwickshire				
Bedworth	2,165	22	253	
Chilvers Coton	3,730	71	178	
N.W. Warwickshire				
Aston (includes Deritend Birmingham)	11,161	250	226	207

(Sources: Acreage – VCH. 1563 returns – Diocesan return transcript loaned by Dr D. Palliser. 1666 returns – Hearth Tax SHC, Warwickshire returns from the work of Mr T. Arkell.)

presumably to swell the expanding industrial parishes of the Birmingham region (Tennant 1977: 9–30). At Pattingham, a village in south-west Staffordshire, the numbers of persons passing through the village increased greatly from 1621 onwards, even when allowance is made for travelling soldiers and Irish (Kent 1981: 36–7). At Sheldon in Arden 15–20 per cent of each generation of the community moved out of the village. The majority of migrants moved no further than they could travel in a day but the more ambitious or physically fit moved further and many young men at this date went to London, others to Warwick, York or Norwich.

Sixteenth- and seventeenth-century midland communities were composed firstly of a stable core of families, secondly of connected groups of the more mobile, and thirdly of a shifting population of wanderers (Palliser 1983: 55). The stable core is evident both in rural parishes, such as Brailes, and in industrialising parishes, such as Burslem, Sedgley and Rugeley. Manor courts tried to impose restrictions on migration. At Claverdon the penalty for encouraging immigrants was 10s. a month and at Snitterfield 20s. a month. At Tanworth it was agreed that no man should take inmates into his house unless he had first had permission – the penalty for non-compliance was 20s. (Styles 1963).

From 1597 the justices of the peace were expected to support the parish officers, but the first cases reported to them seem to have been those aggravated by special circumstances. Thus, Hugh Bold of Little Sandon was summoned to the Quarter sessions at the petition of his infuriated neighbours. He had not only built a house for himself and five cottages on a scrap of land 'insufficient to maintain two beasts', but he had brought in five families, thirty-five persons in all, to whose manner of life and morals his neighbours objected strongly and in detail (SHC, 1935: 95–6). Likewise the complaints of the inhabitants of West Bromwich, that they were overcharged with poor to the number of sixty persons, were embittered by the fact that two of the bastards they were expected to maintain were fathered by one of the overseers of the poor, who refused to contribute to their maintenance (SHC 1935: 189).

The problem of the vagrant poor did not pass away with the troubles of the 1590s; instead, the numbers of migrants increased markedly in the seventeenth century. Justices of the peace became increasingly concerned at the numbers of migrants being brought before them and they frequently gave orders to send persons back to whence they had come. In the early years the landlord or harbourer was punished for taking migrants; in the later years the migrants themselves were punished for moving. In 1661 Edward Fairfax removed with his wife and child to Tanworth having 'of late got into the parish of Solihull without any lawful authority being poor and so may prove a charge of the parish'. A year later the hardening attitude of the justices was enshrined at national level in the Settlement Act (Styles 1963).

The overall growth of the population and even the rapid growth in rural industrial parishes did not lead to any noticeable increase in the size of the individual household but rather to the increase in the numbers of houses and householders. Moreover, rising prices and diversification of trades meant that while some suffered the pressures of poverty others profited from new opportunities and were able to spend money on improving their standard of domestic comfort. While the problems of the poor were recorded in the burial registers and the poor law accounts, the comfort of the more prosperous was recorded in their probate inventories and in the houses which they built, some of which are still in use.

Houses continued to be built of stone with stone tiles or thatched roofs. Many yeomen were adding additional rooms to their houses in the seventeenth century (Husbands 1980–1: 206–7). At Stoneleigh, for example, all the late medieval cruck-framed and boxframed houses had staircases and floors inserted to provide chambers in an upper storey. Brick or stone chimneys were built within the walls to provide fireplaces in both hall and kitchen and some warmth in the upper storey. In general in the Midlands all new houses were of boxframe construction and of two storeys (Barley 1961: 101). The plan was either rectangular or T-shaped with a hall or cross wing.

As the numbers of rooms increased from an average of four to an average of six, so there was also an increase from the 1640s of the numbers of rooms set aside for a particular purpose (Husbands 1980–1: 206–9). Cooking was more and more concentrated in the kitchen, the parlour on the ground floor gradually ceased to be used for sleeping, as in the home of Thomas Woodward of

Butlers Marston. When he died in 1615 his parlour contained a drawing (or leaf) table and six joint stools, a screen and four green cushions but no bed (Lane 1971: 17). Service rooms, such as the buttery, the brewhouse and the malthouse, were often either separate buildings in the yard or leanto buildings erected behind the house.

In the towns the larger houses were of two or even three storeys with upper rooms jettying over the street as in the case of the High House in Stafford (1555). On the ground floor were the hall, kitchen and workplace or shop often fronting the street, and above were the sleeping rooms. The maids and apprentices slept in the cocklofts in the roof. At Lichfield some of the town houses had a piped water supply from the conduit with a lead standpipe in the yard behind the house. In town houses fireplaces and chimney stacks were sometimes ranged along the rear wall and there was a passage giving access to the upstairs rooms. The town houses tended to have more decoration on the brackets supporting the upper storeys, the barge boards, doorframes and porches and the wealthier townsmen imitated the gentry by having wood-panelled rooms, inside walls decorated with paintings, and plastered ceilings with strap work and mouldings.

The peers, baronets and the wealthier gentry of Staffordshire and War-wickshire almost all built new houses or greatly elaborated older ones between 1560 and 1620. By the reign of Elizabeth the timber-framed house had become old-fasioned and the upper classes aspired to build with brick or stone. Their homes were further distinguished from those of lesser men by their fine frontages, rational planning and dignity, and by their symmetrical architecture. Even if old timber-framed buildings continued in use, to the outward view at least they presented a modernised frontage. The finest houses however were wholly new. They were large mansions with three storeys, the roof and chimneys concealed behind a balustrade, and the central projecting porches had classical pediments. The windows were wide, symmetrical, with mullions and transoms, like the great gatehouse at Tixall (1570), Lord Robert Dudley's additions at Kenilworth (1563 to 1570) and Charlecote (1558). In north Staffordshire Wootton Lodge was built for Sir Richard Fleetwood in about 1600. It was a compact building with kitchen and service rooms below, twenty-five steps leading up to the grand entrance to the ground floor and two upper floors. The porch had Ionic columns and the facade was topped by a balustrade. The frontage had three rows of symmetrical large transomed windows with a fourth line of windows at ground level giving light to the service rooms. On every floor the outer windows of the frontage and the side windows were projecting bays, still further increasing the appearance of a delicate and elaborately shaped box of stone and glass (Pevsner 1974: 328).

In the reign of James I the new baronets and other landowners often made use of brick which was readily available and not too expensive, and enabled the builder to elaborate the mansion with stepped gables, bands of contrasting colours, and decorative chimneys. Aston Hall built for Sir Thomas Holt 1618 to 1635 was of brick with stone facings and quoins. The entrance porch had Doric columns, a tablature pediment and the Holt arms above the door, and gave access to a central hall. The house had a ground-floor hall with a screens passage in the old manner, with service rooms at the lower end and the parlour at the upper end. Despite the brick exterior, the inner structure was of timber frames and the plasterwork and wood panelling were firmly in the Elizabethan tradition. Nevertheless the house was in the grand manner with a gallery 136 ft long and a dining room on the first floor which were reached by a great oak cantilevered staircase with carved balustrade and stands for lights. The Hall was visible on the skyline from the main road between Birmingham and Lichfield through a long avenue of trees (Fairclough 1984: 57–73). Other large houses of brick built in the Midlands about this time included Salford Hall (1602) and Wormleighton (1613).

The costs were kept down by using timber, stone and clay from the estate, re-using materials from older houses and employing local labour. Building a great house does not, in itself, seem to have placed an undue strain on the finances of the families concerned. Sir Thomas Leigh, with money made in London commerce, was able to build three separate houses one for each of his three sons. Other men besides the heads of old families were building mansions, among them Michael Purefoy, a younger son, at Caldecote, and John Fisher, a manorial steward who built the first Packington Hall. The pace of building was rapid until about 1620 but only one new great house was built in Warwickshire thereafter until after 1660 (Tyack 1970: 50–67).

In both town and countryside those who prospered, whether from rising rents, commercial farming, or increasing trade, used their profits in part to provide themselves with homes in which there was more privacy, more separation of work and leisure, and more comfort. As a result more carpenters, tilers, glaziers and plumbers were able to make a living. Dennis Napper, who died at Lichfield in 1660, for example, at his death had in his yard 1,500 bricks, 3,000 tiles, 240 gutter tiles, 72 crest tiles, and at his clay pits were 2,500 raw bricks and his moulds, wheelbarrows and spades (SHC 1969: 122–3). He was probably one of many for whom the doubling of midland population between 1560 and 1660 had been an opportunity rather than a threat.

Chapter 13

Agriculture: feeding a growing population

By the sixteenth century most demesne lands were leased out and landlords were in effect rentiers. At Sedgley most of the demesne was leased out to Edward Hall of the neighbouring manor of Tipton, who called himself a gentleman though he was not recognised by the College of Heralds.

Although seventeenth-century tenants continued to rehearse precedents from medieval manor court rolls when in dispute with their lords, the region was nevertheless experiencing a general trend towards leasehold tenure, a process which was necessarily gradual and piecemeal. John Lyttleton (1541– 99) of Hagley converted customary tenures to leaseholds and tenancies at will on his five manors in north Warwickshire. He charged moderate entry fines and rents but introduced regular and systematic accounting and greatly improved his income from the manors (Tonks 1978). The rising value of land and the increasing market opportunities, together with the growth of population, ensured enough tenants willing to undertake leases even on less advantageous terms than before.

Different modes of landholding had legal and economic implications for the tenants concerned, but they no longer represented social groupings within the community. The same individuals frequently held lands of all kinds of tenure which were acquired by purchase, lease and customary inheritance. Moreover, such engrossing of holdings was not confined to opportunities within a single manor. Gentlemen and yeomen acquired land under all types of tenures in neighbouring manors. Thus, a particular copyhold in Sedgley manor in 1614 of 35 acres of open field and a meadow was held in return for a rent of 12s. 2d., two strikes of oats and a hen; the copyholder did fealty and was liable to pay a heriot. However, the copyholder in question was John Pershouse of Walsall, a gentleman, with a coat of arms, educated at the Inner Temple, with good connections by marriage, and experience of local administration ((U) DRO Sedgley Survey). The great majority of the inhabitants were landless cottagers or subtenants of the thirteen or so principal yeomen who held not only the freehold but most of the copyhold land.

At Cannock a survey of unusual detail made in 1554 shows that most of the land was wholly or partly sublet and that some 64 per cent of the cultivated land was in the hands of subtenants. Not all the sublet parcels were small, one tenant leased 200 acres, another 187 acres and also had 118 acres copyhold. One-third of the Cannock landholders were absentees (Harrison 1979a: 86).

It is evident that in these manors men took up land as a commercial enterprise. The principal tenants could be absentees, tenant farmers might be receiving as well as paying rents, and the opportunity for engrossing holdings was being seized by substantial yeomen. On the other hand, the former copyholders were not simply displaced, since they might themselves have become subtenants on a considerable scale. The forms and procedures in the manor courts continued to enshrine ancient ways, the land was delivered by the rod or by the cutting of a sod, but status lay in the possession of money and acres, not in the method of tenure.

Large numbers of families held insufficient land for subsistence. At Brailes 48 out of 79 landowners held less than 30 acres in 1607 and only 6 had more than 50 acres (Tennant 1977: 60). In five Arden parishes 74 per cent of the cultivators had less than 30 acres. At West Bromwich the 'little parcels of waste ground' held by 21 families amounted to only 10 acres altogether. These plots were almost indistinguishable from those of the squatters and cottagers on the waste, who in their turn are hard to distinguish from the wholly landless.

As the population grew, the Feldon parishes experienced some problems in providing for larger numbers. Predominantly arable common field parishes had little opportunity for expansion or diversification. One response was to reduce the proportion of land left fallow, by evolving more complex rotations and by increasing the number of open fields by reorganisation and division.

Villages in the woodland and upland areas had never had the regularity of field systems of the Feldon and their small irregular fields occupied a comparatively small part of the total land used. At Sheldon in Arden there were two irregular groups of fields comprising only 25 per cent of the land. These blocks of land were scattered and held in severalty, but there were nevertheless communal agreements about sowing and reaping, rotation of crops and about grazing, and the arrangements were supervised by the manor courts (Skipp 1960: 20–1). Villages on the south Staffordshire coalfield might have anything from two to seven open fields or might have been wholly enclosed and farmed in severalty (Frost 1980: 31).

At Cannock and elsewhere in mid-Staffordshire there was additional arable land to be obtained from the abundant waste lands and short-term cropping was recorded during the sixteenth and seventeenth centuries. These lands were broken up, ploughed and cropped with a four- or five-year course of rye, barley, peas, beans and oats before reverting to waste. At Sutton Coldfield, which had a vast area of waste, 'lot acres' were allocated to any tenant who wanted them, and the tenants were allowed to make temporary enclosures and grow crops for five years before the land was thrown open again. Other examples of temporary cultivation have been noted at Ilam, Morridge and Staffold in the moorlands, and Iverley and Great Barr in central Staffordshire.

The process of enclosure of open arable, common meadow and common pasture continued despite government anxieties and local disturbances. Enclosure which took place by agreement caused little outcry and only comes to light when manor rolls, leases and field evidence have been subject to close scrutiny.

Thus the whole of the parish of Clifton under Dunsmore in east Warwickshire was enclosed by agreement, a process which took six years to complete from 1643 to 1649. Each freeholder was granted a single consolidated farm and arrangements were made for tithe, for the poor, the cottagers, the roads and ditches, and for building 25 miles of fences. Both before and for many years after enclosure there remained about forty households, of whom about two-thirds were labourers and craftsmen dependent upon employment by their neighbours (Gooder 1965). The forest laws had ceased to be enforced and much former forest land became integrated into the village lands. In 1636–9 the Uttoxeter ward of Needwood Forest was enclosed and disafforested despite local riots. Twenty years later the forest, as Crown land, was in the hands of the commission for forfeited estates who proposed to sell and enclose all the land, 9,220 acres in all. Again the proposal was resisted and a local landowner, Zachariah Babington of Comberledge, petitioned Cromwell against the sale. Local opposition delayed the implementation of the proposed partition, and on the restoration of the monarchy the proposal was abandoned (Thirsk 1969: 1–16).

A form of enclosure which usually went unchallenged was the emparkment of land by landowners who wished to create a private environment. The creation of new parks involved the removal of villages at Wrottesley, Blithefield, Great Sandon and Chartley among others. Such parks stand as a symbol of the growing privatisation of landownership. However, in times of dearth and social disturbance enclosure was seen as a threat, and fences became an object of attack as a symbol of oppression. A detailed analysis of one enclosure riot at Cannock in 1580 reveals that the trouble was precipitated by quarrels between local landowners. Part of the woodlands had been enclosed and common rights of grazing and gathering fuel had been overridden. The riots which were organised on five holidays in January and February were led by a local yeoman and an innkeeper, and did not involve local husbandmen, tradesmen or landless men (Harrison 1974: 158–63).

During the reign of Elizabeth, grain prices remained high and public anxiety about enclosure and conversion abated, and in 1593 the Acts against conversion were repealed. Almost immediately however, the bad harvests of 1594–7 re-introduced a sense of crisis. Two new depopulation Acts were passed, the second of which included Warwickshire but not Staffordshire. High prices of foodstuffs embittered the agricultural labourer against those who appeared to be profiting from the crisis. Sickness and poverty continued and prices of grain again rose abnormally in the spring of 1607. In east Warwickshire and neighbouring Northamptonshire parishes there had recently been many changes of ownership and considerable enclosure and conversion (Martin, J.E. 1982: 258). At Hill Morton near Rugby 250 acres had been converted to pasture and at Kettering and Market Harborough local shortages of grain had been exacerbated by the activities of malsters and London merchants. The district had also been disturbed in another manner by the Gunpowder Plot. In May 1607 local ill-feeling became public protest, and an assembly said to be of 3,000 persons gathered at Hill Morton demanding redress of their grievances. However the rising was brief and did not spread, and on 31 May a proclamation was issued against them. After a clash with mounted gentlemen and their servants at Newton (Northamptonshire), when 40–50 protesters were killed, the assembly dispersed (Tate 1967: 124).

A commission of inquiry made an investigation into seven counties in 1607–8. The Warwickshire returns suggest that, although they had been the leaders of the rising, the Warwickshire men lived on the edge of the region most affected. General anxiety about this problem was decreasing as more specialised use of land was coming to be accepted and the 'rising' of 1607 proved to be the last to attract official notice. Occasional reports of disturbances and destruction of fences continued but were treated simply as local disorders. In 1624 the Acts of 1597 were repealed and although between 1632 and 1641 there was a revival of prosecutions in Star Chamber for enclosing, these may well have been a fiscal expedient, rather than part of a general policy. The official response of central government was more sympathetic to enclosure if it did not cause disturbance, as William Combe of Welcombe, in the Avon valley, found. He was opposed at the assizes when he proposed enclosure of Welcombe, but permission was granted when he appealed to Privy Council. Moreover, enclosures made by local arrangement were given some legal security by registration in the records of the court of common pleas or by Chancery Bill (Tate 1967: 124–9).

Mixed farming integrating cereal and animal husbandry remained essential on all but the most exceptional locations, but the forms of this integration were more and more varied and flexible, with management adjusting to changing market opportunities. The traditional combination of permanent arable land with permanent pasture was modified by 'up and down' or convertible husbandry, where the same land was used for arable for some consecutive years and then put down to grass. In the sixteenth century in central Staffordshire land was being tilled for 2–12 years and then put down to grass for 7–12 years. In the Avon valley near Stratford and at Hampton in Arden, and at Kenilworth, land was under the plough for 2–3 years then used for pasture for 15–20 years (Kerridge 1967: 184–5).

The prices of grain rose faster than the price of wool in the sixteenth century, so land which had formerly been used for pasture was now more profitably used for corn. Barley and flax were being grown on former pasture

near Stafford in 1542 and at Trentham in 1630 meadow land was being used
for oats and barley. The increase of grain production in 'pastoral areas' was
noted by contemporaries.

> The inhabitants of Arden partly by their own industry and partly by the
> assistance of marl and other useful contrivances have turned so much of
> their wood and heathland into tillage and pasture that they produce
> corn, cattle, cheese and butter, not only for their own use but also to
> furnish other counties, whereas in the memory of man they were
> supplied with corn from the Feldon.
>
> (Camden 1586: 50)

Camden's observation is confirmed by probate inventories. In five Arden
parishes the balance between arable and pasture in the sixteenth century had
been 40–60 whereas by the mid-seventeenth century this was reversed and was
by then 60–40 (Skipp 1978: 53).

Winter-sown rye continued to be the main bread grain in the north
Staffordshire moorlands, and rye was commonly listed in inventories from
parishes all over Staffordshire and north Warwickshire both in the lowlands
and the uplands (VCH Staffs IV: 48–64). However there was some increase in
spring-sown barley and oats and on the better soils especially in south and east
Warwickshire wheat was grown. In the inventories from the Trent valley near
Lichfield this is described as 'red wheat' (SHC IV, V, 1969: 20–2). Mixed
grains such as muncorn or mixtum (rye and wheat) and drage (barley and oats)
sown and harvested together were commonly grown and could be used for
human or animal food. Peas were grown in every district and were the principal
fodder crop, while beans were grown in some parishes in east Warwickshire.

There was much variety in the food stuffs grown in gardens and crofts.
Crops assessed for tithe in Warwickshire in the seventeenth century included
apples, pears, cabbages, garlic, onions and even grapes. Orchards were
common in both villages and towns, and the gentry were planting orchards
and growing peaches and grapes, while hops were grown in south-west
Warwickshire (Barratt 1955).

For many midland families hemp was an important additional cash crop.
All over Staffordshire and north Warwickshire small 'hemplecks' were
associated with the cottages. The hemp stems were made up into hanks of yarn
either to be woven into rough cloth or to supply the ropemakers. Flax was also
grown in small garden patches to provide yarn for the linen weaver and woad
in south Warwickshire (Thirsk 1978: 169–74). The use made of pasture
depended upon its quality. Although wool prices declined from the 1550s and
even more in the seventeenth century, wool production was maintained in
some south Warwickshire communities until the end of the sixteenth century
(Thorpe 1964: 52–64). At Wormleighton there were 2,500 acres of pasture
and a great shearing shed, where in 1577 10,000 sheep could be shorn at one

119

shearing. The wool was sold to large-scale wholesalers in London and Norwich in sales amounting to over £1,000 (Finch 1956: 41–4). There were also sales of quality sheep to other estates for breeding. At Burton Dasset Peter Temple kept flocks of Welsh sheep bought in Coventry, mainly of breeding ewes, raised and sold the lambs and the older and barren ewes for mutton in local villages and towns and made a steady income from wool sold to the major wool merchants (Alcock 1981: 78–103). In the moorlands the black-faced, small-horned mountain sheep continued to be kept in considerable numbers for their wool or sent south for fattening. Around Cannock and Rugeley in mid-Staffordshire the yeomen and small farmers between them pastured some 6,000–7,000 sheep on the former forest lands (Harrison 1979: 104).

Sheep markets were held at Newcastle, Tamworth, Lichfield, Birmingham and Uttoxeter where sheep were sold to the town butchers for meat. Worcester and Kidderminster, Burton and Newcastle continued to buy wool, although Coventry presumably bought less than formerly. However, by the seventeenth century sheep farming was declining in the greater part of the Midlands. In the more industrial areas fewer and fewer families kept sheep, and even the Spencers leased their pastures to adventurers by 1640.

In contrast, prices of beef were rising, and the black cattle of the moorlands and the Staffordshire longhorns were becoming more numerous. Black oxen from Staffordshire were sold to the Crown and to graziers from Buckinghamshire and other areas (Thirsk 1969: 6) while Gilbert Markham declared the cattle bred in Staffordshire and Derbyshire were the best in England. There were cattle markets and shambles in every midland town, and cattle fairs in at least eighteen towns in the two counties and midland farmers also sold stock in the cattle markets of surrounding counties. In the Needwood Forest district, in the limestone valleys of Dove and Manifold and even in the neighbourhood of Walsall, pastures were let out to strangers and cattle were brought in for fattening.

Welsh drovers passing through the region added to the numbers of beef cattle on the move. They passed along one or other of a series of drovers' roads which crossed the Midlands from west to east, whether in the north where the road crossed the high moors, or further south through Halesowen. They pastured their cattle along the way, exchanging dung and a small payment for overnight accommodation for themselves and their beasts. Welsh cattle were sold in the markets at Birmingham, Wolverhampton, Coventry, Tamworth, Berkswell Hampton in Arden and Wall (near Lichfield). In the 1540s Peter Temple, of Burton Dasset, grazier, bought lean cattle each spring, fattened them and sold them off from July of each year. At their largest his herds numbered about two hundred with a majority of cows, some oxen and a few bulls. He sold them to butchers in Banbury, Coventry and Warwick but many of his animals were bought by dealers at Burton Dasset and then taken on the hoof to London, Kent and other destinations in the south of England (Alcock 1981: 44–6).

Peter Temple lived in Coventry and it was not uncommon for graziers to be important members of the elite of market towns where they worked in close cooperation with the butchers, tanners and skinners. The Dove valley became a major source of supply of butter for the London market. Rolleston became a specialist dairy community in the late sixteenth century. Small parcels of meadow land were leased for high rents by local yeomen (Yates 1974: 52). Cheese was extensively produced in north-west Staffordshire on the Cheshire border, and dairy farming also increased around Nuneaton and Atherstone in north-east Warwickshire, and Warwickshire was supplying London with large quantities of cheap cheese by 1660.

Pigs were kept in small numbers by most landless labourers and craftsmen on the common waste, or in styes close to the house, while on gentlemen's estates and yeomen's farms swinescotes or pig houses were built, some of them quite elaborate, but there was little large-scale pig rearing in the Midlands (Frost 1980: 38). Rabbits and pigeons were an important supplement to the meat supply in winter and most estates attached importance to the management of their coneygres. Large households maintained fish ponds, while other families bought fish from fishmongers in the towns and in the riverside parishes a few specialist fishermen made a living.

Horses were increasingly being used as draught animals for coaches, wagons and wains by the mid-seventeenth century, were kept by many yeomen as riding horses, and were used by professional men as well as the gentry. Horses were bred in the Cannock Chase area, in Needwood Forest and at Eccleshall where large numbers of mares were kept for work and breeding. Their foals were sold as yearlings or broken in and sold at two or three years old. There were horse fairs in several midland market towns notably Stafford, Penkridge, Rugeley, Eccleshall, Lichfield, Warwick and Stratford. Penkridge Fair attracted buyers from all over central England by the early seventeenth century but Brewood and Eccleshall attracted only local trade (Edwards 1979: 90–100).

Winter feed was a perennial problem and in the majority of villages meadow was not abundant. Hay was increasingly expensive, and frequently one of the most highly valued assets in a yeoman's or husbandman's inventory. Winter sown peas, beans and vetch were the main fodder crop throughout the period, but by the mid-seventeenth century a few new fodder crops were being sown including sainfoin and lucerne.

From the late sixteenth century there is evidence from many places in the region which suggests that agricultural productivity was rising as farmers gradually adapted and improved their techniques in response to the demands of population and industrial growth. Already, on the light soils of south-west Staffordshire and north Worcestershire, mixed farming and crafts were giving way to specialised arable farming, while in the north-eastern valleys farmers

121

were concentrating on supplying dairy products to the local and London markets. Such adaptation was still limited by natural conditions, soils and weather, by the lack of fertilisers and the need for fodder. Even so midland farmers were not slow to profit when new opportunity arose (Large 1982: 169–86; Palliser 1983: 185–201).

Chapter 14

The reformed Church and its critics

The extent and limitations of the Henrician reformation came home most sharply to the bishops. The Protestant Bishop Latimer, faced with the statute of six articles, resigned his see in 1539 and was kept in custody for nearly a year. On his release he returned to the Midlands to live near Baxterly. In 1541 a new diocese of Chester was created. The diocese of Coventry and Lichfield lost Cheshire and its former territories in parts of north Wales and Lancashire, which made the midland diocese a poorer but more manageable unit. Latimer's successor Bishop Richard Sampson (1542–54) had to surrender episcopal estates at Longden, Rugeley, Beaudesert and Hayward to the Secretary of State, William Paget, and received in exchange lands in Derbyshire of lesser value.

From the 1540s Protestant teaching began to be heard in the Midlands and the influence of reforming theologians began to make an impact on the local community. By 1547 Augustine Bernhers from Zurich was living at Baxterly and there were others in the vicinity of like mind: Thomas Bentham, the future bishop, John Hales the 'commonwealth' man at Coventry, and John Foxe at Charlecote. A circle of convinced Protestant devotees began to emerge which included not only clerics but yeomen, weavers and fishmongers living in Coventry and east Warwickshire.

From 1547 the pace of religious change in the midland parishes quickened. The Book of Common Prayer Service was introduced, apparently without disturbance, and altar tables were removed. The churchwardens bought Erasmus' *Paraphrases*, communion books, the Book of Common Prayer and four psalters, and the Easter sepulchre was pulled down and the walls whitewashed. The church furnishings were sold off gradually to local men, the reliquaries to the goldsmiths and the vestments to the mercers and drapers, and the chalices were converted into communion cups (SHC 1915).

The teaching of the Church concerning prayers for the dead, purgatory and indulgences had long been challenged by Lollards and reformers. Between 1536 and 1545 many chantries had been dissolved by royal decree, including Nuneaton, Coventry and Chelmscote, and in 1545 a general dissolution of chantries had been enacted, but the process of dissolution had not proceeded very far when the Act had lapsed with the death of Henry VIII. Now in 1548 a new statute ordered the dissolution of the chantries, religious gilds and colleges. The proposal caused much greater alarm than the dissolution of the monasteries, not because of the doctrinal issue but because it infringed upon the property of the laity and the institutions and rituals which expressed their self-importance. This was especially the case in the towns where the religious gilds and chantries were intimately associated with town government. In 1547 both Coventry and King's Lynn attempted to prevent the passing of the Bill, but were satisfied with the Privy Council's offer to grant them the gild lands 'to stay and content' them.

The dissolution of the chantries and the gilds released money and priests to establish chapels of ease in the more populous places. Eighty-five chantry priests were dispossessed in Staffordshire in 1548 (VCH Staffs III: 45). At Tamworth revenue of over £100 was confiscated, but the town was to be provided with a preacher at a salary of £20 and two assistant curates. At Wolverhampton the college was dissolved, but the collegiate church became the parish church and two of the former prebendaries became vicar and curate and provision was also made for the chapelries of Pelsall and Bilston (SHC 1915). Schools also survived with new foundation charters re-establishing them with part of the funds left for prayers for the dead, as at Wolverhampton, Birmingham and Tamworth.

By 1553 Midlanders had accommodated a considerable degree of institutional change. The visible changes in the parish churches and the liturgy and the dissolution of the religious houses and chantries had brought home the fact of change to every individual and in the towns in particular the role of the church in economic, social, ceremonial and educational activities had been considerably diminished. How far there was a corresponding change in religious belief and loyalty remains obscure. Mary's attempt to restore catholicism in the ensuing six years was to demonstrate that some Midlanders at least were deeply committed to the reformed faith.

Within a few weeks of the accession of Mary the churchwardens were busy in the churches restoring the altars, the images and the holy water stoups. They were sometimes able to recover from the parishioners the items which had been removed only five years before. At Rowington they bought new vestments, a new altar and a pyx, censers, candles and a canopy and began to rebuild the rood screen. At Wolverhampton the old-fashioned hanging pyx was replaced with a new style tabernacle, and the gilded altar of 1533 was rebuilt and at Wolverhampton, Halesowen, Rugby and Coleshill organs were brought back. Bishop Sampson deprived at least fourteen clergy of their livings, including the Dean of Lichfield cathedral, and perhaps one-fifth of the clergy of Warwickshire were also deprived (VHC Staffs III: 46; Strype 1709). In the city of Coventry and in east Warwickshire there was active resistance. Hugh Simmons, vicar of St Michaels, Coventry, was accused of saying that 'he wishes them hanged that would say mass'. Richard Hopkins, sheriff of Coventry, was imprisoned in the Fleet for 'evil religion'. In 1554–5 a number of other Coventry Protestants were arrested, Baldwyn Clare, weaver; John Careless, weaver; Thomas Wilcocks, fishmonger; and Richard Astlyn, haberdasher; all of whom belonged to the circle influenced by Augustine Bernhers. Three brothers, Richard, John and William Glover, close friends of Bernhers were summoned; John and William managed to escape, but Robert was taken and imprisoned at Lichfield and sent back to Coventry to be burnt on 20 September 1556. Lawrence Saunders, a scholar and well-known preacher, was arrested and tried in London and was sent to die in Coventry where his family had connections, no doubt to discourage the Protestant citizens. However, here as elsewhere the deaths of these respected and dignified individuals only deepened the commitment of their co-religionists. Altogether three heretics were burnt at Coventry and three more at Lichfield. The incidence of burnings reflects not only the strength of Protestant feeling but also episcopal policy. Bishop Baynes of Coventry and Lichfield was vigorous in implementing the hersy laws, but Richard Pates, whom Mary had appointed Bishop of Worcester in 1553, was a scholar and a mild man and there are no records of burnings in that diocese (VCH Staffs III: 46; Dickens 1967: 266).

The death of Mary and the accession of Elizabeth soon brought yet another settlement of religion as William Cecil and the Queen set about the task of establishing the uniformity of worship and allegiance they considered essential to good government.

The whole of Mary's bench of bishops rejected Elizabeth, among them Bishop Baynes and Bishop Pates, who were both deprived. Baynes was replaced by Thomas Bentham (1560) who had spent the reign of Mary in exile travelling in Zurich, Basle and Geneva while Bishop Sandys who replaced Pates at Worcester had been imprisoned in the Tower of London as a supporter of Jane Grey. The new midland bishops were thus both unequivocally Protestant. The clergy and other prominent persons were required to signify their acceptance by oath of the Acts of uniformity and supremacy. Of 88 parish clergy in Staffordshire 7 were deprived, and 12 others resigned at this time. Of the 30 diocesan officials 8 were deprived and 10 resigned (SHC 1915: xlvii). In Warwickshire 9 clergy were ejected, but the great majority of the clergy accepted the transition from the mass to the Book of Common Prayer.

The Privy Council looked to the local secular authorities to support uniformity in religion. Privy Council immediately removed from the list of Justices of the Peace some of those who had been most active in Mary's reign, such as Coyney, Draycott, Fitzherbert and Persall and in 1564 enlisted the help of the bishops in classifying the gentlemen according to their religious leanings. Bishop Bentham cannot have taken much satisfaction in the reply he had to make concerning Staffordshire. Seven gentlemen he could describe as 'favourers of religion and meet to be continued in office', but he had to report ten as adversaries of religion. In Warwickshire only eight gentlemen were favourers of religion (SHC 1915: 367–71).

Bishop Bentham was accused of being slow in enforcing good order in his diocese, and by his injunctions of 1565 he attempted to purge the diocese of the remnants of popery. The clergy were to destroy Latin service books and to permit only those rituals prescribed in the Book of Common Prayer. The people were to throw away their rosaries, to work on those days which had formerly been holy days and to refrain from praying for the dead. The churches were to be cleared of holy water stoups, rood screens, Easter sepulchres and bells, and a table of commandments set up. Every church was to have a bible, a paraphrase, a Book of Common Prayer, a psalter, a copy of the royal injunctions of 1559, the Declaration and the Homilies. The clergy were to say morning and evening prayer daily in public, parishioners should communicate at least four times a year and all children over seven years were to be presented for confirmation (Alcuin 1924, 163–70).

It was difficult to reinforce the statutes of central government with effective religious teaching. Vacancies persisted, there was a lack of newly trained young men and there were few whom the bishops could license to preach. Writing from Coventry, 10 July 1560, the archdeacon complained that

> many of our parishes have no clergymen . . . and out of the very small
> number who administer the sacraments throughout this great country
> there is scarcely one in a hundred who is both able and willing to preach
> the word of God but all persons are obliged to read only what is
> prescribed in the books.
> (Robinson 1842: 85–6)

The ecclesiastical courts continued to function much as they had done in the Middle Ages and in addition to the traditional categories of business were now required to deal with the enforcement of church attendance and royal supremacy. Bishop Bentham dealt in the consistory courts with those who continued to hold rogation processions and to carry crosses and banners. However, Staffordshire remained 'hinderly in all good things pertaining to religion' (SHC 1915: 368). In 1573 there were twenty Staffordshire churches which did not have the appointed books and there were complaints about inadequate clergy, infrequent sermons and insufficient celebrations of communion. Bentham suffered constant financial difficulties, found difficulty in collecting tithes and was forced to engage in litigation. He was in debt and there was much friction with the gentry (O'Day 1975: 84–6).

There were many in north Warwickshire favourable to a more Protestant settlement of religion. The Earl of Leicester, a member of the Privy Council and an acknowledged patron of protestants, was living at least intermittently at Kenilworth, and his brother Ambrose, Earl of Warwick, was at Warwick Castle, and between them they controlled a great deal of ecclesiastical patronage. Among the gentry who favoured further reform of the Established Church there were Thomas Lucy at Charlecote, Richard Wigston of Wolfston, six miles from Coventry, and John Hales, son of the Edwardian reformer at Warwick Priory and at Whitefriars Coventry. The mayor of Coventry had returned from exile and the corporation invited Thomas Lever, a friend of Bullinger and another of the exiles, to come with his wife and family and settle in Coventry. He discovered that 'great numbers in this place were in the habit of frequenting the preaching of the gospel' (Cross 1976: 134). Bishop Bentham subsequently made Lever Archdeacon of Coventry. The commitment of the Protestants of Coventry was constantly reinforced by the memories of the holy martyrs now made familiar to all as John Foxe's book was placed in every church. By 1568 the corporation of Coventry had permitted a small community of Protestant refugees from the Low Countries and their pastor Jacob Kunick to settle in the city and in 1578 the active and somewhat turbulent Humphrey Fenn, who had already suffered imprisonment at Northampton, came to Coventry as vicar of Holy Trinity. These and other men of like mind formed the Warwickshire *classis* in 1582. 'Prophesyings' were organised at Southam where the laity prayed and interpreted scripture under the Puritan radical John Oxenbridge, until suppressed by the Bishop (Collinson 1967: 193).

Conflict became more and more bitter. In the last twenty years of the reign the Marprelate tracts attacking the bishops were circulating and some at least were printed in Warwickshire, at Coventry and at Wolfston. Job Throckmorton was believed to be one of those responsible. Meanwhile, Thomas Cartwright came to live under the protection of the Earl of Leicester as warden of the newly founded Lord Leycester Hospital at Warwick. Here he was exempt from episcopal jurisdiction and able to preach, though suspended by his bishop, and he also preached by invitation of the mayor at Stratford on Avon (Savage and Kripp 1929: xvii). Despite the opposition of the council the puritan preachers continued to be supported by the gentry and listened to by the people. From 1590 to 1620 there was an important group at Burton on Trent led by two noted divines, William Bradshaw and Roger Hillesham, both followers of Cartwright.

In the Midlands Protestant opposition to the Elizabethan religious settlement was initiated and sustained by the laity. The Puritan clergy were not native to the area, but were men invited to come to the Midlands to lead already existing congregations or to be chaplains to gentlemen whose own commitment was already established. In Coventry, Burton on Trent, Southam, Stratford and Newcastle under Lyme the congregation took an active part in choosing their preacher and the country gentlemen selected for themselves the man who would live in their homes and write under their patronage.

Meanwhile many of the gentry and yeomen of Staffordshire, south Warwickshire and north Worcestershire held allegiance to the Mass and in varying degrees to Rome. Between 1559 and 1569 a pattern of Catholic resistance began to form, taking the shape that it was to continue until the end of the seventeenth century. In 1562 the Bishop of London was reporting that the former Lichfield cathedral clergy who had been deprived in 1559 were being maintained in Staffordshire, among them Henry Comberford, Anthony Draycott and Alban Langdale, the former chancellor, while the former Bishop of Peterborough was living at St Thomas. The first three named were of local gentry families and their relatives were among those who had been excluded from the commission of peace in 1559. Two Marian priests were apprehended at Comberford in 1572 and another was maintained at Stone. Robert Grey was supported by Thomas Fitzherbert; Robert Buckley, Marian priest, was at Checkley in 1581; and in 1592 Barlow, Barclay and Perton, old priests, were harboured at Stafford by Alice Tully; Thomas Hales, 'a very old massing priest', was at Tanworth; and another Marian priest, Sir Robert Whateley, was at Henley in Arden. In the Midlands, Marian priests were probably more numerous than the newly trained seminary priests and it must be remembered that a man ordained in 1557 was still only sixty years of age in 1594.

Douai College in the Low Countries was founded for training English priests in 1568 and by 1571 the first seminary priests began to enter England. Thirty-one seminary priests have been identified either as having come from the Midlands or being mentioned in association with a house there between 1571 and 1604. All priests, Marian, seminarians and Jesuits, lived a fugitive existence depending on the discretion of the Catholic laity, but although they were never safe from alarms, only four midland priests were caught and executed before 1604 (Anstruther: 1968).

In 1577 the Privy Council required the bishops to make a return of papists in their diocese with an estimate of their annual incomes. Bishop Bentham made two returns for Lichfield diocese and the combined lists provide the names of 172 gentlemen of influence, including the Fitzherberts at Swynnerton, the Heaveninghams at Stone, the Erdeswicks of Sandon, and most prominent of all Baron Paget of Beaudesert. The Bishop of Worcester received the names of only three families of note, but subsequently added those of Lady Windsor, the Throckmortons of Coughton and the Talbots, Mrs Blount and Mrs Heath all of north Worcestershire (CRS 1921: 88).

The laity were constantly called upon to pay fines, double subsidy and extra levies. There were for example the demands for a levy for a light horse made in 1580 and again in 1585 and yet again in 1587. From 1581 the fine for refusal to attend church was £20 a month or £260 a year and Thomas Throckmorton of Coughton was one of the very few landowners who actually paid the full £260 a year. In general however the recusancy payments though onerous did not undermine prosperity and Catholic landowners were able to compound for their fines from the 1590s.

The Elizabethan bishops of Lichfield and of Worcester had a hard task creating a united and loyal church in the Midlands in the face of so much turbulence and opposition. The Bishop of Worcester wrote in 1596 'Warwick and parts thereabout are freighted with a number of men precisely conceited against her majesty's government ecclesiastical and they trouble as much with their curiosity and the other with their obstinacy.' Nevertheless, while both opposition groups maintained an irreducible presence and a constant fire of criticism neither Puritan nor Roman Catholic really threatened the general acceptance of the religious settlement in the Midlands, and the next reign saw a further consolidation of the position and influence of the Established Church.

The Book of Common Prayer not only became the central experience of language of every family who went to church, but was increasingly to be found in the home. The Authorised Version of the bible was obtainable from mercers in the market towns and became a common item in household inventories of yeomen and townsmen. The supply and calibre of the clergy gradually improved. Coventry and Lichfield had proportionately fewer graduate clergy than any other diocese in England and Wales. In 1604, 20 of the clergy listed for Staffordshire had degrees and 69 were non-graduates, but even this was an improvement on the figures for 1574 and by 1631 the majority of the midland clergy were graduates (VCH Staffs III: 57).

Laymen anxious to secure a higher standard of the preaching of the word supplemented the parish clergy by supporting or endowing lectureships. At West Bromwich in 1614 the Stanley family established a lecturer to preach every Sunday and to visit the sick. He was to be a graduate and a bachelor and his salary was £30. Puritan preachers and lecturers were also active at Rugeley, Nuneaton, Birmingham, Sutton Coldfield and many other centres. Individual clergymen exercised wide influence through writing as well as preaching. At Kings Norton the perpetual curate and master of the grammar school was Thomas Hall who built up a reputation as a preacher and as the author of *Historiomastrix, The Beauty of Holiness, Wisdom's Conquest*, and other theological works.

In 1611 the citizens of Coventry were reprimanded by James I for making the town a second Geneva and in 1621 he refused to renew their charter until satisfied that they received communion kneeling (Hughes, A. 1980: 136). The corporation bought and repaired the dilapidated church of St John the Baptist and appointed the Puritan John Oxenbridge to preach there. In 1624 Humphrey Fenn returned to the city after his imprisonment and in 1626 the mayor, aldermen and godly people of Coventry invited Samuel Clarke to preach in the city. Attendance at the weekly lectures was made compulsory and there were public disputes on theological issues between Clarke and the vicar of St Mary's (VCH Warks VIII: 373).

The Burton on Trent Puritans were unfortunate in attracting to their gatherings, Edward Wightman, a Burton mercer who was untiring in expressing his opposition to infant baptism. After a long tussle with the ecclesiastical authorities he was handed over to the secular authorities and executed at Lichfield in March 1612, the last heretic to be burnt in England

(Mathews 1924: 11). Wightman was almost certainly an unbalanced fanatic, but Baptist ideas were circulating in the Midlands and took root in the well-prepared soil of Coventry. By 1626 the pastor of the little congregation was Thomas Helwys, a correspondent of the Mennonites in Amsterdam (VCH Warks VIII: 373).

In general, however, Puritan thinking and attitudes were expressed by individual clergy and laymen within the context of the Established Church. There were many laymen who were seriously concerned with the demands of godly living and who, without adopting a distinctive theological stance, derived their attitudes to political and social matters from their Protestant principles.

Sir John Newdigate of Arbury for thirteen years set himself on a systematic study of Christian morality, English justice, history and husbandry, in a determined attempt to develop his spiritual life and to carry out his Christian responsibilities more effectively. He was a moderate Calvinist by conviction earnestly trying to achieve his salvation by unremitting attention to his soul and his duties, bewailing his lapses and acutely conscious that as a public figure and a Justice of the Peace he must show forth the grace granted to the elect by the probity of his behaviour (Larminie 1982). Other 'godly gentry' of Warwickshire included Sir Clement Throckmorton, William Brawne, William Purefoy (Hughes, A. 1980: 135).

Some laymen among the lower orders took their religion equally seriously. When the young Richard Baxter took his first post in Dudley as a schoolmaster in 1638 he found that the nailers and lockmakers of the area were 'vehement in pleading their cause . . . Godly honest people, yet smartly censorious and made conformity no small fault'. They lent Baxter manuscripts and books and stirred him to examine his own position (Mathews 1924: 14). There are constant references to the circulation of books among the godly of all classes.

There were many who were shocked when instead of leading the diocese towards a purification of teaching and morals, Bishop Richard Wright began in 1632 to emphasise ritual and sacramental teaching. A number of the more unco-operative of the clergy were deprived, including Prebendary Lee of Wolverhampton, William Fenner of Sedgley, and Simon Ashe of Stoke on Trent. When Laud became Archbishop of Canterbury, Bishop Wright was encouraged and supported in his promotion of liturgical worship and sacramental practice. Wolverhampton was the scene of a particularly elaborate service when on 10 October 1635 a new communion table and organ were dedicated 'with incense, organs, singing of anthems and many congies and washing of hands.' The horror of local Puritans such as Prebendary Lee can be imagined (Mander 1969: 73–4).

Archbishop Laud made a metropolitan visitation in the Midlands in 1635 and uncovered many cases of resistance to the use of altars and candles and refusals to doff hats or to receive communion kneeling. The more active

Puritans were cited before the church courts and even the Court of High Commission. Among them in 1641 were John and Robert Ebb, braziers; John Cowper, ironmonger; Thomas Sherratt, blacksmith; Anne Cowper, spinster; Sylvester Pearson and Elizabeth his wife. They were accused of going into the church of Wolverhampton, breaking down the communion rail, destroying the carpet, and moving the communion table into the middle of the church. Examined before quarter session Robert Ebb said 'it was made an idol of and he would do it again if it were to do' (Johnson and Vaisey 1964: 15).

Such townsmen were linked together in networks of kinship and commerce and the teaching of the godly preachers spread readily among them. It was reinforced by the exhilarating experience of flouting the authorities in the name of righteousness. The determined attempt to impose Arminian teaching and practices in every parish brought many more men and some women into the debate and created local leaders who were stimulated to public witness and action against the policies of the Crown.

Meanwhile the Roman Catholic presence in the Midlands was also being consolidated. After the debacle of the Gunpowder Plot Catholics no longer expected a dynastic solution to their problems; instead the new generation were creating the organisation and structures of a Church from within their own body, and in the anticipation that the arrangements they made would have to be long-lasting.

Between 1603 and 1659, twenty-nine men of Staffordshire families and seventeen from Warwickshire families are known to have become priests trained at one of the English seminaries abroad (Anstruther 1975). Many of the better-off families sent their sons secretly to the English school at Douai. English convents were being established abroad and girls from the Giffard, Throckmorton, Fitzherbert, Purcell and other midland families went overseas, either for their education or to become nuns.

Sending children abroad for long periods was beyond the resources of most families and many Catholic boys were educated in England, either at the local grammar schools or secretly by priests. There was a clandestine school at Ashmores near Wolverhampton run by the Jesuits, until it was raided and broken up in 1635 when the priest and eight students were arrested, and three chests of books, vestments and altar vessels were seized (Beales 1963: 211).

Despite occasional alarms midland Catholics were able to continue to maintain their own priests and worship. While they protected themselves by keeping secret matters pertaining to the mass and the education of their children, they nevertheless accommodated themselves as far as possible to the society in which they lived and were able to survive by relying upon the connivance of their neighbours and the inefficiency of the execution of the law. In addition, midland Catholics were able to contribute both financially and in terms of leadership to the colleges and convents abroad. Catholic gentry made themselves responsible for protecting their tenants and in some villages, notably at Sedgley, the yeomen families were sufficiently secure to maintain

Catholicism even when the lord of the manor was not a Papist. The majority of priests were of the secular clergy and in the absence of a bishop were accustomed to organise their own affairs without much reference to outside authority.

For the first forty years of the seventeenth century the Established Church had constantly sought to teach, to watch over clergy and laity, to bring all into an orderly obedience. The Church licensed schoolmasters, preachers and midwives, enforced Sunday observance and tried to suppress immorality, tippling and fortune telling. For Thomas Price, a tailor of Wheaton Aston, it was sufficient that 'the King and his council go to the church and all their followers. It is best in my opinion to observe God's laws and the King's laws and go to church', and most respectable people would have agreed with him (Johnson and Vaisey 1964: 14). Religious books and pamphlets were sold, read, passed from hand to hand and debated. Prayer and catechesis were part of orderly family life, whether the family were Anglican, Papist or 'of the precise sort' and laymen were assuming more and more responsibility in religious affairs. Both Puritans and Papists, when they found themselves in conflict with the authorities, appealed to the overriding voice of conscience and Lord Brook even came near to recognising the possibility that all might follow their rational conscience (Hughes, A. 1980: 215–16). However, even he made haste to exempt Roman Catholics and Baptists from this toleration. All in all, the will to order and unity was stronger than concern for individual conscience. The dissidents did not seek to introduce freedom of belief but to uphold a better order of ecclesiastical government.

Chapter 15

Towns in adversity and recovery

The religious gilds had been so closely linked with town government that when they were dissolved in 1545 and 1548 leading townsmen in many midland towns had to find some alternative means of legitimating their authority and guaranteeing their common ownership of property. At Warwick the gildsmen applied immediately to hold the lands of the dissolved college, but were told by the court of augmentations that they would have to obtain incorporation in order to do so (VCH Warks VIII: 494). At Stratford they were concerned that 'if the gild be dissolved it was likely that the government of the borough will fall into a worse state' (Savage and Kripp 1924: 1–22).

Stratford, Lichfield and Warwick proceeded immediately to obtain a charter of incorporation. At Stratford, fourteen aldermen and fourteen capital burgesses were incorporated and granted former gild lands to the value of £40 a year and took over the almshouses and the grammar school. At Lichfield the town was incorporated and two bailiffs and twenty-four councillors took over the gild hall and gild lands to the value of £20 per annum. Five years later, Queen Mary granted them county status and Lichfield became a 'city and a county of itself' (Heath 1979: 5). At Warwick the burgesses obtained their charter in 1547 and one-third of the former gild land and college lands were transferred to them. They also took over the ancient school of the college and the college church became the parish church. Their powers were consolidated and extended in 1554 by a further charter (Chatwyn 1951: 8). Coventry was profoundly affected by the dissolution of the religious houses. The Benedictine Priory at the centre of the town was dissolved on 15 January and the Carthusian Priory on 16 January. Coventry failed in its attempt to secure the lands of the dissolved Whitefriars and Greyfriars, and, although the mayor and aldermen supported the Bishop of Coventry and Lichfield in his attempt to preserve the cathedral church as a collegiate church, they were unsuccessful. The cathedral church was largely destroyed after the dissolution, the palace fell in to gradual decay and Coventry ceased to be the seat of a bishop. However when in 1546 the Trinity Gild and the Corpus Christi Gild were dissolved and the corporation was able to purchase much of their land for £1,315, it proved a

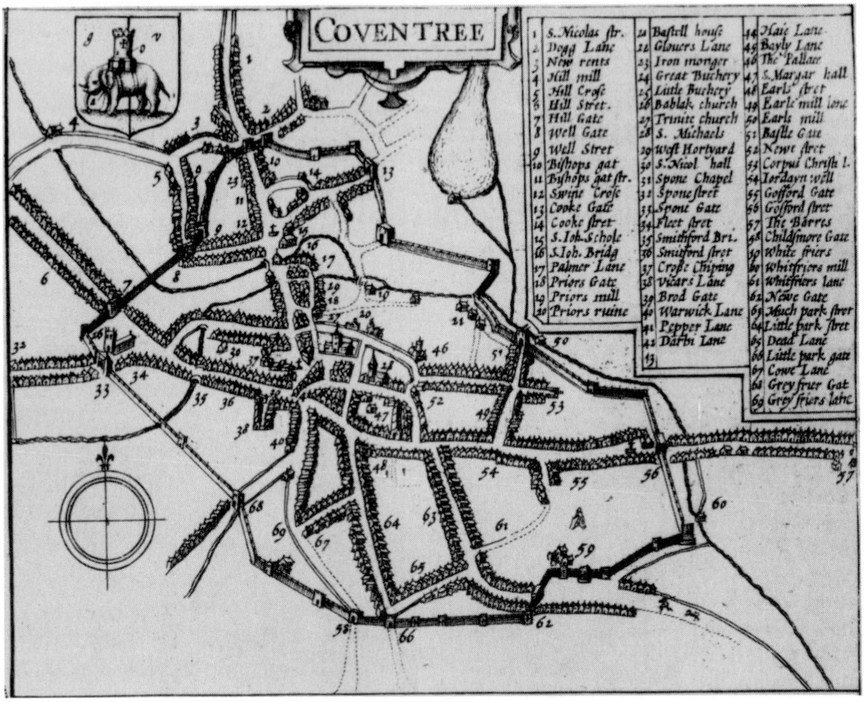
COVENTREE
1 S. Nicolas str.
2 Dogg Lane
3 New rents
4 Hill mill
5 Hill Crose
6 Hill Stret.
7 Hill Gate
8 Well Gate
9 Well Stret
10 Bishops gat
11 Bishops gat str.
12 Swine Crose
13 Cooke Gate
14 Cooke stret
15 S. Ioh. Schole
16 S. Ioh. Bridg
17 Palmer Lane
18 Priors Gate
19 Priors mill
20 Priors ruine
21 Bastell house
22 Glouers Lane
23 Iron monger
24 Great Buchery
25 Little Buchery
26 Bablak church
27 Trinite church
28 S. Michaels
29 West Hortyard
30 S. Nicol hall
31 Spone Chapel
32 Sponestret
33 Spone Gate
34 Fleet stret
35 Smithford Bri.
36 Smitford stret
37 Crosse Chiping
38 Vicars Lane
39 Brod Gate
40 Warwick Lane
41 Pepper Lane
42 Darbi Lane
43
44 Haie Lane
45 Bayly Lane
46 The Pallace
47 S. Margar hall
48 Earls stret
49 Earle mill lane
50 Earls mill
51 Bastle Gate
52 Newe stret
53 Corpus Christi l.
54 Iordayn well
55 Gofford Gate
56 Gosford stret
57 The Barres
58 Childsmore Gate
59 White friers
60 Whitfriers mill
61 Whitfriers lane
62 Newe Gate
63 Much park stret
64 Little park stret
65 Dead Lane
66 Little park gate
67 Cowe Lane
68 Grey frier Gat
69 Grey friers lane

Plate 3.2 Town map of Coventry from John Speed's *Atlas of England*, 1611.

Plate 3.3 Town map of Lichfield from John Speed's *Atlas of England*, 1611.

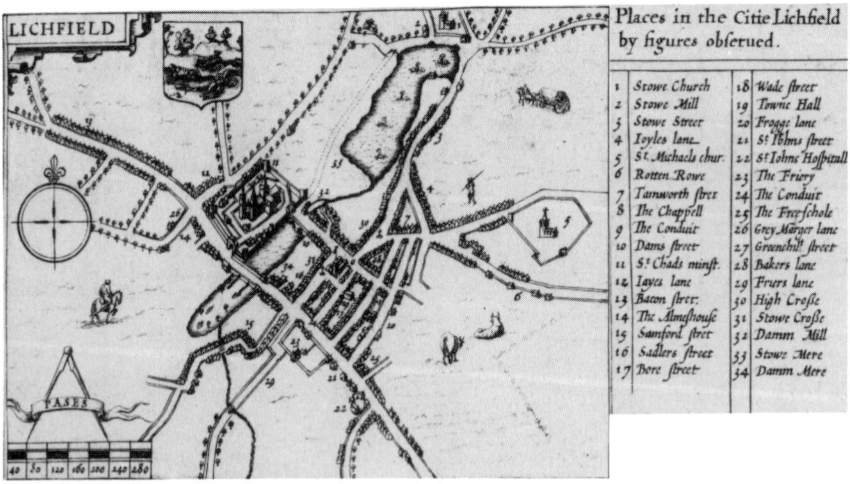
LICHFIELD
PASES
40 80 120 160 200 240 280
Places in the Citie Lichfield by figures obserued.
1 Stowe Church
2 Stowe Mill
3 Stowe Street
4 Ioyles lane
5 St. Michaels chur.
6 Rotten Rowe
7 Tamworth stret
8 The Chappell
9 The Conduit
10 Dams street
11 St. Chads minst.
12 Iayes lane
13 Bacon stret.
14 The Almeshouse
15 Samford stret
16 Sadlers street
17 Bore street
18 Wade street
19 Towne Hall
20 Frogge lane
21 St. Iohns street
22 St Iohns Hospitall
23 The Friery
24 The Conduit
25 The Freeschole
26 Grey Marger lane
27 Greenehill street
28 Bakers lane
29 Friers lane
30 High Crosse
31 Stowe Crosse
32 Damm Mill
33 Stowe Mere
34 Damm Mere

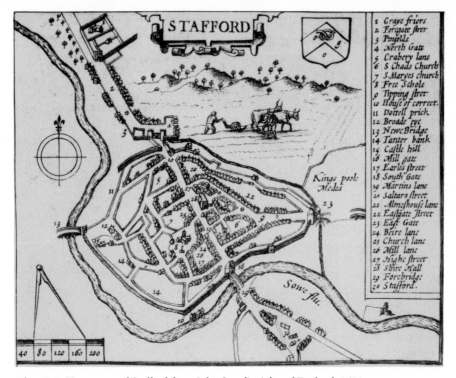

Plate 3.4 Town map of Stafford from John Speed's *Atlas of England*, 1611.

Plate 3.5 Town map of Warwick from John Speed's *Atlas of England*, 1611.

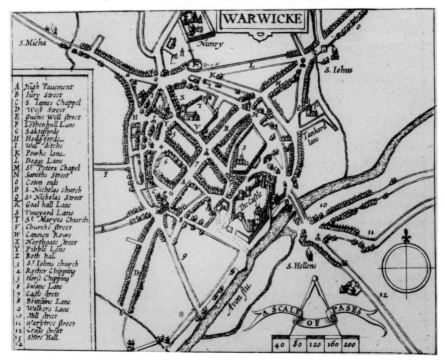

profitable investment but added considerably to their responsibilities, for they had to administer the lands, collect the rents, administer the rectories of St Michael and Holy Trinity and a number of charities. Bailiffs and overseers were appointed for the lands, tithes were farmed, receipts and expenditure began to be entered in the council minutes, and contracts for maintenance of the properties were granted often to the councillors themselves.

There was little change of personnel in town governments at the reformation. The former wardens and masters of the religious gilds became members of the new corporations, and in all towns the same individuals and families occupied the principal offices. There was a marked trend towards greater definition of offices and the concentration of leadership in fewer hands. At Coventry the offices were filled by co-option and the great leet met only twice a year to elect officials. At Stafford the ordinances of 1560 (confirmed in 1590) concentrated power in the hands of the bailiff and the Twenty-Five, and in 1608 the total number of councillors was reduced to twenty-one. In 1613 a prominent townsman, Matthew Craddock, campaigned for a new charter with the professed intention of 'curbing the vulgar burgesses'. He was successful and the new council consisted of Matthew Craddock as mayor and ten capital burgesses and the aldermen (VCH Staffs VI: 212). Central government expected the town leaders to undertake an ever growing list of duties. They were charged under various statutes with the maintenance of the roads, the care of the poor, mustering soldiers, controlling cottage building, supervising constables and controlling vagrants. The chartered towns were responsible for keeping the peace and had their own magistrates, and at Lichfield and Coventry the magistrates had the full powers of county magistrates. The towns collected royal taxes and levies and were expected by Privy Council to keep the town loyal. The townsmen regulated the markets and the shambles, and organised the cleaning of the streets and wells. Coventry had an income of over £1,500 derived mainly from land, market tolls and fairs, but most towns had much less; Alcester had an annual income of only £19 (Dyer, A. 1976–7: 139).

The influence of the laity was increasing at the expense of that of the clergy. At Coventry the town council pursued a vigorous Protestant policy suppressing processions, regulating behaviour, suppressing tippling, removing maypoles and banning football. At Wolverhampton the collegiate church was dissolved and much of the land passed to the Leveson family, while in Lichfield the Bishop had been forced to surrender his manorial rights to the burgesses in return for £50 rent. The power of the Bishop of Worcester over Stratford was similarly diminished.

The processions and public religious celebrations which had been so marked a feature of urban life before the reformation were already in decline before 1540. At Coventry the leading families had shown themselves increasingly unwilling to support the great expense entailed. The membership of the Corpus Christi Gild was declining and it had been amalgamated with Holy Trinity two years before the gilds were wholly dissolved. The drama cycles were abandoned gradually; the last Corpus Christi pageant had been held in 1519 but the craft gild plays continued until 1579. At Lichfield, Wolverhampton, Tamworth and elsewhere, the dramatised rituals of Holy Week and the festivals were discontinued during the reign of Edward VI and not revived. In the place of religious rituals some towns became the centre of secular theatre. Despite Puritan objections, players were licensed to play at Stratford, Newcastle and Stafford. Among companies appearing in midland towns in the early seventeenth century were the King's Company, the Queen's Company, Lord Stafford's, Lord Dudley's, Lord Buckley's and Lady Elizabeth's Company (VCH Staffs VIII; Pape 1928: 90; Savage and Fripp 1924: xxiv–xxxv). Some limited civic rituals continued, such as 'walking the fairs', and the Mayor's processions, but for the most part the celebrations of urban dignity and wealth were transferred from the church and the streets to the privacy of the banqueting chamber.

The parish church and the market remained the social centres of the towns and around the market in the sixteenth and seventeenth centuries substantial timber-framed houses were built and were occupied by mercers, grocers, chandlers, drapers and goldsmiths. Their roofs were of tiles and they were well furnished. In the larger towns they were often of three storeys and some had their own gatehouses and yards. The largest houses were the inns, which were handsome and well furnished, provided accommodation for travellers and their horses and servants, and were convenient places for buyers and sellers to meet outside the public markets to make large-scale credit bargains. The inns kept horses for hire and waggoners set out from the inns to London and the river ports. In the capacious inn yards goods were accumulated and warehoused, and travelling merchants could inspect samples and make orders.

There was a market hall even in small market towns such as Stourbridge, and Dudley. The expenses of building the market halls were met by special town levies and the use of the building was controlled by the town officials. At one remove from the market place craftsmen and labourers lived in smaller houses of one or two storeys, timber-built and with workshops and small gardens behind. The timber and thatch town houses were very liable to catch fire. Stratford had major fires in 1594, 1595, 1614 and 1641 (Porter 1976: 97–100).

By the 1560s there were some fourteen endowed grammar schools in the market towns of Staffordshire and Warwickshire. Warwick, Coventry, Stratford, Solihull, Tamworth, Brailes and Lichfield all had schools associated with the colleges, chantries or gilds before the Reformation and the townsmen were able to ensure their continuance either under groups of feoffees or by transferring responsibility to some other body as in the case of Wolverhampton whose school was taken over by the Merchants Taylors Company. New schools were endowed by wealthy tradesmen at Stone, Uttoxeter and Rugby in the early years of the reign of Elizabeth and there were three more endowments in the seventeenth century. At Newcastle the town council began to employ a schoolmaster from 1565. All these schools were grammar schools for the teaching of Latin. Boys were admitted at about the age of eight having already learned to read and write English and to say the catechism in English and in Latin. Some towns including Stratford had a petty school with a licensed schoolmaster to teach the younger boys.

These town schools brought together the sons of the local elite of both town and country – aldermen's sons and the sons of local gentlemen. The schools retained close links with the Established Church for schoolmasters were ordained and licensed by the bishops and were expected to reinforce the teachings of the established church by precept and example. The schoolmasters of the endowed schools in Warwickshire were almost always graduates or had at least attended university and in the early seventeenth century at least were better educated than many of the parish clergy. The masters were assisted by ushers, also usually graduates, who taught the preparatory classes and sometimes even the three Rs when illiterate boys were admitted contrary to the statutes. Many of the masters and the ushers were young men in their early twenties and the great majority were local men appointed by local patronage. They were drawn from many backgrounds, sons both of shoemakers and of gentlemen. Many, if not most, of the more able remained in the school for only a few years before moving on to ecclesiastical benefices (Orpen 1979: 1076). The endowed grammar schools were all located in towns, part of the service which the town offered to its region. There was a wider diffusion of endowed English schools which were to be found in some fifty or so places in Staffordshire and Warwickshire in the seventeenth century, both in towns and larger villages.

The towns were not as yet densely inhabited. There are many references to orchards, tenter fields, gardens and waste grounds within the towns. However, townscapes were changing, for the empty spaces were filling up and there was increasing use of bricks and tiles. By 1650 it could be said of Walsall that there were no lands in the town, only houses and backsides (Homeshaw 1960: 60).

Population increases were not regarded with satisfaction by the town authorities, but were seen as a threat to food supplies and to the livelihood of the townspeople. When natural increase was compounded by increased immigration of the poor their anxieties became acute. Scattered figures indicate the scale of relief being given. At Warwick in 1582 weekly contributions from 99 persons of St Mary's parish produced 18s. 4½d. a week and a further 26 householders in St Nicholas parish collected 26s. 4½d. a week. The numbers to be relieved out of this sum were 43 in St Mary's and 20 in St Nicholas, most of whom were the very young, the very old and the sick (Kemp n.d.: 47).

There was no shortage of legislation which could be invoked or adapted by the frightened authorities and although each town before 1597 was acting individually there was much that was similar in the means they took to prevent their responsibilities escalating beyond their capacity and to ensure that members of their own community kept control of scarce resources.

In 1586 the Warwick burgesses made a survey of the poor and enumerated 114 adults and 113 children as 'poor', almost a quarter of the population of whom 50 adults and 60 children were beggars. Some families were expelled immediately and expulsions continued in subsequent years. One hundred and thirteen vagrants were arrested at Warwick between 1580 and 1587. They came from near and far. Most of them had travelled the roads constantly, slowly moving from place to place (Beier 1981: 58). More were removed in 1604 after the outbreak of plague and thirty-six in 1605. The town employed a uniformed marshall to keep out beggars and two-thirds of the cases heard by the town magistrate were about vagrancy (Beier 1982: 60–1).

An alternative to ejecting incomers was to bind them not to demand poor relief. In Stratford eighty-one bonds were kept between 1613 and 1662. The security was about £40. The majority of these were persons connected with the land – for example, husbandmen, labourers, yeomen, shepherds and five malsters, and were able to maintain themselves; almost half established themselves permanently in the town (Styles 1963: 181–2).

Some public-spirited individuals endowed almshouses and charities for the poor but Midlanders at this period were not on the whole conspicuous for almsgiving. Lord Leicester established a hospital at Warwick for twelve wounded soldiers, endowing it with an income of £200. Preference was given to men from Warwick, Kenilworth and Stratford in that order (VCH Warks VIII: 548–9). At Coventry Bond's and Ford's almshouses founded in the early-sixteenth century survived the reformation and Bablake boys' hospital was founded in 1560 (VCH Warks VIII: 398–9). At Stratford two modest bequests were used to provide clothes for twenty-four almsmen and women (VCH Warks II: 65–6). Bequests such as these at best assisted a small number of the poor and were enjoyed as a rule by those who could find a patron to prefer them to the place rather than those who had the most need of help.

A number of midland towns were complaining of lack of trade. At Warwick the malt trade and the cloth trade were both in decline and the corporation was in debt. The value of the townsmen's inventories fell relative to north Warwickshire despite the rising values produced by the inflation of prices. Although the population probably doubled between 1560 and 1640 there were a high proportion of poor and husbandmen and the town failed to develop any new trades (Martin, J. M. 1982b). At Coventry the mercers, drapers and dyers continued to monopolise power but there were many complaints of their management. In particular they were accused of interfering with the textile trade by permitting the import of Gloucestershire cloths for finishing. Coventry remained true to its long tradition of internal conflict and disorder, and the management of the town's common field continued to be a cause of trouble.

Despite all the difficulties, there was from 1570 a quickening of trade and commerce, and a degree of economic recovery. Where this occurred it was often attributable in part to the links between the Midlands and the London market for both food and manufactured goods. By 1600 Walsall and Birmingham merchants were beginning to break down the monopoly of the London ironmongers in the distribution of metalware through London and also developing direct marketing to other parts of the country. By 1640 they were exporting independently to Ireland. At Burton on Trent local geological conditions favoured the development of brewing and by 1620 there were forty-six licensed brewers in the town and Burton ale was being sold in Holborn and Gray's Inn Lane, London.

Stratford on Avon in the seventeenth century began to recover from adversity and was becoming an important riverport and the market in corn and malt for the whole of south Warwickshire. In general, the demand for foodstuffs was increasing as population grew and specialist trade and manufactures occupied larger numbers of the people. While towns such as Walsall, Newcastle, Birmingham and Dudley flourished as markets for manufactured goods, the towns in the river valleys and the Feldon became important as suppliers of agricultural produce, as at Warwick, Lichfield and Shipston on Stour, while the production of malt and beer became the principal trades at Stratford and Burton. In general, the economy of towns was becoming more broadly based and varied, as townsmen responded to changing demands and found new openings for their products.

One of the most notable commercial developments of the period was the growth of the retail trade. By 1650 every market town and some of the larger villages had permanent retail shops. The mercers, grocers and apothecaries stocked their shops with goods obtained in London, often imported from abroad and also with goods bought directly from the wholesale clothiers, drapers, ironmongers, pewterers and braziers. The retailers were often the most substantial of the townsmen and occupied places of importance in the local community. Their stock in trade was very various indeed for they depended on selling small quantities of a large range of goods. The value of the stock in trade could amount to £200 or more. They dealt with their own wholesalers and with their customers largely on credit and their shop books of debts owing in trade are often the largest item in their inventories.

In addition to the retail shops in towns there were numerous pedlars or 'petty chapmen' who carried similar goods from fair to fair and to the wealthier houses. These men were by no means only concerned with selling trifles to the poor, but formed an essential link between producers and the gentry, the yeomen, craftsmen and others whose income was sufficient to purchase comfort rather than subsistence. At Lichfield a pedlar's pack contained caps, handkerchiefs, stockings, ribbons, buttons, buckles, gloves, laces, scissors, pins, spoons and laces (SHC 1969: 187–8).

The retail shops of the market towns clearly both stimulated and supplied a demand for goods and were one of the principal outlets for goods manufactured in England as well as for goods imported from abroad. Moreover, they were an important link in the circulation of credit for, whereas the manufacturers sold their goods in London against debts incurred in the country, the retailers' shops bought goods in London and collected cash in the country. They were thus increasingly used to discount bills of exchange, or to provide them for persons wishing to pay off a creditor in London.

The smaller market towns continued to dwindle. Solihull market ceased to trade and Tutbury, Bidford, Kineton, Brewood, and Kenilworth became insignificant and their functions were taken over by their more successful rivals. The recovery of trade and growth of population did not lead to a revival of markets in small rural centres but to consolidation of trading in the larger markets and to the growth in those towns of retail shops. The improvement in roads and the increasing traffic on the long-distance routes encouraged the development of some towns at the expense of others (Dyer, C. 1976: 122–35) and the growing volume of trade outside regulated markets must also have played a part.

In addition to their commercial functions the larger towns were becoming centres for the diffusion of knowledge and ideas. Books and pamphlets were on sale in the shops, the wealthier townsmen owned books, maps and pictures, and the larger towns brought together men who travelled from town to the ports and to the metropolis, men who were literate, and who had contacts in both London and the provinces. The townsmen's opinions might be conformist and conservative as at Lichfield or dissenting and combative as at Coventry, but their voices were beginning to be heard.

Chapter 16

Industry and the national market

The Midlands in the mid-sixteenth century was well placed to take advantage of the growth of trade in manufactured commodities. Commercial organisation was already well established by the drapers and clothiers who had for many generations exported cloth from the region to London, the ports of East Anglia, Southampton and Bristol for shipment abroad. The numerous market towns acted as collecting centres and although the transport of goods by road was laborious there were no obstacles sufficient to prevent trade. Even bulky objects were transported by waggons and wains, and trains of pack-horses carried small manufactured goods from the Midlands to all parts of the land.

Birmingham and midland merchants were importing raw materials, wine and other goods from Spain in the mid-sixteenth century. John Smythe of Bristol (1538–50) was sending a range of goods including bar iron up the Severn to merchants in Birmingham, King's Norton, Wolverhampton, West Bromwich, Tewkesbury and Coventry. Among the Birmingham merchants importing iron were William King, fuller; Humphrey Colchester, tanner; and Nicholas Webster, smith; which suggests that many with an eye for profit were turning to the iron industry from other trades (Royal Commission on Historical Manuscripts 1974).

Scattered references in probate inventories show that midland goods were already being marketed in Yorkshire, East Anglia, Devon, Buckinghamshire, Nottinghamshire, Northamptonshire and Oxfordshire.

Walsall pewter was sold in London and in market towns within a radius of sixty miles. William Nicholas of Walsall, for example, sold pewter ware at Northampton, Coventry, Banbury, Abingdon, Chipping Norton, Wallingford and Hereford (Hatcher and Barker 1974). Trading links with London were well established by 1600. The Walsall, Birmingham and other merchants successfully challenged the monopolies of the London trading companies and by the seventeenth century there were numerous examples of midland merchant families who had one member living in London working in partnership with another member of the family who remained in the Midlands. We have seen that the industrialising parishes were already populous in 1563 and that their populations grew at a rate greater than either town or rural parishes. In many parishes this growth was made possible by the development of crafts based on local raw materials. At Knowle, Yardley, Solihull, Sheldon and Bickenhill families turned to work in building, furniture making, tile making, fulling, and weaving, using local clay, wood and yarn. In the north of Staffordshire an increasing number of families used local clay to make pottery, storage jars and drinking vessels with many handles and simple decoration. The families of Adams and Daniels had been potters for several generations and the Wedgwood family were established by 1650.

Metal working was important in several north Staffordshire parishes and also in Warwickshire in Studley and Atherstone, but it was on the south Staffordshire coalfield that development was most rapid and most sophisticated. There were very real differences in the standard of living of the different kinds of metalworkers, differences which developed in part because of the variety of materials used and the skills required in the different trades.

Nailing was the least skilled of the trades, but the range and variety of types of nail was great and some nailers concentrated on the production of particular types, sprigs, brads, tacks, spikes, sheath nails, clouts, dogeared frost nails, rose, sparrables and others. Each had their own specifications in the trade and standard allowances for waste. Some nailers bought their own rod, but the majority of them were supplied by the ironmongers. The nails were made in small workshops at the back of the nailer's house, mainly in winter and early summer, for nailing was suspended during ploughing and harvest. When made, the nails were bagged, docketed and delivered to the ironmongers' warehouse, then forwarded to the customers. The nailer provided the work-shop, the fuel and the hearth, anvil, hammers and bellows; the total value of the tools was usually given for probate as about £1. Most of the tools could be made or inherited.

Lockmaking provided greater opportunities to the workers. Simple pad-locks and chest locks were made in quantity in much the same way as nails, bagged and sold wholesale by the ironmongers. Highly sophisticated locks were also made of brass as well as iron, incorporating clockwork counting devices, warning chimes, or decorative features, and these commanded high prices from householders with goods to protect and servants to control. They were made to individual order, and the skilled locksmith himself negotiated with his customers and advertised his products. In a few cases locksmiths made reputations which outlived them.

Scythe making was the most skilled of the trades using iron. Different scythes and reaping hooks were made for different parts of England, each requiring a different heat and temper in the process. The scythe required the welding together or plating of iron and steel. The unfinished scythes were sent to the grinding mill to be sharpened at 1s. a dozen, and then returned to the scythe makers to be finished and sold. They sold their own scythes in the

143

market towns in agricultural areas, employing a member of the family or a chapman. As a group they held more land, had more cattle, lived in larger and better furnished houses than any other metal workers. Some of them had larger workshops; sometimes they contained as many as eight anvils and six hearths.

The lorimers of Walsall making metal parts for harness were skilled men with a range of tools and a variety of materials and techniques. They appear from the inventories to be poorer than either the scythesmiths or the locksmiths, but this was because they were essentially urban workers and had no husbandry tools, hay or animals. As early as 1600 there had been complaints of the lorimers refusing to help with the harvest and inciting other smiths to continue work in the shops during harvest time.

The remarkable feature of the trade was the extreme subdivision of process between different workmen (Plot 1686: 376–7). There were four separate stages to the making of a spur, each carried on in a different shop; there were seven different kinds of snaffle, each being made with six variant ends and sides. The subdivision of the work is explicable in terms of the different skills and the different materials required for the separate parts, for example the head and the rowell of a spur. The brass buckles were made by a worker in brass, but the spike had to be of iron and was therefore made by the chapemaker. Some of the more elaborate harness parts for riding horses were decorated and inlaid by lorimers using tin or even silver.

In Walsall there were also makers of brass and copper pans, vessels and other domestic utensils and kitchen tools. The braziers and copper smiths were strong family groups not confined to Walsall but with a representative in several different market towns. The Ebb family for example had a branch in Wolverhampton, Walsall and Uttoxeter.

A great variety of terms of employment existed side by side, and a man might be at the same time an employer and an employed man, a taker-in of work and a putter-out to others. The smith, as well as being responsible for the capital equipment, the fuel, the tools and the maintenance, organised production and trained the workforce. A family of capable sons not only enabled a smith to increase his output, but also to go out on journeys to seek orders or deliver goods. Hours of work, and choice of kind of work were under his own control, subject to the availability of orders. His work and, therefore, his income might fluctuate greatly from week to week and from season to season, and he might have to wait some considerable time before receiving an accountable return on his investment of labour. Broadly speaking the more skilled the worker and the more complex his product the greater degree of independence he could maintain, but much depended on the circumstances of the particular family. Sons usually set up their own workshops when they grew up, but there were many links of kindred and neighbourhood between workshops and in marketing. Expansion was achieved by the proliferation of more and more small units of production, and the investment came from the mobilisation of many small inputs by men of little means (Rowlands 1975).

Tanners and leather workers were among the wealthiest and most influential of the townsmen in Birmingham, Warwick, Stratford, Coventry and elsewhere. Despite the noisomeness of their business their work places adjoined their own homes. The tanners required storage sheds, tan pits and numerous vats, oak bark and a plentiful supply of water, but the total value of their equipment was usually only between £5 and £10. Most of their capital was required for the purchase of stock, since the skins could take weeks or even months to prepare and the supply from the graziers and butchers was to some extent seasonal.

One important manufacturing industry changed its location in order to meet increased demand and opportunity. The glass industry before 1600 had been located in the Cannock Chase area at Abbots Bromley and Eccleshall. It was here that immigrants from Lorraine first settled after leaving the Weald in 1574. Members of the families of Henzey, Tyzack and D'Haux were already making glass at Eccleshall and Bishops Wood. In 1585 Ambrose Henzey agreed to erect new glasshouses and furnace in Bagot's Park. He was joined by Richard Henzey from Eccleshall and other workers were brought into the parish. Calculations based on excavations at other sites of this period suggest that at this date two teams of glassmakers could make 1,000 cases of glass a year, producing an income of £160 to £200 a year. The glassworkers, skilled men from Lorraine, offered an attractive investment to landowners wanting cash and projectors hoping for patents of monopoly (Crossley 1967; Crossley 1972: 426–8).

However, in the Cannock area the glassworkers were competing with the iron makers for supplies of charcoal, and the means of making glass with coal was already being sought. About 1604 some of the Lorrainers moved to new coalfield sites for glassmaking, some to Newcastle on Tyne, and some to the Stour valley which offered the additional attraction of high quality refractory clay. Paul Tyzack had left Eccleshall and settled in Stourbridge by 1612. In Nottinghamshire other members of the Henzey family were making glass with coal for Robert Mansell who secured a proclamation forbidding the use of wood as fuel for glass furnaces. The Stour valley with its coal and clay immediately became the principal midland location of the trade. The Lorrainers were well established in the parishes of Kingswinford, Amblecote and Oldswinford by 1610 and they were joined in the trade by local men, Bradley, Wilson, Piddock, Dixon and Bendy. Mansell's patent terminated in 1642 and was replaced by a duty of 12*d*. in the pound, but this did not inhibit the sale of window glass and bottles. The town of Stourbridge, although it contained no glass works, became the acknowledged market for glass and increasing quantities left the district for the ports of the river Severn and Bristol (Guttery 1956).

During the same period new methods of iron production were introduced into the Midlands, new both in techniques of production and in methods of control and distribution. The first blast furnaces had been built in the Weald of

145

Kent and Sussex and by the middle of the sixteenth century there were about sixty-five works in the south-east of England, but it was not until about 1560 that the first blast furnace was built in the Midlands, almost certainly on the Paget Estate at Cannock Chase while about the same date another blast furnace was built at Shifnal only a few miles to the west in Shropshire. These early furnaces were square structures about 20 ft high and built of local stone. They were built on streams usually under a slope which made it possible to construct a bridge to the top of the furnace, along which ore, charcoal and limestone could be brought in barrows. The daily output of iron at the furnace at Cannock Wood has been calculated as approximately one ton per day and it was tapped every twenty-four hours. By 1603 there were at least nine more such furnaces in the Midlands and a further fifteen had come into production by 1640.

The pig iron was brittle and required to be decarbonised in a finery hearth, to be reheated in a chafery hearth and then by repeated hammering converted into malleable iron. Each of these processes was facilitated by water power. Forges were of necessity more numerous than furnaces, and usually some distance away. Already in the reign of Elizabeth there were hammer mills, fineries and chaferies at Cannock, Little Aston, Bromley, Hints, Brewood, Congreve and Rushall which produced bar iron of varying qualities and types.

In the Midlands the bar iron was still slit laboriously by hand, but from the 1620s water power was also applied to this process and by 1625 there were slitting mills at Kinver, West Bromwich and Abbots Bromley producing standard bundles of iron weighing half a hundredweight of square rods. At Hyde Mill, Kinver, 400 tons were slit each year and delivered to customers in the Midlands (Rowlands 1975).

The initiative in erecting an iron mill was usually taken by a landlord anxious to make an investment which would bring in a cash return. The Willoughbys of Nottinghamshire, the Pagets of Beaudesert, Lord Dudley, the Holts of Aston, the Lyttletons of Hagley, the Wyrleys and Whorewoods of Handsworth all proved willing to make the preliminary investment required. Groups of linked furnaces and forges were built and then leased to specialist ironmasters, who built up the trade and extended the networks, sometimes becoming builders of mills in their own right, sometimes continuing to lease all their mills. In the early seventeenth century the many mills originally established by the Earl of Dudley, and the Wyrleys and Whorewoods of Handsworth in the Tame and Stour valleys, were gradually leased by Richard Foley of Dudley who built up the network which his son and grandsons were to turn into an unprecedented business empire (Johnson 1952).

A group of mills comprising furnace, forges and slitting mill was usually managed by a 'clerk of the ironworks'. A man of 'government, skilled and painful', he had to maintain stock, obtain raw materials, hire the workmen, appoint each to his daily work, receive the work, check the tallies and pay the men. He was responsible for sales, carriage of iron between the works and keeping accounts. Pay day was once every three weeks and was complicated by advances to the workmen, and arrears (Harrison 1978: 795–810).

The men who managed and worked in iron mills were to some extent a separate community of their own, forming their own networks of kindred, trade connections and credit. The mills were sited away from settlements and the workers worked unsocial hours, lived in provided accommodation and did not take part in husbandry or harvest. The ironmasters and the clerks spent much time away from home and deals were negotiated with customers at inns, in London and Bristol, as well as at the works. Iron in the process of manufacture was carried many miles and the carriers had wide ranging contacts.

In contrast the mining of coal remained closely related to the local community, it was dug by local people and sold to local industry and to local householders for domestic fuel.

The capital costs of setting up a mine varied very greatly. In Darlaston's open fields the villagers could dig down from the surface and the cost was trivial. In contrast a litigant in a dispute in 1620 claimed that he had spent £800 on providing a new gin and gin shafts, digging a pond, diverting a stream, making a water mill and a horse mill for a large coal works near Coventry. The Warwickshire coalfield was more difficult to work than the Staffordshire coalfield and in the late sixteenth century attracted a number of ambitious adventurers and projectors who found the problems exceeded the profits (White 1970: 12–24). Meanwhile other less ambitious but more successful coalmasters were at work supplying the market for domestic fuel and for industrial uses in Coventry and also carrying some coal into Leicestershire and south Warwickshire.

In south Staffordshire where the coal was easier to obtain, the majority of the lessees were local men usually of yeoman status who put in simple gins and gear, provided horses and paid pikemen to work underground and banksmen above. Sometimes a lease was subdivided between three or four sub-lessees. Small partnerships began to be identifiable between associated families who took leases of parcels in adjoining parishes, sometimes building up a connection which continued for three or four generations. At the same time Lord Dudley, the Pagets and the Vernons and other large landowners continued to exploit the mineral resources directly ((U) SRO Paget Mss).

Both skilled and unskilled workers were required. Sinkers and borers were specialists who were employed to find and open up the pit and then move on. The pikemen who dug out the coal and the banksmen above ground were local men, but experienced in this work and paid above the average of agricultural wages. They worked in teams and were paid as a group according to the amount they got. There were constant stoppages and interruptions to the work and since they were producing for a mainly local market there was little incentive to get a greater quantity than could be sold. Much work, such as the clearing of soughs, the mending of gins and buckets, and the loading of waggons, was done by unskilled labourers hired on a day-to-day basis, whose tools were simple mattocks, picks, mandrels, wedges and shovels made of wood 'shod' with iron, but in underground working great quantities of candles were consumed ((U) SRO Vernon Mss).

While the metalworking, glass and pottery industries were developing to meet increasing consumer demands, the old textile industry was surviving rather than developing. Weavers were still to be found in the great majority of towns and villages, and weaving continued to be an important element of Coventry's economy. The decline of the traditional woollen cloths was to some extent offset by the introduction of crimpelists and ultrafines. Drapers and mercers continued to dominate the town. The silk industry was introduced and spread to the surrounding villages. A silk weavers gild was established in the City in 1610 and there were also silk weavers at Lichfield and Wolverhampton. The weaving of 'tammies' was carried on around Tamworth and at Tutbury, while at Bedworth the miners' wives wove duffle and spun worsted.

William, Lord Paget, among his many enterprises built a new fulling mill in 1560 on the Trent and leased it to the Lowe family of Burton, and his son Thomas built a second nearby in 1574. Their investment was rewarded with a substantial increase in the clothmaking industry in Burton. One of the most prominent clothiers of the period was John Clarke who had a weaving workshop in High Street and a dye house which processed all the cloth made in the town. The Burton clothworkers produced kersies which were carried to Blackwell Hall in London. In the early seventeenth century the industry was thriving and although the trade suffered during the civil wars there were still about forty clothiers and perhaps three hundred clothworkers in and around the town in the 1660s. The associated trade of spinning leaves less indication in the records but many homes contained a spinning wheel (Owen 1978: 130–1).

At Lichfield a cappers' company was founded in 1576 and a company of dyers and weavers in 1610. Stafford set up a Drapers' and Clothiers' Company and a Glovers' Company in 1609, but although there were some substantial craftsmen they did not dominate the town, and the companies contained members of other trades. However, Midland industries on the whole were comparatively free from regulation. The trading gilds in the corporate towns controlled access to trade, sought to limit the numbers of apprentices and laid down rules of working. The Mercers' Company of Lichfield also attempted in 1624 to restrict entry to the retail trades, the mercers, grocers, drapers, hosiers and salters. The Coventry gilds continued to exercise their traditional controls.

The development of manufacture necessitated a corresponding increase in carrying services. Much carriage was done by the farmers, husbandmen and labourers, especially for short hauls and where demand for carriage was especially great. In the Potteries, on the coalfields, near ironworks, and near the river ports such as Bewdley and Bridgnorth work was always available, and an army of men underemployed in agriculture met the fluctuating demand for carrying services, providing an amorphous and flexible work force, costing nothing between jobs, and yet immediately available when required. By the mid-seventeenth century there were regular carriers with four to eight pack-horses making regular journeys to London from the main market towns, namely, Newcastle, Lichfield, Stone, Stafford, Birmingham and Coventry. Among them was William Hill of Oldswinford, waggoner, who had a substantial house in Oldswinford with hall, parlour and rooms over. His equipment included a wagon, cart, tumbril, wheels, gears, dassels and hampers worth £6 10s. and seven horses worth £20 ((U) WRO Probate William Hill).

It is clear that by the middle of the seventeenth century industries in the Midlands were serving a national market and were organised with commercial professionalism. Both investment and profit were widely diffused through society and men of all conditions were accustomed to manufacture standardised articles for customers they never personally met. Every stage of buying and selling was conducted on a credit basis with raw materials being advanced upon credit to facilitate production and customers being given extended credit facilities to return payment.

Development had been achieved mainly by the growth of industries indigenous to the area and with little in the way of technical or commercial innovation. It was a growth in scale rather than a change in kind. If there was a revolution it was in the changing habits of consumption and the extending marketing opportunities which created the demand to which Midlanders of many different social levels responded along traditional lines.

Chapter 17

The country gentry and the local community

The early sixteenth century saw the eclipse of several of the leading families of the Midlands. The third Duke of Buckingham had been beheaded in 1521, and although his son recovered the castle and manor of Stafford, the power and lands of the barony were much diminished. Edward, the seventh baron Dudley, died in 1532, and his heir was a simpleton and much impoverished. Meanwhile, some lesser midland families were able to secure royal favour and to accumulate manors and power in the Midlands. The arch climber was John Dudley, son of Edmund Dudley, Henry VIII's tax collector. Despite the execution of his father in 1510 he was able to enter royal service and was successively Viscount Lisle (1542), Earl of Warwick (1547), Duke of Northumberland and Lord Protector of England (1553). He sought to fix in the minds of the public his connection with the medieval Earls of Dudley and of Warwick. Dudley Castle was acquired in 1532 and extensively rebuilt and Warwick Castle also taken over 'for the name of the thing'. He accumulated manors and monastic property on a grand scale, but his empire was destroyed when on the accession of Mary he raised a rebellion in favour of Lady Jane Grey. Although he fell, lesser men survived. William Paget entered royal service in 1530 and in the last years of Henry VIII was First Secretary. He acquired monastic lands, and a new estate called Beaudesert in Cannock Chase. He was consistently a conservative in religion and became a Privy Councillor in the reign of Mary.

Another conservative midland family who thrust their way into Court favour in the latter part of the reign of Henry VIII were the Throckmortons of Coughton. George Throckmorton was a member of the Reformation Parliament and was associated publicly with opposition to the breach with Rome. He survived considerable suspicion and attached himself to Thomas Cromwell, but turned against him in 1539 and with Thomas Rich supplied part of the evidence which led in 1540 to Cromwell's fall from power and execution. He was rewarded with manors and monastic lands and during the reign of Mary he and his allies controlled most of the offices of importance in the Midlands.

Staffordshire members of Mary's Parliament were drawn from Catholic families such as Draycotts, Giffards, Littleton of Pillaton and Fowler, but the Catholic gentlemen were not able to control the town elections to the same extent as the county. Newcastle elected one Catholic, but the second member was a Protestant, Thomas Bagnel, who refused to accept the restoration of England to the Roman Catholic Church in 1554 and went into exile. Coventry was advised by its recorder and former member of Parliament to proclaim Mary not Queen Jane and under his influence elected John Throckmorton as one of the city's members for Mary's three parliaments but the second member was in each case a Protestant city tradesman.

The close links between royal office, and the Privy Council at national level and the web of local power and patronage were evident at every turn in the sixteenth century. The accession of Elizabeth saw a considerable shift of power in the Midlands, as Catholic gentry were displaced by Protestants. The sons of John Dudley, Earl of Northumberland, were in the ascendant. Ambrose, his eldest surviving son, became Earl of Warwick in 1561, residing in the remodelled castle where he received the Queen in 1566 and again in 1577. Robert Dudley became Earl of Leicester in 1564 and made Kenilworth his headquarters in the Midlands, spending £60,000 on rebuilding it in medieval style. He was a recognised leader of Protestant opinion and patron of intellectuals and the arts. Among the Warwickshire gentlemen who allied themselves to him were Sir Thomas Lucy of Charlecote, and Job Throckmorton of Haseley, the most Puritan member of that divided family, and Nicholas Throckmorton of Coughton, a Protestant who had taken part in rebellion against Mary. He was now in high favour and accumulated offices and lands until his position was jeopardised by suspicion of his Catholic relatives and associations in 1569 (Rowse 1962: 51–2). The Lord Lieutenant of Staffordshire from 1585 was the loyal and anti-Catholic George Talbot, sixth Earl of Shrewsbury. Between 1569 and 1605 the midland Catholic gentry, now excluded from power, were again drawn into and implicated in plots and conspiracies against the Crown. Each successive episode followed a common pattern. In every case the connections of kinship and religious allegiance drew into alliance Privy Councillors, hot-headed and footloose sons of respectable midland landowning families and busy go-betweens of doubtful integrity. Every plot was discovered; the maximum propaganda value was extracted from the situation and each episode was a political victory for the Crown.

During the war years the Midlands was dominated by the young second Earl of Essex and by his loyal supporters, the Bagots of Blithefield. Anthony Bagot had been a close friend of the Earl at university and the head of the family; Richard (1541–97) was twice Sheriff of Staffordshire and at various times Justice of the Peace, Deputy Lieutenant Commissioner of Array and Collector of Taxes. He sat on most of the special commissions of the reign, including the commission for recusancy (SHC 1979: xv). Other supporters included the wealthy Sir Walter Leveson of Trentham, Sir John Lyttleton of Frankley (north Worcestershire) and the raffish Earl John Dudley who had recovered the castle and estates but not the wealth of his forefathers. The power of the Earl of Essex was all the greater after the deaths of the Dudley brothers. Robert Dudley died in 1588 and Ambrose in 1590 and although Sir Robert Dudley inherited the Kenilworth estate he lived mainly in Italy, while Warwick Castle and its estates reverted to the Crown from 1590. The Earl of Essex dominated Staffordshire elections, intervening especially in the by-election of 1593. He made himself acceptable to the boroughs of Tamworth and Newcastle by helping the burgesses to obtain their charters. He became Lord Lieutenant of Staffordshire in 1594, made his servant John Lynacre Clerk of the Peace and built a new Shire Hall at his own expense (SHC 1927).

When he was sent to Ireland in 1595 as Governor General to suppress the rebellion of Tyrone there was much activity raising soldiers in the Midlands. His fall from favour was caused by his failure in Ireland and had nothing to do with the Midlands, but when subsequently he made his dramatic bid to seize London with six hundred men on 7 February 1601, he was surrounded by some of his most excitable midland adherents, not only Antony Bagot but also John Lyttleton of Frankley, Robert Catesby of Lapworth, and Thomas Winter of Huddington, all members of malcontent Roman Catholic families of the Midlands. Against this background it is not surprising that the Privy Council intervened in the 1601 Worcestershire elections to secure the choice of loyal Protestants (Durst 1970).

The execution of Essex left the politically minded papists of the Midlands frustrated and angry. James I on his succession raised exaggerated hopes of a political settlement in the minds of men like Catesby, the Winters and Tresham, and the Papists of Worcestershire made a determined attempt in 1604 to secure the election of a Catholic candidate. Despite a bitterly fought campaign they failed, and their frustration became more acute as James I reverted to a policy of repression of papists (Gruenfelder 1976: 4). The Worcestershire, Staffordshire and Warwickshire Catholic families were closely linked with each other and with the Treshams and Catesbys of neighbouring Northamptonshire and their long experience of turbulence and political frustration goes far to explain why the more hot-headed among them were by 1605 willing to go to extremes. It was the men who had been associated with failure of attempts in 1586 and 1602 to secure a negotiated solution, with the failure of Essex in 1601 and the failure of their party in the Worcestershire elections, who, in the summer of 1605, began to consider the legitimacy of assassination.

Princess Elizabeth, the daughter of King James, was living at Combe Abbey under the guardianship of Sir John Harrington and it was at Dunchurch near Rugby that the rising was planned, to follow the death of the King and the rest of the royal family, the Lords and the Commons when they had all been blown up with gunpowder at Westminster. After the discovery of the plot the conspirators fled through the Midlands to Holbeche House on the borders of Staffordshire and Worcestershire, where they made their last stand. Even at this stage there was some reluctance on the part of the midland sheriffs to pursue the traitors and some Justices of the Peace with Catholic associations found it expedient to be absent from duty. The conspirators were rounded up in January 1606 and their executions marked the end of plots and conspiracies in the Midlands. Government was thenceforward in the hands of the wealthy and the godly, and a period of comparative peace ensued.

Many of the families now achieving prominence had been able to acquire the lands of the dissolved monasteries by a gradual process of purchase between 1540 and 1560. Some new men had come in; William Sneyd, Mayor of Chester, had bought Keele Manor for £334 in 1543 and thousands of acres in north-west Staffordshire − but on the whole the monastic lands in the Midlands were distributed among the established gentry of the area, and many of the gentry made further purchases of episcopal collegiate and chantry lands with the result that there was a major shift in landholding to the lay nobility and gentry from the Church and the Crown. The impetus to purchase seems to have died down somewhat after 1590 and the gentlemen of the seventeenth century were more concerned to improve their rent rolls than to purchase more lands. The Spencers were able to increase their profits threefold between 1520 and 1630 (Thorpe 1965). At Frankley John Lyttleton consolidated his estate, bought more land in 1565 and by good management and personal attention was able to increase its annual value from £1,400 to £2,000 (Tonks 1978). Sir Clement Throckmorton at Haselour increased his income from about £1,000 to £2,000 a year. Some of this apparent increase in the wealth of the midland gentry must be attributed to inflation, but in general the value of land was rising and families who combined political prudence, advantageous marriages and attention to management prospered. Those who failed were often the victims of circumstances, overburdened with jointures and portions, while the Gregorys of Stivichall lost their wealth when they became too heavily involved in public office at Coventry (Bearman 1972: 49–50). There were few families of really large fortune in the Midlands in the seventeenth century. On the eve of the Civil War only about a third of the Warwickshire gentry had incomes above £250 a year and only seventeen more than £1,000 a year (Hughes, 1982). The general trend was stability and modest increase in prosperity as the long leases prevalent in the adverse conditions of the fifteenth century were replaced by leases for lives or shorter periods and the traditional copyhold and other tenures were gradually rationalised. The gentleman of the early seventeenth century expected to live on rents collected for him by his bailiff. He also expected to spend his income mainly on housebuilding, portioning his daughters, educating his sons, dispensing charity and maintaining the high profile required to support his responsibility for law and order.

The kings and Privy Council relied more and more upon the justices of the peace in the counties to maintain order, supervise parish officials, execute legislation, and to respond to a constant stream of particular orders and instructions. To their number was added in the sixteenth century the lords lieutenant and the deputy lieutenants of the counties whose responsibility was primarily for the county militia. All these offices were normally filled by lesser nobles and gentlemen resident in the county, who exercised power through their local connections, influence and presence, and while strengthening the power of the Crown in the locality, also enhanced their own status. The role of sheriff was diminishing in importance and he was usually appointed from the same social group as the JPs. As the appointment was only for a year, involved heavy expense and much administration, it was not much sought after.

A minority of those nominated in the Commissions of the Peace sat regularly at Quarter Sessions. In Warwickshire the number was rarely more than ten. Those who did so were required by Privy Council and by statute to carry out an ever widening range of duties and to exercise more and more influence over the day-to-day lives of their neighbours and inferiors. They were responsible for the main highways and county bridges, supervised the surveyors of highways from 1530, they licensed the increasing numbers of ale houses and dealt with a growing range of felonies. They were expected to enforce uniformity of attendance at worship from 1581 to 1586 and again from 1593, and to carry out the provisions of the statute of labourers from 1563. They supervised the Poor Law overseers from 1597. They supported the deputy lieutenants in their efforts to collect soldiers to go to the Low Countries in 1586, to stand to the defence of the realm in 1588 and to go to Ireland in 1598 and 1601.

Since their work was voluntary and the expense allowance only 4s. a day for the days of their attendance, they exercised a good deal of discretion in respect of which statutes they chose to enforce, and how thorough they were in their attention to the requirements of Privy Council, and so in practice provided both an arm of central authority in the local community and a buffer against centralisation.

It was from this elite group of locally active families that members of Parliament were drawn. Many were peers' sons, relatives or close associates of the peers, and were always substantial landed proprietors. In Warwickshire the names of Lucy, Throckmorton recur and in Staffordshire Bagot, Chetwynd and Crompton. The members for the boroughs of Staffordshire in the reigns of James I and Charles I were on the whole much under the influence of the peers, especially the Earl of Essex, while Warwick MPs were almost always gentry and the townsmen were virtually excluded (VCH Warks VIII: 496). Coventry as a city and county in its own right with its own sheriff and magistrates remained largely independent and its members of Parliament were usually drapers and mercers of the City (Hughes 1970: 150–60).

Despite wide variations in wealth and status the midland gentry formed a closely meshed group, linked by marriage and kinship. Of 152 Warwickshire gentry, 43 per cent took brides from Warwickshire families, 34 per cent from contiguous counties, and 24 per cent from further afield. One-third of the eldest sons had been at the inns of court (Hughes 1982: 47–9) and in later life

Plate 3.6   Memorial to Sir Thomas Lucy and his wife, in the parish church of St Leonard Charlecote, Warwickshire. The Lucy family held Charlecote from the early thirteenth century to the mid twentieth century. The books behind Sir Thomas are Horace, Virgil, Cato, Xenophon and Winter's Ayres.

they visited London for business and pleasure. Their contacts at home were based upon the circle of neighbouring families accessible by road; the southern Warwickshire gentry were linked with those of Oxfordshire and Northamptonshire and those of north Staffordshire with Cheshire and Derbyshire. Neither county had much sense of county community.

The great estates were concentrated along the valley of the river Trent in Staffordshire and in the Feldon in Warwickshire, and although about 300 families in Warwickshire and 250 families in Staffordshire were recognised by the College of Arms it was the 40 or so families of these areas which provided the majority of justices of the peace and members of Parliament (Hughes, A. 1980: 150).

The persistence of families, such as the Bagots and Giffards, tends to lead to the assumption that the midland gentry were a stable group, whereas in fact there was a constant change in the composition of the community. Of the Warwickshire gentry in 1640 only one-quarter had been seated in the county before 1600 (Hughes 1982: 46).

By 1625 the dominant family in Warwickshire was the wealthy Spencer-Comptons of Compton Wynyates – the Earls of Northampton who were loyal supporters of Charles I. Baron Feilding, first Earl of Denbigh, who was also enriched and ennobled by service to Charles I, had his seat at Newnham Paddox in the south of Warwickshire.

Robert Greville, of Warwick Castle, who succeeded as second Lord Brooke in 1626, was at odds with both the Court and his own community. He was a consistent opponent of the Crown, an intellectual, a convinced Puritan, and alienated his Warwickshire neighbours by protracted lawsuits against the Verneys (Hughes, A. 1980: 46–50). In Staffordshire the third Earl of Essex had been restored in blood and honour, but became embittered against the Court when he was the victim of the Carr scandal of 1614 and from 1628 onwards used his influence in opposition to King Charles. After 1629 there were no great men in Privy Council or at Court who had their main seats in Stafford-shire and Warwickshire, and as Parliament did not meet there was a degree of dissociation from central government. Moreover from the 1630s the loyal gentry of the Midlands found themselves quite frequently at odds with the Crown and Privy Council, as the financial demands of the Crown aroused hostility among peers, gentlemen and town councillors alike.

In 1616 Sir Walter Bagot, member of Parliament for Staffordshire, was infuriated by the grant of the glass monopoly to the courtier Robert Mansell when he and his ancestors had been making glass for many years (Johnson 1964: 16). The forced loan of 1627 was opposed in Warwickshire by the justices of the peace, and 231 gentlemen were distrained for refusing knight-hood (Hughes 1980: 172). Ship money was collected reluctantly – 94 per cent of the levy was paid in Warwickshire in 1635, but in the following years more and more people refused and less than 3 per cent was collected in 1639 (Heap 1975: 55; Hughes, A. 1980: 59). In Staffordshire large sums were already outstanding in 1636. Coventry, Birmingham and Warwick all protested against their assessment and demanded abatement, Warwick offered only £40 instead of the £100 assessed (Mosler 1974: 50–2). By 1639–40 the lack of co-ordination between Privy Council and local administration became manifest. The Privy Council tried to raise soldiers, money and horses to repel the Scots invasion, but could get no co-operation from the local authorities. Coventry as usual was particularly recalcitrant, partly out of opposition to the Crown, and partly out of their usual determination to be independent of the country gentry. All through the year gentlemen in both Staffordshire and Warwickshire refused to pay coat and conduct money and as soon as the troops were assembled they dispersed again, and constables refused to pursue deserters. There were serious riots at Uttoxeter when the town was terrorised by the militia for days and similar disturbances occurred near Walsall. The Puritans, William Combe of Stratford and Sir Thomas Lucy, were removed from the Commission. The elections of the short Parliament in March and April 1640 were held in an atmosphere of conflict with the Court and the attitude of the Warwickshire gentry was demonstrated when they elected Combe and Lucy as members of Parliament while at Warwick two close associates of Lord Brooke, Bosville and Purefoy, were elected, and Coventry rejected the royal nominee and elected Sir Simon Archer and Purefoy's stepson, George Abbot, even though he was a foreigner from Yorkshire.

Chapter 18

The Civil War and the Interregnum in the Midlands

Between April and July 1642 the gentry of the Midlands found themselves faced with contrary directions and divided leadership. They remained for the most part more concerned with their own affairs than with the coming of the conflict. The sheriffs in both counties were King's men, but the Lords Lieutenant were both opponents of the Court. Lord Brooke began to hold musters in June and by the end of August he had taken the magazine at Coventry to Warwick Castle and an active militia committee had been formed to raise men and arms.

In the meantime the Royalists received commissions of array from the King, empowering them to organise troops of volunteers. Although the commissions were declared illegal by Parliament they were issued to men of influence including several justices of the peace and the King's Commission still carried weight. The Commission of Array for Warwickshire meeting at Coleshill in June and July received the adherence of 2 peers, 78 gentlemen and their followers (Hughes, A. 1980: 230–1). Of the 18 Catholic gentlemen of the county, 11 gave support to the Commission of Array (Mosler 1974: 73; Hughes 1982: 59). In Staffordshire on the other hand the King's Commission of Array refused to act 'without greater motives of more demonstrable dangers'. William Paget raised a regiment of 1,200 foot at his own expense under the Royal Commission, many of them from his own estates.

The majority of gentlemen in both counties were Royalists by instinct and neutral by preference (Pennington 1966: 16). They responded to the situation as individuals and as the situation changed they altered their response. The towns were by no means unanimous in their allegiance. Lichfield was Royalist, Stafford neutral and Coventry strongly supported Parliament, but in each town there were a few wealthy townsmen who opposed the prevailing stance (Mosler 1974: 101).

Fighting started in the Midlands in July when Prince Rupert was staying for a few days at Aston Hall near Birmingham and attempted to pre-empt the situation by attacking the home of one of Warwickshire's most conspicuous Parliamentarians, William Purefoy at Caldecote. In August Charles I at the head of an army tried to enter Coventry, but the Mayor sent to London for a relief force, and he was forced to withdraw (Hughes 1982: 59). Meanwhile, the more bellicose local Royalists had ridden to Nottingham to join the King, among them the Catholic Peter Giffard of Chillington and his sons.

The King left Nottingham with his forces on 13 September and moved slowly through Tutbury and Stafford to reach Shrewsbury by 19 September. At Uttoxeter he met a gathering of freeholders and gentlemen who sought to negotiate with the King to preserve the peace (Pennington 1966: 16). Meanwhile, the Earl of Essex had gathered the main parliamentary army in Northamptonshire and he, too, marched westwards, crossing Warwickshire and reaching Worcester by 23 September. The royal army turned south-east again in October and began to march on London, passing slowly through Bridgnorth, Wolverhampton and Aston. Rupert meanwhile had taken a small body of soldiers south to the Stour Valley to collect iron, grenades, shot, pikeheads and nails from the metalworkers. By 22 October he had rejoined the main army at Edgecote on the Warwickshire–Northamptonshire border and the Earl of Essex had moved eastward and was camping at Kineton a dozen miles away.

On Sunday, 23 October, the first major engagement of the war was fought on the ridge of Edgehill. The outcome was indecisive and both Charles and Essex moved southwards. On both sides the men were hungry, ill-equipped and after the first clash unwilling to follow up the enemy. The local people proved hostile to both armies and unwilling to produce food for several thousand men. The soldiers were strangers and regarded as a scourge in the villages through which they passed. It was to be another two and a half years before another large scale battle took place in the Midlands, but the main armies were constantly passing through the region, and their movements were always marked by complaints of looting and overbearing behaviour (Sherwood 1974: 31–41).

In the winter of 1642–3 parliamentary organisation began to take shape. County committees were appointed for various specific purposes such as assessments, sequestrations, payments to militia, but in practice the membership of separate committees and their functions overlapped to such an extent that the same active Parliamentarians carried out most of the financial, military, and administrative tasks (Hughes, A. 1980: 291–5; Pennington 1966: 16–18). In Staffordshire all business was carried out by the Committee of Stafford, in Warwickshire the Committee was variously called the Committee of Safety, the Committee of Sequestrations and the Committee for the Militia (SHC 1957: xxi–xxii).

The first lists of members date from February 1643 and in both Staffordshire and Warwickshire there was a core of hardworking, diligent committee members who by the frequency of their attendance effectively dominated policy. They were for the most part lesser gentry with a strong religious commitment to Calvinism, godly magistrates in action. Such were

William Purefoy of Caldecote, Richard Pyott of Streethay and Edward Leigh of Rushall (SHC 1957; Hughes 1982: 81). By 1644, however, the committees included a number of wealthy tradesmen, among them Henry Stone of Walsall, John Simcox of West Bromwich, Roger Wilmot of Smethwick and John Barker of Coventry (Hughes, A. 1980).

In the early months of 1643 the Parliament at Westminster issued a series of ordinances which provided the county committees with a programme of action. In February the committees were required to collect the weekly pay for the armies. Staffordshire was assessed at £212 a week plus £5 for Lichfield, and Warwickshire and Coventry at £562, an indication of the relative wealth of the counties. It is instructive to compare this with the £1,800 required from Devon and the £10,000 from London. The money collected was assigned to local commanders who used the soldiers to assist the constables in the collection. Local taxpayers found weekly pay both more onerous and more difficult to evade than royal taxes, and having paid they felt entitled to some protection. When the forces occupying the Leek area were called away for service elsewhere the weekly tax was resisted. On 27 March a general sequestration order created national and local committees for sequestrations to take over the estates of all delinquents and two-thirds of the estates of all Papists. Thus, by spring 1643 the county committees were committed to a heavy programme of administration which was to occupy them for many years to come.

The Royalists meanwhile were also raising money. Even before the war started the Catholics of the two counties had contributed about £5,000 to the King's cause. In July 1643 Charles imposed an excise on alcohol and in May 1644 demanded that all persons worth £10 a year in land or £100 in personal estate should make a loan to the Crown. Individual loyalists like Richard Gough, draper, of Oldfallings, Wolverhampton, came with personal gifts of money and plate. Both Parliamentarians and Royalists began to issue sequestration orders from spring 1643. Thomas Leveson of Wolverhampton, for example, was issued in July 1643 with a warrant to seize the goods and estates of disaffected persons. Both sides also requisitioned premises and materials. Leveson compelled the local people to supply Dudley Castle with wheat, malt, butter and cheese and scoured the countryside for teams of horses and wagons. Foley's iron was seized in transit between the mills and carters, and smiths and nailers were forced to live inside the garrison and to manufacture shot and weapons. In the Tutbury area the people were paying their weekly tax to Captain Snow for the committee and also £50 a month to the Royalists in Tutbury Castle and supplying oats, cheese, butter and sheepskins.

Under the ordinances of association the parliamentary forces of Staffordshire, Warwickshire, Lichfield and Coventry were all placed under the command of Lord Brooke, who took Northampton Castle and then returned to Warwickshire to take Stratford and Kenilworth. However, the Royalists were garrisoning Tamworth, Lichfield and Stafford, and Royalists of

Nottinghamshire and Derbyshire were threatening. A bold but futile attempt was made by the Moorlanders to take Stafford early in February 1643, armed only with clubs, scythes and birding guns. They failed, but their attack brought into the area both the able parliamentary commander from Cheshire, Sir William Brereton, and his associate from Derbyshire, Sir John Gell, and their forces. Lord Brooke moved from Coventry to Lichfield and began his bombardment of the Royalists on 2 March, but he was killed early in the attack and the capture of the garrison was completed by John Gell. On 19 March a second battle was fought at Hopton Heath four miles from Stafford. This time it was a Royalist commander, the Earl of Northampton, who was killed (Sutton 1967). Thus, at the end of March 1643 the local armies on both sides were without a leader. There was considerable delay in appointing a successor to Lord Brooke, and Sir William Brereton stepped into the gap, mainly because of his force of character and military efficiency.

The Earl of Essex issued a commission to Brereton who with Purefoy, Gell and Haslerigg took command of the Midlands (Hughes, A. 1980: 360). Brereton's importance in both Staffordshire and his home base of Cheshire was steadily growing and all through the spring of 1643 his horse and dragoons were attacking Royalist garrisons in the north-west and in Staffordshire. He and his associates gradually took over Staffordshire. Gell captured Burton on Trent in April, leaving a garrison of 200 foot and 60 dragoons; on 16 May Brereton occupied Stafford, entering in the early hours of the morning and meeting almost no resistance, and he repeated the strategy at Wolverhampton a week later, while Newcastle and Leek were also taken for Parliament. Prince Rupert returned to the Midlands and provided a counterpoise to Brereton's successes, by occupying Burton, Stratford and Henley in Arden. He then marched north, burning parts of Birmingham as he passed through and reached Lichfield on 8 April. He besieged the Parliamentary garrison in the Close for twelve days, finally achieving its capture by undermining the walls and making a breach with gunpowder (Sherwood 1974: 58–62).

The royalist Earl of Denbigh died at Cannock in June 1643 and was succeeded in the earldom by his son, a Parliamentarian who was appointed commander of the associated counties of Staffordshire, Warwickshire, Coventry and Lichfield. He never gained the support of the parliamentary committees for they could never forget that he was the son of an aristocrat and a Royalist and that his mother was even then in France with Henrietta Maria. They always suspected that he was using his position to seek a peace settlement with Charles and his activities as military commander were never sufficiently successful or vigorous to compensate in their eyes for his Royalist connections. His appointment marked the beginning of a struggle for power between Denbigh and Brereton which was to be carried on in the Midlands and at Westminster for another twenty years.

In most parts of England and Wales the Royalists were gaining the upper hand in 1643, but in the Midlands and the north-west Brereton and other parliamentary commanders were increasing their control. In August 1643 Brereton captured the Bishop's town and castle at Eccleshall, a strongpoint to the west of Stafford. He was soon in dispute with the county committee who were unwilling to assign pay for his soldiers separately from the rest of the county and who placed their own man in command at Stafford in opposition to Brereton. Brereton went over the heads of the committee to secure the continuance of his forces from the House of Commons and a grant of the rents and profits of the Bishop's estates to maintain them. The Earl of Denbigh opposed Brereton and made his ally Lewis Chadwick governor of Eccleshall.

In the spring of 1644 the Earl of Denbigh was seeking to lead his armies of the associated counties westwards into Shropshire. Colonel Purefoy and Colonel Barton of Warwickshire refused to take their regiments out of the county and Brereton who wanted to march east appealed to the National Committee of Public Safety. Both sides then appealed to Westminster, and petitions and counter-petitions were heard by the House of Commons. Denbigh secured a petition of 2,000 moderates from Warwickshire and of 3,000 from Staffordshire in his support, but the Committee of Both Kingdoms was becoming in general more hostile to the aristocratic commanders of the parliamentary forces and Brereton could rely on their support. He entered Stafford with 200 foot and 100 horse, recaptured it from the county parliamentary committee, removed the commanders appointed by the committee and replaced them with his own ally, Captain Henry Stone of Walsall, ironmonger. Meanwhile Denbigh spent much time arguing his case in Westminster where the Earl of Essex was also coming under attack.

Having established his position in Staffordshire Brereton moved north into Lancashire and north Wales and then returned to defend Nantwich, a few miles north of Newcastle under Lyme. There were frequent excursions into north Staffordshire and some fighting in the moorlands. Meanwhile further south the royalists captured the important parliamentary garrison at Rushall near Walsall, and there was much skirmishing around Dudley Castle; Aston Hall was besieged for three days by 1,200 men, and 12 royalists and 60 parliamentary soldiers were killed, 5 of whom were buried in the parish churchyard. In south Staffordshire and north Worcestershire the parliamentary Captain John Fox was harassing the Royalists. He seized Edgbaston Hall and Hawkesley Hall from the Catholic Middlemore family and made Edgbaston Hall his headquarters (Hughes, A. 1980: 512–13). In July 1644 he had there three troops of horse, two companies of dragoons and 256 soldiers. He was an ironmonger of Walsall and Tamworth in civilian life and hence always known as Tinker Fox. He was an ally of the Earl of Denbigh and a moderate, but often seems to have been acting almost independently of the main command. He captured Stourton Castle near Kinver and lost it again. He harassed the Royalist garrison at Worcester, and captured supplies of iron at Cannock. His most significant victory was the capture of the river port of Bewdley which he took by surprise in the night with a force reputedly of only six men, and captured the governor, Sir Thomas Lyttleton, as he lay asleep (Sherwood 1974: 127–30).

By June 1644 the efficient movement of troops in the Midlands was being rendered almost impossible by the differences between the Earl of Denbigh, Sir William Brereton and committee men. Of Staffordshire it was said that there were more commanders than troops. A council of war was held at Stourbridge between the leaders in an attempt to resolve the problem, but without success. Meanwhile, however, in the north of England all the main parliamentary armies were gathering including the East Anglian army under Fairfax and Oliver Cromwell. The national policy of the Committee of Both Kingdoms was taking over control of the military situation from the local organisation and leadership. While midland commanders spent their time in lobbying and making representations, central government was taking vigorous measures. Denbigh and Brereton did eventually join the parliamentary armies in York- shire, but played little part in the decisive defeat of the royal forces at Marston Moor on 2 July 1644. The Earl of Denbigh was deprived of his command in December and in April the self-denying ordinance removed the Earl of Essex. Both Brereton and Purefoy were among those who kept their seats and posi- tions (Sherwood 1974: 153–5). The new model army was formed, paid by the central treasury for war and directly controlled by the Committee of Both Kingdoms, and Parliament pressed forward to a decisive military solution. Peace negotiations started with the King, but the talks broke down. In the spring Charles marched northwards through south-west Staffordshire intend- ing to break Brereton's control of the north-west, and raise the sieges of Chester and Hawarden. Parliamentary forces were massing in the north and Charles turned at Market Drayton, changing direction to reach Tutbury by 25 May. At Tutbury he turned south to be decisively defeated by the new model army at Naseby on 14 June 1645. The battle marked the end of all real hope of a Royalist victory, but it was only gradually that the Royalist garrisons in the Midlands accepted the inevitable and surrendered. Indeed, the King had already given himself up to the Scots when Dudley surrendered on 13 May 1646, Lichfield on 1 July, and Worcester on 23 July. The committees faced the task of finding the money to pay off their armies; in Warwickshire William Purefoy was particularly active in ensuring that they were not disbanded unpaid. Warwickshire troops were disbanded by August (Hughes, A. 1980: 329) and Staffordshire troops by October 1646 (Pennington and Rootes 1957).

The four years of hostilities had been a disturbing experience for the towns and villages. There had been constant demands for money and for food, bedding, shelter and supplies for the troops and their horses, there was much movement of men through the area, mutual suspicions and local conflicts were encouraged by the rival claims on men's loyalties. Trade was interrupted, and at Burton the decline in the kersey trade was attributed to the war. Men and women travelling about on business were turned back if they could not produce a pass. There was a shortage of sheep for sale at the sheep fairs and at Warwick there were complaints of a shortage of chapmen. The roads became even more dangerous as soldiers lay in wait for carriers and seized goods, waggons and horses. Throughout the war the people found themselves paying taxes to both sides (Sherwood 1974: 98–123). The towns suffered much from plundering armies, quartered soldiers and plague. At Tamworth, Burton and Stafford the mortality was especially high and infection was particularly difficult to control in wartime (Hughes, A. 1980: 407; Mosler 1974: 457).

The battle of Naseby decided the issue between the Royal and the New Model armies, but it left all other matters unresolved. Local leadership was divided between the activists, Calvinists in religion and independent in politics, and the moderates who looked for the continuation of government by the Long Parliament and King and a return to the predominance of the gentry in local affairs. From 16 October 1645 elections were being held to recruit members to fill places in Parliament which had become vacant since 1642. Although Brereton in Staffordshire and Purefoy in Warwickshire were very active in trying to influence the elections in both counties, hardworking moderates were elected (Mosler 1974: 190; Pennington 1966: 22).

The county committees continued to administer civilian affairs, supervising the constables and churchwardens, and listing popish recusants while subcommittees of accounts were appointed to manage finance. On 17 March 1643 the local county committees had been ordered to sequester the estates of all who took arms against Parliament, contributed to the King's army or assisted his cause. They also took over the duty of compounding with papists for two-thirds of their estates. By 1646 sixteen Roman Catholic gentry and twelve Protestant gentry of Staffordshire had had their estates sequestered and from 1646 to 1650 fifty-six Roman Catholic landowners in Staffordshire were sequestered (Smith 1979). In Warwickshire over the whole period sixty-one Catholics were sequestered (Mosler 1974: 261). In 1652 a halt to further sequestrations was called and three acts of sale were made covering 680 properties. In Staffordshire of forty-six sequestered Roman Catholic estates twenty-eight were actually sold.

A matter of immediate concern at the end of the war was the settlement of religion. At the beginning of the war many enthusiastic ministers had joined the army as garrison chaplains or as personal chaplains to the officers. The church courts had ceased to operate in 1642 and both bishops had died during the war. In some parishes the Laudian clergy simply withdrew, leaving a clear field to Puritans and several of those who had been ejected by Laud and Wright were now able to return to the parishes. Between 1645 and 1650 about forty of the former parish incumbents were replaced by Puritan preachers such as Obadiah Grew, George Bryan and other men of established reputation. The presbyterian Directory of Worship was issued in 1646 and changes were again required in the furniture and ornaments of parish churches. Much depended on the temperament and personal religious commitment of the incumbent. At

Yoxall the Book of Common Prayer continued to be used in defiance of the ruling. At Claverdon Thomas Pilkington carried out the changes without protest (Styles 1978: 110) and at West Bromwich the minister Edward Lane was pulled out of the pulpit and the Book of Common Prayer was burnt. When it came to making a declaration in favour of the Presbytery as required by the Westminster Assembly a number of midland parishes recorded their support – Draycott, Kinver, Madeley, Uttoxeter and Womborne among others, parishes of many kinds rural and urban, large and small. At Coventry in the 1650s the town corporation and ministers co-operated to enforce godly discipline and true religion (Hughes, A. 1980: 433). The influence of individual divines can often be traced, forming a network of mutual support and influence for the godly and zealous independently of parish structures or local landowning. Richard Baxter of Kidderminster in Worcestershire was particularly influential. He was a moderate Puritan who had accepted, not without scruple, ordination in the Church of England and who continued to support a modified Episcopal Church promoting unity and comprehension and trying to build up the Worcestershire Association as a formal organisation of moderates. Meanwhile laymen and even some laywomen raised their voices to preach without check or control, and Warwick, Henley, Alcester and other places became known for the activities of 'ranters' (Hughes, A. 1980: 433–5).

By 1648 divisions within the parliamentary ranks were sufficient to encourage Charles to make an attempt to regain power. His alliance with the Scots led to a full-scale invasion in August 1648. The main body of Royalists was defeated in Lancashire, but at Preston a section of the foot turned south and reached Warwick before they surrendered, while 3,500 soldiers of the horse also turned south and were cornered at Uttoxeter on 25 August. The fear of a Royalist rising led to a hardening of attitudes at Westminster and in the army. Midland members of Parliament were among those purged from the Parliament by Colonel Pride as too moderate, leaving only the influential independents, William Purefoy and Geoffrey Bosville, members of the Rump Parliament. Both men were committed opponents of the Crown, and voted for no further addresses to be made to the King, and for his trial (Hughes, A. 1980: 341).

The indestructible Earl of Denbigh had survived three years of public discussion of his actions and loyalties and was now employed in last-ditch negotiations with the King. After the trial and execution of King Charles, he and William Purefoy both took their places on the new Council of State, thus epitomising the forces in contention at the time (Pennington 1966: 22).

After the death of the King the Rump Parliament authorised the justices of the peace to continue to govern and they again met in quarter sessions. The justices commissioned after the execution were men who had served on the many administrative committees and commissions during and after the war. The most diligent member both of the committees and of quarter sessions was William Purefoy, notwithstanding that he was also a member of Parliament, and other activists were John Hales, Thomas Broughton and Anthony Stoughton. The militia was reformed under the commissioners Baker, Peytoe, Purefoy and Hawksworth, and promptly refused to leave Warwickshire for Ireland. Their anxiety to stay and guard their homes was not without foundation, for the Midlands were kept in constant fear of Irish and Scottish invasion, fears which were realised in August 1651 when Charles II marched south from Scotland. He arrived at Worcester on 22 August. The parliamentary armies under General Lambert, Thomas Harrison and Oliver Cromwell made a rendezvous at Warwick on the 24th, gathering 30,000 men, and moved on Worcester, defeating Charles II decisively on 3 September 1651. Charles escaped from the battlefield and the story of the six weeks he spent moving secretly from house to house in the Midlands was to become the best known and most lovingly remembered midland tradition (Bond 1927).

The justices of the peace found themselves taking on a wider range of responsibility, especially since the abolition of the bishops and the bishops' courts. Their duties now included the appointment and supervision of churchwardens and the collection of tithes, and they found that they had a greatly increased case-load in the aftermath of war. They ordered thirty-nine collections in eleven years for poor and distressed persons and places, and attempted to modernise the collection of assessed taxes and to ensure payment by persons formerly exempt. They dealt with three times as many cases concerning poor relief and many more cases concerning vagrants. In all these matters they worked within the existing framework of society and relied to a great extent upon traditional sanctions (Beier 1966: 75–100).

In February 1652 the Committee for the Propagation of the Gospel was set up against a background of debate concerning the nature and structure of a settled ministry. In Warwickshire the clergy drew up a petition which proposed that there should be a single visible Church with common practice and ordered belief. They proposed that there should be a public maintenance of the clergy, and also of schools and universities.

Lay control over the Church was re-emphasised in 1654 by the order ejecting scandalous ministers. Ejections took place at Walsall, Tamworth, Sutton Coldfield, Lichfield, Burton, Newcastle, Coleshill and Wolverhampton. The commission responsible was an interesting mixture of Protestant gentry such as Sir Charles Wolsley of Wolsley, the Protestant head of a Catholic family, the moderate Swynfen, the activist ironmonger Henry Stone, Captain Fox of Tamworth, and Walter Wrottesley of Wrottesley, the former ally of Lord Digby. All were Parliamentarians, experienced committee men and administrators rather than zealots.

In the towns independency began to challenge moderate Presbyterianism. Baptist congregations were established at Coventry, Stafford, Walsall, Berry Hill, Alcester and Burton. George Fox spent much time in Warwickshire and Staffordshire from 1646 and Societies of Friends were established in both towns and villages, and drew their members from a wide area (Hughes, A. 1980: 436).

In comparison with many parts of the west and south of England the Midlands remained quiet, despite the presence in the area of many determined and prominent Royalists. Sir William Compton, third son of the Earl of Northampton, the Lyttletons of Hagley and the Vernons of Hilton were active members of the Sealed Knot and were involved in planning an armed rising intended to take place in February 1655. In the event, however, the plots were well known to Cromwell's Council of State for some time before the intended date and the midland leaders were among the many imprisoned in January and February 1655. Despite secret preparations and rumours it was only in Wiltshire under Penruddock that there was any real threat to order.

The suppression of Penruddock's rising was followed by a determined attempt to strengthen and supervise local government. Cheshire, Lancashire and Staffordshire formed a district under the supervision of Major General Sir Charles Worsley, a soldier and administrator, who had served Cromwell well in the dismissal of the Rump Parliament. He was an austere fanatic, reputed to be the most severe of all the major generals. He worked hard rounding up Royalists great and small, discovering Cavalier plots, collecting taxes, suppressing horse races and other dangerous opportunities for Royalists to gather, and he demanded equal rigour from the justices and constables. Warwickshire was placed under the rule of Major General Whalley, another enthusiast who stirred up the justices of Warwickshire to even greater zeal.

The rule of the major generals did much to prepare the way for the restoration of the King by making Cromwell's rule unpopular and demonstrating to moderates that liberty might usher in a tyranny. Mr Swynfen, Justice of the Peace and member of Parliament for Stafford, was certainly of this opinion by 1659 when he urged that 'boundless liberty may destroy liberty. There is much tyranny in liberty as otherwise, I would not stir up that liberty that leaves no liberty here' (SHC 1922 II: 105). Anthony Stoughton, a Warwickshire supporter of both the Earl of Denbigh and the County Committee, now in 1656 expressed himself convinced of his errors and appointed as trustees of his will two moderate Parliamentarians (Hughes, A. 1980: 454).

The trend towards the restoration of the monarchy became apparent as more and more local landowners disentangled themselves from the committee of sequestrations and salvaged their financial affairs. By 1658 Robert Holt of Aston Hall was back on the Commission of the Peace for Warwickshire.

In the period of uncertainty and anxiety after the death of Oliver Cromwell on 30 September 1658 the extremists made their last attempt to seize power, while on the other hand moderates were determined to return to a more normal government. In 1659 the Royalist George Booth, MP for Cheshire, who was training forces in the north-west of England, seized Chester and occupied Cheshire in favour of Charles. This was too close to the Midlands to ignore. Thomas Gent, Mayor of Newcastle, led a thousand moorlanders against Booth and in support of General Lambert the Parliamentary leader. Coventry was garrisoned with seven companies of foot and two of horsemen. The new Royalists were defeated by Lambert at the battle of Winnington Bridge in August 1659, but the move by moderate men to restore the King was unchecked. The leading county gentlemen of Warwickshire were among those who petitioned Monk to move south in January 1660 (Hughes, A. 1980: 455) and by the spring the Earl of Denbigh was a Royalist.

Charles II returned to London on 19 May 1660 and took up the reins of government. Midland families basked in their Royalism and besieged the restored King with petitions for pensions and rewards for services rendered to him in his wanderings in 1651. Charles II himself seized upon the propaganda value of the story and had it written up by Samuel Pepys, Lord Claverdon and others. It remained to be seen whether the events of the Interregnum were to prove to have been a temporary aberration or a permanent shift of power in the Midlands.

Part four

An Industrialising Society

Chapter 19

Population growth and industrialisation

Between 1662 and 1679 the constables made lists of the households assessed for payment of Hearth Tax, the number of hearths for each house and the households exempt from payment. The total number of households for Staffordshire and Warwickshire in any one year was about 40,000, the two counties together thus recording 26 per cent of the total number for the whole of England and Wales in a geographical area which was only about 10 per cent of the whole. The houses were most numerous per thousand acres in south Staffordshire and north Warwickshire, while the agricultural areas of central Staffordshire and south Warwickshire were relatively more thinly populated. Thus a trend which had been evident since the early sixteenth century was now becoming clearly marked, and the links between industrialisation and population were more and more apparent ((U) BRL Hearth Tax).

In many rural parishes the trend to later marriage continued. At Fenny Compton in south Warwickshire few people married before the age of 29 (Styles 1951) and similarly at Bidford on Avon, Napton on the Hill and Old Stratford couples tended off put of marriage until the age of 27 or 28, and although the numbers of baptisms continued to exceed burials the death rate among infants and children remained high, and the communities showed little overall growth. In Arden parishes such as Fillongley, Berkswell, Meriden and Tamworth, although the rate of growth was much less than in the early seventeenth century it was still greater than in comparable communities in the Feldon (Martin 1976).

The pattern was very different in the industrial towns and villages. Birmingham showed a 'massive upsurge' in population, especially between 1695 and 1710. In the 1690s the number of baptisms each year averaged 172, by the 1720s this had risen to an average of 279 a year and these figures do not include the populous suburb of Deritend, which was in Aston parish. Birmingham baptisms exceeded burials every year except in 1695, 1698 and 1701 ((U) BLR Birm. Parish Registers). During the 1720s Dr Thomas, the antiquary, recorded the total number of households as 1,786, a figure which was more than twice the number of households recorded fifty years before

171

(Dugdale 1730). Most of the industrial parishes on the south Staffordshire coalfield – for example, Wolverhampton, Wednesbury, Dudley and Sedgley – registered more baptisms than burials in almost all years between 1690 and 1720. Similar growth was taking place at Nuneaton in the east Warwickshire coalfield, and in north Staffordshire at Stoke on Trent.

There was much movement from village to village and from village to town. At Lighthorne, an open-field village, about one-third of the families of 1662 had come into the village since 1600. At Barcheston, an enclosed pasture village, only one-seventh of the families were of long standing (Styles 1951: 33–51). In most rural villages there was a core of yeomen families who remained generation after generation in the village, while the cottagers, apprentices, servants, labourers, craftsmen and carriers came and went (Martin 1981–2: Table 1).

In Birmingham a correlation of the names of householders in the Hearth Tax returns suggests that about one-third of the householders moved away from the town in a ten-year period (1664–74), one-third or rather more remained resident taxpayers in the same street, and about one-third were new taxpayers with new family names ((U) BRL Hearth Tax). Between 1686 and 1725 the 718 Poor Law certificates issued to immigrants into Birmingham showed that one-third of the immigrants came from immediately adjacent parishes and rather more came from parishes within a 50-mile radius. One-quarter, however, came from further afield, including sixteen people who had journeyed from London. Immigration from rural parishes was much less marked than immigration from neighbouring industrial parishes. One-sixth of all the registered immigrants came from the south Staffordshire coalfield, coming in a sense from a wider Birmingham (Pelham 1937).

The numbers of people moving into rural villages with a Poor Law certificate were much fewer. The rural parish of Checkley recorded seventy-nine incomers by certificate between 1665 and 1800, Hatherton only ten between 1734 and 1770 ((U) SRO Hatherton and Checkley Certificates).

Although in many midland parishes the pattern was one of growth by natural increase and by immigration, there were frequent 'crisis' years when harvests were deficient, food prices rose and famine and fever again took toll of the population, especially the infants and children, the labourers and the old. Solihull suffered in 1698, 1708 to 1711 and in 1714. The worst crisis came in 1727 to 1730 when most midland parishes suffered 'great dearth'. Along the river Avon, at Bidford and at Stratford, 30–35 per cent of the population died. At Alcester 21 per cent of the population died. Birmingham, Audley, Stoke, Madeley and many other parishes saw a dramatic increase in the number of burials. Mortality rates were highest among labourers, paupers, cottagers and orphans; more infants died and fewer were conceived. The price of grain and the cost of poor relief were both higher than usual, the number of paupers on parish relief increased and the justices of the peace for the first time in years sanctioned a small and temporary increase in wages. There were reports of disease, but these may well have been the result of food shortages (Gooder 1972: 1–22). The Midlands' population crisis of 1727–30 was paralleled in Worcestershire, in the West Country and in parts of Yorkshire. A few years later outbreaks of smallpox caused great alarm at Shipston on Stour in 1731 and 1744 (Gooder 1972: 6), and at Wednesbury in 1755 and 1760, where the vicar attributed the greatly increased number of burials in those years entirely to smallpox and epidemical fever. However, in general it seems probable that in the Midlands smallpox was neither so frequent nor so mortal as was once thought (Skipp 1979).

From the middle of the eighteenth century many midland communities experienced rapid and sustained population growth. Maps of Wolverhampton published in 1750 and 1781 include the information that the population was 7,454 on the first occasion and 11,361 on the second; by 1801 it had risen to 12,565. Birmingham's population was given by a 1750 map maker as 23,688 and by the compiler of a 1770 directory as 30,804; this figure had doubled by the time of the 1801 census, and between 1780 and 1800 baptisms registered exceeded burials by 14,064 (Duggan 1975). At Bedworth in the mid-eighteenth century, where the numerous inhabitants earned their living from agriculture, coalmining and silk spinning and weaving, the age of marriages fell. Consequently families were larger, three-quarters of the families having over six children (Martin 1981–2). Moreover, the number of children born out of wedlock also increased. Similarly, in many rural south Warwickshire parishes the age of marriage fell among all classes, and the number of births per marriage increased to six; illegitimate births and bridal pregnancies also increased (Martin 1977a: 526–7). Some parishes exported their surplus population; Bickenhill, Elmdon and Sheldon in Arden, for example, all recorded more baptisms than burials, but their total populations remained small. Audley, in north Staffordshire, regularly exported its young to Newcastle and the Potteries (Speake 1971: 65). The parish registers of Napton, Bidford and Priors Marston suggest a pattern of late marriage and low baptism rates, but closer study of the families reveals that the villages contained a high proportion of older people and of older-marrying eldest sons and that the younger sons had already left the village before marriage.

The most readily available population figures for the period 1760–1801 are those drawn from the estimates provided by parish incumbents for the Registrar General in 1831 (see Table 4). These estimates have been accepted as broadly reliable by the most recent study of population and the general pattern can be accepted without attempting to evaluate the accuracy of the figures in detail and it is clear that between 1760 and 1801 the population of the Midlands increased by about 60 per cent compared with 45 per cent in the country as a whole.

From 1801 onwards the government sought to take account every ten years of 'the population of Great Britain and of the increases and diminution thereof' (see Table 5).

Table 4   A summary of the parish register estimates and the census of 1801 for the midland counties

	Staffordshire	Warwickshire	England and Wales
1750	151,051	134,070	6,467,000
1781	188,977	171,816	7,953,000
1801 (Census)	242,693	206,796	9,200,000
(1801 (Wrigley)	239,153	208,190	

(Source: Lawton 1958: 165.)

Table 5   Summary of census totals for each county, 1801–31

Year	Staffordshire	Warwickshire	England and Wales
1801	242,693	206,796	9.2 million
1811	290,595	227,895	10.2 million
1821	344,838	274,482	12.0 million
1831	409,480	336,338	13.9 million

(Sources: *VCH Staffs*, I; *VCH Warks*, II).

Between 1801 and 1831 the population of England and Wales rose some 51 per cent, and the annual growth rates were in the region of 1.6 per cent. The total population of both Staffordshire and Warwickshire increased through the same period even more rapidly than the national average; during the third decade of the nineteenth century Warwickshire's population increased about 2 per cent per year and Staffordshire's 1.8 per cent. Rural communities in the Midlands still grew, if only slowly, and only sixteen parishes in Warwickshire and eleven in Staffordshire actually declined in total population between 1801 and 1831.

Stafford, Lichfield and Warwick each felt some quickening of industrial development in the general growth of the early nineteenth century and by 1831 Warwick had over 9,000 people and Stafford and Lichfield more than 5000. Stratford, Tamworth and Newcastle also had more than 5,000 inhabitants but these towns changed little, deriving much of their importance from their administrative functions, their links with the aristocracy and the marketing of agricultural produce. In contrast Leamington, a small village in the eighteenth century, was successfully promoted as a Spa town and was launched into its rapid rise to wealth and importance, growing from about 543 people in 1811 to 6,209 by 1831. Meanwhile, the industrial towns had grown much larger than the older urban centres. Rising birth rates, falling mortality rates and an earlier age of marriage all made their contribution to natural increase, but it is apparent from parish registers, town directories and the multiplicity of the early histories of firms and undertakings, that immigration, however difficult to quantify, was also very significant.

A listing of those midland parishes which showed the greatest increase between 1801 and 1831 is sufficient to illustrate the point (see Table 6). Birmingham increased by about 80 per cent in thirty years; the fastest period of increase was in the decade 1821–31. Wolverhampton, Burslem and Dudley all grew at some 3 per cent per annum, greatly exceeding national growth rates from at least 1801. Coventry, on the other hand, only began to grow at a rate faster than the national average from the decade 1821–31. Some Black Country industrial parishes grew at an extraordinary rate; for example, Tipton's population increased 96 per cent between 1801 and 1811, Smethwick's by 47 per cent between 1811 and 1821, West Bromwich by 61 per cent between 1821 and 1831 and Stoke on Trent by 37 per cent between 1801 and 1811 (Barnsby 1980: 2–6).

Table 6 Midland industrial communities' census totals, 1801–31

Town	1811	1821	1831
Willenhall	3,523	3,965	5,834
Walsall	4,881	5,585	6,647
West Bromwich	7,485	9,505	15,327
Tipton	8,407	11,546	14,951
Burslem	8,625	10,176	12,711
Dudley	13,925	18,211	23,043
Wolverhampton	14,836	18,380	24,732
Coventry	17,923	21,292	27,070
Stoke on Trent	22,495	29,333	37,220

(Sources: *VCH Staffs*, II; *VCH Warks*, II).

By 1831 about 45 per cent of Midlanders lived in towns, that is considerably more than the national average of 36 per cent. Six of the fifty towns in England and Wales with more than 10,000 population were in the Midlands, namely, Coventry, Birmingham, Wolverhampton, Dudley, Halesowen and Stoke on Trent. Birmingham was the third largest provincial town in the country, and was smaller only than Manchester and Liverpool. Nevertheless, Lancashire and Cheshire had more town dwellers than the Midlands (Wrigley and Schofield 1981: 533–6).

The three industrial regions of the Potteries, the Black Country and Coventry, with their hinterlands of industrial villages, had experienced a very rapid, absolute increase of population and concentration of settlement by 1831, often without any corresponding growth of services such as shops, entertainment, public markets, religious and education facilities. As a result Burslem, Tipton, Bedworth and many other places were large aggregates of families, both rich and poor, concerned with the production of manufactured goods, but with none of the amenities traditionally found in towns. The industrial traditions of these areas reached far back into the past, but the size and concentration of their populations were of a new order.

Chapter 20

Agricultural development

By the end of the seventeenth century midland farmers were supplying both the local and the London markets. They gradually adjusted their methods and organisation of tillage and stockrearing to take advantage of expanding opportunities. Throughout Staffordshire and Arden and as far south as the Avon valley, cattle rearing was the mainstay of middling and small farmers. For example, Edward James, farming in mid-Staffordshire from 1662 to 1704, used his arable crops of wheat, barley, muncorn, peas, turnips and clover mainly to feed his family and his animals. His main business was buying cattle at the Staffordshire and Shropshire markets and fattening them for sale to the butchers in the same area (Yates 1975a: 31).

Sheep continued to be kept in some parts of the region in even larger flocks than before. The Moorland sheep of north Staffordshire had a coarse, fine wool which was used by the feltmakers and hatters of Newcastle under Lyme. Wool for cloth weaving was still produced in the vicinity of Burton and Tamworth, and some wool was sent to Kidderminster and Worcester. Increasingly, however, sheep were kept for their mutton. There were butchers' shambles in every market town and most large villages. Weekly sheep markets were held in Newcastle, Leek, Uttoxeter, Lichfield and Tamworth, and farmers continued to buy sheep for fattening and selling to the butchers at the annual sheep fairs at Newcastle, Stone, Stafford, Albrighton, Cannock and Newport.

The rich pastures of the Dove and Trent valleys enabled farmers to take advantage of the growing London market for butter and cheese. In Rolleston arable land was converted to pasture and by 1700 the probate inventory of many a yeoman referred to cheese and butter-making equipment in the dairy house. John Smith of Timore, near Lichfield, had a herd of twenty-four cows and calves, cheese presses, cheese vats, sieves, milkpans and butter pots, and twenty-two cheeses worth £1 when he died in 1675 ((U) LJR Probate John Smith). Uttoxeter and Newcastle were the main marketing centres for the dairy farmers of the Dove valley and south Derbyshire. The butter was packed in standardised clay pots each containing 14 lbs and then taken to London by waggon. The north-western parishes of Staffordshire, such as Audley, participated in the cheese trade of their Cheshire neighbours, sending their products north to Manchester and Liverpool (Henstock 1969). North-east Warwickshire also developed as a cheese-making area, supplying a modestly priced article to London; the main centres of production were around Atherstone. By 1682 the activities of the London cheesemongers in Warwickshire were threatening the profits of the Warwickshire merchants (WCR III 1946: 254).

The farmers of north Worcestershire parishes, south of the Staffordshire coalfield, at Belbroughton, Chaddesley Corbett, Broome, Clent and Hagley, concentrated more on their arable products. Greater production was achieved by more complex rotations and by converting waste into tillage. In 1675 Clent Common was enclosed and was wholly converted to arable. Indeed, by the eighteenth century these parishes were slowly shifting from a predominantly dual economy based on agriculture and the edge-tool industry to a more specialised agricultural economy (Large 1982: 169–87). In the areas closest to the industrial parishes, farms were being advertised specifically as offering opportunities to the purchaser to make profits by supplying food and carrying services to industry.

Widespread efforts were made to improve grassland, whether pasture or meadow. Clover grew well in the Midlands, especially in south Staffordshire and north Worcestershire. Clover seed could be bought by 1700 in all the west Midland towns, including Kinver, Dudley, Tamworth, Lichfield, Walsall and Wolverhampton, and the larger landowners sent to London for seed. Other common 'artificial' grasses included sainfoin and rye grass. Wood and heathland were cleared and manured in order to extend the area of grassland. Although the Midlands contained some of the finest natural grassland in the country, in some areas meadows could be developed only by irrigation. Thus, Thomas Foley the ironmaster invested £500 to convert 400 acres of poor arable at Chaddesley Corbett into good meadows at 30s. an acre, thereby increasing their value sixfold. Hay for winter fodder was valued at £1 a load and £4 in time of scarcity, and peas, beans, oats, barley, turnips and vetch were all grown as fodder crops (Large 1982: 179).

Although stockrearing predominated in most of the region, arable farming was important in south Warwickshire and west Staffordshire and there was some development in the organisation and methods of tillage. The types of corn grown in Staffordshire included lammas, pollard or bearded wheat, french, white and red beans, white and grey peas, and buckwheat was grown on temporary clearings on Cannock Chase. Most of the seed corn was still obtained by setting aside a part of the crop, but special seed corn was purchased either from London suppliers or from market towns such as Lichfield (Plot 1680). The open-field Feldon parishes of south Warwickshire had no reserves of untilled lands, so that recourse was made to ever more complex rotations of crops. For example, four-course rotations of wheat, peas

Plate 4.1 Windmills at Wolvey in north-east Warwickshire.

and beans and fallow were enforced by the court leet at Dorsington (1679) and
Burton Dasset (1714).

Hemp and flax continued to be grown widely and production appears to
have increased in the early eighteenth century. Small parcels of land were
leased out at 45–50s. an acre for flax growing (VCH Staffs iii: 67) and flaxmen
visited the farms to purchase yarn for most market towns had one or two linen
weavers or threadmakers. Some landlords, however, believed that flax, hemp,
rape and coleseed impoverished the soil and so they prohibited their
cultivation. The gentry took great interest in planting fruit trees to provide
them with dessert. Sir Samuel Clarke at West Bromwich planted peaches,
apples and pears, and a fine cherry plantation thrived at Packington. A wide
range of vegetables, including potatoes, turnips, carrots and cabbages, were
grown in cottage gardens and on small plots of land, not only for food for the
family but also for sale in the town markets.

The fertility of the soil was increased by both traditional and new
methods. Lime from Caldon Low was widely used in north Staffordshire, while
in south and east Staffordshire and north Worcestershire lime was obtained
from outcrops near Dudley and Walsall. Lime was burnt at the Wren's Nest
limeworks of the Lords Dudley, for sale to farmers, from at least 1680. Plot
referred to five different types of marl and distinguished their properties in
enriching the soil. He noted that good-quality marl was sold at prices varying
from 4s. 6d. to 9s. the load. Fern, ash and pitcoal ash were also used as
fertilisers, bracken was burnt on Cannock Chase and peas and beans ploughed

in for fertiliser at Harborne and elsewhere. Heaps of animal manure in the yard and on the fields were a noteworthy feature of most midland probate inventories, where they were listed respectively as 'in-muck' and 'out-muck' and carried high valuations. Landlords were very aware of the need to maintain the fertility of the land and encouraged good farming by reliefs of rent allowed for liming, mucking and other improvements. Some land was farmed not on traditional rotations but by alternations of several years of tillage and several years of grassland, adjusted in accordance with local and metropolitan market demand. Such land required very heavy dressing with marl, clay, lime and manure, but could yield crops for six, seven or eight years before being put down for grass. The Moorland farmers used more lime and burned turf. They grew in succession barley, oats, rye and oats again on the land as long as it would bear crops.

The flexibility of the farm economy on an individual holding is demonstrated by the case of Richard Pyott, who farmed at Streethay from 1699 to 1727. He had differing amounts of land under tillage from year to year, from a minimum of 20 acres to a maximum of 43 acres in 1712, before returning to the smaller acreage. He grew wheat, barley, blendcorn, rye and peas. Part of his farmland had formerly been pasture which he broke up to grow as many as seven successive crops before it was returned again to pasture (Yates 1975a: 32–3).

Open fields were gradually enclosed at Madeley (by 1708), Drayton Basset (by 1714), King's Bromley (by 1730), Wrottesley (by 1731) and Shenstone (by 1745). The thirty-eight tenants and five copyholders of Meretown petitioned for a general enclosing of the fields in an almost peremptory manner on the grounds that all the neighbouring fields had already been enclosed (Yates 1975a: 39–41). By 1760 the enclosure of the common arable was already far advanced in Staffordshire but perhaps one-third of the county still consisted of communal open pastures, heather and gorse (Pitt 1796). Some of the largest enclosures for pasture were made in the Moorlands; at Cheddleton, for instance, 2,300 acres of pasture were enclosed in 1735 (Johnson, 1964: 173–4).

In industrial parishes the common fields and pastures gradually became a patchwork of closes, cottages, gardens, pits and works. Communal farming persisted at Bilston, where the curate noted in 1717 that 'today we reaped the coalpit field'. In Aston parish the townships of Bordesley, Nechells and Duddeston became industrial suburbs of Birmingham, while Erdington, a village on better soils in the same parish, remained an open-field community under common management until 1802 and the village of Saltley, also in Aston parish, remained open until 1817.

There was much piecemeal enclosure in the Feldon and in the Avon valley, at Bidford, Claverdon, Temple Grafton and Great Alne, for example. Many of these enclosures were made by groups of freeholders in the period 1750–80. From the 1780s the influence of a growing food market and rising land prices led to more arbitrary actions, and larger landlords were prepared to face the difficulties involved in tackling the enclosure of large populous parishes with a view to increasing rents.

In south-east Warwickshire crafts and bye-employments declined and rural villages specialised in agriculture perhaps for the first time. This left the labourer more than ever dependent upon casual employment. How far arable farming, parliamentary enclosures and improvement increased or decreased his opportunities of employment has always been and still is subject for debate (Martin 1981).

The enclosure of heath and waste was an exercise different in kind as well as in degree. Gailey Common, 500–600 acres of waste land, on which five vills had common grazing rights, was enclosed by an Act of Parliament of 1770 in 'cold barren land but not so flat but that it may easily be drained and made profitable'. The land had been enclosed as a temporary intake seventy years before. Five enclosure acts were completed for Lord Dudley's manors and all were to some extent concerned to facilitate canal building, access to minerals and the industrial development of the areas concerned (Raybould 1973: 52–89). All the enclosures made by the Leveson-Gowers in Staffordshire before 1800 were of waste land. Lightwood Forest enclosure in 1736 added 650 acres, Northwood enclosure in 1757 149 acres, and Lightwood Common 198 acres; Tittensor waste was enclosed in 1828, and the waste of the manor of Burton was enclosed piecemeal (Wordie 1982: 177–8).

The costs of enclosure in Warwickshire rose considerably during the last years of the eighteenth century. In the 1750s, it had averaged 11s. an acre, by the 1780s 19s. an acre and in the 1790s it reached 34s. an acre, as the exercise became more complex and prices rose (Martin 1967). By the 1830s landowners like Oswald Mosley were becoming critical of the 'enclosing mania when every spot of ground supposed capable of growing a blade of corn must be converted to tillage' (Thirsk 1969: 5). The last open-fields in the Midlands to be enclosed by Act of Parliament were at Alstonfield (1839) and Yardley (1847). Some enclosure of common pasture, woodlands and heath continued spasmodically for a little longer.

From the mid-1750s the price of grain at market began to rise, and after 1790 the French wars created such difficulties in importing cheap foreign corn that the price of grain rose steeply. A series of bad harvests from 1794 to 1800 drove up the price of wheat still further to famine levels, and in 1801 bread was rationed by royal proclamation. Thus farmers had every incentive on financial and social grounds to increase their production of grain and between 1790 and 1815, in the Midlands as elsewhere, farmers grew corn on land which, under normal circumstances, they would have considered ill-suited for the purpose. In 1801 it was said that Wootton Wawen had twice as much land under wheat as was customary, and attempts were even made to grow wheat in the Moorlands. In 1800 and 1801 the government enquired into the amount of crops grown in each parish. Staffordshire made only 66 returns, but these sufficiently indicate the distribution of the main crops. Oats was still the main bread crop in the Moorlands, especially in the more remote parishes. From the vicinity of Newcastle and southwards wheat and barley and some oats were cultivated. In the river valleys on the heavier soils beans were grown. Much barley was produced in east Staffordshire, partly because of the soil, and partly in response to the demands of the brewers of Burton, Stone and Lichfield (Pelham 1951). In Warwickshire wheat, barley and oats were grown in every one of the parishes making a return. Wheat was the predominant crop in the Feldon, where soils and hours of sunshine were conducive to its cultivation, and it was grown especially in the remaining open-field parishes (Pelham 1952). By 1820 a notable rise in the yields of corn per acre and a great improvement in the ratio between seed corn and corn harvested had occurred. This had been achieved by an all-round improvement in techniques rather than by any single innovation.

Seed continued to be sown broadcast and although the virtues of drilling were known and praised, a good deal of scepticism was expressed about the real value of the new technique, except in the case of root crops and beans. About twelve estates in Staffordshire had introduced drill sowing by 1800 and the technique gradually spread in association with horse hoeing. Harvesting too was carried out largely by hand, for abundant supplies of seasonal labour were available. Threshing machines, however, were generally adopted, ploughing was increasingly done by pairs of horses instead of ox teams, and harrows were also widely used by the 1830s. A number of midland firms manufactured agricultural machinery at this period. Three firms, notably Cornforths, were based at Wolverhampton, and others were established at Longton and Brewood (Sturgess 1960: 77).

By the 1820s many four- and six-course rotations had been adopted. Beans formed part of the rotations on heavier soils. The Norfolk system which eliminated bare fallow was followed in the Midlands, but for the most part the claylands were not suited to the 'turnip–fallow' which was an essential element of the Norfolk system. Improving landlords and agricultural writers extolled those who attempted it, but it was mainly in north-east Warwickshire and south-west Staffordshire that the system could be used successfully. Elsewhere the traditional system of at least one course of bare fallow together with one year's corn, wheat or oats or barley, and then one or two years of legumes persisted (VCH Staffs vi: 102–6).

Between 1790 and 1830 many field drains were laid. Trenches were dug, filled with furze or small stones, and covered by stone flags or turf, which was kinder to the plough. Tiles were manufactured locally and provided a cheap and efficient improvement after the removal of the duty on them in 1815 at the instance of Sir John Wrottesley, a local member of Parliament.

The Potteries, the Black Country, Birmingham, Coventry and Burton on Trent were encircled with parishes where land was cultivated intensively in order to supply a wide range of vegetables to the town markets. Market gardens had been cultivated on the outskirts of Wolverhampton from at least 1700, and the good light soils of the parishes to the west of the town, namely, Wombourne, Himley, Patshull, Pattingham and Tettenhall, enabled them to take full advantage of local demand. 'Immense quantities' of cabbages, onions, carrots, early peas and potatoes were grown in the valley of the river Trent around Lichfield and Tamworth. By 1845 Lichfield and Tamworth had sixty-eight market gardens. Fruit was not cultivated on a commercial scale in the west Midlands, however, for good supplies came in quantity from Evesham, Pershore and the Worcestershire part of the Avon valley.

The keeping of poultry, though universal, remained in a fairly primitive state and Midlanders showed little interest in large-scale production or scientific management. The only notable exception was Lord Aylsford, who produced turkeys at Meriden for the London and Birmingham markets (Pitt 1796; Wedge 1794; Murray 1813).

The demand for horses multiplied many times during this period, with the increasing use of farm horses, riding and hunting horses, stagecoach and mailcoach horses, the huge army of waggon and cart horses, pit horses and a new demand for canal boat horses. Horses were bred in Warwickshire from Leicester stallions, but most were brought in from Leicestershire and Derbyshire to the great horse fairs at Penkridge, Stafford, Burton and Rugeley. Rugeley Horse Fair, which was held in May and June, was said to be one of the most important in the country.

On the great estates which covered so much of central Staffordshire and central Warwickshire, gentlemen proprietors took great interest in maintaining and developing their timber as a source of income and as an environmental asset. Oak trees were both sold and planted at Chillington, Beaudesert, Ragley Hall, Stoneleigh and Abbots Bromley. Walnut, elm and beech wood were used for furniture and gunmaking. Underwood was cut every six years and sold for making baskets and pottery crates. Coppice woods, which were cut in rotations of from ten to twenty years, had long been a major feature of the countryside, and though demand for charcoal for the ironworks had virtually ceased by 1790, there was much demand for wood for fences and hurdles. Certain small farmers near Tamworth specialised in providing quickset plants for the hedgemakers and enclosers.

Needwood Forest was finally enclosed in 1801, after years of debate about the value of the timber for the navy and the value of grazing for the commoners' cattle. The Enclosure Act passed in 1801 declared that the area should cease to be Royal Forest and in 1805 half the land was awarded to the Duchy and half to the twenty-one villages that claimed common rights. In 1811 awards were made to individual freeholders and commoners. In 1802 58,621 oak trees worth £86,000 and 148,000 holly trees were growing in the forest area. The freeholders received one tenth of the trees, most of which were cut down and sold; the holly went to Manchester traders to be used in the printing of cotton (Thirsk 1969: 5–6). The other old forest lands in the region had ceased to be regarded as Royal Forests from the mid-seventeenth century and they were enclosed gradually during the eighteenth century.

By 1815 the purchase price of land in Staffordshire had increased from twenty-seven years' purchase to thirty years' purchase. Rents in Warwickshire averaged 29s. per acre and in Staffordshire 25s. per acre. Market-garden land made the highest prices of all at £3 an acre.

By this time the largest proprietors in the Midlands had rent rolls in the region of £8,000–10,000 per annum. Their midland estates were merely members of great empires that were spread over many counties and were managed by professional agents. They began to increase investment in drainage and in tenants' buildings. However, they expected their tenants to pay interest on the capital that was advanced. The cash outlay of the Leveson-Gowers on their Trentham estates increased dramatically from 1805 onwards, exceeding £7,000 in some years. Tenants usually paid all rates and taxes on the land, and also all tithes, which at this date were often being revised upwards. Rents too showed a marked upward trend and, although tenant farmers could prosper, the demands being made upon them were increasing.

Between the late-eighteenth and the mid-nineteenth centuries a major change took place in the pattern of leasing. The old tenancies for years and for lives were largely replaced by annual tenancies, which not only provided opportunities for regular adjustments of rents but also enabled the landlord to introduce cropping and other improvement clauses into the leases (Wordie 1974: 177).

In the years after 1815 the high grain prices of the Napoleonic war period fell to more normal levels, but the Midlands was affected less adversely than many other areas, for farmers shifted from grain to livestock production which in many cases was more appropriate to the clay soils. By the 1830s in most of northern and central Staffordshire and much of north Warwickshire much of the land was permanent pasture and only in the south-west, south-east and parts to the west of Stafford did arable land still predominate.

In the depression after 1815 the condition of the agricultural labourer worsened. They were still 'an indispensable class of society', but with the rise in population labour remained cheap. At Alton daily wages per man were 2s. 6d. from 1807 to 1816, 2s. from 1816 to 1821, and 1s. 9d. from 1822 to 1824. On the other hand, the falling price of bread was of some assistance and at least on the large estates much attention was paid to cottage building. The Midlands was comparatively free from agricultural riots and agitation in the 1830s except for an isolated instance of rickburning at Himley in 1831. Wages in the vicinity of industrial areas were always higher than in purely agricultural areas (Pitt 1796: 155–6) and they rose by as much as 10 per cent in the 1790s because of the demand for corn and the increasing opportunities to obtain labouring work in canal and house building and it seems probable that agricultural labourers in the Midlands did not suffer as much as the farm workers of the south of England.

Corn prices continued to fall in the 1820s, but this was not matched by a reduction in rents, for lords of great estates expected their agents to manage the lands commercially and to keep up the rent rolls and profits. Tenant farmers were under pressure to maintain cultivation and pay their rents, and increasingly the larger tenant farmers were prepared to adopt innovations to increase productivity. Good practice spread and there was a gradual elimination of customary practices. In the Midlands the changes were derived from an improvement of management and the acceptance of higher investment rather than from the introduction of new ideas.

Chapter 21

The changing towns: 1660–1830

In May 1661 warrants were issued to a body of commissioners for Warwickshire, Worcestershire and Staffordshire to receive the oaths of allegiance of the burgesses in corporate towns. The commissioners were Royalist gentry who had suffered during the republic as delinquents. At Coventry, Walsall and Newcastle under Lyme the majority of the council refused to take the oath and were removed from the councils, but since they continued to live and exercise influence locally their removal only increased hostility to the restored regime. As their next mayor Coventry elected Thomas Hobson who had not only refused to take the oaths of allegiance but was an anabaptist and a fifth monarchy man. He was unable to serve but the gesture of defiance demonstrated the strength of local feeling.

Newcastle under Lyme was forced to accept a new charter which required among other constraints that the persons appointed to the offices of justices, recorder and town clerk must have royal approval in writing before being allowed to take office. In the first five years of the reign all the midland boroughs accepted new charters, albeit with varying degrees of willingness.

By 1665 the first onslaught of the restored Cavaliers had slackened and the dissenters had begun to recover ground. At Stratford two of the ejected burgesses were elected without intervention from the Crown, and at Coventry a number of dissenters were elected and conventicles met openly. On their side, the suspicions of Whigs and Dissenters were being daily aroused by the popish proclivities of the court of Charles II and the conversion of the King's brother, the heir to the throne. The popish plot of 1678 to 1679 and the political struggle between the Earl of Shaftesbury and the Court were reflected by dissensions and tension in the Midlands. In Walsall, town government broke down altogether, no mayor could be elected and the town charter was invalidated (Homeshaw 1960: 59–64).

The Duke of Monmouth gained considerable support in the towns of the Midlands as the champion of the Protestant cause against the follies of the popish court. At Stafford he was made high steward and he was given an enthusiastic welcome when he visited Coventry and Newcastle in 1682.

Meanwhile, at Westminster and Oxford, King Charles II successfully rode out the crisis and by devious means secured the dissolution of the exclusion parliaments, the disgrace of Shaftesbury, the peaceful succession of his popish brother James and the suppression of the Duke of Monmouth's rebellion in 1685. The last four years of his reign produced a remarkable Tory reaction in the midland towns as well as at Westminster. At Coventry the new Tory mayor and council agreed to a new charter which gave the Crown the right to remove corporation officials. There followed a purge of the dissenters who had been elected to the council despite the Corporation Acts (VCH Warks).

The reign of James II opened with a flurry of loyal addresses from corporate towns, including Stratford, Tamworth and even Coventry. Under the new King the town corporations appeared to be falling under the control of central government. At Stafford the new mayor was Benjamin Thornbury, a doctor of medicine, who had attended the royal family, a known Papist exercising office by virtue of a royal dispensation from the oaths of allegiance and supremacy. At Coventry, although the mayor was a Presbyterian, three of the aldermen were royal nominees. The constant negotiations with central government, the surrender and renegotiation of charters and the seeking of patronage caused not only political but also financial problems. Newcastle borrowed money, at Coventry the mayor could not be paid, and at Walsall 'anarchy' continued.

The revolution settlement of 1689 marked the end of direct intervention by the Crown and the county authorities in corporate borough affairs. The years after 1689 saw no changes in the structure and organisation of borough government and the closed corporations consolidated their hold on the leadership of the towns, concentrating on regulating markets, maintaining order, controlling the poor and administering town finances which had suffered greatly in the previous years. The councillors formed a small self-perpetuating elite and demonstrated little initiative or enterprise. Almost every town suffered financial difficulties. Coventry witnessed constant litigation and accusations of corruption; financial difficulties led the councillors to take over various small charities, and bribery cases were brought in 1726, 1728, 1737 and 1741 (VCH Warks VIII: 267–9). In Walsall leadership was exercised by a very few families, and riots and political disturbances broke out in 1714 and again in 1743, 1750 and 1756; the council appeared increasingly isolated from the townsfolk, inept and unwilling to take responsibility (Homeshaw 1960: 82–117). At Stratford it was difficult to persuade leading men to take office, and meetings were adjourned for lack of business or of attendance and the borough court ceased to function (VCH Warks III: 40–2).

The seigneurial boroughs saw little change in government. At Halesowen, Birmingham, Burton on Trent and Alcester the principal officials were the high and low bailiffs, elected by the annual town meeting. The vestry officials, the constables, churchwardens and the overseers of the poor provided sufficiently, if unimaginatively, for immediate needs.

186

Some rural towns in the Midlands declined in importance, among them Abbots Bromley which by 1717 was 'a very poor town and its market very mean' (Defoe 1724 (1971)). Markets virtually ceased trading at Solihull, Southam, Kenilworth and Bidford. Rugby scarcely increased in population while Sutton Coldfield, though a post town and turning point for coach traffic, remained small and its town council functioned principally as a charitable trust. Brewood had a magnificent medieval church, four streets, a grammar school and a market cross, but Gregory King, riding through in 1696, recorded only sixty houses and the market had ceased trading in 1673. Towns such as these became increasingly dependent on the county towns for services.

The corporate towns did not decline but they grew only slowly in population and enterprise. By 1697 Lichfield had 3,085 people according to Gregory King, and by 1781 this had increased only to 3,771. Nevertheless, it continued to support a variety of luxury trades; tobacco pipes, bone lace and silk were made and sold, and the tailors, booksellers and parchment makers were busy. Great aristocratic estates at the height of their grandeur surrounded Lichfield, and clergy, gentry and literary leaders were numerous in the town. Elias Ashmole, William Camden and Gregory King were all Lichfield men, and a generation later the town produced Samuel Johnson, David Garrick and Anna Seward.

Warwick was not on a main post road but nevertheless attracted gentry and professional men. Lord Brooke continued to reside in the castle, and the meetings of quarter-sessions, assizes, and occasional parliamentary elections made the town a place of resort. After the Great Fire of 1694 the town was rebuilt under the supervision of a body of commissioners empowered by a special Act of Parliament. The commissioners laid out wide streets and required builders to conform to rigid building specifications with uniform frontages and dignified, restrained ornamentation. The new houses were all built of brick or stone and roofed with tile or slate. The work was carried out by skilful local builders who established Warwick as a centre of fine craftsmanship. In contrast the industrial towns were increasing rapidly in population and wealth. In the later seventeenth century Birmingham, Wolverhampton, Coventry, Newcastle and Dudley were still dominated visually and socially by wealthy retailers, who lived above their large shops around the central market place and parish church. Their homes were the largest in the town and their furniture as grand as anyone could show. The craftsmen lived in smaller streets at one remove from the centre, in smaller houses and with domestic furnishings of lesser value.

A hundred years later the industrial towns presented a very different aspect. The wealthiest men were by now the ironmongers, metal merchants and wholesale traders in locks or guns, or (in Newcastle) the felt makers and hatters. New churches had been built and each of the industrial towns also had several small but well-endowed dissenters' meeting houses. The ancient grammar schools had all been rebuilt and supplemented by the provision of

Plate 4.2 The Church, mills and houses of Burton on Trent in 1743. Detail from Buck's prospect of Burton on Trent.

Blue Coat schools. In all four towns assemblies, public balls, musical concerts and plays were held and Wolverhampton and Birmingham had cold baths, coffee houses and assembly rooms. All the industrial towns had booksellers, dancing masters and stationers, and visiting teachers offered lessons in French, book-keeping and mathematics. There were numerous attorneys concerned with commercial and business transactions as well as conveyancing and litigation. They drew up agreements, arbitrated disputes and brought together investors and investments, mortgagors and mortgagees.

The pace of urban building speeded up to meet the needs of the growing population. Clay suitable for building was available locally, in some cases the clay dug out for the foundations was made into bricks on the site, and much timber was imported into the area from the Baltic by way of Burton on Trent.

In Coventry the persistence of the early layout of the town was caused partly by the Lammas and Michaelmas grazing rights of the burgesses on pastures to the south of the town which could not be extinguished. On the west side of the town expansion was inhibited by Cheylsmore Park and Whitley Park. To the south-east an entailed estate could not be built upon. The town walls had been destroyed in 1662 and the gates were removed in 1781 (Gooder 1967: 40) but development was easiest and cheapest within the lines of the old

188

walls. Former gardens, yards and open spaces were filled in with small houses, weaving shops and watch shops, with access through back passages. The south of the city saw the growth of some areas of high-status housing and to the north in 1828 a new area, Hillfields, was laid out and was occupied chiefly by ribbon weavers. Many of the leading manufacturers of the first generation of the Industrial Revolution still lived adjacent to their premises; nevertheless the growth of the high-status suburb, once begun, steadily accelerated and by 1820 Lord Calthorpe had already started to make Edgbaston into a green suburb for Birmingham business men.

As Midlanders formed clubs to buy watches or books, and to pay sick and funeral expenses, so they clubbed together to facilitate the raising of capital to build houses. The earliest recorded building society was Ketley's in Birmingham in 1775 and numerous others were soon established at Dudley, Wolverhampton, Burslem, Handsworth and Coventry. The building society brought together perhaps 20–50 tradesmen, small masters, small provision merchants and other better-off working people and they contributed 4–6s. a week to a common fund. With this security they were able to borrow sufficient capital to build. As the houses were completed the members balloted for ownership and paid off the price in a lump sum and when all members were provided with houses the club was wound up. Very often the house provided a basis for further development as the new owner filled up the back courtyard with very inferior housing to rent to the poor. About 10 per cent of the stock of new houses in Birmingham from 1780 to 1790 was provided by building societies (Chalkin 1974: 175–8). In 1807 the Burslem Building Society aimed at producing planned groups of houses of good quality and sound construction (VCH Staffs VIII: 114–16).

Apart from the building societies and the larger developments most of the building was carried out by small-scale developers who abounded in both town and countryside. When the Gooch estate was leased for building 139 leases were made to 129 different lessees who in turn brought in the builders. They obtained short-term credit from the builders' merchants, and built perhaps three or four houses at a cost of less than £500. After 1790 the scale of undertakings increased as attorneys facilitated credit by arranging mortgages within the area, but the overall increase in the housing stock was achieved by the input of large numbers of small investments derived from the savings and profits of small manufacturers.

The industrial towns developed a social role by providing for the industrial classes, rich and poor, the same services which the country towns provided for the gentry and farmers. Birmingham had two theatres by 1807. The New Street Theatre, licensed as the Theatre Royal in 1807, was elegant and refined, a supporter of good causes such as Sunday schools and the new Hospital. Swann's Theatre on the other hand offered circus stunts, lampoons, and a pantomime. At Newcastle under Lyme a company of shareholders erected the Theatre Royal in 1787, Coventry had a Theatre Royal from 1815 and at

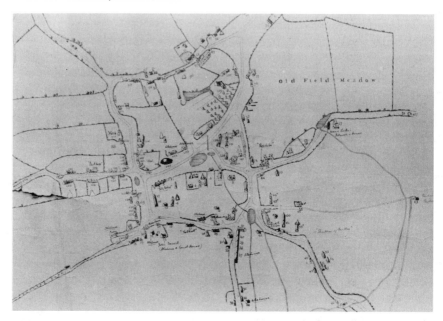

Plate 4.3   Map of Burslem reconstructed from contemporary deeds and estate maps by R. Simms
c. 1880.

Plate 4.4   Burslem Town Hall and Market Place about 1830.

Warwick a building called Cocksparrow Hall was regularly used for plays. Touring companies to suit all tastes proliferated and the names of Siddons, Kemble and Macready were as familiar in the industrial as in the county towns. At Stratford David Garrick organised the first of the Shakespeare jubilee festivals in 1769 and by 1830 Shakespearean processions and performances were well-established in the town. Orchestral concerts and choral festivals became a regular part of town life and all towns had permanent bowling greens and pleasure gardens.

Towns were centres of the distribution of knowledge, news, and intellectual attitudes through newspapers, libraries and public gatherings. *Aris's Birmingham Gazette* and *Jopson's Coventry Mercury* were both founded in the 1740s and achieved a wide circulation in the Midlands. They reported foreign and London news and perhaps more importantly provided a medium for the advertisement of goods, services, social and public gatherings, houses and businesses for sale, employment opportunities, notices concerning workhouses, absconding servants and lost and found animals.

They contained many advertisements of lectures and classes in scientific and commercial subjects, exhibitions of electricity, magnetism and other phenomena and sales of books of instruction, dictionaries, and encyclopaedias. *The Wolverhampton Chronicle, Warwickshire Weekly Journal* and *Staffordshire Advertiser* were founded in the 1770s and became well-established periodicals and provide evidence of widespread interest in science and commerce. After 1800 newspapers were founded which sought to discuss local issues and to offer a political judgement upon events. Forty-five such papers came into existence in Birmingham between 1800 and 1835, but many were very short-lived. In the 1820s the quickening of political debate in the town led to a greater interest in political newspapers. The *Birmingham Journal* became the organ of the Birmingham political union and the Birmingham *Argus* offered a critique of local society and politics (Briggs 1949).

During the 1770s several towns saw the formation of subscription libraries. At Birmingham the charge was 8s. and the librarian opened the door for three hours every weekday. It became a recognised meeting place for the like-minded and acquired purpose-built premises in 1790.

The first Midland bank was opened in 1765 in Dale End, Birmingham, by the partnership of Sampson Lloyd, the ironmaster, and John Taylor, the button maker, on the basis of their credit and experience in industry. Other manufacturers and merchants followed their example in the 1790s, including Molineux and Hordern in Wolverhampton, Patten and Company in Cheadle and Charles Forster and Sons in Walsall. Soon family partnerships were opening banks in every large town in the Midlands, discounting bills, issuing their own bills of exchange, providing overdrafts and loans, and gathering the money of large numbers of small investors from a wide spectrum of occupations and varied social status. The banks also acted on behalf of the town commissioners and of large-scale undertakings such as the hospitals. After a period of great difficulty from 1815 to 1825 they became Joint Stock Companies after 1826.

The towns saw the meetings of the Ironmasters Associations, the Master Potters' Associations and others who maintained agreements about wage fixing and undertook common representations to the government and to the public on commercial matters. The attempt in 1782 to found a Birmingham Commercial Committee and to extend this to a national Chamber of Manufacturers was shortlived, but manufacturers were increasingly consulted collectively and individually. They met frequently in running common enterprises such as the Assay Office, the Proof House, and the Brass Company; they corresponded as a group with colleagues in Manchester, London and Sheffield, and began to think themselves as a significant 'interest' within the national community. In order to improve the roads or build a canal, it was necessary for them to work together to obtain a private Act of Parliament, enabling them to override the property rights of their neighbours or to collect rates and tolls. In the same way leading townsmen obtained Acts which enabled them to establish town commissions to collect a rate to be used for the better paving, lighting and cleaning of their towns. The first such Act was obtained by Coventry in 1763. The commission set up under the Act did not derogate in any way from the powers of the Corporation but simply acted alongside the older body, collecting a rate and undertaking a limited programme of improvement. Birmingham held its first town meeting to discuss obtaining an Act in 1765, but it was not until 1769 that the Act was passed. This was to be the first of five Acts extending and adding to the powers of the Commissioner. Wolverhampton secured its Act in 1777 and Dudley in 1784. By 1825 all the larger industrial centres had their own commissioners, including Burslem, Fenton and Hanley. Other parts of the Potteries were more laggardly and Trentham, Fenton, Stoke and Longton did not establish town commissions until 1839.

At first the powers obtained were limited. The commissioners were only allowed to collect a rate of a few pence in the pound, and their borrowing powers were very modest. The experience of functioning within these limits led the commissioners to extend their powers by successive Acts of Parliament. Larger designs began to suggest themselves, but the basic principle of limited powers for specified purposes remained; there was no open-ended entitlement to act. The commissioners were men experienced in industry, and local leadership. In Wolverhampton the familiar names were Fryer, Jesson, Molineux and Horden the banker, while the Birmingham commissioners included Ryland, Galton, Lloyd, Smith and Russell. The objectives of these commissioners were clearly linked with the demands of their daily lives.

Lighting the streets in the centre of the town was an immediate objective of the commissioners. Whale oil lamps were used and lighting was at first confined to three weeks in the month, for the full moon was regarded as sufficient illumination for travellers by night. In Wolverhampton the 460 street lamps were lit only from November to March and from sunset to 4.00 a.m.

Street cleaning was also undertaken on a limited scale and scavengers were appointed. Clearing obstructions caused conflicts between local residents and the commissioners, and brought to light difficulties of title. In the case of a really obstinate resident, who simply refused to obey the commissioners' ruling, or to accept the compensation and get out of the property, the only appeal was to the sheriff of the county.

In 1814 Wolverhampton extended its powers by a new Act and tackled the difficult question of market rights by appointing a surveyor and a clerk of markets. Birmingham had been negotiating with the lord of the manor for the lease of market rights for some time and was able to purchase them in 1806. The old moat of the former manor house was built over and space cleared for the market, a new market hall was built and the market place ornamented with a statue of Nelson and an Egyptian pyramid. By 1827 the market tolls were bringing in the commissioners £1,000 a year. By 1833 the total reached £14,970, of which almost £3,000 came from market tolls. They maintained three separate markets, spent nearly £6,000 on lighting and watching and nearly £2,500 on scavenging. The new generation of commissioners gradually developed a series of committees, each with its particular function and procedures. Regular minute-keeping, accounting and formal action were established and there were an increasing number of paid employees and officials. There were watch committees in Wolverhampton and from 1826 a finance committee (Smith 1967: 26–48).

In Coventry the minutes were particularly well kept, accounts were regular and presented to the clerk of the peace, vacancies were advertised in the press and employees were supervised (VCH Warks VIII: 271–2).

The town commissioners did not see themselves as forerunners of local government, their function was administrative and limited in its objectives. Government involved the exercise of authority and power, and the maintenance of order, and this was emphatically not their role. Their willingness to serve and to carry considerable responsibility was derived from the practical needs of their commerce rather than from any principle of local self-government.

Chapter 22

Churchmen, evangelicals and men of reason

After the Restoration of the Church of England in 1661, the authorities made a determined effort to maintain uniformity of worship as a concomitant and test of public order and the unity of society. The first midland bishops after the Restoration were men reared in the Laudian tradition. Worcester had a succession of five bishops in twenty years who were associated with the Court and who were hostile to dissent. At Lichfield on the other hand the accent was on moderation. Bishop John Hackett made great efforts to restore Lichfield Cathedral, to ensure uniformity and to revive liturgical worship, but he respected the integrity of the dissenters and made efforts to protect them from ejection. Nevertheless eight Staffordshire clergy lost their livings immediately and 34 more were removed after the passing of the Act of Uniformity in 1662. In Warwickshire the incumbents of Atherstone, Long Compton and several other parishes were also removed or resigned (Morgan 1970: 3). Meanwhile the justices of the peace, notably Sir Bryan Broughton and Sir Charles Holt, were zealous in fulfilling their duties of breaking up conventicles and prosecuting those who dissented from the Re-established Church. The shortlived declaration of indulgence of 1672 revealed 17 centres of dissent in Staffordshire and 28 in Warwickshire. Between 1669 and 1687 no less than 219 persons from Birmingham alone were indicted at Quarter sessions for dissent. The majority were Quakers whose way of life brought them into collision with the law over a wider range of offences than the Presbyterians or Baptists. Nevertheless there was a sense in which dissent was becoming more respectable. The conduct and quality of many of the dissenting ministers won them respect and some powerful friends, and, as hostility to the Court increased, an alliance was created between the new Whigs and the old dissenters.

As anxiety grew at the prospect of a Roman Catholic inheriting the throne, fear and suspicion of Papists in the local community became more marked even in the Midlands where Catholics could normally rely on a measure of tolerance. It reached a crisis in the years 1678–80, during the 'Titus Oates Plot'. That storm raged in the Midlands more furiously than anywhere else outside London, since one of Titus Oates's principal fellow informers was Stephen Dugdale, the dismissed steward of Lord Aston of Tixall. William Ironmonger, SJ, chaplain of Lord Aston was the first priest to be arrested in London, followed soon afterwards by John Gavin, SJ, of Wolverhampton. Meanwhile five peers including Lord Stafford were imprisoned in the Tower, accused of plotting to raise a huge Catholic army to seize power once the King had been killed by the Jesuits. In November trouble came nearer home with the arrests at Rushall of Francis Leveson, OFM, and his brother Edward Leveson, SJ, both of Willenhall. Andrew Bromwich, a young secular priest living with relations at Perry Barr, was imprisoned with several of his family, and three other Jesuit priests and another Franciscan were arrested in the Midlands. Many laymen were imprisoned, houses were searched and long lists of Papists were made and presented to quarter-sessions and to the House of Lords (Rowlands 1965: 4–8). Lord Chief Justice Scroggs came to Stafford for the assizes and William Atkins, SJ, Andrew Bromwich, priest, and others were tried and sentenced to death. In London the trial of Lord Stafford by his peers in the House of Lords began in November (Cobbett 1809–20, VII: 715). The last of the midland Jesuits to be taken was Richard Giffard who had been hiding at Alveston for eight months (Roberts 1963: 3–18). By then the tide had turned, Charles II had secured the succession and routed the Whigs. No more arrests were made and the dissenters rather than the Papists were again the main target of attack in the interests of public order. However, five midland priests had been executed or had died in prison, and Andrew Bromwich and nine laymen remained in Stafford gaol ((U) PRO Privy Council Mss).

Between 1681 and 1685 the changes made in the ranks of local office showed the tightening hold of the Court upon local influence and leadership. By the time Charles II died in 1685 the way had already been prepared at local as well as national level. The accession of James produced a supportive and enthusiastic Parliament and the appointment of Tories and Roman Catholics to every position of authority and influence. Humphrey Wyrley, William Bromley and Francis Hanson were added to the Warwickshire commission and so, after his conversion to Rome, was Robert Feilding of Solihull, a relative of Lord Digby and a 'bully, bigamist, wife beater, heiress hunter and arch libertine' (WCR VIII: xxiv). By 1687 44 per cent of the justices of the peace in Staffordshire were Roman Catholics, an even higher proportion than the national average of 23 per cent (Browne 1939). The lord lieutenants of both Warwickshire and Staffordshire were also Catholics. Even such wholesale promotion of his co-religionists did not win James any real support, any more than his attempt to win over the dissenters by a declaration of indulgence. By October 1688 at local as at national level James' attempt to create a broad base of support had finally broken down, and in November William landed in England to protect Protestantism and accept the throne.

However a scapegoat was necessary. On the night of 12–13 December wild rumours spread that the Irish had fired Birmingham and that

Staffordshire was blazing, and the people of Lichfield and Burton prepared to defend themselves. Lord Delamere set out from Cheshire to join William and passed through Staffordshire with about 500 horsemen. At Stafford the troops encouraged the mob to pull down the Roman Catholic chapel, and they went on to attack the gaol and release the prisoners. At Wolverhampton the church books and furniture were pulled out of the Jesuits' house and burnt on High Green, and the disorder was so great that a man was killed (Roper 1960b). At Birmingham the six-month-old Catholic chapel was totally destroyed, and Edgbaston Hall and the chapel wing of Coughton Hall were attacked.

The attempt to create a single instrument of policy combining central and local politics had been destroyed by being wrested to a purpose impossible of achievement. Some limited degree of plurality of faiths had to be accepted. The Toleration Act of 1689 enabled the main groups of dissenters, Quakers, Presbyterians, Baptists and Congregationalists, to register their places of worship; 42 places were registered in Staffordshire and 67 in Warwickshire. Presbyterian and Quaker congregations were by far the most numerous.

Coventry remained the chief stronghold of dissent in the Midlands. In 1715 an estimated 200 general Baptists, 50 particular Baptists, 200 Congregationalists, 1,000 Presbyterians and 50 Quakers worshipped in the town. The city had a succession of eminent Presbyterian ministers, and The Great Meeting was owned by the corporation, who appointed a body of trustees. Midland Quakers included among their number many leading local business men, Ambrose Crowley of Stourbridge and London and Newcastle, the Lloyds, the Fidoes, the Parks of Birmingham and the Paytons of Dudley. These families were bound together by a network of marriage, meetings for Quaker business and worship, 'meetings for sufferings' and women's meetings. They were distinguished from others by dress, deportment and forms of address, they used their own system of dating and forms of correspondence, they provided their own schools, including one at Hartshill, Coventry – all helping to reinforce their separateness and their sense of mutual responsibility. A similar network of connections can be traced among Presbyterians, Roman Catholics, Anglicans, but none was so exclusive and supportive as the Quaker network. Their cohesiveness as a religious group contributed to their material prosperity, which in turn contributed to the strength of their religious community (White 1873 (1894)).

The Baptists were of lower social status and on the whole they operated within a particular locality. The records of the Baptist meeting at Netherton show vividly this sense of the importance of belonging to a distinctive group. The members included Dixons, Bufferies, Tibbets, Bloomers and Hornblowers, none of whom was really poor, for all played a significant part in local industrialisation. Their pastor was a local member, John Newey. Fifty-six people were baptised between 1697 and 1712; all adult members were expected to conform to moral norms and were expelled for fornication, drunkenness and irregular attendance; the elected pastor and deacons spent

Plate 4.5 Thomas Howell, blacksmith, of Albrighton near Chillington Hall, Staffordshire, and his wife Lydia. Thomas Howell was born in 1797. His family were among those who remained Roman Catholics from the reformation to the twentieth century.

much time in domiciliary visits of exhortation, rebuking the ungodly and arbitrating between accusers and accused, but suspended members who reformed were readily readmitted ((U) DRO Netherton Chapel Records).

The Roman Catholic congregations of the Midlands on the other hand, once they had recovered from the aftermath of the Revolution, showed signs of growth and development. Their numbers increased, especially in Wolverhampton, Burslem and Sedgley, and kept abreast of the growth of population. The rural papists living and working on the great estates of the landowning Catholic families found that they were able to worship with comparative freedom. In most cases the landowners ceased to provide Mass in their houses; instead chapels were built to which the tenants could resort independently for worship. At Brailes a substantial new church was built in 1727 and at about the same time the clergy and people of Wolverhampton organised and provided funds for the building of a combined residence for three priests and a chapel in North Street which was 'openly resorted to'. At Edgbaston the Franciscans had a Mass House in Pritchatts Lane which drew its congregation mainly from Harborne, Tanworth and King's Norton.

It would be a mistake to try to associate any particular kind of dissent too closely with any particular section of the community. Industrial towns often supported several different chapels of different denominations and dissent could also take root in rural parishes. Moreover the congregations who met at a particular place were often drawn not only from that place but from surrounding parishes. Napton Priors, Marston and Newbold on Avon all had large Baptist congregations drawn from several parishes and several large Quaker meetings were established in south Warwickshire, for example at Brailes and Ettington, and in north Staffordshire at Carlton, Shallowfield and Fradley.

Broadly speaking, the numbers and importance of Papist and Protestant dissenters over the whole area were not dissimilar. The wealth and influence of the leading dissenting families and the thoroughness with which the Quakers, in particular, recorded their proceedings has probably exaggerated the significance of dissent in the Midlands in the eighteenth century. Even at Coventry the dissenters represented at most one quarter of the population and in Birmingham not one in a hundred. By the 1730s the original momentum of old dissent in the Midlands was slackening. Many of the Presbyterian ministers were moving towards Unitarianism; almost every Presbyterian and Congregational meeting declined in numbers while Quaker numbers remained stable.

In urban and industrial parishes the older social controls of uniform belief and practice no longer operated, and by the middle of the eighteenth century churchwardens had ceased to make returns of those who did not come to church. By 1760 these parishes were larger than any rector or curate could administer properly. In Birmingham, Coventry, Wolverhampton, the Potteries, Bedworth and Sedgley, men adhered to particular religious congregations as they saw fit. Already many probably had little to do with organised religion except when, constrained by Hardwicke's Marriage Act (1753), they repaired to the Church of England to solemnise legal marriages. In rural areas on the other hand the influence of the squire, his lady, and the rector was becoming even more dominant.

The Augustan age of the Church of England in the Midlands was not so static as might be thought. Churches were built or rebuilt as wealth accumulated and populations grew, especially in the towns and industrial areas. After the fire at Warwick in 1694 the great church was rebuilt on a magnificent scale at a cost of £12,000. About twenty midland churches had been extensively or completely rebuilt by 1760 and many others repaired or improved. At Birmingham the new church of St Philip was designed by Thomas Archer and is recognised as an important example of the English Baroque style. New churches were built at Wolverhampton, and in the rapidly growing industrial villages of the Potteries and south Staffordshire. Churches were also built in rural Warwickshire at Lightbourne and Honnington, and a very elegant new chapel was built at Hall Green, Yardley. In the towns, the wealthier inhabitants took the initiative, as in so many other areas of life, by obtaining private Acts of Parliament to establish new churches and parishes – for example, St John's (1766) and St George's at Wolverhampton (1830), or St Bartholomew's (1749), St Mary's (1772–9) and St Paul's (1777) at Birmingham. These new churches were dignified buildings, reflecting the aspirations and tastes of the families of ironmongers, bankers, lawyers and merchants, who were responsible for their erection. They were almost always surrounded by superior new houses and assisted in establishing the district as an elegant neighbourhood. However, despite a great deal of church building the number of places still fell far short of what was required. The accommodation the churches could offer for the burial of the dead was also lamentably less than what was needed, especially in towns, where additional land was not readily available.

The shift from public communal religion to individual adherence and private belief was paralleled by increasing emphasis on individual religious belief within the churches, challenging the older emphasis on community, state and family. Individual aspirations were expressed in an emotional and spiritual commitment rather than in the regular fulfilment of public and family duty, challenging rather than conforming to the social order. This movement, known as the evangelical movement, can be recognised in all denominations from Roman Catholic to Baptist.

The first prophets of enthusiasm were John and Charles Wesley, who visited the colliers of Wednesbury, Tipton and Darlaston in the 1740s. Working people responded immediately and by 1742 a group of a hundred members met regularly at Wednesbury. However, in May and June 1743 and at intervals through 1744 violent anti-Methodist riots broke out, especially at Wednesbury, Darlaston, Walsall and West Bromwich. The Wednesbury riots were particularly vicious. The riots only confirmed the zeal of the converts and the Methodist circuit system was established in the Midlands between 1746 and 1750; by the 1780s every town and industrial village in the Potteries and the Black Country had its Methodist chapel. It was not exclusively an urban phenomenon, for Ridgeacre Chapel at Quinton was an important rural chapel, established in 1780. From 1770 to 1830 Methodism attracted a steady number of converts, chapels were built and circuits organised by ordained ministers and lay preachers. Although in the eyes of many these congregations were formed of men and women without civility or refinement, they were nevertheless collectively substantial and socially secure. After the death of Wesley the Methodist Conference became more 'respectable' and anxious to maintain a firm grip upon individual vagaries. This led to a number of secessions which originated in the Midlands. Alexander Kilham and his followers were expelled by the 1796 Conference, and within a year five Methodist chapels of his New Connexion had been established in the Potteries. The Kilhamnite Connexion flourished and by 1822 Hanley circuit had 19 societies, 17 chapels, 5 circuit preachers, 39 local preachers and a membership of 1,916.

In 1807 Hugh Bourne, a Methodist preacher, attracted large crowds 'singing, praying, preaching, exhorting, speaking experience, relating anecdotes from morning until night at Mow Cap in north Staffordshire'. These meetings aroused anxiety in the Methodist Conference and Bourne and his Primitive Methodists were expelled in 1808. Primitive Methodist societies spread rapidly, appealing strongly to the poor urban and industrial workers. Their meetings were frequent, exciting, emotional and intensely personal. In the Midlands they were most numerous in the industrial villages in both south and north Staffordshire. By 1818 Tunstall circuit alone had 690 members (Morris 1969: 62–72). Primitive Methodism did not displace Wesleyan Methodism or really compete with them for members, rather, both bodies grew in cohesiveness and self-confidence, but among different social groups.

George Whitefield visited Gornal, Wednesbury and Wolverhampton in 1743 under the patronage of the Countess of Huntingdon. The most note-worthy of the Countess's converts was William Legge, Earl of Dartmouth, of Sandwell Hall, West Bromwich. He was one of the leading evangelical laymen of his day and did not neglect reform in his own neighbourhood. He appointed able evangelical ministers to the living of West Bromwich. They held services on Sundays and prayers on Wednesdays, Saturdays and Holy Days, and lectures were given on Wednesdays at 6.00 p.m. for the instruction of the inhabitants after work. Children were catechised publicly before the congrega-tion and the parish officers were vigorous in enforcing church attendance, reporting all those found drinking, dicing or playing cards during divine service.

'Old Dissent' was revitalised as the Quakers, Presbyterians, Baptists and Unitarians grappled with new problems in a changing society with renewed energy. Birmingham Quakers were leaders in the campaign for the abolition of slavery; John Lloyd, brother of the banker, had lived in North America and on his return joined forces with the Barclays, his cousins, in public opposition to slavery and was supported in Birmingham by Priestley, Russell, Garbett, and Spencer Madan, the Tory Anglican, all very active in fund-raising, publicity, lobbying and fact-finding. New and gifted young Baptist preachers came into the Midlands from Leicestershire. The old Calvinistic exclusiveness of the particular Baptists was gradually forgotten and instead there prevailed the softer creed of the general Baptists, who allowed that all might see salvation. In Coventry a new Baptist chapel was opened in Corns Lane in 1793 and another in Whitefriars Lane in 1824. Nuneaton saw a revival in the 1790s and Stratford in the early-nineteenth century. New village Baptist communities sprang up in Wilmecote, Loxley and Aston Cantelow. Much of this success was due to the initiative of a lively group of ministers of whom the two Sibrées, father and son, were the most active (Sibrée and Caston 1855). Unitarianism in the late-nineteenth century was vigorous and intellectual, closely linked to currents of thought in science and politics. It remained illegal until 1816, and the Unitarian teachers presented a very real challenge to established values and social norms.

The influence and experience of Joseph Priestley in Birmingham show clearly how the new spirit in religion, politics, science and industry interacted at this time to present challenges to the established order. He was patronised by Lord Shelburne and wrote prolifically, his *Institutes of Natural and Revealed Religion* bringing him into national prominence. He wrote as a rationalist, entirely rejecting the mystical and miraculous in the Christian religion, even to the denial of the Godhead of Christ. He was invited by leading scientists and intellectuals of the Birmingham Lunar Society to take over the New Meeting in 1780. He was generously supported by them and became the leader of an intellectual elite. Magistrates and clergy looked askance. They were startled by his choice of books for the new Birmingham Library and by his support for the teachings of the French revolutionaries. A dinner was held at the Hotel in Birmingham on 14 July 1791 to celebrate Bastille Day, but Priestley did not attend. The magistrates were dining nearby at the Swan with the usual toasts – 'Huzza for church and King'. A lawless mob milled about outside the Hotel and the Swan during the dinners, but the gentlemen got away without attack. However, the mob broke into the Hotel and then proceeded to the New Meeting Chapel and went on to the Old Meeting Chapel. At both places pews, cushions and books were destroyed and the chapels set on fire. The next day they proceeded to Priestley's house at Fair Hill, one and a half miles from the town at Sparkbrook, destroyed the laboratory and its equipment and carried off the furniture and the contents of the cellar. They were harangued by the magistrates, but nevertheless went on to the house of another dissenter, John Ryland, on the western edge of the town at Easy Hill and Kingswood Methodist Chapel four miles to the north-east of Birmingham. Thereafter, they became less religious in their choice of objectives to attack.

Six days after the trouble broke out, sixty-four soldiers of the light horse were sent from Nottingham. Together with the special constables sworn in by the magistrates they were able to disperse the mob and arrest twelve persons. Priestley left Birmingham never to return, but Unitarian influence remained very strong indeed. Carrs Lane Chapel became its main centre in Birmingham under the new minister, John Angell James, whose spirit was far more characteristic of evangelical dissent, for he was able and willing to communicate a personal faith and as a preacher he drew crowds.

The position of Catholicism in the Midlands changed quite fundamentally during the period from 1770 to 1830. The Catholic Relief Act of 1778 enabled Catholics to register their places of worship. Catholics were still subject to many legal disabilities, but in 1791 Catholic chapels and worship were legalised and schools were permitted, provided that an acceptable oath of loyalty was taken to the Crown. By 1834 nearly 50 Roman Catholic chapels had been built in the Midlands, especially in the towns. Some gentry enclaves remained, for example at Coughton, Tixall and Wappenbury, but the driving force of Catholicism was now in the towns. In the Potteries the old Catholic centre of Burslem was the mother church for new foundations in the north of Staffordshire while Wolverhampton created new filiations in every Black Country centre of population. In Warwickshire the old centres at Studley formed the stem from which a new parish was formed at Alcester. The sheer growth of the general population led to the establishment of centres in Birmingham and Coventry, despite their traditional hostility to Catholicism. These town missions grew by natural increase, by immigration and by conversions. They were lively and often aggressive in their assertions of their new freedom. Many of the secular clergy who were appointed to them were men of independent thought and action who had been much influenced by the spirit of 'enlightenment'. John Kirk of Lichfield, Joseph Berrington of Oscott and the 'Staffordshire clergy' espoused liturgical change, scriptural studies and vernacular prayers, played down papal authority and autocratic decision-making, and cultivated ecumenical contacts. Parish fund-raising committees made their appearance in the early-nineteenth century in order to build large churches at Walsall, Leek and many other centres, while in the industrial villages hard-worked, English-trained clergy taught working-class congregations, made converts, built churches and schools, set up Catholic friendly societies and engaged in public controversy.

By 1830 the religious scene in the Midlands had been transformed. In common with the rest of the country there were now no legal constraints on the proliferation of varieties of faiths. Unitarians had been accepted in 1813 by the repeal of the relevant clause in the Blasphemy Act, Protestant dissenters had at length been admitted to public office in 1828 and Roman Catholics in 1829.

In the same year as the Priestley riots, Birmingham saw the opening of the first Irvingite or Swedenborgian chapel in the world at New Hall Street, offering its congregation a religion of eclectic intellectual mysticism and demonstrating that even the more eccentric vagaries of private judgement could be tolerated by the community. The midland community also accommodated the religions of immigrant groups, such as the European Jews who had first arrived in the early-eighteenth century. The 'Jews' House' was listed in the 1751 rate book and by 1780 the Jews had a regular synagogue in the Froggery. This was rebuilt in Hurst Street in 1791 and then again in Severn Street in 1810 under Rabbi Isaiah Philips.

By 1830 the long-standing concept of a local community united by religious belief and practice had lost all relation to reality except in some rural parishes. For the most part religious congregations were sub-groups of the population to which individuals adhered according to their own needs and preferences. Moreover, the religious groups appealed to different socioeconomic groups within the communities and emphasised social divisions and the boundaries between the sects, rather than acting as a force for social unity.

The churches were still seen as the appropriate organisation for educating the young, and especially the children of the poor and the working classes. The old endowed grammar schools in the towns continued to provide courses based on Latin grammar and literature and to prepare boys to enter the universities, but they catered mainly for the middle and upper classes. Blue-coat schools were endowed by the Church of England in the early eighteenth century in Wolverhampton, Dudley, Birmingham and Coventry. They prepared respectable if impoverished orphans to take employment in domestic service and manual trades as well as rearing them in piety. Many parishes had a village school associated with the parish church and new parish schools were endowed by individual benefactors, at Penn, Hampton Lucy and Tysoe, among other places.

In the towns Sunday schools were provided by every parish and religious congregation for their own children and for those of the poor of the area. Birmingham had 24 by 1784 and by 1838 20 per cent of the children and young people under 20 years of age had some Sunday school education. Girls and boys were equal in number in the Sunday schools. The total number in any one school averaged about 200. They offered a range of subjects in addition to religious instruction and provided books, tracts and such fringe benefits as outings and treats as inducements to attendance.

Most urban centres had at least one British and Foreign or National Day school by 1833 and with the added support of government grants the churches built day schools rapidly in the 1840s and 1850s. The Roman Catholics meanwhile had been making their own provision and from 1847 they too began to receive grants. By 1850 Stoke on Trent had 28 national schools, 5 Wesleyan, 4 other non-conformist and 6 Roman Catholic schools, and there were also two non-sectarian schools, one founded by the Ridgways at Hanley and one by the Wedgwoods at Etruria.

Not all educational activity was in the hands of the churches. There was a great appetite for the acquisition of knowledge and in the towns lectures, courses and classes were advertised.

New proprietary schools proliferated in this period. Such seminaries of literacy and social aggrandisement could be set up by any person and they succeeded through advertisement and personal recommendation. The sheer number of such enterprises is astonishing and suggests that some of them must have been ephemeral. In 1838 Birmingham had a total of 541 private venture schools with nearly 8,500 children between them. About 8 per cent of the population under twenty years of age had attended some such school, boys and girls in about equal numbers (Journal of the Royal Statistical Society 1840: 25–49).

From 1766 onwards the Lunar Society brought together informally in Birmingham men distinguished in their own fields of medicine, botany, engineering, chemistry, education and manufacture. Their discussions ranged over both theoretical and applied science and their minds were occupied with canals, balloon transport, instrument making, assaying and engineering as well as the pure sciences. Individually they made important contributions to theoretical science and to its industrial application, as a group they demonstrated that a provincial industrial town could both produce and sustain men of genius. They were no longer empiricists, but were men consciously seeking to experiment, theorise and apply knowledge. Innovation and discovery were more highly regarded than authority and tradition (Scholfield 1963).

The late-eighteenth century saw the growth of a spirit of rational enquiry at many levels of society. Intellectuals like Joseph Priestley increasingly emphasised Reason rather than Revelation in religion and while there were few, if any, who would have been prepared to set up Reason as the Supreme Being, there were increasing numbers who concentrated their thoughts upon the natural universe and the organisations of man on Earth rather than on the consideration of life after death and the mediation of grace to the soul.

Chapter 23

The ruling classes and those they ruled: 1660–1830

The Restoration had proved to be not only a restoration of King Charles and the Church of England but also of the aristocracy and gentry. A list made in 1662 of the gentlemen of Staffordshire shows Biddulphs, Giffards, Digbys, Astons, Shirleys and many other Papists and Royalist delinquents restored to their homes and estates. William Orme of Hanch Hall near Longdon was one of the many; he had spent his personal estate on supplies for the garrison at Lichfield and had his estates sequestered, but by 1662 he had recovered his lands in Staffordshire and Derbyshire, was estimated to have an income of £500 a year and was providing for his fourteen children (SHC 1958, 4th Series Vol. II: 7–41). In Warwickshire the Earl of Northampton despite his family's great losses during the war and the interregnum was still the wealthiest of the peers.

In Warwickshire there were 12 peers, 41 baronets and about 120 esquires resident in the county and between them they held nearly three-quarters of all the manors in the county (Mimardière 1963: 7–24). It was difficult to determine how many 'gentlemen' there were since the term was increasingly used for any man of wealth. The Bracebridge family of Atherstone bought land in east Warwickshire and build a handsome residence and lived as gentlemen but not long since had been wholesale hatters organising the manufacture of hats in the Atherstone district. By 1700 lawyers, ironmasters, wholesale ironmongers, stewards of manors, constables of hundreds, mayors and aldermen of towns and many others called themselves, and were called by their neighbours, 'gentlemen', while the term Esquire or Squire was used for the wealthier gentry with landed estates.

There were no outstandingly wealthy landowners in the Midlands at the restoration. Only 6 men in Staffordshire were believed to have an income of more than £1,500 a year in 1662, 64 were set down as worth between £500 and £1,000 and 46 at less than £500 (SHC 1958). Many landowners were experiencing financial difficulties in the 1660s and 1670s. At Burton Dasset Sir Richard Temple's rents fell by about 15 per cent between 1661 and 1667 and rents were also falling on the six estates of Sir Richard Newdigate of Arbury.

205

There were complaints of non-payment of rents and agricultural prices for agricultural produce were falling. Moreover many estates were still suffering from the expenses incurred in recovering them from sequestration (Davies 1977: 86–97).

Landowners were making determined efforts to increase the rent rolls by converting the old long leases to tenancies at will. William Sneyd wrote that he was anxious

> to increase my estate for the benefit of my posterity by increasing my rents. When leases expired I would not renew, but kept my tenants on a reasonable and easy rack, allowing those that were ancient tenants above a third part of the yearly value of their livings, most of them holding for lives upon an old rent.
>
> (Kolbert 1976: 8)

The larger landowner at this date showed little or no interest in commercial farming on his own account and there was a widening distinction between the 'farmer' who leased land and cultivated it and the landlord who leased it out for others to cultivate. The aristocrats began to invest in the funds and government securities. The Leveson Gowers made a 300 per cent profit on their investment in the South Sea Company and sold out before the bubble burst in 1720.

The larger landowners consolidated and secured their estates by advantageous marriages for their sons and daughters, and by entering into strict settlements so that all the legitimate long-term demands on the state for jointure and pensions were secured and the head of the family became virtually a trustee of the estate for the heir and for other members of the family dependent upon it. The aristocracy built up marriage alliances throughout England, Wales and (after the Union) in Scotland, they had land in many counties, and several great houses as well as a house in London where they spent much of their time. No family in the Midlands achieved a more remarkable rise to power and status than the Leveson Gowers of Trentham. Sir John Leveson Gower became a peer in 1702 and Baron Gower of Stittenham in 1703. His son John was created Viscount Gower of Trentham and Earl Gower in 1746, his son Granville a Marquis in 1786 and finally George Granville Leveson Gower (1788–1833) became Duke of Sutherland in 1833. At each stage the family gained thousands of acres and increased political power by successive marriages to great heiresses. By 1833 they had 32,000 acres in England and over a million acres in Sutherland and an income of £141,000 a year (Wordie 1974: 595). They continued to make Trentham Hall their principal country residence, but also maintained Stafford House in London, Dunrobin Castle in Scotland, Cliveden and Lilleshall Hall (Wordie 1982: 1–16).

There was a widening gap between the education of the nobility and of the majority of the esquires and gentry. The sons of the nobility were sent to Westminster and Eton while the sons of the esquires and gentry continued to attend the grammar schools in the market towns, living either with relatives or boarding with the master. Rugby School was especially favoured and unlike other grammar schools its foundation was managed by a board of trustees of local gentlemen, the Caves, the Bromleys, the Feildings and the Skipwiths. Younger sons of gentlemen went on to the university, graduated and entered the church and more and more often were placed in a living in the gift of a relative, thus developing the long-lived alliance between the squire and parson. Other sons of gentlemen became lawyers (Mimardière 1963: 75–84) and others went to London to be apprenticed to merchants and large-scale traders, an opportunity which could cost their fathers as much as £500 or even £1,000.

The most favoured form of higher education for all who could afford it was the grand tour, in which the young man travelling with his tutor carried introductions to political, intellectual and social circles in Paris, Rome and other cultural centres, making important contacts. Daughters were educated at home or sent to boarding schools and still more often spent time in the households of relatives of superior wealth and status.

Between 1660 and 1720 most of the homes of the nobility and wealthier gentry were rebuilt in a manner intended to demonstrate their wealth and dignity and also their learning and classical taste, following the designs in the seventeenth century of Wren and in the early eighteenth century of the revived Palladian style. Most of the work was carried out by local builder-architects. The Smith brothers of Warwick made their name rebuilding Warwick after the Great Fire of 1694, and one or other members of the family were subsequently employed on large-scale projects at Stoneleigh Abbey, Oakley Hall, Newbold Revel, Sandwell, Chillington and Swynnerton among others. The houses were on the grand scale, with plain exteriors, huge symmetrical windows and great porches with columns and pediments. Inside they were decorated with the utmost elaboration with plaster ceilings, stucco work, and painted and papered walls following the fashions of France and London. Furniture and decorations were imported from abroad – even from China – or bought in London, and skilled craftsmen were also summoned from London or Italy to embellish the houses with wood carving, plasterwork, gilding and chimney pieces, and to furnish them with vases, fine furniture and hangings. Many of these houses were remodelled again in the late eighteenth century as rent rolls continued to rise and taste became even more sensitive to fashion. In south Warwickshire at Radway on Edge Hill lived Sanderson Miller, a man early possessed by enthusiasm for the revival of gothic styles. He built a thatched cottage and a tower on Edge Hill in 1744 and added gothic adornments to his house at Radway Grange. In 1748 he assisted Sir Richard Newdigate to remodel his house at Arbury Hall, turning it into one of the most influential gothic houses in the country.

All the houses were set in grand landscaped parks, and the views from the house were controlled and managed to the benefit of the landowner. At Chillington, Shugborough and Sandon and elsewhere, villages were removed to improve the vista from the windows of the hall, trees were planted or cut down, water was diverted to make lakes and cascades. At Tixall even the canal was widened in the interests of the picturesque. At the Leasowes near Hales-owen the poet Shenstone laid out his grounds to create a romantic walk with sculpture and stones carved with literary quotations to encourage artistic and literary reflection. Lancelot Brown was often called in to plan the landscaping of the park, notably at Ragley Hall, Compton Verney, Chillington and Tixall (Stroud 1950). New plants and trees were imported at first from Europe and by the mid-century from America, Asia and India, and green vistas, trees, sheets of water, bridges, model temples and marble seats and balustrades combined to impose order, and beauty upon the environment of the noble household (Tyack 1970: 60–154).

It was in these great houses that the political groupings which ruled the nation and the local community were formed, reinforced by marriage alliances and consolidated by patronage and mutual benefits. The gentlemen of the midland shires did not immediately consider themselves Tories or Whigs but, as lawmaking, taxation and political opportunity increasingly centred on Parliament, so they were gradually drawn into more or less long-standing political alignments.

In 1690 there was still in the Midlands considerable underlying opposition to the new regime. The Earl of Stafford (son of the 'martyr' of 1681) left England and accompanied James to France and Ireland. His estates and

---

Plate 4.6 'A sight of the Banging Bout at Lichfield'. A cartoon sold in London referring to the 1742 election at Lichfield when the Gowers began to establish their interest.

those of his two brothers were sequestered. Charles Aston died fighting at the battle of the Boyne, and John Gifford went to join the Court at St Germains. There were some twenty families of Roman Catholic gentlemen in Staffordshire and Warwickshire and for them James was the only acceptable King, however unsatisfactory his government. In addition about twenty-one of the Anglican clergy of the Midlands found it against their consciences to swear loyalty to William while James was still alive, among them the influential and respected John Kettlewell who went to Coleshill to live with the Jacobite Lord Digby.

By 1710 the latent Jacobitism of some Tories came into the open and men such as the Bagots of Sudbury, Ralph Sneyd of Keele, the Pagets, Lord Uxbridge and William Bromley of Bagington and Sir John Packington thought that a legitimate monarchy might yet be restored without endangering the power of their class.

The loyalties of the midland Jacobites were put to the test when a year after the accession of George I James Edward Stuart invaded from Scotland. All over the Midlands mobs were stirred up to attack the Protestant meeting houses, and there was more damage done in Staffordshire than in all the rest of the country put together. In June and July there were attacks on chapels and on the homes of Protestant dissenters in Walsall, Nuneaton, West Bromwich, Wolverhampton, Stafford, Stone, Cradely Burton, Leek, Coseley, Oldbury, Uttoxeter, Dudley and Birmingham. The rioters were accused of having raised cries for James III, the newly enacted Riot Act was read and the *posse comitatus* was called out. The mobs were generally believed to have been set on by their betters and Mr Sneyd of Keele in particular was held responsible for inciting the Newcastle mob.

Toryism was increasingly the party of the lesser gentry and of the country critics of the great Whig association of landed power and government office. Jacobitism lost its force even in Staffordshire. In 1745 Charles Edward and his forces reached Derby and Scottish Highlanders were seen in Leek. However, this time the Midlands were anxious to demonstrate their loyalty to the Hanoverian monarchy. Lord Lieutenant John Leveson Gower forgot his Tory youth and became a vigorous supporter of the Crown, coming up from London to raise a regiment at his own expense. Even the Catholic gentlemen kept a low profile, and by the 1750s they had embraced the concept of 'providential allegiance' with equanimity (Rowlands 1965: 231–2).

In 1744 the Whig admiral George Anson brought his prize money home to Staffordshire and with his elder brother Thomas at Shugborough Hall created a huge estate and a political empire. John Leveson Gower transferred his allegiance to the Whigs in the election of 1747, and took with him the Chetwynds and the Wrottesleys. From 1747 to 1820 one of the two county seats was always in the pocket of the Leveson Gower family although the other remained Tory. Together the Ansons and the Leveson Gowers set to work to build up control of the Boroughs. It was not difficult to obtain property and therefore freehold votes in Lichfield, but it was more difficult to control Stafford and Newcastle, and in those towns the freemen had to be persuaded by paying annuities to faithful supporters, collecting rent arrears only from opponents, and giving lavish entertainment at Trentham. By these means the Leveson Gowers could usually rely on six and often on eight of the Staffordshire seats. Similarly, in Warwickshire Lord Brooke transferred his political allegiance to the Whigs in 1741, a change which by his own showing was engendered by his ambitions for advancement in the peerage and from then until 1768 Lord Brook and Henry Archer were able to share patronage in Warwick. The second Earl, who succeeded in 1778, further extended the influence of the castle over the town and was able to form an alliance with the corporation which enabled him to dispose of both seats (VCH Warks VIII: 500–2).

By the 1770s the dominance of the Whigs and landed interests began to weaken. Disputed elections became more frequent, the members of the House of Commons were drawn from a wider range of families. There was for example Richard Brinsley Sheridan who was MP for Stafford from 1780–1802. He owed his introduction to politics to his writing and association with Charles James Fox rather than to any Staffordshire connections.

After the Revolution the Justices of the Peace continued to be the principal agency of administration of the law in the counties but they received far less direction from Privy Council. Both Charles II and James II had attempted to increase their authority and control of national politics by manipulating the membership of commissions of the peace but after 1688 the appointment of a justice of the peace again depended principally on local standing, effectiveness and acceptability to the lords lieutenant. About six to ten of the numbers of justices regularly attended quarter-sessions in each county and carried real responsibility for local order and administration. They were occupied with breaches of the peace, especially petty larceny, personal attacks, hedgebreaking and theft. During the reign of Charles II there was much activity following up dissenters, suppressing conventicles and listing papists. In the last years of the seventeenth century the justices were especially concerned to improve the highways, ordering roads to be levelled, and foot bridges to be replaced with cart bridges. Increasing attention was paid to the suppression of poaching on the estates of landed gentlemen and the taking of game by persons possessing less than £100 a year in property.

Justices of the peace of the late-eighteenth century found that their workload was greatly increased. A number of new responsibilities were thrust upon them, as for example inspecting madhouses (1774) and prisons (1791), registering friendly societies (1793) and savings banks (1815), supervising the affairs of the Turnpike Trusts (1823), Combinations (1822) and electoral registers (1832). On the other hand they were no longer required to regulate wages (1779) or to register apprenticeships (1815). The new Poor Law reduced their responsibility for the poor by introducing Boards or Guardians but justices of the peace were *ex officio* members of these Boards. The increase in the number of cases brought before quarter-sessions made their work much more onerous. The number of larceny convictions in Warwickshire increased from three in 1773 to 445 in 1837. The notable increase in the number of juvenile offenders from about 1810 was greater than can be accounted for by the rise in the birth rate. In order to meet these problems Warwickshire Justices awarded exemplary sentences and made more use of the punishments of imprisonment and transportation. Petty session courts were held from 1795 in every hundred in order to deal with increased business, and by the early-nineteenth century these courts were held in sixteen county divisions. Special licensing sessions were held from 1828 onwards. In addition, by 1837 the justices had set up thirty special committees for specific business. The county assessments were reorganised in 1815 and separate finance committees met from 1820 (Styles 1934).

More and more clergy became magistrates and Church and state were visibly aligned to maintain order. In Warwickshire twenty-one out of the fifty-four acting magistrates in 1830 were clergy, many of them residing in the Coventry area. Magistrates, clerical and lay, were also active and capable leaders of county institutions and charitable funds and they took a lively interest in local politics (Stevenson and Quinalt 1982: 187). In the 1790s fear of increasing crimes against property and persons and of the dangerous influence of the French Revolution alarmed respectable inhabitants to such an extent that in many towns and populous districts local volunteer defence forces were formed to control disaffected subjects at home and to defend the country against possible French invasion. They wore uniform, met regularly and paraded on Sundays.

Loyal and respectable gentlemen also established associations for the prosecution of criminals, though many proved to be ephemeral. The Bloxwich association of 1814 sought 'the more speedy and effectual apprehending and prosecuting of persons of every description who shall commit any felony or larceny upon any of our persons or property', and rewards for convictions were offered to achieve their aims (Homeshaw 1955: 150). The members included all the leading inhabitants, ladies and gentlemen of independent means, farmers, industrialists and shopkeepers, all with property to protect.

The villages and manorial towns continued to be organised by the vestry of churchwardens, constables, Poor Law overseers and surveyors of highways. The constables continued to collect levies and taxes, make reports to Quarter Sessions, and deal with disorderly persons and places. They maintained the wells and pumps, bought fire-fighting equipment, organised public rejoicings and investigated suspicious and untoward circumstances. They were expected to prevent outbreaks, fighting and riots, though in this last duty they were usually unsuccessful, and rioting was a common and recurring feature of life in the industrial communities of the Midlands in the eighteenth century. Local roads continued to be the responsibility of the surveyors of the highways who organised statute labour, and local bridges were usually repaired by contract with a local builder.

The Poor Law overseers wrestled with ever greater and more intractable problems in attempting to carry out their duties under the terms of the Poor Law of 1603 and the Settlement Acts of 1662 and 1697. The movement of the poor was permitted but controlled and even quite substantial tradesmen sometimes found it advisable to procure a certificate while some of the better-off continued to enter into bonds. Ratepayers were required by the same laws to take in parish apprentices. Under the statute of 1697 those in receipt of relief were to be identified by wearing a brightly coloured badge bearing the initial of the parish and the letter P. From time to time resolutions would be passed to insist upon this distinction, and at West Bromwich in 1766 they were still trying to ensure that the poor wore their badges.

From the 1770s onwards the rising population, rising prices and the changing economic organisation of many parishes put an increasing strain upon the Poor Law system. The dual economy of trade and agriculture was being superseded by specialised employment in either one or the other. In south Warwickshire the numbers of villagers with income from sources other than husbandry declined to the point of extinction (Martin 1981). Between 1759 and 1766 a variety of difficulties caused distress in urban and industrial areas. The price of raw materials and the cost of transport of goods rose, but the prices of remuneration for piecework rose less quickly. In 1766 riots were reported in forty-one separate towns and industrial areas in the Midlands (Williams 1976: 256, 298). Further food riots occurred in Birmingham in 1782 when the Wednesbury colliers came to town in threatening mood to insist that the price of malt and flour be reduced. The gentlemen of the association (for the prosecution of felons) paraded and the colliers were sent out of town (Ede 1962: 122). Distress was again acute in the years 1795 to 1800 when drought, bad harvests, severe winters and cold summers led to high prices and food shortages. Grain prices reached unheard of levels and prices in Birmingham market were even higher than the national average.

At Warwick in 1795 a public fund to relieve famine was set up, and in 1800 Lord Warwick provided a soup kitchen where between 1816 and 1817 4,000 persons were issued with beef soup. In 1800 and again in 1816 soup kitchens issued broth in West Bromwich. Further riots broke out in Birmingham in 1795 when a mob attacked the corn mill of James Pickard at Snowhill, Birmingham; the mob was dispersed only after the dragoons had been called in and two rioters killed. The corn mills were again attacked in 1800, Pickards for the second time.

The end of the war again brought great distress and the total amounts collected and disbursed for poor relief rose dramatically. In nine north Warwickshire agricultural parishes about 16–25s. was expended for every person in the parish (Martin 1981). At Burslem £2,125 was spent in 1802 and £7,400 in 1817, at a time when the total population was about 9,000. In most communities distress was at its worst and the poor rate at its peak in the period 1817–20 and the problem persisted throughout the 1820s.

By 1815 rising population and economic difficulties were creating a crisis in local administration and in the Midlands this was exacerbated not only by industrialisation but also by the decline of industry in rural areas. To well intentioned gentlemen, lovers of order and tradition, the growth of the poor rate, the increase of crime, and the frequency of political and economic riots must have appeared a threat to the whole social order. Little wonder that so many of the aristocracy and gentry of the post-war decades thought it neces-sary to support the forces of order, to band together with the like-minded to resist change, and to control radicals and demagogues by means of restrictive legislation.

The numbers of freeholders were rising dramatically with the growth of population and wealth, and the freeholders, with the example of Middlesex before them, were increasingly difficult to persuade. Elections became more and more expensive (they could cost £25,000 and more) and charges of 'corruption' were raised after almost every borough election. The industrial interest was becoming more articulate. Lord Dartmouth and Lord Shelburne associated not only with Lord Anson but also with Josiah Wedgwood of Etruria and Mathew Boulton of Birmingham and corresponded with them on political and commercial policy. Samuel Garbett was developing the art of political lobbying in the industrial interest. The attempt to form a General Chamber of Manufactures to act with government on commercial matters failed, but its proposers did not cease to exercise influence by other means.

In 1774 the Birmingham freeholders allied with Sir Charles Holt to thwart the traditional control of the Marquis of Hertford and the Earl of Aylsford (Money 1977: 158–85) over the Warwickshire county elections. George Granville Leveson Gower was expected to combine the highest office with control of local elections. However, he retired prematurely from politics in 1812 and his son, the second Duke of Sutherland, withdrew ignominiously from a vital Staffordshire election in 1820 when it became obvious that there was substantial opposition from the south Staffordshire ironmasters among others (Wordie 1982: 258–71).

Meanwhile there was a growing demand for change not only in the personnel of the House of Commons but also in the method of its election. It is not clear how much support there was in the Midlands for Wilkes and for the early demands for parliamentary reform. Tokens and medals attest the exist-ence of corresponding societies until 1792 and there were debating societies in the main public houses in Birmingham. However, the mood changed with the outbreak of the French Revolutionary wars and support for radical reforms of Parliament became disloyalty almost amounting to deliberate treason.

Many of the leading midland political families became Tory once more and although individual gentlemen might support the intellectual concept of reform, most of them as members of the House of Lords or the House of

Commons, or as magistrates and local rulers sought to control the voices of protest and to strengthen the arm of the Home Office.

On the other hand some saw constitutional reform as a means to economic recovery and rational government as a means of modifying the ills of society. In the towns leaders emerged who organised the discontented artisans to demand political solutions to their economic grievances. George Edmonds, son of a Baptist minister, gained great support among the Birmingham artisans organising meetings, lectures and petitions. Major Cartwright visited thirty-five midland towns in 1816 addressing reform meetings. In 1821 George Edmonds was arrested under the act forbidding assembly and imprisoned for a year at Warwick, greatly enhancing his status and leadership. Newspapers stamped and unstamped proliferated, and encouraged debate. In 1823 according to the London Gazette the 'lean unwashed artisan' of Birmingham was constantly engaged in discussion of the 'maxims of government and the conduct of their rulers' (Briggs 1949: 18).

Meanwhile Thomas Attwood, banker and ironmaster, was evolving the critique of the currency policies of the government which was eventually to lead him to found and lead the Birmingham Political Union, a union which for a short period brought together middle-class leadership and mass support in a demand for reform of the House of Commons. Political unions were formed between 1829 and 1831 in Coventry, Wolverhampton, Hanley, Stourbridge, Warwick, Kenilworth, Alcester and in almost every town in the Midlands. They gradually gathered into their ranks all the critics of Tory government, radicals, utilitarians, industrialists, bankers, artisans and journalists. Highly organised mass rallies with banners and brass bands, badges and speeches drew in the unemployed and the distressed. Between 1831 and 1832 it seemed that the whole energy of the industrial areas was concentrated upon support for the Whig reform bill. The Midlands saw the passage of the Reform Act in 1832 as a triumph of their organisation and political power. They believed that the artisans of Birmingham and Coventry had put down the power of the Duke of Wellington and the House of Lords. It did not take long to discover that their victory was without substance. The position of the landed classes, though under fire, was still secure (Flick 1978).

Chapter 24

Industry: 1660–1760

By the late seventeenth century more and more midland families were concentrating on the manufacture of articles for wholesale outlets. Pottery, glassmaking, and especially all the metalworking trades depended essentially on the production of a mass of simple and traditional goods. Nevertheless, an increasing emphasis on creating as well as supplying demand encouraged innovation. New materials were introduced, the range of goods was extended, new customers were sought out and the network of trade was extended both spatially and socially. All the midland industries from 1690 onwards, especially in the period from 1720 to 1755, saw a marked diffusion of innovations. The impact was undramatic and gradual, but none the less significant. Moreover, by the 1750s the growth in the scale of many undertakings was leading to innovations in management.

The process of change is clearly evident in the well-documented cases of the metalworkers and the pottery trades, but it was by no means confined to these sectors. Growth and the diffusion of innovation is also perceptible in glassmaking, brewing and even coal mining. The causes of this growth were many and complex, but among the principal factors were the opening up of the West Indies and mainland America, the growth of population and consumer demand in England and in Europe, and the increased availability of raw materials. In addition to the demand for traditional products a new market for 'decencies' was built up both at home and abroad. The small consumer was buying more and cheaper cloths, more buttons and buckles; he had pottery and glass drinking vessels instead of treenware, and his house contained a clock and small ornaments. Midland metalworkers tempted the fancy with more and more new items of domestic and personal adornment, brass candlesticks, snuffers, painted or decorated metal boxes for snuff, cosmetics, playing cards, spectacle frames, watch chains and ornaments and so on.

The trade continued to be organised and led by the commercial capitalists, the wholesale ironmongers. The principal contribution of the ironmongers was extended credit, the ability to manage the long-drawn-out sequence of credit payments, discounts, advances and allowances which

215

enabled the trade to develop in size and in geographical range. They handled a variety of paper instruments of credit – debts recorded on speciality, with and without interest, overt or concealed. They became skilled in manipulating discounts and in the management of the inland Bill of Exchange. The discounting of bills was done to a great extent in London, but also at fairs, especially Bristol Fair, and in the larger market towns such as Lichfield and Stafford. Birmingham was a centre of credit and the mercers and grocers performed an important function in their willingness both to provide bills which could be drawn on London and in cashing bills when small change was needed (Rowlands 1975: 72–5).

The improvements in roads and the ever increasing use of long-distance waggoners enabled all producers to despatch goods far afield. James Sylvester of Birmingham, jeweller, for example, had trade debts in market towns all over England and even in Edinburgh and Aberdeen. He also exported to Europe by making use of the merchanting firms of Cugnoni in London and of Winkleman of Brussels ((U) BRL Warwick Gift).

Manufacturers were able to respond readily to changing demands. Gunmaking, for example, developed very rapidly in the last years of the seventeenth century during the wars of William III. The first government contract for snaphance muskets for the Board of Ordnance was obtained in 1689 and in the following years the Treasury paid out over £1,000 to the

Plate 4.7 The London Road near Burton on Trent in 1743 with pack horses and foot travellers. Hay is being made in the background. Detail from Buck's prospect of Burton on Trent.

Birmingham gunmakers. The trade spread rapidly in the parishes of Wednesbury, Darlaston, Harborne and Dudley. By 1750 the large Birmingham firm of Farmer and Galton were sending 12,000 guns a year to Africa and this was only one of their outlets. Exports were handled by agents in the ports, in Bristol, London and Lancaster as well as Liverpool. The agents secured orders for the stocking of a particular ship, not only with guns but also with nails and as many as forty different types of metalware. The gunmakers then bargained with the workmen, negotiating customary prices and discounts, brought the orders into the warehouses and despatched them to meet the sailing time of the vessel ((U) BRL Galton Mss). The making of the gun was divided between the gun lockmakers, the gunbarrel forgers and the stockmakers. Sometimes the process was further subdivided and the work went to specialist filers, rufflers and finishers; fourteen stages might be needed in the manufacture of a gun.

The making of small fancy goods in metal was known as toymaking, and the earliest reference to the trade in the Midlands occurs in 1710. It spread rapidly in the Midlands and between 1750 and 1760 thirty Birmingham toymakers took between them sixty-eight apprentices. In the 1740s the toy trade was further diversified by the introduction of the enamel box manufacture in Birmingham, Wednesbury and Bilston. In 1759 Sam Garbett and John Taylor, giving evidence to the House of Commons, claimed that 20,000 people were employed in the trade in Birmingham and its neighbourhood. However exaggerated this figure may be, all contemporary observers agreed on the extraordinary growth of both the home and the export trade (Rowlands 1975: 134–69).

Most development took place in areas which had already had a long history of industrial activity, but certain new centres of metalworking became established, notably along the valley of the river Arrow on the Warwickshire–Worcestershire border where needlemaking was introduced. It seems probable that the search for additional water power might well have been part of the reason for this extension. The forge mill at Redditch was converted into a needle scouring mill about 1734 and Ipsley, Hoo and Oversley mills were also adapted for needle scouring shortly afterwards. The area also provided supplies of suitable pebbles for scouring. By 1757 it was claimed that more sewing needles were made in Worcestershire and Warwickshire than in the rest of the kingdom put together (Jones 1978).

Changing market conditions, combined with the shift to more malleable metals, had far-reaching effects on the modes of production. In the first place, the introduction of new tools was encouraged. The stamp, and dies, the turning lathe and the drawbench appear in inventories from 1712 onwards and specialist die sinkers are recorded in the 1740s. The stamps were very simple, being little more than a block of stone in a wooden frame controlled by a rope. The wooden lathes were made by a carpenter and their metal parts by the smith himself. It became common for workmen to have a casting shop and a stamping house as well as an old workshop containing the hearth and bellows (Rowlands 1975: 124–45).

The ironmongers and manufacturers believed that they kept ahead of their competitors only by means of 'the particular arts in Birmingham that foreigners are quite strangers to' and also by the use of 'machines and engines which lessen much the manual labour and enable boys to do man's work'. They were in a perpetual fever of anxiety lest their secrets should become available to competitors, and their anxiety seemed to be justified in 1753 when Michael Alcock, a Birmingham buttonmaker, went to France with eight skilled workmen and, with the support of the French government, undertook to make La Charente the Birmingham of France (Harris 1981).

Agreed price lists existed but 'special' prices were always being discussed in an atmosphere of secrecy and favour. The orders came back in one month in the home trade and six months in the foreign. The merchant charged a fixed commission, and regular customers were allowed six months' credit. In brisk times there was great pressure to get the work done to meet the sailing times of vessels. In slack times goods were stockpiled in order to retain the services of skilled men. Just when pressure was acute key workmen fell sick or decided to go off on a visit. The workmen determined their own hours of work and in any case if they did work over long hours the quality of the work suffered. The more skilled the worker the less control the manufacturer could exercise. Rival manufacturers competed by offering higher prices or by stirring up ill-feeling among the workmen ((U) BRL Galton Mss).

In view of the difficulties it was natural that in some cases there was a move away from the family workshop and a tendency to gather the workmen into one place of work. Such large manufactories were few in number before 1760 (and indeed were *still* few in number in 1830), but they were a significant development for the future. In a large manufactory the workman with special skills, the box painter or die maker, gave all his time to skilled work, simpler jobs were done by boys, or by unskilled men with the help of machines. Overall production was increased, the skilled man earned high piecework wages, and a variety of raw materials could be stocked and controlled.

The function of the manufacturer in these workshops changed. He provided the premises, often an old domestic house, he also provided the stamps, lathes and workbenches, the lighting and heating costs. Instead of riding round the countryside seeking orders he stayed at home supervising production, designing new products and maintaining correspondence. He kept a showroom and welcomed visitors, especially aristocrats and writers, and he spent time and money entertaining visiting merchants. He employed warehouse keepers, clerks and riders to go out to solicit orders, and he sought out and sometimes brought from a distance skilled workmen and designers.

The large workshops did not displace the small. Manufacturers continued to place much work with outworkers and the traditional products continued to be in ever greater demand as the population grew. The domestic shops themselves were not only becoming ever more numerous but they also contained more places of work at the benches, and whereas formerly there used to be two men to a hearth, by 1770 it might be four or even six (Rowlands 1975: 156–69).

The north Staffordshire pottery industry was also responding to the demand for cheaper, more varied and attractive domestic goods. Robert Plot, FRS, described the processes used by the potters at the end of the seventeenth century in great detail. He listed four kinds of clay worked for the body which was made on the wheel and three decorative slips, orange, white and red which produced a glaze of yellow, orange and black when fired. The clay was steeped in water in a pit, beaten on a board, rolled and cut up. It was first moulded by hand and then on a wheel by the potter. In addition to the decoration with slip, Plot refers to the potters using lead glaze and manganese to produce a 'motley colour'. The slip ware pots could be placed directly over the heat. To fire the glazed pots they had to be put in clay containers or saggars (Plot 1686: 122–4).

White clays from Devonshire were imported from the 1720s onwards and many experiments were made with colour. Scratch techniques of decoration, where the underlying colour was revealed by 'scratching the glaze', and sprigging (laying white decoration on coloured backgrounds) were developed in the 1740s, and a fluid lead glaze was in use by 1755. The making of small decorative figures and models was facilitated by the introduction in about 1750 of plaster of Paris moulds, which made possible standardised designs and cheap production of 'runs' of a particular model. The equipment that was used changed little, although various potters made claims to have improved the lathe, the wheel and the flues of the kilns. Some of the larger scale potters maintained contacts in London; others welcomed visitors to the Potteries as potential customers. John Baddeley's firm had an agent in Amsterdam and cargoes of a hundred crates and more were regularly shipped abroad every two months (Mallet 1966 and 1967). Josiah Wedgwood was the fifth generation of his family to be a master potter and he came into an industry which was already extensive, highly capitalised, innovative and international – very different in reality from his own characterisation of it as 'primitive, peasant pottery'. The works were sometimes elaborate; the workshops of a pottery in Shelton which employed ten men in 1720 contained lathes, stamps, mortars and stoves, and models, moulds, boards and stools. In addition to the stock of clay brought from the south by way of Liverpool and Bridgnorth, panned flint, clay and 'greenware' were listed. The whole stock was valued at £100. Twenty-five years later, the schedule of stock at this same pottery included two lathes and appurtenances, a vice, a throwing wheel, a clagger wheel and a separate workshop called the slip house (Rowlands 1967–8: 51).

In about 1700 the Elers brothers introduced fine finishes in imitation of china, and the lathe for better quality ware, but it is evident that a wide range of local potters were already turning their attention to producing goods for the growing home market in 'decencies'. Small decorative figures became popular from about 1700. By 1710 thirty-five potteries were operating in Burslem alone, and a further four at Cobridge, one at Rushton Grange and two at Brownhills. By 1715 seven of the Burslem potworks made stoneware, the most profitable branch of the industry (Weatherill 1971).

A number of important innovations in technique were made at this time. Coal was used in the firing and from the 1660s salt was used to glaze the pots. Finely ground flint was introduced as an important constituent of the earthenware body from about 1710. By 1715 flints were being imported from Lincolnshire, and the stream of the Moddershall Brook in Stone parish was turning the wheels of several flint grinding mills. James Brindley, millwright, was employed to build four mills between 1753 and 1763 (Sherlock 1976: 41–3).

Silk weaving had been established in Coventry in the early-seventeenth century; in the eighteenth century more and more weavers specialised in ribbon weaving, adapting new ideas from France and seeking to tempt the fashion conscious. The trade spread to the surrounding suburbs and nearby coalfield villages. Six of the twenty-four Bedworth men entitled to vote as £10 freeholders were silkmen. Silkmen taking apprentices in Warwickshire included William Villiers, John Dudley, Nathanial Alsopp, Thomas North and Abraham Ellis of Coventry and Joseph Bacon of Nuneaton (Smith & Williams 1975).

The main centre outside Coventry was Leek, which lay on the road between Macclesfield and Congleton, and Derby and the Moorland, and the silk industry developed as a southern outlier of the Macclesfield industry (Wilde 1979: 45–6). In 1740 Dr Pocock could still describe Leek as a town of little trade except the making of thread, buttons and some ribbon (Pocock 1740). However, seventy years before, in 1673, the inventory of John Wood shows that he was a well-established silkman. His shop goods included looms and the wheels worth £4 1s., dyed silk worth £179 1s., buttons worth £100, more silk worth £144, more silk at London £18, more silk for woofing £6 and more silk 'to be changed' [sic] valued at £110. His total debts in trade, good and bad, totalled £356 ((U) LJR Probate John Wood).

Unlike any other midland manufacture the silk trade enjoyed state protection. The import of French silks was prohibited in 1698 and Indian and Chinese silks were banned in 1701. In north Staffordshire and in Coventry the silkmen found trained weavers and supplies of coal for their dye vats. Around Leek water power was also available, but when in 1724 John Lombe set up his water-powered twisting mill twenty miles away at Derby, the Leek silkmen saw it as a threat, not as an opportunity, and in 1734 joined with the Macclesfield, Stockport and Manchester silkmen in petitioning successfully against the renewal of his patent.

The Burton on Trent brewing industry developed rapidly in the eighteenth century, taking advantage of its natural resources and of the opening up of the Trent navigation which gave the town's brewers access to the Baltic and to London markets. By 1700 the town already possessed a small industry that had achieved a national reputation for high-quality products which had the important virtue of carrying well. Burton ale sold in London at 7s. 6d. per dozen bottles. However, the industry of Derby was at this time considerably more important than that of Burton. Nevertheless, the numbers of Burton brewers was growing and at least one London brewer moved to Burton to develop his trade. Coastal trade with London had reached almost 1,000 barrels in 1722 and exports overseas through Hull had been established. In the 1740s a number of the old, small inn brewhouses were converted into large, well-equipped premises and taken in hand by men who established large-scale export business to the Baltic. The Derby trade was declining and among the incomers were several established Derby brewers. Hull exported much more beer than formerly, and it has been estimated that half of its exports may have been brewed in Burton. Benjamin Wilson, who made and exported rope, began to brew and export beer and by 1750 had built up his trade to around 1,000 barrels exported per year with a workforce of thirty men. He dealt with established merchants in Hull and Gainsborough and concentrated on supervising the brewing at his premises in High Street, Burton. By this period Burton had probably some ten to twelve large-scale breweries.

During the late seventeenth century the hatmaking industry spread to the provinces, when the London company which had hitherto exercised a monopoly proved itself unable to supply rising demand at home and overseas. At Burton the opening of the Trent Navigation and the growth of the Baltic trade encouraged a number of local clothiers to take up this new trade, so that by 1720 there were over 20 feltmakers in the town; the industry continued to grow until it reached its peak in about 1770 with about 60 concerns (Owen 1978: 155–61). In 1734 Newcastle had 27 hatmakers and fell mongers and 11 journeymen hatters listed in the town's poll book as voters in the parliamentary election and some of the largest probate inventories were those of the town's feltmakers and hatters. Whereas the feltmakers' premises were usually part of their home, the hatters' workshops were often separate and 9 or 10 journeymen were employed there; Astle's workshop was large enough for 24 men. Here they took the loosely matted felt, transferred it to the moulds, and shaped, baked and varnished the hats. The hats made in the Midlands were the cheap kind made of wool felt, and they ranged from children's hats retailing at 1s. to fashionable hats for men which cost 16s. In addition to wool the feltmakers used rabbit fur and the dyes in their workshops included logwood, redwood, galls and cheen (Rowlands 1967–8: 54–5). The journeymen hatters had a highly organised system of 'tramping' in the summer. Young men would travel from one hatmaking centre to another, sure of a welcome at certain recognised inns and some temporary employment by local hatters. This practice was reflected in the Newcastle parish register by occasional entries of hatters who were also 'strangers' (Giles 1960: 104).

The growth of the metalworking, textile and brewing industries in the

221

Midlands were all contingent upon increasing supplies of raw materials, drawn from an ever widening geographic range of sources.

The Midlands metalworkers consumed a large proportion of the iron manufactured in England, especially that made in the Forest of Dean, Shropshire, north Staffordshire and Cheshire. The supply of iron was organised in the main by great interlocking family partnerships of ironmasters, of which the most notable was that of the Foleys. Thomas Foley of Stourbridge had profited from the opportunities of the Civil War, from investment in the new world, and above all from the twenty-five iron mills he leased with his father Richard Foley of Dudley. By 1660 he was ready to retire to live in gentlemanly ease at Witley. He divided his mills and iron interests between his sons, Paul and Philip. Philip first undertook the management of some of his father's mills at the age of sixteen. The brothers proved to have a genius for business and they combined their holdings in a series of partnerships, whose stock was valued at £68,000 in 1669. In 1672 Thomas, the father, suffered a stroke and from then onwards Paul and Philip built up their organisation, taking into partnership from time to time a few capable shareholders and evolving techniques of accounting and supervision which have been described as the first example of modern business management. They kept daily control in their own hands and those of their principal partner-managers, Henry Glover and later John Wheeler. In 1692 Philip Foley retired to a great house at Stoke Edith in Herefordshire and his brother became Speaker of the House of Commons. The partnership continued and although in 1705 the Foley Stour Valley Works were given up, the Forest of Dean and south Wales works were extended (Schafer 1971: 19–38). The Stour valley works on which the Midlands drew so heavily, passed to new partnerships, and by 1736 the Knight family of Wolverley and Abraham Spooner of Birmingham were dominant. The north Staffordshire works were also reorganised, passing from the Foleys to a partnership which included members of the Hall family. The Staffordshire works were in turn linked with the Cheshire works which were mainly the concern of the Cottons and Halls (Awty 1957: 71).

Not all furnaces, forges and slitting mills were operated by national networks and great partnerships. Families like the Rock family of Brewood and the Downings of Cradley built up and maintained ownership of two or three linked mills for several generations and a number of new ironmasters appeared in the Midlands in the 1740s, among them the Kendalls and the Manders.

Much iron was imported from Sweden and later from Russia and North America. Ironmongers who imported American iron included Homfray of Stourbridge, Seney of Walsall, Molineux of Wolverhampton and the Knight partnership. Russian iron came in mainly through London, but Hull and Gainsborough were the most advantageous ports for Swedish iron.

The midland toy trade could not have expanded as it did without the increased availability of the more malleable metals, especially copper, brass, lead, tin and zinc. Seventeenth-century probate inventories for braziers and coppersmiths contain small quantities of brass but give little indication of where it was obtained. Plot says that the copper came from Sweden. Between 1690 and 1720 the position was transformed by the revival of mining of non-ferrous metals in England and Wales, and by innovations in the techniques of smelting. The midland ironmongers had many family and commercial links with the partners in the brass works of Bristol and the tin works of Wales. Sampson Lloyd, for example, was apprenticed at the Bristol Brassware house, later married Rachel Champion and eventually joined the Walmley company as a partner in 1746 (Lloyd 1975: 131–2).

In north Staffordshire copper and lead mining were revived in 1692 when the Earl of Shrewsbury set up a partnership which included both London and local investors; lead and copper ore were mined at, among other places, Ribden and Swinscoe in Alton parish, at Ilam and at Onecote. The lead seams were leased out in the traditional manner of the Stannaries to free miners, the Earl receiving royalties ((U) SRO Bill Papers). Eleven miles away at Ecton in Wetton parish copper mining was revived by an Ashbourne company and later by the Duke of Devonshire. By 1760 the Ecton copper mine had become one of the largest and most elaborate in England and yielded copper worth £57,000 in eight years from 1760 (Robey and Porter 1972: 2–10). Meanwhile Thomas Patten and Company from Warrington built a brass works at Brookhouses south-west of Cheadle in 1719 and another at Farley in Alton parish in 1734. They produced mainly brasswire using both local copper and copper imported from Cornwall (SRO Bolton Deeds). Both Warrington and Cheadle supplied the midland brassworkers. By 1746 Birmingham had its own brasshouse in Coleshill Street, a large enterprise with nine furnaces producing 300 tons of brass a year. At Wednesbury John Wood also produced brass, using copper from Bristol and calamine from Derbyshire. Other semi-prepared materials which became available in the Midlands in the early-eighteenth century included rolled iron plate from south Wales and from Shropshire, and tinned plate from Shropshire and Worcestershire.

A great range of decorative materials such as gold, silver, dyes, oils, and acids were required in the toy trade and many of these posed special problems of storage and distribution. Specialist suppliers soon made their appearance, especially in Birmingham. Alexander Seaman concentrated on the supply of enameller's colours, Samuel Banner sold gold and silver leaf to the button-makers, Samuel Garbett, a Birmingham brassworker, went into partnership with a Scots chemist to produce sulphuric acid at his works in Steelhouse Lane, and John Bedford imported ivory from Africa through Liverpool.

All the midland industries depended upon readily available supplies of cheap coal, and coalmining was an attractive investment to men of many different conditions and degrees. In the north Staffordshire coalfield landowners who exploited coalmines included Lord Stafford, the Leveson Gowers, Lord Macclesfield (né Parker, a lawyer), Sir John Bowyer and the Egertons.

Plate 4.8 'A Bilston Chap' is the title of this cartoon of the early nineteenth century. His pick and basket suggest a collier, but this is somewhat belied by his clean smock and shining shoes.

Coalmines were also leased by yeomen and potters. When William Bourne of Wolstanton died in 1696 his inventory listed nineteen cows and other farm stock, but also details of the goods at his coalpit, namely, 'coals gotten and standing on the bank £28, two delph ropes, two windbarrels, one byng, one stone tub, turnells, barrels, one delph pick and four corves'. The equipment was valued at only £1 1s. 4d. ((U) LJR Probate William Browne).

The south Staffordshire coalfield was similarly exploited by men drawn from a great variety of backgrounds. In 1701 the four coal works of Edward Ward, Baron of Birmingham, were worth £1,514 a year. Other pits in the area were worked by yeomen and lesser gentry, families such as the Pershouse family of Sedgley and the Gibbons of Ettingshall. Others were held by individual craftsmen and colliers or by partnerships of two or three neighbours ((U) DRO Earl of Dudley Mss).

The Warwickshire coalfield presented greater difficulties of exploitation and the demand locally for coal was not so great. The principal coalmaster in the early eighteenth century was Sir Richard Newdigate of Arbury who inherited the estate in 1665 and embarked upon an ambitious programme of estate development, mining and house building. Between 1700 and 1709 he tried to develop his coalmines on the largest scale. He introduced new devices for test boring and blasting through hard rock, constructed deeper pits, and recruited specialist labour from south Staffordshire. He used water, wind and horse-powered machinery for a wide range of tasks, and he organised and managed a large force of surface and underground workers. Other individuals and partnerships, including both local yeomen and investors from a distance, leased the mines at Coton, Griff, Bedworth, Hawksbury, Nuneaton and Fackley (White 1970: 25–36).

Specialist partnerships of coalmasters began to take short leases of mines in many different areas and exploit them to their utmost. An early example of such a partnership was that of Bate and Tandy, who from 1654 to 1702 leased Coneygre mines from Lord Ward on a succession of three-year leases. Coalmining was a risky and uncertain venture. The choice of site for experimental boring was based on guesswork and local tradition rather than proper information, and even when coal was found there was constant danger that the works might collapse or set on fire. The specialist coalmasters were often men of little capital, running very close to the wind. They competed with each other fiercely, even violently, and sought to make quick profits. One of the most prominent of such partnerships was that of Richard Parrot of Audley and his partner George Sparrow of Wolstanton. They undertook leases of coal and ironstone mines in Audley, Talk, Wolstanton, Darlaston and in Derbyshire and Warwickshire (Rowlands 1968–9: 965).

In the deeper mines men and horses were lowered on an open platform by a windlass and coal was raised in the same way. Larger pits were worked by horse-drawn gins. There was virtually no systematic ventilation, though some crude methods of keeping the air moving by fires or by doors were employed.

The Newdegate mines at Griff had three adjacent pits, each served by a general-purpose shaft to the main seam, which was about 37 yards deep and from this shaft underground roads ran to a deeper part of the mine. Separate drainage shafts were 48 yards in depth.

As mining became deeper, conditions of work deteriorated. The burial registers in coalmining parishes record accidental deaths of men falling down pits, being crushed by falls of coal or being drowned, and at Kingswinford a parish charity of £10 was endowed for the benefit of colliers' widows. Wages are difficult to evaluate since men were employed either on day labourer's wages or in teams paid according to the quantity of coal obtained. It is not clear how or when the 'butty' or 'charter' system was introduced. Before 1750 where men worked in teams, it appears that the leader of the team himself worked at the coal face. In 1751 John Smallman and John Clark of Bilston undertook to get and sell coal for Mr Robins and this agreement was called a charter ((U) WSL Hand Morgan Collection). It may be that the later 'butty' or charter system began about this time but at least until the middle of the eighteenth century the terms and conditions of hiring colliers were exceedingly variable and largely determined by the individuals concerned. A small proprietor planning works at Halmer End in Audley, for example, produced two sets of calculations to consider whether he would profit more by paying for coals got by the dozen, or by making a 'partnership' with the colliers ((U) SRO Aqualate Mss). The Newdigate pits made use of both direct and indirect employment of labour. The underground workers were organised into teams of faceworkers called companies and others called wage men. The former were of higher status and better earnings. The assistants were paid by the day. The Leveson-Gower pits at Meir Heath in north Staffordshire used the same combination. Some of the companies were hired directly by the landowner, others were subcontractors working measured lengths of the seams. Sometimes independent operators hired pits for a short period at an agreed rent. From 1705 onwards Sir Richard Newdegate sent out specialist agents to recruit labour, attracting them by high wages, lodging allowances and bonus payments (White 1970: 31).

As the pits varied from single digs worked by a copyholder in the open fields to elaborate coalworks, the amount of coal produced cannot be estimated. Plot wrote of some pits producing 200 tons of coal yearly, others as much as 5,000 tons (Plot 1686: 127–8). It was sold for the most part in the immediate locality of the pits. In the north of Staffordshire the purchasers were the potters and increasingly the saltmakers of Cheshire and Staffordshire who used 2 tons of coal to every drawing. In the south the coal was consumed by the metalworkers in the workshop forges and in the Stourbridge area by the glasshouses. Coventry coal was sold for domestic and workshop use in the city. Coal from Griff was sold to the brick and tile makers of Nuneaton who used 7 tons of coal to every 16,000 bricks produced, and it was also transported 14 miles to Lutterworth. Some was delivered to Chilvers Coton Workhouse. Coal was occasionally sold in the seventeenth century in Oxford, Leicester and

Northamptonshire, but it was the local sale which was important. Wednesbury and Hawksbury coals sold in Coventry in the summer of 1684 for 7½–8*d.* a hundredweight, but coal from Bedworth three miles further away than Hawksbury cost 10–12*d.* a hundredweight and more in the winter. Coventry market was only profitable to the Staffordshire coal owners if they could charge 12–14*d.* a hundredweight (White 1970: 8–9).

For some years a series of attempts had been made to use steam power for drainage. Thomas Savery had patented a steam engine in 1698 and one of his engines was reputed to have been erected at Darlaston in about 1706. Thomas Newcomen of Devon, ironmonger, developed an engine on an alternative principle in the south-west of England. He had family links with the Baptist congregations of Bromsgrove and of Netherton, Dudley, though how he came to be employed by the trustees of the seven-year old Lord Ward remains obscure. It is certain, however, that he erected the first successful steam engine at Coneygre near Dudley in 1711. The cylinder was 7 to 10 ft long, 20 in in diameter and the pump drew 10 gallons at a stroke and made 12 strokes per minute. It could do work equivalent to the power of 5½ horses (Rolt and Allen 1977: 24–44). The engine aroused great interest and in 1713 the partnership of Sparrow and Parrot, now joined by Richard Parrot's son, Stonier, agreed with Thomas Newcomen for the erection of an engine at Griff. In the following year the ownership of Newcomen's patent had passed to a board of London businessmen known as the proprietors of the patent, who agreed to allow Parrot and Sparrow to take over the engine at Griff and to erect engines at other mines. By 1733 when the patent expired they had been concerned in varying degrees with at least 14 engines, though many of their projects were not brought to completion (Rowlands 1968–9: 49–67).

Meanwhile, other coalmasters in the Midlands were erecting Newcomen engines and 20 were at work by 1733 out of a total for England and Wales of 110. After the expiry of the patent the numbers of engines in the south Staffordshire and Warwickshire coalfields continued to increase (Rolt and Allen 1977: 61–89). Development was slower in north Staffordshire but in 1756 James Brindley built an engine at Great Fenton for Thomas Broad for £700. Despite the introduction of steam pumping, the difficulties of extraction, especially in Warwickshire, were still very great. Between 1730 and 1744 the three largest collieries in Warwickshire all ceased working. The introduction of the Newcomen draining engine was a major portent of technological innovation but exploitation on all but the most accessible seams required great capital investment, greater than the available markets could always justify. The greatest need was not for power but for a means of transporting coal cheaply and easily to wider markets (Grant 1982: 329).

Chapter 25

Transport by land and water

In the course of the eighteenth century every possible means of carriage was exploited to the utmost and carrying employed huge numbers of the population full-time and part-time. Burslem supported an exceptional number of carriers even in the 1660s. Seven who left probate inventories between 1662 and 1720 were described as yeomen or husbandmen, but the number of their horses varied from four to ten. Professional waggoners were found in all midland towns and many large villages by the early-eighteenth century, some with their own warehouses. Ralph Leigh, for instance, earned 10–12d. to go for coals two or three times a day to Norton; his six horses each carried 2½ hundredweight of coal on its back. He also carried crates of pottery to Winsford and brought back ball clay from Cornwall. Every horse had a crate on a pack saddle, and a small pannier on each side which held two to three balls of clay each weighing 60–70 lbs. In later years Leigh had a cart and went to Winsford with his crates, and brought back a ton of Chester clay to Burslem. He also made longer journeys and took four days to take crates of pottery to Bridgnorth (35 miles); on other occasions he took crates of pottery to Willington, Derbyshire (16 miles) and returned with flints, plaster and stone. He had occasionally been as far as Exeter and Liverpool, and also brought back goods for the mercers, grocers and apothecaries (Shaw 1829: 148–9).

Grain and malt were brought into the industrial parishes and sold at the weekly markets and the number of badgers and corn carriers licensed by quarter-sessions increased. Foodstuffs were carried out of the Midlands to London and to the ports of Bristol, King's Lynn and Hull. Burton had seven regular carriers and Ralph Hancock specialised in taking ale and beer from Stone to London. Cheese, another midland commodity much in demand in London, was mostly transported by land. The waggoners and carriers brought back from London, from the ports, and from all over England a wide range of cloth, luxury goods, imported spices and foodstuffs to stock the retail shops or to deliver directly to the gentry and farmers. The smaller items were distributed by pedlars and local chapmen who travelled round the villages and farmhouses.

228

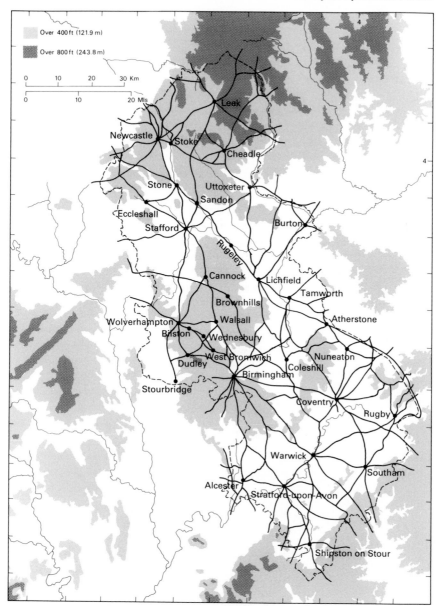

Figure 4.1 Turnpike roads in Staffordshire and Warwickshire in the eighteenth century (based on Slater 1981: 84; and Greenslade and Stuart 1965: 48)

An important group among the regular pedlars and chapmen were the 'scotchmen' or, as they preferred to be called, 'North British chapmen' who sold Manchester and Scotch cloth and haberdashery in the market towns and industrial areas. They had regular routes, recognised divisions and officials and some degree of supportive organisation among themselves.

Many foot bridges were converted to waggon bridges and the access to them raised or lowered and the surfaces gravelled in the late-seventeenth century and local justices became interested in enforcing legislation aimed at reducing wear and tear on the road and bridge surfaces. From the 1720s onwards turnpike trusts were formed in the Midlands. They were of course only concerned with specified sections of the most used roads and county justices and the surveyors of highways remained responsible for all other routes.

The first turnpike in Staffordshire was established in 1714 to improve the main London to Chester road from Darlaston-by-Stone to Talk in north-west Staffordshire. In 1729 the whole Staffordshire section of the road was turnpiked, together with the Lichfield to Burton road (Owen 1978: 20–1). Similarly in Warwickshire the early turnpikes were on the main roads which were part of the national network. The road from Dunchurch to Meriden through Coventry was turnpiked in 1723, and the Birmingham to Banbury road through Warwick and the Birmingham to Oxford road through Stratford were improved soon afterwards. The Birmingham to Bristol and the

Plate 4.9 A Toll House on the Alcester to Worcester turnpike road.

Birmingham to Holyhead roads were also turnpiked by 1730. Then after a lull of twenty years, turnpike activity was renewed between 1750 and 1770 and again between 1800 and 1820. During this last phase many cross routes and extensions of existing stretches were put into the care of turnpike trusts. The difficult high ground in the north-east was tackled in 1762 when a trust took over the Macclesfield–Leek–Ashbourne road. Many turnpike trusts were created for comparatively small stretches of road in the south Staffordshire coalfield and the Potteries. The extension of the turnpike road to the six towns did much to make the Potteries more independent of Newcastle but nevertheless Newcastle remained in its own right an important coaching town with twenty-nine daily coaches in 1830.

The river Avon was made navigable as far as Stratford on Avon and from the 1660s coal was brought upstream from Bristol and malt and other agricultural products went downstream. The Stour was improved as far as Stourbridge and used by coalmasters and ironmasters.

By 1690 the river Trent had been made navigable inland as far as Wilden Ferry, and this provided an additional outlet for midland goods, especially cheese for London. After some difficulties the navigation was extended further upstream to Burton, and by 1720 was providing a vital link between the Midlands and both the Channel and the Baltic. It was of course of major benefit to the brewers of Burton ales, but some of the most important Birmingham exporters sent metalware to Europe and the Baltic by this route. Raw materials came down the Trent into the Midlands, including flints for the potters, iron from Sweden and Russia, and much Baltic timber, hemp and tar for the builders.

The widespread trade of the Midlands could never have been sustained without an adequate postal system. The origins of the service go back to the reign of Henry VIII. The main post route through the Midlands went from London through Daventry, Coventry, Coleshill, Lichfield, Stone and Newcastle under Lyme to Holyhead. Along the route the masters of the posts kept horses in readiness and passed on the royal letters. In the early-seventeenth century more private and commercial mail was carried and additional routes and posts were set up.

By the end of the seventeenth century, Birmingham had three posts a week to London and regular arrangements were made for these posts to connect with the sailing of mailboats to France on Mondays, Holland on Thursdays and Flanders on Fridays. The service was essential for the rapidly growing commerce of the region and the post included merchants' letters, accounts and invoices, bills of exchange, bills of lading, letters giving or soliciting orders, letters of complaint and letters arranging for buyer and seller to meet ((U) GPO Peover Mss). From 1696 a much more complex and useful network of postal routes and cross routes was developed and by 1746 Birmingham had postal departures six days a week. All mail was carried by riders who were required to travel at six miles per hour on the main roads.

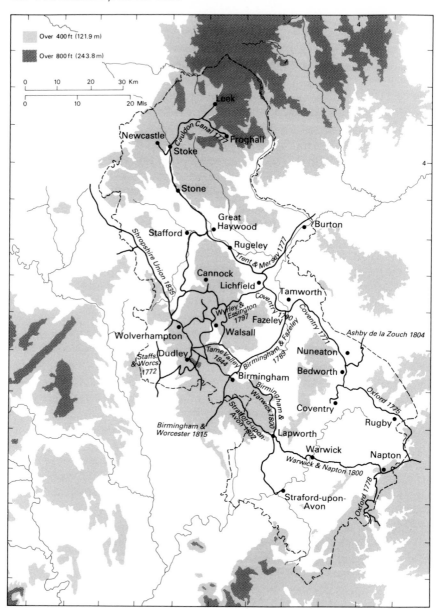

Figure 4.2 Canals in Staffordshire and Warwickshire, 1768–1830 (based on Greenslade and Stuart 1965: 48; and Slater 1981: 96)

For certain categories of goods water transport was evidently more convenient than land transport, especially for large quantities of heavy, loose materials such as salt, coal, clay, sand, flints, grain, lime, gravel and stone, and above all coal. On the coalfields the coalmasters were already constructing stretches of canal in the early-eighteenth century and in 1717 Thomas Congreve of Penkridge produced a detailed plan for artificial waterways across central Staffordshire, linking the rivers of Derbyshire, Staffordshire and Lancashire to provide transport for coal, ironstone, timber and fullers earth. However, the real problem was not the construction of the waterway but access to the land rights along the proposed routes. The early canals, Newdegate's at Arbury and John Wood's at Wednesbury for example, were built on the land belonging to the coalmaster. The third Duke of Bridgewater's canal from Worsley to Manchester was financed by the Duke himself, but pointed the way to securing compulsory purchase rights by private Acts of Parliament (Richards 1973, 42–3).

His example was quickly followed in the Midlands and three canals were commenced almost simultaneously in 1766. The Birmingham to Wednesbury canal was the first to be completed. It was only 22 miles long and although there were difficulties caused by the gradient required, these were small compared with the building of 93 miles of waterway and the Harecastle Tunnel for the Trent and Mersey Canal, which was started in the same year. The Birmingham Canal was open to traffic in 1772, the Trent and Mersey not until 1778. The third canal, the Staffordshire and Worcestershire, presented less difficulties and by 1772 forty-six miles of canal had improved access to the river Severn and had linked the Trent and Mersey at Great Haywood.

The sheer size of such undertakings forced committees to raise capital through publicly advertised shares, sharing risks and profits very widely. Lobbying was required to secure Acts of Parliament and these had to be worded to the best advantage of the promoters. They needed to be accountable in the handling of money and in meeting the professed objectives. They became adept at advertising, and the manner of presenting projects to minimise opposition and maximise support. Industrialists, engineers and local banks worked together, plans and estimates proliferated, and the opposition was compensated or persuaded.

The midland canals were immediately profitable to the share-holders. The price of coal fell dramatically. Whereas carrying coal from Birmingham to Liverpool had formerly cost £5 per ton, now it cost only £1 5s. per ton. In general, carriage on the Birmingham canal cost only 2e. 6d. a ton per 10 miles for perishable goods and even less for goods such as roadstone, lime and manure. Birmingham goods could be taken in bulk to London in four days, and midland manufacturers were quick to take advantage. Soon the Birmingham canal was the busiest in the kingdom with 300 tons of goods going daily to London, while by 1798 a hundred boats a day went over Smethwick Summit, carrying 20 tons of coal on every journey. By 1838 the Birmingham canal carried over 3 million gross tonnage per year and the bulk of this was coal (Broadbridge 1974). The Trent and Mersey carried over a million tons of local pottery and raw materials. So great was the traffic that delays and hold-ups occurred, particularly at the Summit Locks near West Bromwich and through the Dudley and Harecastle legging tunnels (SHC 1934 (I): 101–15).

Competition for canal-side industrial sites had started even before the canals were completed and by 1798 1,500 collieries and ironworks in the Black Country were linked with canals. In the Potteries new communities of works and houses sprang up alongside the Trent and Mersey at Longport and Etruria. In rural areas too industries were sited along the routes of the canals. In north-west Staffordshire the Froghall brass and copper works were built beside the Uttoxeter canal and ironstone quarries used the Caldon Canal into the Churnett valley. Stone quarries, lime works and cement works were opened near the canals at Stockton, Napton and above all at Rugby; even Warwick developed an industrial suburb, as a woollen mill, iron foundry, a hatmaking works, a brickworks, and a silk works were all established at the canal wharfs (Ardafyio 1974).

At Burton on Trent, the Trent and Mersey canal joined the Trent river navigation, thus making possible a great expansion of road and canal services without any fundamental change in the system. Prime barley could be brought from eastern England and hops from Kent and Worcestershire. The main export trade in ale shifted from the Baltic and the connection with London thus became more and more important as Bass, Worthington and Alsopp laid the foundations of the trade with Calcutta (Owen 1978: 18–20).

Canal carriage soon became as important a form of employment as road transport. Pickfords added water carriage to existing land carriage services, and soon had wharfs in all principal centres, but how many lesser firms followed their example is not yet clear.

The canals became important customers for large cast-iron bridges, lock gates and gear, boats and boat fittings, and pumping engines to maintain the water supply. Once they were built, however, canals required comparatively few permanent officials. Engineers earned £400, the chief clerk at a central office and the 'walking surveyors' earned £200 to £300 a year, and their assistants £70 to £100. Lock-keepers, night watchmen, loaders and wharfingers earned about 10s. a week (Broadbridge 1974).

The next period of rapid development was between 1790 and 1800 when the length of waterway was nearly doubled in the Midlands. The most important new canals during this period were the Birmingham and Fazeley Canal linking the industrial north-west of Warwickshire with the Oxford Canal and London, and the Warwick and Napton Canal which also joined the Oxford Canal further south, passing through Lapworth and Warwick.

By 1820 the canals had had some fifty years of intensive use and the problems caused by delays, curving and twisting lines and old-fashioned locks were becoming acute. From 1824 to 1829 Thomas Telford was engaged by both the Birmingham and the Trent and Mersey companies to overhaul and improve their canal navigations. He did so in a grand manner, widening canals, making new straight cuts wherever possible to replace the old winding lines, building a new straight tunnel at Harecastle and achieving wonders in the organisation and management of large-scale constructions. Telford was also largely responsible for the construction of the Macclesfield canal in the north of Staffordshire and the Birmingham and Liverpool junction canal (later known as the Shropshire Union) which provided the industrial districts with a shorter and less congested route to the port of Liverpool and north Wales. Meanwhile, in the industrial areas, innumerable small access canals were built to link factories and collieries with the main routes (Hadfield 1966).

By 1830 the canals themselves were increasingly regarded as insufficient and the potential of steam-driven locomotion by railways was already being discussed, especially in the Trent valley and in south Warwickshire. However, the canals, like the roads before them, were not declining in importance, rather they had assisted in making possible a rate of economic growth which was now outstripping their fullest capacity. While their greatest significance was undoubtedly economic, they also left permanent marks on the landscape and the pattern of settlement. Their offices and warehouses were often gracious and dignified buildings, and land near wharfs attracted housing development as well as commercial buildings.

Meanwhile road services continued to be extended. In 1767 fifty-five different carriers advertised at least weekly services in Birmingham and between them they covered all the main overland routes from the town. The wagons set out to regular timetables from seventeen of Birmingham's inns, including the George in Digbeth, the Red Lion in Digbeth and the White Hart.

All this activity was in aggregate a good deal more important to the economy of the town than the weekly departure of Birmingham's five stage coaches from the Swan and the Dolphin to London, Bristol and Worcester. The Royal Mail was carried by coach from 1784. Businessmen still rode long distances on horseback – indeed commercial travellers were called riders, and new large works commonly had stables built for the owner's and manager's horses. In Birmingham a town service of hackney carriages was provided by 1820.

Travellers were assisted by a growing volume of printed maps, guides and trade directories aimed mainly at merchants, riders and potential customers for local products. They were published from 1770 onwards for virtually every town and industrial district and by 1830 county directories such as *Wests* for Warwickshire were also beginning to appear. Such publications indicate a growing mobility and accessibility to strangers. It was only in the small villages and industrial hamlets that strangers were still greeted with scorn and derision as alien beings.

Chapter 26

The Industrial Revolution and the Midlands: 1760–1830

Between 1760 and 1830, the Midlands experienced both revolutionary change and a high degree of continuity in the organisation of production. Among the significant contributions which the Midlands made to the Industrial Revolution as a whole was the new development, application and diffusion of steam power, either to supplement the existing resources of wind and water power or as a means of using power in locations where there was no natural power available. By the 1760s the Newcomen engine had been applied to a variety of enterprises as well as draining mines, and there was much experimental work in progress. In 1769 in Scotland James Watt patented the single-action steam engine, and in 1775 entered into partnership with Matthew Boulton, the Birmingham toymaker, to develop and market engines under the patent. In 1783 James Watt patented a rotative engine which greatly increased the range of functions to which steam power could be applied, and by 1795 the partnership had erected 143 reciprocating and 139 rotative engines for use in a wide range of industries throughout Britain and a further 16 for use abroad. On the expiry of the patent they built a carefully planned foundry at Soho near the toy manufactory, and placed it under the charge of their sons, M. R. Boulton and James Watt. Even under patent, the partnership had many rivals and imitators and the number of engines emanating from the Midlands must have been considerably greater than those documented by the Boulton and Watt partnership (Tann 1978a: 42–8).

In the Midlands steam power was put to work in blast furnaces and in textile mills and in some other large works, but many of the midland manufactures had no use for such a large measure of power which could not easily be turned on and off. For the majority of processes and in many works the traditional power of wind, water, man and animals continued to be used not only because they were cheaper but also because they were more appropriate and efficient in the particular context.

In the Midlands, as in the country at large, the most rapid and far-reaching changes were in the iron and textile industries. In little more than thirty years charcoal iron smelting was replaced by coke smelting, steam power replaced water power for producing the blast, and new techniques of refining were introduced to convert pig into malleable iron. At the same time the industry moved to the coalfields and output and diversification increased dramatically.

The first Midlands furnace to use coke which can be dated precisely was that of Partridge Nest at Springwood, north of Chesterton, in 1768–9. This disputes the honours with the establishment about the same time of Wilkinson's coke-fired furnace at Bradley, Bilston. Neither site had sufficient water power for bellows and the inference must be that in both cases a Newcomen pumping engine was used to create an artificial fall of water to move the bellows wheel.

By 1788 Staffordshire had six coke furnaces and three more were being erected, five on the south Staffordshire coalfield, and the sixth at Apedale in north Staffordshire (VCH Staffs II: 133), which was founded by the Parker family from Tipton (Lead 1977: 10).

The Napoleonic wars proved a great stimulus to the iron industry and by 1805 there were 31 Staffordshire furnaces producing 49,460 tons of pig iron a year, about one-fifth of the total production of England and Wales. Expansion continued until the end of the war when 55 furnaces were producing 115,000 tons. By then the newer blast furnaces were making use of double-acting steam engines for blast and also for hoisting the filling to the top of the furnace (Gale 1966: 37–56).

The coke-smelted pig iron required more refining than charcoal iron to eliminate silicone, manganese and carbon, and new techniques were required for the further processing of the pig. At Wednesbury John and Charles Wood carried on the family tradition of enterprise and innovation and took out patents for converting coke pig into malleable iron in 1761 and 1763, and analysis of slag at one of their forges, namely, Little Aston, has shown that they were successfully carrying on the process there (Morton 1973). At Coalbrookdale in Shropshire, Thomas and George Cranage established their process in 1766, but in Staffordshire five years later Jesson and Wright at Wednesbury took out a patent for an alternative method known as 'potting and stamping' and although it was very laborious the method was adopted by other Black Country firms. Meanwhile, Onions at Merthyr Tydfil and Cort at Ketley, were perfecting puddling and rolling methods using a reverberatory furnace, and soon made the old charcoal iron chafery and finery obsolete (Morton 1967: 723–5). Joseph Hall of Tipton introduced an alternative method of puddling, which became the principal method for high grade irons in the Black Country (Morton 1967: 723–5).

There was a dramatic development of the foundry industry, to meet a great demand for heavy castings for iron canal bridges, road bridges and for cylinders for steam engines. The Boulton and Watt foundry at Soho, the Eagle

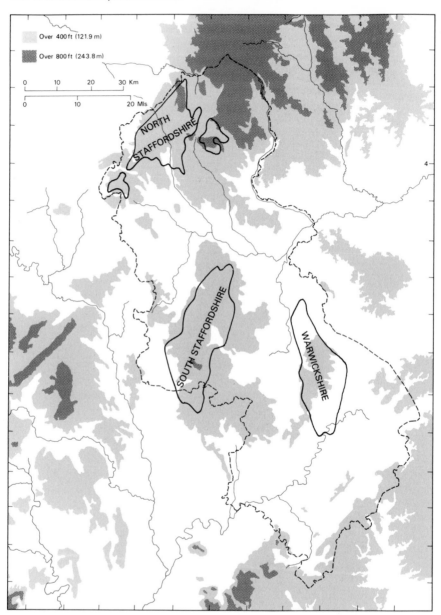

Figure 4.3 Midland coalfields

Foundry at Birmingham and the Horsley iron company at Tipton specialised in sophisticated heavy castings. Meanwhile cheap malleable iron was being introduced to take the place of brass for all kinds of small metal containers or hollow-ware. Kettles, pots and pans were cast, annealed, turned on steam driven lathes and tinned; handles and decorations were added by hand and goods sold in vast numbers to the home and overseas market. Izons and Kenricks established canalside firms at West Bromwich and were both soon selling hollow-ware to the value of £2,000 a year. A whole range of new uses for cast iron were developed, cast-iron hinges, cast-iron ploughshares, kitchen grates, ovens, chapes, nails and window frames. Iron was developed for building construction by 1820, and even grave slabs and church decorations were made of iron (Timmins 1865: 103–9).

Any one of these stages of iron processing could be established as a separate unit, but by 1830 about 50 integrated works combined coalmines, ironmines, coking, furnaces, refineries, puddling furnaces (10–12 to each blast furnace), rolling mills, slitting mills, forging shops, steam engines, stores and blacksmith's shops. In addition 95 firms rolled and slit 2,160,000 tons of malleable iron per annum at 2,100 puddling furnaces. Such works poured forth smoke and fumes which transformed the landscape and darkened the light of the day and illuminated the darkness of the night (Timmins 1865: 54–77).

The depression at the end of the Napoleonic wars caught some of the ironmasters unprepared and caused a number of spectacular bankruptcies. The leaders who survived strengthened their position and continued to increase output. The introduction of hot blast, the gradual adaptation and improvement of the size and shape of furnaces, greater use of steam lifting machinery and steam hammers all made possible the handling of larger quantities, bigger structures and the continued growth of output, but the real transformation of the industry had already taken place.

The revolution in the textile industry also made itself felt in the west Midlands. By 1839 fifteen textile factories were operating in Staffordshire and sixteen in Warwickshire, including cotton, woollen and silk mills. These mills were for the most part founded as an extension of the Lancashire and Yorkshire industries, the outermost ripples from the high tide of the northern flood or as suppliers of the Leicestershire hosiery trades. They were established as the search for suitable water power extended further and further afield. Richard Arkwright built an early cotton mill at Rocester in 1781–2 near the river Dove and by 1815 it had 133 carding machines and 7,151 spindles (Sherlock 1976: 57–9). The earliest cotton mill in the Midlands was established by Robert Peel. After thirty years in the cotton trade he was driven out of Lancashire when his efforts to concentrate and mechanise the various processes of cotton aroused the opposition of domestic workers. Peel moved to Burton where he leased two large houses in Horninglow Street. The town was already linked by a waterway to Liverpool, whence he obtained his raw cotton, while the east midland hosiery district lay conveniently along the Trent. Three cotton spinning mills were set up on the sites of old fulling mills. In 1792 Peel returned to Manchester, leaving the enterprises in the hands of his sons. His seventh son, John, eventually became the main manager of the mills for twenty years. His third son, Robert, became the proprietor of profitable cotton spinning and bleaching mills at Fazeley and Bonehill in 1795 and calico printing works at Tamworth in 1791. He acquired the Thynne estates around Tamworth, lived at Drayton Manor, represented Tamworth in Parliament from 1790 and became a partner in several local banks. By the early-nineteenth century, Peel, Yates and Company had become one of the largest industrial concerns in the country, employing 15,000 workers (Owen 1978: 127).

At Cheadle in 1747 J. and N. Philips installed Dutch swivel looms at Tean Hall for the manufacture of tape and rented out looms and loom sheds to the country people. By 1811 they had 129 looms at Cheadle, 217 at Tean, 40 at Kingsley, 8 at Draycott and a further 35 which they rented out. Anything between 1 and 10 looms were lent out to particular weavers and in the phraseology of the day the looms 'employed' 2,000–3,000 people. This probably means that 400 families were in some way dependent upon them. Be that as it may, they claimed to be the largest tape manufactory in Europe. They used brown yarn imported from the Baltic and from Ireland and this was bleached at Teanford by a process involving the purchase of large quantities of milk from the local dairy farmers. In 1824 450 looms were collected together at Cheadle and Tean mills and steam power was introduced. The estimated cost of the building was £6,400 with a further £2,000 for mill gearing. The steam engine and its engine house would, it was estimated, cost £3,600 (Sherlock 1976: 61–6).

The few wool and worsted spinning factories in Staffordshire, Warwickshire and north Worcestershire were outliers of the main industry. William and John Parkes, bankers, and John Brookhouse, engine builder, opened a wool spinning mill at Saltisford, Warwick, in 1797. They installed a 30 hp Boulton and Watt engine and brought the coal in by canal at 2s. 9d. a ton. They employed 500–1,000 hands and by 1823 were selling 4,800 lbs of yarn a week to the Leicestershire hosiery trade and to the Kidderminster carpet manufacturers.

Between 1790 and 1815 cotton and wool spinning and weaving was a significant employer of labour in the Midlands, especially in the valley of the Trent, but after 1815 the midland mills rapidly lost ground to other districts and most of them were converted to other uses.

The well-established silk industries of north Staffordshire and Coventry reacted more slowly to the option of technical innovation. Between 1750 and 1825 silk thread was produced in Leek in the shed or shade. The threads were hooked to the circumference of a large gate or wheel and then passed round the 'cross' at the opposite end of a long, narrow building. Boys (known as Staffordshire trotters) ran to and fro carrying the bobbins as they went. The distance between gate and cross was about 30 yards, a roll was complete after 36 journeys and 12 rolls were made in a day. Thus the boys ran 15–16 miles a day. Silk weaving on the other hand was carried on in the upper rooms of domestic houses in specially built workshops with large windows which ran the width of two adjoining homes, and which had separate access by an outside stair. Here the weavers produced ribbons, ferrets, sewing silk and buttons. There were perhaps 80 single hand ribbon weavers by 1818 and about 200 Dutch engine looms. The principal suppliers of raw silk and purchasers of the final product were merchants from Macclesfield only 13 miles away. Transport between the two centres was improved when the road was turnpiked in 1762 and the canal was opened in 1797; the prohibition of the import of foreign silk in 1768 proved a real encouragement to home industry.

In Coventry, Bedworth, Nuneaton and in the surrounding villages, ribbon weaving had become the most important trade by 1770. The weavers produced plain ribbons on Dutch engine looms and on single looms and they also elaborated a variety of fancy weaves with 'purled' and embossed edges.

The leading silk merchants distributed ready-made yarn and orders to the undertakers or middle men who employed the weavers. The undertakers provided shop room, looms, materials, winders and throwers and quills and the weavers worked in their shops or in their own homes. They employed apprentices on the traditional seven-year term, taking them into their families. However, a system of half-pay apprenticeship had been introduced in this as in other trades, in which the apprentices lived out and paid for their own maintenance, many of them girls aged 11–18. Undertakers also employed journeymen as and when required. By 1818 9,412 persons were employed in the Coventry silk trade, of whom 5,054 were men and 4,358 were women. Women were employed on the plainer work in their own homes in the villages using the single looms, whereas the Dutch engine looms, which enabled 5–28 ribbons to be woven at once, were all used by men and were concentrated in the city. All work was piecework and printed price lists were issued. In 1816 91 masters worked in Coventry, 6 in Nuneaton, 2 in Bedworth and 1 in Coleshill. In the post-war period the small masters found themselves faced with competition from the large silk brokers in London, who attempted to employ the weavers directly and to set up work places with large numbers of hand looms. However, the small masters had the support of the city council and were able to remain competitive. The Jacquard looms were introduced about 1820. There were 5 in Coventry in 1823 and 650 by 1831.

The pottery industry has often been studied as the prime example of revolutionising methods of production, of management and of the introduction of factory discipline. This picture needs to be modified in the light of two considerations. In the first place, as we have seen, the pottery industry before 1760 was emphatically not as described on Wedgwood's tombstone, 'a rude and inconsiderable manufacture'. Secondly, most of our knowledge of the industry is derived from the exceptionally well documented works at Etruria and from Wedgwood's own presentation of his work as innovative and revolutionary. In fact there was much continuity, and development continued along lines already laid down. Baddeley introduced transfer printing in 1775 and copper plates, steel engravings and lithography were in widespread use to prepare decorations. Booth introduced fluid glazes and an ever wider range of colours and finishes were used. Fine china was successfully and commercially produced from 1781 by the New Hall Porcelain Company under the Cookworth/Champion patent using kaolin. Spode began making bone china in 1794. A wider range of clays were used; south-west Cornwall became the major supplier, but clay was also imported from America and Europe. The kilns remained essentially the same, while ware continued to be pressed by hand and turned on lathes. Water and wind power was applied to the grinding of flint from about 1775 and John Turner at Lane End introduced a Newcomen engine to pump water over a water wheel in 1775 while Spode had a similar arrangement at Stoke. Wedgwood ordered his first Boulton and Watt engine in 1782 and used it to drive a clay mill and a colour-grinding mill, and Spode and Minton used steam power for grinding (Thomas 1971: 52).

Steam power was little used in the Potteries except for grinding flint and colours. A steam-powered machine called a jigger was introduced in the early-nineteenth century to press ware and the possibility of turning the thrower's wheel and the turner's wheel by power was certainly known, but in the days of an abundant supply of cheap child labour diffusion was slow, and most of the work was still carried out by hand. By 1829 the Potteries had only

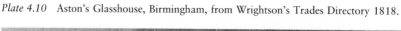

Plate 4.10 Aston's Glasshouse, Birmingham, from Wrightson's Trades Directory 1818.

seven large-scale integrated works and about 120 small works, and in these there had been little change in techniques, location or layout (Lamb 1977: 50–3).

In the glass industry the main changes were in the extension of the industry to new locations and in the development by some firms of new products. It is thought probable that the glass cone was introduced into the Midlands in the 1750s. The older glasshouses had an overall roof to reduce heat loss, but the cone provided not only protection from the weather but also a chimney to carry off waste gases. Up to ten or twelve pots, each with their teams of workmen, were arranged in a circle in the centre of the kiln.

Separate hearths were also required for pre-heating the pots in the pot arch, for reheating the glass during the working, and for annealing. This structure did not represent any major technological advance upon the older types of furnaces, but did require the investment of much more capital, justified by the expectation of expanding demand (Sherlock 1976: 25–40). Glass furnaces became larger and were capable of producing the higher temperatures required for the production of flint glass. By 1796 the Stour valley had 8 firms with 11 houses and 65 pots. Between them they employed 520 men. Far more people were employed in an area in clothmaking and in metalworking.

The numbers of glassworks in the Stour valley remained constant, but many new glasshouses were built beside the canals in places where cheap coal was available. These houses often specialised in the newer products. By 1797 Dudley had 3 firms with 5 houses and 49 pots between them. In Birmingham a Jewish immigrant, Meyer Oppenheimer, set up a works for the manufacture of a patent red glass in Snow Hill. By 1808 the Birmingham glassmakers included Hughes, who produced cut glass, and Oslers, who made trinkets, chandeliers and toys, and monopolised the production of glass eyes for dolls and humans with an output of many millions of eyes per year. Five other large firms operated in the town and another at Aston, the huge concern of Jones, Smart and Company, who made glass in a three-storey building lit by gas. The firm of Thomas Shutt and Partners, established in 1814 at Smethwick beside the Birmingham Canal, remained undistinguished until taken over by Chance Brothers in 1828, who built up a huge manufacture of sheet, optical and plate glass. They paid more duty than all the Birmingham firms in 1832 and the Birmingham firms in their turn paid more than the Stourbridge firms (Timmins 1866: 147–53).

The chemical industry was completely new. In 1741 Samuel Garbett and James Roebuck had established the large-scale manufacture of sulphuric acid in Birmingham for the brass workers. In 1773 James Keir, a Scottish scientist, established works at Tipton, supplying alkali, potash, soda soap and red lead to the glass industry. In Wolverhampton the Mander family developed the manufacture of chemicals and dyes mainly for the japanning industry. In every case scientific enquiry was consciously linked with the needs of industry. The traditional sources of chemicals, human, animal and vegetable, could no longer supply the growing manufactures, although they continued to be exploited alongside the newer sources of supply. These chemical works were laid out from the beginning to produce large quantities and the owners and the workers all had to learn new techniques and processes.

In the early 1760s three or four large-scale toy manufactories were already established in Birmingham; by far the best documented was the Boulton and Fothergill Manufactory at Soho. Matthew Boulton had learned his trade and built up his connections in the Snow Hill works of his father, but he acquired considerable capital through marriages and inheritance. He bought a site in the south of Handsworth parish, adjoining the turnpike road with a water mill on the Hockley Brook. The Soho works was innovative in that it was purpose-built, though the layout was reminiscent of older patterns with workshops around courtyards. In the works the traditional stamp, press and lathe were used by the workers, some of whom lived on the site, but most of whom came in by the day. Boulton frequently assured his customers that the work was all done on his premises and under his supervision, but in fact he continued to contract with independent workshops, especially when under pressure to deliver. A water-powered rolling mill and eventually a small steam engine were introduced as the range of products was extended. Boulton's innovations in the toy trade lay mainly in his vigorous development of new products, marketing techniques and extension of the overseas trade. He had many very active competitors and in order to secure orders he had constantly to produce new goods, create as well as follow fashion, and meet orders as quickly as possible to forestall change in taste. He aimed both at the largest possible market for cheap goods and at introducing new and elaborate fashionware, silver and ormolu for example. He placed great emphasis on advertising through the patronage of royalty, ambassadors and the wealthy and fashionable, through newspapers, displays and exhibitions of ware and through advertising 'stunts' (Robinson 1965–6). In spite of his enormous energy and creativity the manufactory did not make large profits and the original capital investment in the works proved a burden on the partnership (Hopkins 1984: 43–59).

In the trades of brass, copper, plating, gunmaking and watchmaking, skilled handwork continued to be the basis of most production and large output was achieved by multiplying small workshops. Gradually steam power was applied where possible to stamping blanks. However, most operations needed very little power; and in both Birmingham and Coventry it was usual to share power among several works or processes. In many cases steam power was introduced to supplement water power not to supersede it, and many long-established industrial sites were further developed with new buildings, and old water mills became large rambling works. Many new works were sited alongside canals or on open heath or newly enclosed land, and in the towns dwelling houses continued to be used as workshops. The parliamentary reports of the 1830s and 1840s bring vividly to light the crowding together of small metalware workshops indistinguishable from shabby private houses except for the noise and dilapidation. The tools, processes and internal trade relations changed very little. The large firms, such as Soho, Thomasons, and Rylands, led the way and their enterprise opened up markets, set on foot new products, provided models for imitation and encouraged cut-price competition by their very success.

Silver plating followed a similar pattern at least until the introduction of electro-plating in 1840. When Boulton began to exploit its possibilities there were perhaps half a dozen other shops in Birmingham. The provision of the Assay Office, and Boulton's enterprise and contacts enabled many small men to operate. The work remained highly skilled and laborious, most of the operations were carried on by hand with small hammers – for example, soldering handles was done with the aid of a blow pipe and a single tureen might take a week to make.

In all these trades the workmen operated at their own bench or forge, spare space was hired out to young men, and workmen offered themselves as 'casters for hire' or 'stampers for hire'. They worked irregular hours and kept 'St Monday'. Their prices were based on traditional lists of prices for all the different processes and products, but the lists were increasingly subject to negotiable discounts.

In some trades the introduction of simple machinery assisted the survival of the domestic workshop. In lockmaking the introduction of Mason's fly press in 1794 enabled the homeworker to cut out the parts more speedily. The domestic lockmakers, nailers, chainmakers and boltmakers all adopted various forms of the Oliver or foot-operated spring hammer in the early-nineteenth century and this enabled a smith to work single-handed. These crude machines greatly facilitated work in the domestic workshop and it became possible in some cases for the 'unit of production' to be one old woman. Until well into the second half of the nineteenth century the small workshop with 'oliver' hearth anvil and bellows was to persist as the character-istic mode of production of simple iron goods. Between 1760 and 1830 the number of nail shops increased, and the trade spread into the rural villages of north Worcestershire and west Staffordshire.

In 1840, only 4 of about 150 locksmiths in Wolverhampton had premises larger than a single shop. In Willenhall, where cheaper locks were made, there were only 2 large works to 260 shops. Even Chubbs produced their whole output in 1840 without machines, though foot-operated stamps were used for piercing. In Walsall bits and spurs were produced in exactly the same way in the 1840s as had been described by Dr Plot in 1686 (BPP 1843: xv).

Chainmaking was newly established as a separate trade in the Midlands in the early-nineteenth century, when many nailers became chainmakers. The composition of wrought iron made by the puddling process from coke pig was particularly suitable for welding into chain and the demand from pits, factor-ies, ships and agriculture increased. A few large workshops had been estab-lished by the 1830s when the heaviest chains were made, but most of the chain came from the three hundred or so domestic workshops in Cradley, Old Hill, Netherton and Quarry Bank (Timmins 1866: 99–100). In both large and small workshops the men operated their own 'standing', agreed prices with the gaffers, chose their own hours and employed and paid their own assistants. They made their own tools and resisted all factory discipline, even into the 1970s when puddled wrought iron ceased to be produced, and the hand-made chain industry died out.

Another 'new' industry established in small workshops in Darlaston in the early-nineteenth century was nut-and-bolt making. The only large employer was Alexander Cotterell who employed 14 men in 1851, but 75 by 1861 (Morton 1972: 11–16). However, the subsequent history of the nut-and-bolt trade saw a transition to large factories.

The coal industry experienced great growth and development but only a limited degree of technical innovation or restructuring. The great landowners continued to take the lead. By 1800 Lord Gower was making £3,000 a year from his pits at Brereton where he employed 227 men and this pit was one of many on his estates in north and central Staffordshire. Lord Dudley and Ward was investing much money in sinking new pits, building canals and railways, introducing new systems of ventilation and producing 400,000 tons a year from his collieries. In Warwickshire Sir Richard Newdigate invested £20,000

Plate 4.11   The Prince and Princess of Wales visiting Gillotts' pen factory in Birmingham in 1875. The women are slitting nibs using a press.

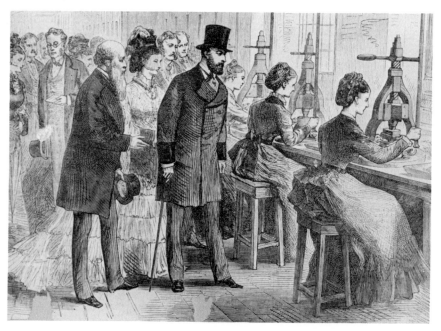

opening a new colliery at Griff, and brought in engineers from Newcastle on Tyne to build a double-acting steam engine (White 1970: 61). Much of the development in Warwickshire was by specialist coalmasters, notably Richard Parrot, the third generation of that enterprising family. Despite difficulties the number of pits increased and the coal was carried from the mines not only by road but also by the new Birmingham and Fazeley canal which gave an outlet to Oxford, London and the south-east (Grant 1982).

The Staffordshire coalfields were exploited not only by the great land-owners and the yeomen partnerships, but also by the ironmasters. Virtually every furnace had its coal and ironstone mines and employed indirectly hun-dreds of colliers. By 1830 the ironmasters were said to control the south Staffordshire coal trade. At Bilston for example the principal coalmasters were Lord Ward, Burslem Sparrow and James Bagnal, ironmaster. By 1840 Staffordshire had 400 large and small collieries which employed on average about 60–70 men and boys each.

In all the midland industries there was considerable continuity of lead-ership. There were new men coming into the district and making great fortunes but many of the leading entrepreneurs were members of families prominent in midland industry for five or six generations by 1760. The Gibbons family had been yeomen lockmakers in the early seventeenth century, built up their family fortunes in coal and ironstone mining, entered banking before they leased the New Level furnace and continued their traditional ironmongering trade until 1808 (Smith 1970–1). Other familiar names in the iron industry included Elwall, Fereday, Turton and Bickley. Wedgwoods, Daniels and Warburtons had been potters of enterprise in the Potteries since the early seventeenth century, Samuel Galton of Birmingham was the third of his name in the gunmaking business and his grandfather had known the names of Garbett, Lloyd and Boulton among his fellow industrialists. Most notably of all the industrial interests of the family of Lord Dudley and Ward went back to at least the thirteenth century.

Management of even the large works continued to be based upon the family, with brothers, cousins and sons forming reliable networks of kin and connection. There were more new partnerships but these too were often reinforced by marriage or neighbourhood. The detailed study of the Kenricks of West Bromwich shows the extent to which capital and management were still drawn from family resources (Church 1969).

By 1830 the Midlands had some works where large numbers were employed under one roof, hired and paid directly by the management, super-vised closely and kept to a disciplined routine. At Gillotts' pen factory in Birmingham women workers sat in rows using simple hand machines, paid by the hour and kept in order by a male overlooker. At Etruria Wedgwood glorified his methods of controlling his workforce, declaring that he was making his factory a 'place of hope and progress' and offering the prospect of 'making of men such machines as cannot err'. Workers were trained to predetermined tasks, old hands were retrained and a school of art established for apprentices from twelve years old. Wedgwood employed many girls, 25 per cent of whom were trained in the works. Output was maximised by setting workpeople to constant employment at a particular task, and time and money was saved by the layout of the works. The workers were closely supervised, mainly by his partner Bently and his nephew Brierley, assisted by specially appointed clerks and supervisors. Instructions issued in 1780 required the potters to respond to a bell summoning them to work at 5.45 a.m., to clock in by means of a ticket system, to eschew careless work, waste, fighting, drinking and dirt; the rules were enforced by heavy fines. However, such organisation was far from typical in the Midlands. Even in the great integrated ironworks there was much subcontracting and teamwork. The bridgestocker at the top of the furnace contracted with the employers and in turn took on his own team while the Founder did the same at ground level. The puddlers and shinglers brought in and paid their own underhands and boys (Gale 1966). Enterprises such as Hunts of Brades in Oldbury combined on the same site large-scale production of basic materials or semi-finished goods with finishing by hand in small workshops located on the employer's premises. These workshops were controlled by workmen who hired their own assistants, worked piece-work, kept their own hours and identified their shops by their own names. This was also true at Kenrick's hollow-ware in West Bromwich, although by the 1890s the employers were already deliberately trying to limit their independence (Church 1969: 20–4).

By this time the majority of pikemen and hewers of coal were not employed by the mine owner but were hired as a team by the butty. The butty negotiated for a price for the ton of coal got and then collected his team. Most men, therefore, could only presume upon employment a fortnight at a time. Butties generally employed a number of teams; supervision and leadership of each team underground was carried out by the 'doggy'. The butty relieved the coal owners of the management of labour and took about a quarter of the earnings of the team. He provided tools, skips, horses and wages for the men. The butties on the coalfields enforced a work discipline, conducive to the economic advantage of the employer. Their manner of conducting the discipline and the lack of equity in their dealings soon became notorious, but their sanctions were effective and ruthlessly applied.

In most trades in the Midlands payment was by piece rates and special rates for particular jobs. This meant that hours of work could not easily be defined, for when there was a press of work, hours were longer, but low prices also encouraged the working of long hours, especially in the domestic trades. The standard shift in the iron mills, coalmines and other trades was about 12 hours; in the flint glass works the men worked their shifts in two sessions of 6 hours on and off. The crown and plate-glass workers worked only 9–11 hours. The hours worked by the small metal workers were much more variable and could be as much as 16–18 per day, hours which were worked not only by the brass workers but also by their juvenile assistants (Hopkins 1982: 52–63).

Voluntary societies were formed to provide against difficult times by saving in more prosperous times and became very numerous among town workers. Friendly societies were registered with the justices of the peace from 1794 and were encouraged by the churches, the local magistrates and industrialists as a more constructive approach to poverty than ever-rising poor rates. Wolverhampton already had 34 friendly societies by 1794, only one of which registered (Eden 1797). Birmingham had 239 such societies registered between 1794 and 1826. Working men in the towns clubbed together to obtain clothes, burial funds and lying-in benefits. There were at least 800 such clubs in Birmingham by 1820 (Glover 1979: 42). Staffordshire had a larger number of such societies than most areas, among them the Female Friendly Society at Longton which collected voluntary contributions for the relief and maintenance of its members and provided also for the interrment of deceased members.

Friendly societies had a strong social element, reinforced their bonds of friendship with banners, processions, annual feasts and frequent convivial meetings, and they also provided opportunities for some of their members to practise skills of organisation and leadership. The societies generally paid out about 10s. 6d. in case of sickness or accident and £1 for burial expenses. Despite their well-publicised limitations they provided a real support for the 'respectable' artisan and remained an integral part of the family economy in the Midlands until the development of commercial insurance.

Friendly societies were often linked with specific trades and fulfilled an important role in institutionalising and organising industrial relations. When the price of raw materials rose in 1759 many small trade societies advertised in *Aris's Birmingham Gazette* demanding that the merchants should raise the prices for work and threatening collective refusal to work. In 1772 a rival manufacturer, Thomas Hadley, stirred up the Society of Gunmakers at the Nag's Head in opposition to Galton ((U) BRL Galton Mss). Such societies were recorded only sporadically and usually in the course of some dispute. They survived the anxieties and reactionary mood of the 1790s to re-emerge in the period of the orders in Council. In 1810–12 twenty-seven Birmingham societies advertised in the newspapers to demand price increases. During the post-war depression a number of strikes occurred; evidence has been collected of 103 strikes between 1800 and 1850 in Birmingham alone (Behagg 1979: 460). The trade societies of the 1820s were small and local in leadership but they began to try to establish links with similar societies elsewhere. The Wolverhampton tin-plate workers sought connections with those in Lancashire and the Birmingham fitters declared themselves united with their opposite numbers in Derby, Leicestershire and Nottingham. The trade societies exerted sanctions over their members who failed to respond to a strike call and struggled to provide benefits during strikes. However, their resources

were limited and their legal position vulnerable. The Potters' Union commanded widespread support in 1824, but collapsed after the ill-timed and badly
organised strike of 1825 (Owen 1901). The miners' strikes in the south
Staffordshire collieries in 1815 and 1822 led to riots and the military were
called out (Barnsby 1977: 16–17) and Lord Stafford's agent in 1815 was able
to break the combination of the colliers (Richards 1974a: 419).

Trade societies addressed themselves not only to price lists and piecework rates but also to the comparatively new practice of offering work at a
percentage discount on the list prices. By the 1820s the practice had become
widespread and oppressive in the metal trades, notably in lockmaking, spring
making and cinder sifting making. The discount undermined traditional price
lists and made it extremely difficult for the societies to maintain uniformity of
payment among their workers. There were complaints too of the increasing use
of casual labour taken on for short periods instead of employing journeymen
through the traditional source by applying to the 'Houses of Call'. Apprenticeship was becoming another name for cheap labour. The practice of truck
was also a frequent cause of grievance, especially in the Potteries and the
colliery districts. The rapid growth of population, the siting of new communities in areas without traditional retail shops, the shortage of small coin during
the French wars and the difficulties of many coalmasters and ironmasters after
the war, all encouraged the practice of paying men partly with foodstuffs sold
through the tommy shops. The practice became illegal in 1831 but nevertheless
it remained widespread.

Any attempt to summarise the social changes in an area of such diversity
must be very tentative. There had been an evident increase in the numbers of
individuals wholly dependent upon industry and upon the payment of piecework wages. There had been an increase in the use of machines, and also many
more men, women and children were performing mechanical tasks. By 1830
the lives of many were conditioned to an economic imperative outside their
own control, yet the widespread use of sub-contracting and the increase in the
numbers of small workshops make it necessary to qualify any too simplistic
proletarian model. Clearly there was not a 'working class' but many working
classes and a multiplicity of sub groups each with their own cohesiveness and
sense of identity.

At the other end of the social scale were certainly some great 'capitalists'.
The capital investment stock and turnover of the great integrated firms, the
largest manufacturers and the aristocratic coal works were on a scale new in
kind as well as in degree and these works required the development of new
systems of management. In a period when Parliament would only sanction
joint stock companies in areas of public utility most of the capital was derived
from family resources and accumulated within industry itself. There were
partnerships of two or three families, and individuals entered into a variety of
partnerships for different if related enterprises, so there was thus a fairly
close-meshed net of outstanding industrial leaders. Between these men and the

wage workers was an uncountable number of medium and small-scale capitalists and semi-independent small masters. In varying degrees they derived their economic success and social status from their participation in and exploitation of the same innovations, technical, managerial and entrepreneurial, as the large capitalists. Large and small enterprises stood or fell together rather than competing with each other, and the large manufacturers created opportunities which the small firms could exploit, even to the extent of undercutting their rivals.

Part five

The Midlands in the Age of Capitalism

Chapter 27

Population and housing: 1830–1914

The changing patterns of population size, distribution and structure in the Midlands in the nineteenth century were broadly the same as in the country as a whole. Differences were of degree rather than of kind. The population of England and Wales increased by about 42 per cent between 1841 and 1871 while the total population of Staffordshire and Warwickshire increased by about 63 per cent. Most of this increase was concentrated in urban areas. Forty-six agricultural parishes in Staffordshire and eighty-five in Warwickshire reached their peak aggregate populations during this period and thenceforward declined until the coming of the motorcar began to change the patterns of distribution. Most of these parishes were in mid-Staffordshire and south Warwickshire. In contrast towns and industrial villages continued to grow rapidly. By 1851 Staffordshire had seventeen towns whose populations exceeded 10,000 and in north Worcestershire on the edge of the Black Country Dudley, Halesowen and Kings Norton were in the same category. The megatown of Birmingham far exceeded all other midland towns and continued to grow at annual rates of more than 2 per cent. Birmingham overtook Manchester in 1861 and Liverpool in 1881 to become the largest provincial town in England. By 1871 some 231,000 people lived within its 3,000 acres, and 15,000 more in Duddeston, Nechells, Deritend and Erdington in the neighbouring parish of Aston. The central areas of the town had long reached saturation point, and growth in the contiguous parishes was much more rapid than in the town itself, reaching 3.5 per cent per annum in the 1850s.

Rugby had only 2,150 people in 1831 but grew rapidly with the development of railway engineering and also of the public school to reach a total of 16,830 by 1901. Leamington Spa continued to grow and by 1891 had doubled its permanent population. After the coming of the railway to Leamington in 1841 it developed a winter as well as a summer season and broadened its appeal to include not only the sick but also gentlefolk of all ages and an increasing number of American and continental visitors (Baxter 1975–6: 15–37).

Much of the increased population was the result of immigration. Birmingham and the Black Country were attracting the most migrants, mainly from other parts of Staffordshire, Warwickshire and Worcestershire. In addition Birmingham and the Black Country attracted migrants from further afield, from Lancashire, Yorkshire, East Anglia, Wales and London (Lawton 1958: 168–76).

The Potteries had its own pattern of immigration. The majority of the potters were born locally, but a significant number of people came from Lancashire, Flintshire and Denbighshire into the expanding coal and iron industries of north Staffordshire. A small number of immigrants came from Cornwall, the source by this date of much of the potters' clay (Dupree 1977). The east Warwickshire coalfield was attracting immigrants mainly from Warwickshire, Leicestershire and Northamptonshire, and people were moving into Burton on Trent from Staffordshire (Lawton 1958: 174). The Cannock area developed large-scale mining from the 1850s, and mid-Stafford-shire industrial villages, such as Hednesford and Chasetown, grew rapidly. The population of Cannock itself grew by 137 per cent in the decade 1871–81.

The overall growth of population was checked in the 1870s in those villages dependent upon the primary iron industry. Some Black Country towns recorded a net population loss in the decade 1871–81. However, this setback was short-lived and the majority of the older industrial areas continued to grow as a new range of large scale industries was introduced. Nevertheless, the 1860s saw the beginning of a movement away from the Black Country to the newly developed coal and iron areas in north-eastern England, and this movement accelerated in the 1870s (Lawton 1958: 164–77). Coventry suffered some loss of population in the 1860s in the aftermath of the collapse of the silk trade, but this was short-lived.

During the middle years of the century the Midlands received considerable numbers of immigrants from overseas, in particular Jews from Europe and large numbers of Irish.

Jews had lived in Birmingham since at least 1751, but the community was much reinforced in the nineteenth century. The town had 730 Jews in 1851 and 2,360 twenty years later. The majority were from Poland, Russia and Germany; the turnover of families within the group was high and many of those who stayed in the Midlands married a British-born Jew or a native. The main concentration of Jews was around Hurst Street where the poorer immigrant Jews clustered in old houses. The wealthier Jews established a separate community in Hagley Road and Edgbaston and a small group of families lived in Handsworth (Josephs 1980). A comparatively new group in the Midlands was formed by the arrival of large numbers of men and women born in Ireland. Until the 1830s an Irish name was uncommon even in Roman Catholic registers in the Midlands, but by 1861 every large town had its Irish quarter. In Birmingham the Irish born formed 4 per cent of the population of

Birmingham by 1851. Wolverhampton had one of the largest concentrations of Irish people, mostly famine refugees from Roscommon, Sligo and Mayo. In Burslem they settled mainly in the central part of the town, and comprised 8 per cent of the population by 1851. They settled in large, closely-linked communities, intermarried and continued to speak Gaelic for at least a generation. For a time they included large numbers of unattached men and many who married late. Irish families offered homes to lodgers and non-kin dependents but these characteristics gave way by the 1870s to a more conventional pattern of family life. Nevertheless, a strong sense of community and separateness remained, reinforced rather than modified by the development of schools and parishes serving their particular needs (Swift 1980: 1).

From the 1880s the basic patterns of births, marriages, fertility and deaths began to change. The regular reports of the medical officers of health drew attention to infectious disease, overcrowding, bad water supplies and sewage problems. Large hospitals were erected in all the major towns and in the counties, and doctors and trained nurses fought dirt and disease with ruthless determination. Cleanliness, sanitary reform and control of infection became fashionable creeds, and the mass production of soap, washing soda, chlorines and disinfectant, and changing standards of domestic housing also contributed to reducing the death rate. The Birmingham death rate had been 25.7 per thousand during the years 1871–5, which was 3.2 per cent above the national rate, but this was reduced to 20.7 per thousand from 1881 to 1885, only 1.3 per cent above the national rate. While this initial victory did not lead to a continuous decline of the death rate, contagious diseases were gradually brought under some degree of control (Woods 1978: 35–57).

From the 1870s the birthrate also fell, though less rapidly than the death rate. The spread of acceptable forms of birth control, changing economic pressures, the fall in the death rate, changing nutrition, environment and expectations of comfort and leisure all made some contribution to the change. In the Midlands the decline of the birthrate did not affect the continued aggregate growth of the county populations or of the larger towns before 1914 since it was compensated for by immigration. The proportion of the total population of England and Wales resident in Staffordshire and Warwickshire remained the same, at almost 8 per cent throughout the nineteenth century. In contrast the south-east and the north-west were both increasing their share of the total population by 1900.

Just as population growth in the early modern period had put critical pressure upon food supplies, so in the 1840s population growth put pressure on the supply of shelter, water supplies and sewage disposal. The labourers, the poor and the migrants were inevitably most at risk.

In West Bromwich in 1837 at a time of very rapid population growth a local survey revealed:

16 families had 1 room
418 families had 2 rooms
578 families had 3 rooms
1,181 families had 4 rooms

and 70 per cent of all houses had gardens. In general the ratio of population to houses in the decade 1831–41 was 5:1 (JRSS I 1837). Coventry had many old and neglected houses, more multi-occupancy and more back-to-back houses than Birmingham or Woverhampton and even recently-constructed houses were of poor quality and had an overall size of only 18 ft by 12 ft. At Stourbridge, on the other hand, many of the houses built in the 1840s were modest but well-built with good flooring and windows (Hopkins 1978: 232–4). Throughout the Midlands, the floors, walls and yards were made of brick from the abundant red, blue and grey clays of the coalfields. Houses in Staffordshire were said to cost £20–80 for two-roomed cottages and £35–100 for three-roomed cottages. Rents were in the region of 1s. 6d. to 3s. a week for most of the nineteenth century, rising in the first years of the twentieth century to 5s. 6d. and 7s. 6d. (BPP XIII 1843a: 70).

The supply of drainage and water for the unprecedented numbers of people was an even greater problem than the provision of shelter. Sanitary enquiries revealed that in the more crowded areas of the towns attempts to cope with such problems had virtually broken down. Wolverhampton had 38 miles of streets, 26 of them with no drainage at all, Hanley and Shelton had 4,663 houses of which only 1,200 had piped water, for which the residents paid 12s. a year or 21s. for a larger supply, and the 2,039 houses in Newcastle had 215 taps, 14 standpipes and 17 public pumps between them.

Unplanned development was seen at its most chaotic in the industrial villages in the Potteries, the Black Country and at Griff and Bedworth on the east Warwickshire coalfield. On the coalfields groups of cottages were built around mines, kilns and furnaces on open ground. The layouts of the settlements were irregular in the extreme and they had no links with the original villages. In Tipton the central village remained a small shopping centre, while new houses clustered around the ironworks, which were sited on the canal network that virtually enclosed the parish. In Longton, Burslem and Tunstall new streets and courts spread over open land until they met. However, the industrial villages had very few back-to-back houses and very few cellar houses, and the total lack of organised supplies of water or of sewage disposal was somewhat mitigated by the great acreage of waste space and tips. The typical plan of houses in the industrial villages was two rooms up and two rooms down, with no entrance hall or separate kitchen. In a small yard at the back were a privy and ash pit and in the Black Country the workshop, nail shop, chain shop, key or lockmaking shop as the case might be. Houses were also built in short terraces with wells, pumps and communal bakehouses. These areas characteristically had remarkably little social or economic zoning.

Plate 5.1   A Black Country nailworker at home.

Although the wealthiest industrialists looked for some domestic comfort and dignity, many of the better-paid artisans and middle managers lived as neighbours to the poorest of their workforce. The large butty's house and the smaller houses of the miners were sometimes all part of a single block of development, and small retail shops and industrial premises jostled for space at road junctions and near canal wharves (Cadman 1977: 15–26).

The pressure of population on housing stock was much less severe in rural parishes. As population levels stagnated or even fell, the older cottages became increasingly dilapidated. The mid-Victorian period saw a great deal of remodelling of farms and the rebuilding of larger farmhouses. After enclosure many farmhouses were rebuilt on new sites, only the church, the rectory and workers' cottages remained in the old village centre. Model estates and model cottages began to exercise the minds of rural philanthropists from the 1860s, including Lord Hatherton at Teddesley and the Lucy family at Charlecote and Hampton Lucy. Model cottages usually had a large family room, wash-house, pantry and kitchen on the ground floor and three sleeping rooms and a garden, and were built of brick, and roofed with tiles and supplied with pumps for water.

From the late-eighteenth century onwards the wealthier men of business and commerce aspired to large villas isolated in extensive gardens or miniature estates. This development was not wholly a reaction to smoke, dirt and noise since it was a feature of many non-industrial towns such as Warwick, as well as of the Potteries, Birmingham and Burton on Trent (Slater 1978: 129–44). The most extensive and well-known of the high-status neighbourhoods was Edgbaston to the south-west of Birmingham, where the Calthorpes made a green suburb for Birmingham business men. Strict management and control was achieved by means of highly restrictive 99-year leases and the landlords were able to exclude industrial premises and even shops for about 50 years. The houses were gracious, two- or three-storey detached dwellings with stuccoed porches, sash windows and conservatories. Edgbaston had three elegant churches in dignified squares, fine walks and many trees (Cannadine 1977: 457–82).

The growth of high-status suburbs separated the middle classes from the home-life and conditions of the workforce. Moreover, it isolated the wives and children of business men from the competitive world of commerce, marking boundaries more distinctly than in any previous generation or social group between the worlds of men and of women. These households were maintained by an already diminishing number of living-in servants, but food and other goods and services were brought to the doors by vanboys and delivery men. Whatever problems existed in reality within the family, the pleasing fiction was strenuously maintained that all the inhabitants of these neighbourhoods were opulent persons of elegance and ease who could keep carriages and servants and enjoy an elaborate and highly ritualised social life.

The majority of the urban and industrial workers still lived close to their work. In Coventry a deliberate attempt was made to maintain the association of home and work. Many ribbon weavers' houses were built with spacious shops on a third floor above the home with large windows to provide good light for the work, and the watchmakers had similar premises in the Chapelfields district (Prest 1960: 96–113). At Cash's new Kingsfield works a hundred premises with homes and workshops were planned, but only forty were actually built. Much of the capital for building smaller houses continued to be provided by innumerable building societies through which an artisan could acquire a small house by paying 5*s*. a week for 14–15 years. His furniture might cost another £10–30. The work of building societies was supplemented from the 1840s by the Freehold Land Societies, which aimed at encouraging the building of freehold houses to be let to suitable respectable householders who would thus be empowered to vote in parliamentary and borough elections.

Very little was done before 1875 by midland voluntary bodies to provide good houses for the poor. In Wolverhampton thirteen model cottages were built and rented at 3*s*. a week by the Metropolitan Association, and a Dudley branch was also active for several years. Stratford on Avon ordered their medical officer of health to inspect newly built houses and Lord Granville laid out model working-class houses at Shelton in the 1850s. Some good, simple housing had been built at Cobridge with front gardens, washhouses and entrance hall and three bedrooms, and even water closets and piped drainage.

The 1870s proved to be a watershed in the provision of housing for the majority of the growing urban populations. The Artisans' Dwellings Act (1875) did rather less than is usually claimed for it in that it permitted compulsory purchase and clearance of insanitary dwellings, but made no real provision for the alternative housing of those whose disgusting shelter was pulled down. Building new houses was still left to private enterprise. Clearance and improvement schemes made only a modest contribution to the improvement of housing. The much publicised improvement scheme in Birmingham led to the destruction of 600 buildings, of which only 375 were dwelling houses, not all of them slums. The Wolverhampton improvement scheme cleared an area between Queen Square and Stafford Road, including the notorious 'Carribee Island'. This area, before clearance had 632 inhabited houses which had only 39 water-closets and 366 privies between them. The Springfield Estate in the north of the town was planned, but private developers here as elsewhere in the late 1870s were reluctant to build, and the scheme was wound up in 1880 when only 75 houses had been built (Barnsby 1975: 19–20).

More important were the model bye-laws issued by the central board of local government which the majority of midland borough councils adopted. These established the principle that new housing must conform to certain minimum standards of height of ceiling, access of air and light, and quality of materials. In 1869 Hanley town council issued a bye-law requiring all new houses to have an area of at least 500 sq.ft, bedroom of 100 sq.ft, ceilings 9 ft high and windows one-twelfth of the floor area. Contractors offending against the bye-laws were fined 40s. a day (Warrilow 1960).

Private developers leased increasingly large areas on the fringes of towns and cities. The connecting link with places of employment was provided from the 1870s by horse-drawn and later electric omnibuses and trams, and before the end of the century by the bicycle and suburban railways. New suburbs followed the lines of tramroads and railways leading out of the town. Roads were longer and wider, their plan was rectilinear and corner shops and public houses were sited at the intersections. Domestic houses usually comprised one or two sitting rooms, a kitchen and scullery on the ground floor and two or three bedrooms and an attic above. They cost from about 5s. to 9s. a week in rent, i.e. about 15–25 per cent of the average wage (Board of Trade 1907).

In the new working-class suburbs the breadwinner 'went to work' each morning at 8.00 a.m. and returned after 6.00 p.m. and the women and children stayed within the suburban environment, with the street as their public forum. Small food shops, dressmakers and sub-post offices served their daily needs. These communities often developed a marked cohesiveness reinforced by the common struggle to maintain solvency, independence and respectability. The development of Whitmore Reans to the north of Wolverhampton by the

Hordern family produced a characteristic community of this type, inhabited by clerks, skilled manual workers and petty manufacturers. Social boundaries were rarely crossed and in the larger towns quite separate and distinct communities lived within half a mile of each other.

Meanwhile older housing in the town centres continued to be occupied and to deteriorate. Reports dating from 1900 to 1914 emphasised the prevalence of overcrowding in town centres. Birmingham had 43,366 back-to-back houses occupied by 200,000 people in the central areas and 58,000 houses without water closets. The most overcrowded area in the Potteries was in the centre of Hanley. The average density of population was 38 per acre, but the parish contained much derelict land and in places the density rose to 250 people per acre (Warrilow 1960: 321).

The garden city movement was part of international developments in aesthetics, architecture and social planning. In the Midlands it took the form of planning garden suburbs to counteract the overcrowding of city centres and the monotony of bye-law housing. George Cadbury had a lifetime's experience of the problems of the inner city as he encountered them in his work as a Sunday School teacher and campaigner for adult literacy. The planning and completion of the garden suburb of Bournville was undertaken in 1895 when he was aged sixty-two. He had moved his chocolate factory to the suburbs fifteen years before and Bournville Village was from the first an experiment in social planning, not a 'factory village'. It aimed at providing a healthier living environment which would enhance the lives of the inhabitants and improve the health of minds and bodies. Bournville Village Trust was established in 1900 and by 1904 400 houses and a school had been built at a cost of £30,000. The roads were wide and each house occupied only a quarter of the site; all the rest was garden ready planted with quickset hedges and fruit trees. In 1910 the rents in Bournville ranged from 4s. 6d. to 8s. a week. Only 40 per cent of the householders were employees of the chocolate factory and Cadbury sought to mix social classes in the village by juxtaposing large and small houses and houses offered at high and low rents. George Cadbury was not alone in his determination to translate idealism into bricks and mortar. J. S. Nettlefold created the Harborne Tenants Association housing scheme and later became chairman of Birmingham's first housing committee. In Wolverhampton R. A. S. Pagett started to build a garden suburb at Fallings Park (Barnsby 1975: 20).

From the 1890s local authorities began to make attempts to provide new housing at low rents. In Coventry the corporation erected 48 houses and some two-roomed flats, rents were from 4s. 3d. a week but other accommodation in the courts of the city cost only 2s. a week.

Despite the very limited achievements in terms of the enlargement of the housing stock, there was nevertheless a growing sense that local government had a responsibility to achieve better provision. A growing volume of public legislation and of private initiative prepared the way for large-scale, planned housing schemes. The Housing Act of 1890 gave powers to local authorities to clear slums and build working-class houses with a public subsidy, and the 1910 and 1911 Planning Acts enabled larger authorities to purchase land and plan large estates. Birmingham was one of the first large cities to take advantage of the new acts and the corporation purchased land in the west of the city at Harborne, Quinton and part of Edgbaston. Thirty-three housing schemes were planned with a strictly limited density of population, roads 30–40 yards wide, separate tramways and much tree planting. However, planned developments were still in their early stages when work was halted by the outbreak of the First World War (Macmorran 1973: 89).

Chapter 28

High farming on the midland claylands

By the mid-nineteenth century there was a marked distinction between parts of the country with light soils on which the technological innovations of the agricultural revolution could be implemented and the claylands which had proved a less suitable environment for the newer types of cultivation and rotation. Some areas of Staffordshire and Warwickshire came into the category of light lands, namely, the Trent valley, south-west Staffordshire and the Avon valley from Stratford to Rugby, but much of the Midlands lay on clay. By the 1850s increased yields of wheat and fodder were being produced on light soils by management based on the Norfolk system, for example on the estate of Lord Hatherton at Teddesley; in north Warwickshire, Meriden Heath was enclosed and, by intensive inputs of capital, Lord Aylesford was able to make it a wheat-growing area on the Norfolk system. Most of the Midlands was clayland and in this area much was expected from drains. Drainage tiles and drainpipes were manufactured in the Potteries from the 1840s onwards and government grants became available from 1846. Lord Hatherton, the Earls of Harrowby, Lord Lichfield and other lords of large estates increasingly made themselves responsible for the cost of deep drainage with the help of grants from the government and improvement companies (VCH Staffs VI: 98–9). A variety of manures were laid to improve the land. Town manure and street sweepings continued in use, despite problems of distribution and quality. Guano was imported from South America in the 1840s and was quickly adopted in the Midlands, at Seisdon, Swynnerton and Chillington, for example. Lord Hatherton was among the first to encourage the use of bone meal, and it was widely used by the mid-nineteenth century. The Birmingham firm of Proctor and Ryland were among the main producers and all market towns had retail suppliers of artificial fertilisers by the 1860s. Government grants were available for manures from 1856 (VCH Staffs VI: 95–7).

The mid-nineteenth century saw the general adoption of seed drills, horse hoeing and winnowing machines. Mechanical reapers appeared in the 1860s and stationary engines and steam traction engines in the 1870s. A wider range of plough types was used, though the traditional heavy plough requiring four horses to drag it along was displaced only gradually by lighter two-horse ploughs. Much of the encouragement to innovation came from firms of agricultural machine manufacturers who not only constantly offered 'improved' machines, but supported their trade by attractive advertising campaigns.

Large landowners continued to take the initiative in improvement. Land prices were high and, at 2½ per cent, profits were modest, less than could be obtained in industry, building or 'the funds'. However, a well-managed estate was still an enormous social asset and the gains in status and public esteem were reinforced by the moral imperatives of the mid-Victorian sense of public responsibility. On social rather than commercial grounds, therefore, Lord Anson, the Earl of Bradford, the Earl of Harrowby at Sandon and Hugh Sneyd at Keele were absorbed in agricultural improvement. Rents moved slowly upwards and the scale of landlord investment in tenants' land increased. Gradually the balance of responsibility for capital investment in land shifted from tenant to landlord. In return the landlord expected good, sophisticated farming from tenants to enable them to pay higher rents. Broadly speaking, the same policies were pursued by gentry families such as the Wrottesleys, the Fletchers of Aqualate, the Tollets at Betley and the Fitzherberts at Swynnerton. The gentry were more particularly dependent upon agricultural income than the peers, so their need to maintain good tenant farms in order to keep up rent rolls was even more acute.

Farming improvements did not depend upon any particular innovation, but upon the management of the interaction of land, crops and stock. R. W. Sturgess has claimed that during the 1850s a technological revolution took place on the midland claylands, in the form of the development of an intensive grassland husbandry on newly drained farms. By feeding cattle more grains and oilcake farmers became less dependent upon hay. Meadow land could therefore be released for pasture, and more livestock could be kept, which in turn yielded more manure. More artificial fertilisers also became available, so the arable acreage was rendered more productive and could, therefore, be less extensive. Fewer horses were needed to cultivate the land and consume fodder, which facilitated an even greater increase in livestock and increased dairy farming (Sturgess 1966).

By 1875, 62 per cent of Staffordshire was under grass, half of it in pastures. Much of the pasture was being improved with manuring and the sowing of selected grass seeds. In central Staffordshire the number of cattle per acre had been increased and the size of herds had doubled, especially on the larger holdings. Beef and dairy cattle were fed intensively on oilcake, maize and rice, and around Burton on the valuable brewers' grains. Longhorns were replaced by shorthorns, whose carcases not only supplied meat for the local towns but were exported to the north-east and north-west by rail.

The numbers of sheep in Staffordshire fell slowly from 317,400 in 1870 to 210,000 just before the First World War. Most of them were kept to supply mutton and lamb to the towns. Many sheep were fed not only on grass but also on oilcake and a range of root crops including carrots. Dairy farming became the mainstay of Staffordshire farming in the 1850s. One gallon of milk was required to produce a pound of cheese, which to the farmer was worth 60*s*. a hundredweight. Much attention was given to improving the milk yield of cows, and by the 1860s the best milkers were each giving a thousand gallons a year. Dairy farming was labour-intensive. At Tutbury a dairy farmer with 61 cows needed to employ 7 labourers, 4 lads and 3 women. He and his son also worked on the farm and had to keep 8 horses. Dairying in the parishes within reach of the populous areas was encouraged by the rising consumption of milk as a drink and by the gradual disappearance of the cow from towns. The cow plague of 1866 was particularly severe on stall-fed cows and the introduction of regulations in the interests of public health and pure food operated in favour of the rural producer. In the Midlands rural dairy farmers were rarely more than two or three miles from a railway, while smallholders on the edge of the towns kept small herds of dairy cattle to retail milk in the local suburbs (Evershed 1856, 1859).

Smallholdings remained numerous in the Midlands, especially where the proximity of large towns provided a market for garden produce. Tamworth and Lichfield were centres for onions and other vegetables, Wombourne supplied early potatoes to Wolverhampton market and Sutton Coldfield supplied cabbages to Birmingham. Vegetables were distributed by canal and later by rail, but the local carrier's cart remained an important element in the distribution network. It was still difficult for vegetables to be transported for more than a few hours without losing freshness and the urban housewife continued to make much use of open markets and small greengrocers in towns and suburbs. By this period the rivers Trent and Tame and their valleys were heavily polluted with sewage. The dangers to health were beginning to be appreciated, but the soil on the banks of the Tame was enriched and enabled local gardeners to grow flowers and flower roots, especially gillies, for the townspeople. Greenhouses were quickly introduced into the Midlands, for the skills of ironworkers and glass manufacturers had already been employed on building the Crystal Palace in London and New Street Station, Birmingham.

In most of Staffordshire and north Warwickshire the arable acreage declined as grain became less profitable, and more and more ploughed land was used for producing fodder crops. In the Feldon, on the other hand, grain remained important, with an increase in wheat compared with other grains in the mid-nineteenth century. The 'great depression' in agriculture in the Midlands was less serious in its impact than in the south and east of England. Since much of the land was pastoral and since demand from the industrial and urban workers was buoyant the main effect of the depression was to intensify changes that were already taking place, rather than to cause a restructuring of the agricultural economy.

From the 1870s the profits, organisation and policies of farming were increasingly influenced by factors of international development and competition, technological innovation and changing habits of consumption. The profitability of arable farming declined even further as wheat prices fell (Jones 1967: 60–4). More food was imported and the price of agricultural labour doubled. A series of wet harvests from 1875 to 1879 made matters worse, especially in the Feldon. Twenty years later the harvests were adversely affected by summer droughts.

Pastoral farmers in the north continued to develop their milk production, sending increasing quantities by rail to the towns. Milk prices kept up while beef and mutton prices fell in the face of imported frozen meat and by 1910 dairy cattle outnumbered beef cattle. In the pastoral areas farmers gradually ceased to cultivate a grain crop for cash and instead concentrated on growing oats and other fodder crops for their own herds. Straw-cutting machinery was also introduced by many tenant farmers to provide additional fodder. Smallholders and horticulturalists suffered less than larger farmers as long as they could find the resources to pay the increasingly high wages for labour. Vegetables, eggs and poultry meat found a ready sale in the expanding consumer market of the towns and suburbs. Potatoes, peas and other field vegetables became more profitable with the development of cheap road transport.

Although not so hard hit as farmers elsewhere, the midland farmers suffered considerable difficulties. In the 1880s large landowners were forced to make rent allowances and eventually to accept rent decreases (Robinson 1978: 165). This clearly could be at best only a temporary expedient; the long-term remedy was to encourage greater efficiency and intensity of farming and to select tenants who were capable of maximising returns. By 1905 landowners had recovered to the extent that rents returned to the general pattern of the 1870s. Despite these difficulties landlord investment on the large estates remained high and to some extent was shouldered as a public duty by the aristocracy at least. Even before the First World War, however, there were signs that this pattern would not continue. The Sutherland estates centred on Trentham were sold ostensibly because of local industrial pollution, but for the most part as building plots. Trentham Hall itself was turned into a public amenity. Lord Ferrers sold the Chartley estate in 1904 and Lord Macclesfield the Croxden estate in 1914. The break-up of these estates sometimes resulted in opportunities for new farmers to move in from the north and west. These men were often of lower social status, doing most of the work themselves in order to reduce labour costs and accepting a limited standard of living (Thompson 1963: 152).

By 1914 more land had been laid down to grass, farmers relied more than ever on dairy farming and imported foodstuffs and the labour force had been reduced. There has also been a marked shift from cash crops to fodder though potato growing and market gardening had increased. Farmers formed co-operatives or commercial ventures to market products, and several cheese factories were established in Staffordshire; although only three became long-term ventures (Henstock 1969: 42). In 1897 the Staffordshire Dairy Farmers Association was founded to promote their interests in general but also to organise sales of milk to London.

Despite all the difficulties of the 1880s and 1890s the remuneration and conditions of the comparatively few agricultural labourers and craftsmen who were employed appears to have improved, although pay still remained very low compared with town workers. Staffordshire labourers on the Trentham estates were paid 17–19s. a week for 63 hours labour and skilled men earned 2s. or so more a week. In Warwickshire in the 1890s agricultural workers' wages ranged from 16s. to 19s. a week for skilled workers but only 9s. 6d. for the lowest paid labourer (Ashby 1961: 158). Labourers usually had free accommodation even though it was in tied cottages, lacking main drainage and piped water.

There was growing concern in the late nineteenth century about the migration of the rural population from the land. An Act of 1908 enabled parish and county councils to purchase land for allotments and smallholdings. In south Warwickshire the allotments were made and worked with determination by the villagers of Tysoe supported by their Smallholdings and Allotments Association. They dug the land with spades, dibbled in beans by hand, planted corn and potatoes, with the whole family helping with the work (Ashby 1961: 134). Elsewhere some small ventures were made often by urban district councils but the Act did little to retain farm workers on the land.

The countryside changed only gradually before the First World War and the most important changes were invisible. The land was no longer the basis of wealth, power and daily bread for the majority of the people. Agriculture was becoming a business to be managed, a subordinate service to industrial society. Land no longer supported effectively the grandeurs of the great house and the majority of people knew nothing at first hand about the cultivation of the land or the rural way of life. For the people of the towns the countryside was becoming an amenity, a place to visit for rest and recreation.

Chapter 29

Public transport, national and local

By 1830 the midland coalfield districts had hundreds of miles of railways along which horses or stationary engines pulled wagonloads of coal, ironstone and clay to the canal wharfs or to the industrial works. These railways were privately developed and managed, but closely integrated with the canal system. An early example, opened in 1777, linked the Caldon Canal at Froghall with the Caldon Low limestone quarries. A line of 16 miles was opened in 1826 from Stratford to Moreton in Marsh. The wagons were horsedrawn and carried coal and ironware from the canal to the Cotswolds, returning with agricultural produce, lime and stone (Slater 1981: 88). Three years later the Shut End railway opened on the Dudley estates to connect pits at Kingswinford with the Staffordshire and Worcestershire Canal (Raybould 1973a: 66). Between 1825 and 1830 there was a growing recognition of the immediate need to develop a public railway network, especially after the Rainhill trials had vindicated the steam locomotive.

The first attempt to secure a public line linking Birmingham with the Mersey was made as a result of the dissatisfaction of the south Staffordshire iron masters with the canal company's freight rates. The London–Birmingham Railway was built under the supervision of Robert Stephenson, and the first section, from Rugby to Birmingham, opened for passengers on 9 April 1838. Meanwhile, the Grand Junction Railway linking Liverpool and Manchester with Birmingham was completed under the supervision of Joseph Locke. The two lines were not continuous, but passengers could transfer at the stations of the two companies in Curzon Street. The early trains travelled the 97 miles from Birmingham to London in $4\frac{1}{2}$ hours at an average speed of $22\frac{1}{2}$ miles per hour (Sherlock 1976: 130). Four major Railway Acts received royal assent in 1836 authorising the Birmingham–Gloucester line, the Birmingham and Derby junction, the Midland Counties, and the North Midland Railways (Clinker 1956: 7). The main-line stations in the Midlands were at Rugby, Hampton in Arden, Coventry and Birmingham. The Grand Junction skirted the north of Birmingham, missing Walsall and Wolverhampton, but had

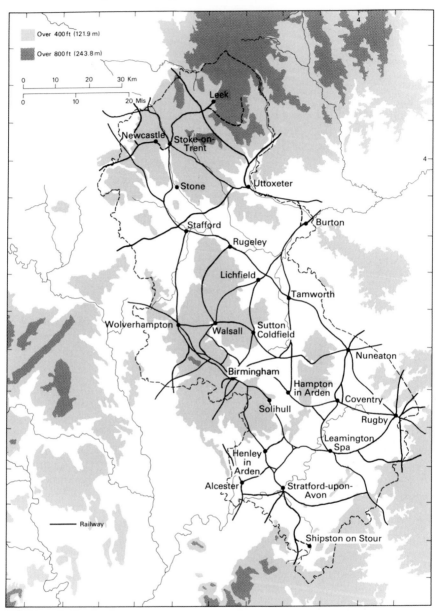

Figure 5.1   Railways in Staffordshire and Warwickshire, 1835–1880 (based on Greenslade and Stuart 1965: 48; and Slater 1981: 89)

stations at Penkridge, Stafford and Madeley before going on to Crewe, well to the west of Newcastle and the Potteries.

Between 1839 and 1843, despite the lull in railway investment in national terms, there was much activity in the Midlands, and even more development between 1844 and 1855. Birmingham was linked to Derby (1842), Gloucester (1840) and Oxford (1852), lines were laid from Rugby to Leicester (1840) and Derby (1847), and in 1848 the North Staffordshire Railway was built through the Potteries, connecting with the London and Manchester line from Crewe, through Stoke to Uttoxeter, Burton and Derby. The main stations were at Etruria and Stoke, both close to the Trent and Mersey Canal, and in 1849 the connection was completed when Macclesfield and the Potteries were linked with Colwich near Burton. The Churnett Valley Railway was completed between 1849 and 1852 (Christiansen 1973).

The separate promotion and ambitions of the many railway companies were encouraged by Parliament who feared a monopoly. The Great Western Railway came into the Midlands with its wide gauge (7 ft 0¼ in) between 1846 and 1849 when the company built a line from Oxford through Banbury to Leamington Spa, Solihull and Birmingham and thence to Dudley Port, Wolverhampton and Shrewsbury. In 1854 the former London and Birmingham and Grand Junction Line combined in a single London and North Western Line with a new station in central Birmingham at New Street. In the 1850s the Great Western Railway and the London and North West companies competed fiercely with each other for midland traffic and the result was two separate but parallel systems with duplicate railway stations at Wolverhampton, Dudley and Birmingham (Davies 1976: 140–60).

Meanwhile, in 1847 the Trent Valley company had made a new route to the north from Rugby to Stafford, by-passing Birmingham. By 1855 a complex and elaborate network of main lines connected with towns and industrial centres of the Midlands and linked them with London and the ports. Many of the routes followed those of the canals. Both the Shropshire Union Canal and the Birmingham Canal Navigation were bought by the London and North Western Railway Company and continued short-haul traffic and an intensive use of their own water to bring goods to the railways for transhipment in the specialised interchange basins. On the other hand, the Trent and Mersey was bought by the North Staffordshire Railway and in a different geographical situation the railway company collected goods on their comparatively short mileage, but were able to undertake long-distance deliveries by canal.

The impact of the railway's arrival on other services was variable. Stage coaches stopped running to Leamington as soon as the railway was built and long-distance services rapidly closed down, with a corresponding change in the type of services offered by the town coaching inns. However, services plying to and from the railway stations increased. Regular horse omnibus services for this purpose were introduced in Longton during the 1860s. The number of long-distance horse waggoners declined sharply but every small village and town without 'railway privileges' still needed carriers to take goods and animals to and from the railway stations and freight yards. In 1850 over 360 carrier's carts left Coventry each week from the principal inns of the town.

Even in 1900 330 weekly cart services still supplemented the carriage services of the Midland Railway. At Warwick, on the other hand, the number of carriers dropped from 62 in 1851 to 36 twenty years later. The daily coach services to Cheltenham, Oxford, Stratford and Alcester also rapidly declined after the coming of the railway and all had ceased to operate by 1874.

Post was carried by the railways from 1840, but large numbers of mail carts were required to distribute mail from the trains to the post offices. Alongside the railway lines telegraph wires were erected by a great number of small local companies, and by the 1860s the United Kingdom Telegraph Company had taken over the earlier companies and was busily establishing telegraphic communication throughout the Midlands.

The engine shed which had been built upon the opening of the railway in Rugby in 1838 was enlarged in 1855 to hold 25 locomotives and in 1878 was replaced by one holding 125 locomotives. By 1881 Rugby railway station had six main lines. In 1892 erecting shops for the LNW Railway were opened, followed by Hunter's Wagon Works, and railway workers and their dependants comprised one-fifth of the inhabitants by the end of the century (Simms 1949).

The coming of the railways changed the pattern of building development in many towns. Hotels for passengers and carrier depots and warehouses for goods were soon associated with the stations. Stoke station, which cost £30,000 to build with its flanking hotel became a social centre in an area notably short of such amenities. The building of New Street station in Birmingham involved the clearance of some of the worst slums and set a precedent for the compulsory purchase and demolition of property (Kellett 1969: 144–5).

Passenger fares in the early days were far from cheap. It cost 10s. to travel first-class from Birmingham to Derby and £1 10s. to London, and the 'parliamentary trains' at 1d. per mile ran at inconvenient times. It was mainly the upper and middle classes who used the passenger services, but they were a numerous and growing body.

Excursion trains from north Staffordshire went on weekdays to Liverpool and London, to Buxton and Matlock and increasingly to north Wales. Excursions to the Isle of Man and to Blackpool were popular by the end of the century. The railways linked with the steamship ferry services from Holyhead, and with the emigrant traffic from Liverpool.

The multiplication and extension of lines continued in conjunction with industrial development. Between 1859 and 1875 the Midland Railway Company provided a network of lines for the Burton on Trent brewers. In 1872 they took 616,000 tons of freight from the town and in 1895 921,000 tons. Meanwhile the great increase in production on the Cannock Chase coalfield was proving too much for the existing canal and rail transport systems, which became so congested that companies were forced to work short time because of delays in getting coal away. In 1880, after many difficulties and false starts, the

LNWR line from Sutton Coldfield at last provided the necessary outlet. In the 1860s the Black Country ironmasters were accustomed to attribute their problems to the high freight rates charged by the LNWR and the GWR. The Midland Railway penetrated the area in 1872 by building the Wolverhampton to Walsall line and advertising lower freight rates. However, within seven years their freight rates were the same as the other railway companies and the Black Country iron industry was still in decline.

By 1875 virtually every Staffordshire and Warwickshire town, including rural market centres, were within reach of a main-line station, and in the 1870s the main developments were of suburban railways. The Potteries loop line had been the subject of acrimonious discussion between Hanley and Burslem ever since 1854, but was opened at last in December 1875. It connected the six towns with stations at Burslem, Hanley, Kidsgrove and Cobridge, and was an immediate success (Christiansen 1973).

However, the large railway companies continued to show only limited enthusiasm for developing cheap local railway travel. Soon the suburban railways were in competition for local passenger traffic with horsedrawn and steam trams and omnibuses and by the turn of the century with electric trams. As early as 1886 the Darlaston passenger service was closed for lack of passengers and although in 1908 230 trains a day left Stoke they were by no means full. Suburban railways in the Midlands succeeded in attracting substantial passenger traffic only in less urbanised areas where competition from trams was not as fierce (VCH Staffs II: 328–30).

The mainline railways and their branches played an ever more important part in carrying freight, including manufacturers' raw materials, manufactured goods and agricultural produce. The carriage of fresh food by railways remained important, and midland farmers and townsfolk were almost entirely dependent on the milk trains. The bulk transport of domestic and industrial fuel was also largely by railway, though some transport of coal by canal barge continued until well into the twentieth century (VCH Staffs II: 331–3).

The larger towns had a service of licensed cabs for the wealthy from at least the 1820s and the extension of the horsedrawn omnibus plying a fixed route and picking up and putting down passengers developed from the 1850s. From 1839 onwards an omnibus ran from the King's Head, Newcastle, to the railway station at Whitmore five miles away. The introduction of steam trams in the 1880s caused controversy, for in Coventry, the Potteries and elsewhere the intrusion of steam engines into streets full of pedestrians dismayed the respectable and frightened the horses; however, as many as 23 million passengers were carried by them in the Potteries in 1899 (Warrilow 1960). By this date, though, the electric tram had already been introduced. In Wolverhampton the rival claims of the older systems of electric power points laid in the road and the newer Lorain system of overhead cables deeply divided the town (Jones, G. W. 1969: 41–2). By 1912 Coventry Corporation had electrically powered trams running on eleven miles of track, and in the following year they were among the first to introduce public motor buses. All forms of municipal transport aimed at providing cheap transport for large numbers of workers and their families. By the beginning of the twentieth century very few people were limited to pedestrian travel.

Chapter 30

Power, politics and the people

The aristocracy were still a force to be reckoned with in the Midlands in the nineteenth century. Staffordshire had the second highest number of country houses in the whole of England. There were 129 estates of at least 2,000 acres or which yielded over £3,000 a year in Staffordshire and 111 in Warwickshire (Bateman 1883). The wealthiest landowner, not only in the Midlands but in the whole kingdom, was the Duke of Sutherland and in the south of the county the Earl of Dudley ranked sixth. However, the majority of estates in the Midlands were of only middling size. Staffordshire ranked eighth and Warwickshire 17 in the table of counties with estates of over 10,000 acres (Thompson 1963: 32). Both counties had just over a quarter of their land held by gentlemen of between 1,000 and 10,000 acres and both had only about 10 per cent held by gentlemen of small estates (Thompson 1963: 117) although there were considerable numbers of small freehold properties in the north Staffordshire moorlands and Cannock Chase (VCH Staffs VI: 116). By far the greater part of the aristocracy and gentlemen of the Midlands derived the principal part of their income from their rent rolls but non-agricultural income formed an increasing proportion of the total wealth of the dukes of Sutherland, the earls of Dudley and of Dartmouth, Lord Hatherton and Lord Anglesey, and the earls of Harrowby were linked by marriage with Coutts the city bankers (Sturgess 1971: 178–87).

The lifestyle of the peerage was still that of their eighteenth-century predecessors. The larger landowners of Staffordshire at this time have been accused of maintaining their personal spending at a higher level than their estates could really support (Sturgess 1971: 201). The earls of Dudley spent £668,000 on buying the palatial Witley Court in Worcestershire which was elaborated with a colossal frontage, porches, orangery and fountains 26 ft high and copied from Bernini and Michelangelo. Most of the other wealthy landed families extended their houses, adding new wings, conservatories, gun rooms, carriage houses and stables and the houses were made more comfortable with the addition of water-closets, bathrooms, central heating and gas lighting. They continued to give great house parties at their various residences, and spent the 'season' in London. They travelled on the Continent and even further afield (Tyack 1970: 160–92).

In income and wealth the peers surpassed all but the wealthiest industrialists but men like Sir Alfred Hickman, Sir Benjamin Hingley and J. H. Chance far exceeded in wealth the majority of the gentry (Trainor 1982: 75). In the course of the nineteenth century the towns and the industrial areas developed their own elite groups and organisations. The Ironmasters' Associations, the Chambers of Commerce and the party political organisations were gatherings of the rich and powerful. Wealthy businessmen built great houses, some of them in the countryside amid parks, kept large numbers of servants and entertained on a lavish scale, and their sons were educated at public schools and attended universities.

The Reform of Parliament Act of 1832 made only very limited changes in the Midlands. Staffordshire and Warwickshire were each divided into a north and a south district with two members from each district. In the counties the electorate of 40s. freeholders and £10 rent payers comprised only about 5 per cent of the adult male population. In south Staffordshire for example there were 3,000 voters in 1833, rising by the following election to 7,871. The county representation in the mid-Victorian period remained on the whole in the hands of Conservatives and the members were nearly all connections of the local landed families – Viscount Ingestre and the Right Honourable Littleton both served as members of Parliament for Staffordshire South and members of the Mordaunt, Shirley, and Brooke families represented Warwickshire South. The older boroughs, with the exception of Sutton Coldfield and Stratford, all kept their two members and the electorate increased by about 50 per cent. The towns newly enfranchised were Wolverhampton, Birmingham and Stoke on Trent. In Coventry and other towns both Conservative and Liberal registration associations were formed to make sure that no potential support was lost. The emergent party organisations were used not only to ensure support in parliamentary elections but also in elections to the boards of Poor Law, and other local administrative bodies. Nevertheless it was still from the ranks of the landed families that virtually all the county and many of the borough members of the House of Commons were drawn.

Large landowners who had the desire and the talent to do so continued to play a major part in national affairs. The earls of Harrowby, the Lyttletons of Hagley and the third Earl Dudley were all in various capacities directly involved in public affairs as members of the cabinet, the privy council, holders of state office or governors of Empire.

By the 1880s a combination of agricultural depression, industrial crises and rising cost of wages meant that many landowners were beginning to find that their incomes no longer supported their expenditure. The Dudleys weathered the difficulties better than most but even they experienced some decline in receipts from the 1880s while the Dartmouths, the Sneyds and Hathertons and others were complaining of indebtedness. However, their anxieties did not lead to any noticeable retrenchment (Sturgess 1971: 170–210). Ralph Sneyd was passionately interested in racehorses and shooting and maintained a breeding stud and a race-course on his estate. In 1904 he solved his financial problems to some extent by leasing Keele Hall to the Grand Duke Michael, a cousin of the Tsar of Russia, and lived in London enjoying 'a brilliant social life' (Kolbert 1976).

New forces were at work in politics which did not so much challenge the landed interest but entered and occupied the place of leadership which it had formerly held. In 1867 the electorate had again been extended and Staffordshire was divided into three constituencies: north, east and west. The temperance issue and the new boundaries brought in the brewers Bass and Alsopp as the new members for Staffordshire East, and another brewer, Salt, was elected at Stafford borough. In Birmingham Schnardhörst created the Liberal voting machine and applied it not only to ensure Liberal representation in the parliamentary elections but also to bring Chamberlain and other Liberals on to the council of Birmingham Corporation and the new School Board. The management of a growing electorate was increasingly a matter for dedicated daily work by local agents rather than the exercise of lordly influence. When the Conservative party was refashioned between 1874 and 1880 it was as the party of wealth in all its forms, landed, industrial and commercial, and it also sought to secure the adhesion of the new enlarged electorate which after 1885 comprised the great majority of adult men. In the last decades of the nineteenth century the influence of Joseph Chamberlain, first as Liberal then later as Conservative Unionist, dominated Birmingham and the Black Country constituencies, carrying them from Liberalism to Conservative-Unionism, and keeping their allegiance until 1914 (Green 1973). Those whose power was derived from ancient landed wealth and those whose power was derived from recently acquired commercial and industrial wealth could find much common ground and the two aristocracies were increasingly assimilated.

The force of a self-conscious and organised Labour movement among the working-classes was another matter and, in the first half of the century at least, appeared as a threat to all order and dominance. The presence of the small master economy and the prevalence of subcontracting stimulated rather than reduced assertiveness and debate, and resistance to the pressures of industrial society emanated from a determination to be respectable and respected in the local community as well as from a desire to overturn the power structure. Among the loudest and most articulate voices was that of Samuel Cook, the draper of High Street, Dudley, who campaigned against church rates, parsons, mine disasters and truck, and in support of Chartism, political reform and the equality of women.

For a time Owenism had a considerable appeal in the Midlands. Followers of Robert Owen were active in the Potteries from 1825 and in the other industrial districts from 1832, surfacing in the aftermath of the struggle for political reform. The National Union of Co-operative Potters was formed and delegates were sent to a three-day co-operative congress in 1836. The Association of Classes of All Nations was founded in 1835 with branches in Dudley, Wednesbury, Walsall, Wolverhampton and Stourbridge, and the Social Institute was set up in Stourbridge in 1840. Meetings were frequent throughout the 1830s and the *New Moral World* circulated in all the towns and large villages. Local clergy became alarmed at this challenge to established religion and many denunciations were made from the pulpit and public meetings. The potters tried to establish a New Moral World in America by organising the emigration of potters to found a new community there. Land was bought and £5,000 expended, but in the event the scheme failed disastrously (Owen 1901: 63–78).

Between 1823 and 1875 one of the principal means of controlling relations between employer and employed was the Master and the Servant Act. A contract was presumed to exist and a workman could be prosecuted in the criminal court for not working up materials, for leaving his employment without fourteen days' notice or for encouraging others to do so. Between 1858 and 1875 in Wolverhampton alone there were 3,000 prosecutions, and in 1875 the number of prosecutions represented 4.51 per 1,000 of the population. In Staffordshire as a whole 10,000 people were prosecuted between 1858 and 1867 (Woods 1982: 93–116).

Between 1825 and 1871 few years went by without some form of strike activity, but the nature and purpose of these episodes needs to be examined with some care, for in the Midlands strikes were scarcely ever a simple withdrawal of waged labour. The prevalence of subcontracting and the persistence of the small family workshop in semi-independence meant that a striking nailer or collier was in a sense refusing to work not for his master but for some intermediary or for himself. The phrase 'playdays' for the days when a nailer refused to work persisted throughout the bitter strikes and demoralisation of the trade in the nineteenth century, since in theory the nailer had the independent choice of accepting or refusing work. Negotiations often centred on adjustments of the traditional price lists, resistance to the drastic lowering of prices when times were bad, or claims for a percentage increase on the lists in times of good trade. In Coventry strikes were aimed at maintaining domestic work and the price lists against the attempt to introduce waged factory work. Some strikes were organised in an attempt to maintain control over entry to the trade and others against particular practices such as discount, or truck.

Strikes were sometimes on a large scale and sustained for long periods. In 1834 a potters' strike lasted ten weeks, and two years later another major strike involved an estimated 20,000 men, who refused to work for sixty-four of the master potters. Between 1825 and 1844, even small-scale strikes had an atmosphere of confrontation with the state since the only resort of the magistrate was to call out the military. In December 1831 the Wolverhampton troop of yeomanry was on duty for fourteen days during a colliers' strike. Troops were also stationed at Bilston, Dudley, Oldbury, Stourbridge, Kidderminster and Halesowen. Moreover, the Home Office and the magistrates both saw any form of industrial action as indicative of a riotous spirit and a challenge to their control (Philips 1974: 150).

Meanwhile there were those who sought a further reform of the electoral machinery, and there was a renewed demand for male adult suffrage and more frequent elections. The Reform Act of 1832 was a profound disappointment to those who had been active in the midland political unions and they were embittered by the Whig policies of 1833–8. New political unions were formed in Birmingham and Coventry and the radical Whig alliance of 1832 could no longer be sustained. Initially they took up the 'people's charter' but the middle-class leadership soon found the bitterness and the growing threats of physical force too much for them. In Birmingham, Muntz and Attwood lost control of the movement, and the Coventry leader Taunton got little support for his reluctant advocacy of a limited and preventive use of force (Searby 1964: 14). In the depression of 1837–8 Chartist groups of working men with skilled artisans as leaders appeared in the majority of industrial towns and villages in the Potteries and in the Black Country. Signatures were collected for the national petition and delegates elected for the national Chartist Convention (Barnsby 1977: 75). The Convention transferred to Lawrence Street chapel in Birmingham in a gathering atmosphere of crisis. Several leaders, including William Lovett, were arrested in June and every night restless and angry crowds gathered in the Bull Ring in Birmingham. There were several violent episodes culminating in the riots of 15 July 1839, when not only the special constables, the militia and the dragoons were called in but finally and devastatingly the new metropolitan police who arrived by railway train at the height of the riots. In many midland towns there were protest meetings, but the wealthier political leaders withdrew and Chartism was left to the tallow chandlers, the screw turners, the hammer makers in the Black Country and to the potters and colliers in north Staffordshire. They collected signatures for a new petition, organised rallies with banners and bands, some of them tried to set up a Chartist church, a Chartist school and Chartist shops. There was a female Chartist association at Bilston led by Mrs Langston. From May to September 1842 political agitation was combined with the prolonged widespread and bitter strikes by the colliers, the metal workers and the potters. Meetings were held and groups of colliers marched from place to place, building up a sense of solidarity and publicising their demands for a nine-hour day with 4s. pay and two quarts of drink, fire coal every four weeks and one hour's dinner break; they also wanted the abolition of half days and bildasses (work without pay). There were serious riots in the Potteries (Briggs 1983: 42–6). Everywhere the magistrates called out the military. At Coventry and at Bedworth the presence of the yeomanry proved a good deal more inflammatory than the speeches of the Chartist orators (Quinault 1974: 204–

279

6). In the Midlands known Chartists such as Cook and Linney were imprisoned, but the strike continued throughout the summer and autumn. In September a major attempt at mediation was made under the chairmanship of the Earl of Dartmouth, but the butties and the largest ironmasters and coalmasters held aloof and in the event they only had to wait until the colliers' resources gave out and with the advent of the second winter the men drifted back to work.

In October 1842 274 prisoners were tried at Stafford Assizes for offences connected with the strike, 55 from south Staffordshire and 200 from the Potteries: many of them were transported, others received sentences of between six and twenty months' hard labour. In autumn 1843 Parliament set up a commission of enquiry into the troubles of the south Staffordshire mining region. Iron prices fell again in 1848 and the ironmasters promptly reduced the wages, in the case of the puddlers by 15 per cent. The puddlers struck for many weeks rather to the advantage of the ironmasters than otherwise, as there was little demand for their product (Worpell 1976: 34–8). In Stourbridge in 1858 the flint glassworkers' union, founded in 1851, came out on strike, not about wages but about the management of the industry. As skilled specialists, well organised and not without funds, the flint glassworkers' purpose was to maintain control of appointments to the trade, thus ensuring that only their own members were taken on (Hopkins 1973: 21).

In the early 1860s the conditions of the domestic workers deteriorated in the context of increasing mechanisation and a series of bitter strikes, with violence and intimidation, expressed frustration without achieving any improvement in their condition (Barnsby 1977: 170–5). Although most midland unions were still strongly local and centred on particular crafts, they nevertheless benefited from the trade union legislation of 1867–75. The Trade Union Act of 1871 protected their legal position and their funds, and control of picketing was determined by the Criminal Law Amendment Act of 1875. Existing societies developed new confidence and, whereas in 1870 Richard Juggins had been the only professional trade union organiser in the Black Country, by 1914 a new class of paid union officials had appeared. The Amalgamated Society of Railway Servants was established in Birmingham in 1871 and became a national organisation by 1913. The National Society of Amalgamated Brassworkers, organised by W. J. Davis, gained a 15 per cent increase on the price lists in the prosperous period of the early 1870s (Dalley 1914). The tinsmiths, electro-plate workers, wood turners, file smiths and the fire iron forgers all made similar gains on the piece work lists. These societies consisted of subcontractors who made a deliberately moderate and reasoned appeal to the employers, seeking to convince them that the agreed price would be paid by the customer. They combined against the underhands and small garret masters who undercut price lists and offered 'unfair' competition, and operated through pressure groups rather than by means of strikes.

It began to seem possible that a permanent and peaceful relationship could be established between the employers and organised labour. Arbitration boards and joint activities were tried in many industries, but the new alliances were put under severe strain in the late 1870s. In the Black Country and north Staffordshire the iron industry collapsed dramatically between 1875 and 1880 and in the Stour Valley the glass industry also suffered severe reverses and glasshouses were closed. The gains of the early 1870s were reversed and the brassworkers, tinworkers, the file smiths and the potters found that arbitration meant a cut in their rates when trade was bad. Arbitrators like Lord Hatherton and Brassey saw the debate in terms of a constant share of fluctuating profits, whereas the trade unions and their members were looking for a larger share of profits for their members on a permanent basis.

From the 1860s trade societies had begun to combine forces in local trades councils. They collected money and appealed for support for the member societies both in the Midlands and in other parts of the country, they trained and assisted small unions and took part as middle men in negotiations and arbitrating disputes. An early example was that founded at Birmingham in 1866 when thirty-five delegates met to establish a council to watch over social and political rights and to press for the legal protection of trades unions. The Midlands Trades Federation was founded at Darlaston in 1886 and by 1891 claimed a membership of 14,000. They were involved in 160 different deputations to employers in the first three years of their existence (Taylor 1972b: 26–41).

During this period public opinion increasingly came to support the claims of the lowest paid and the unskilled. The conditions of the domestic handworkers deteriorated in the face of competition from the machine throughout the period, but most rapidly from 1875 (Hopkins 1982). Human labour was only employable if it was offered at the cheapest rates. Handmade nailmaking and small-chainmaking were by this time the resort of the poorest and most vulnerable, especially women workers. Their sufferings usually found an effective voice only when they aroused the concern of some outsider who could mobilise public opinion through the press. The nailmakers' strike of 1869 had something of the bitterness and desperation of the Sheffield outrages, and the strike of 1878 lasted for sixteen months, yet they achieved little and the Nailers' Board of Conciliation and Arbitration, set up in 1880, collapsed after only five months. The women's chainmakers' strike in 1906, led by Mary MacCarthy, was followed by another in 1909 led by Julia Varley and Billy Bamford, all socialists and outsiders. The Royal Commission on sweated trades publicised the conditions of some of the lowest paid and in 1909 the Trade Board Act laid down a 2½*d*. an hour minimum wage and made Wages Boards mandatory in all trades.

Meanwhile, the agricultural workers had declined in numbers and status as machinery and new types of farm organisation displaced them. In Warwickshire in 1872 Joseph Arch gathered 500 of them into a Union of Farm Workers to press for an increase of 6*d*. a day and the establishment of a nine hour day.

281

Strikes were organised in the 1870s in Tysoe, Claverdon, Kineton and Wasperton, and the movement spread. However, it proved difficult for the union to sustain its influence in the face of dwindling opportunities for employment on the land and by 1892 the National Agricultural Labourers' Union had little or no support in Warwickshire. Between 1893 and 1897 the Warwickshire Agricultural and General Workers' Union attempted to establish a more effective body. Much of the impetus and support came from various intellectual pressure groups such as the English Land Restoration League and from political parties with an eye on the new parish council elections of 1897 (Horn 1972: 23–37).

The concept of a minimum wage for the unskilled spread during the 1880s. When a minimum wage was discussed in industries where rates had been traditionally negotiated on the basis of price lists, considerable difficulties arose. The skilled men wished to retain piecework and price lists, but the underhands and assistants would have benefited from a minimum wage. There was a struggle for power within unions such as the brassworkers between older men, who still sought a negotiated alliance with the employers, and the thrusting younger generation, who based their support on large, well-organised numbers of wage earners. The larger unions attracted increasing support in the period immediately before the First World War. The railway men and the miners were organised by 1906 in national federations. National unions of gasworkers and general labourers were established in 1907. Many workers in different specialist firms joined them and the various employers in

Plate 5.2 Railwaymen on strike in 1911, assembling at the corner of Eaton Road, Coventry.

the different trades proved willing to enter into negotiations with them. Negotiations now took place between delegated groups, committees and representatives of national bodies, and there were fewer face-to-face negotiations between men who, however different their status, shared experience of a particular skill. The National Union of Women Workers (1906) and the Workers'
Union (1907) attracted considerable numbers of unskilled workers. 1913 saw
strikes lasting six months of coalminers, railway workers and craftsmen,
mainly on the minimum wage issue.

Increasingly some people saw trade-union membership and activities as
only part of a wider and more direct attempt to alter the relationships of
society. Socialism spread both as an educative agency and as a motive for
action. Fabians, Communists and even anarchists had small groups of supporters in the Midlands but their influence was slight. In the Midlands it was only
very gradually that a specifically labour presence began to be felt in politics.
Very few Labour politicians stood in either municipal or national elections
before the First World War. Robert Toller represented Saltley Ward on Birmingham Council, and W. J. Davis and Eli Bloor stood for Parliament at the
1892 General Election as Lib-Lab candidates without success. From about
1900, however, the midland Labour Movement began to work for separate
Labour representation and in 1906 T. F. Richards was elected at Wolverhampton, and John Ward at Stoke on Trent. James Holmes stood in Birmingham
East but was beaten by Chamberlain's ally Sir Benjamin Stone, and in general
in the Birmingham area the Liberal Unionist alliance with working men was
still strong (Roberts 1982: 12–21). In 1910 Richards lost his seat at Wolverhampton but Ward retained his at Stoke on Trent. Meanwhile four Labour
councillors had joined Birmingham City Council (Roberts 1983: 9–15).

One of the principal concerns of government had always been the
maintenance of order. During the nineteenth century the increasing numbers of
people and the increasing varieties of crime made necessary a corresponding
increase in the numbers of magistrates, especially in urban and industrial areas.
In the counties the reins of local authority were still firmly held by the
aristocracy and the landed gentry. Lord Dartmouth was a hardworking and
imperious Deputy Lieutenant of Staffordshire, and in Warwickshire the Earls
of Warwick continued to exercise that office. In Warwickshire five of the
county magistrates were peers or baronets and by 1868 seventy of the County's
active justices of the peace each owned over 500 acres. The number of clergy
magistrates was still high but the Earl of Warwick, as Lord Lieutenant,
succeeded in reducing the number by 1858 and by the end of the century the
clerical magistrate was a rarity (Quinault 1974: 189). As the towns acquired
corporate status a body of magistrates was appointed on the recommendation
of the new councillors to the Lord Chancellor. They held office for life and
were almost all local industrialists, members of town councils, the boards of
guardians and in due course of the watch committees and the school boards. In
practice they determined local policies and executed national law and local bye

283

laws. Like the landowners in the counties they formed an almost impenetrable elite and their view of justice was coloured by their private role as employers of labour and by their personal convictions about religion, order and the economic process (Philips, D. 1975).

The development of a permanent civilian police force was a major innovation which created a new relationship between the individual and the law and a new uniformity of law enforcement. In 1833 any town with more than 5,000 population was permitted to appoint and pay watchmen. Coventry established a paid police force in 1836 under the Watch Committee, consisting of one superintendent, one inspector, one sergeant and twenty constables. In 1839 the Police Act enabled the counties to set up their own forces and despite some opposition Staffordshire, Warwickshire and Worcestershire immediately did so, but for some years police forces remained small and lacked resources and experience.

The Watch Committees and the police forces in the industrial towns undoubtedly saw some sections of the community as more disorderly and more criminal than others. The Irish in their ghettos in Wolverhampton, Walsall, Birmingham and Dudley received more than their fair share of police attention (Swift 1980: 1–10). The Watch Committees and the police were also particularly determined to control prostitution, sabbath breaking, and bad language and drunkenness in public places. By the 1850s the police were beginning to be successful in reducing offences against public order and were gaining acceptance among all classes including the working classes. The yeomanry were not called out after 1848 and the military were occupied in maintaining order in the colonies rather than at home.

Chapter 31

Municipal self-government

While reform of Parliament had attracted much political support in the Midlands the reform of municipal corporations aroused comparatively little public interest. There was a Whig party of reform in Warwick and individuals like the utilitarian Joseph Parkes were active in seeking reform and supporting the investigations of abuses but there was no general organised campaign in the Midlands (Finlayson 1973). In the Potteries there were proposals for some form of local government which would incorporate the six towns but local opinion soon swung away from the idea and at the time of the Municipal Reform Act petitions were sent to Parliament praying that the Potteries might be left out of the list of places proposed for incorporation. Coventry, Warwick, Stafford, Stratford, Walsall, Newcastle and Tamworth and Lichfield were reorganised as municipal corporations on the new model. Sutton Coldfield was rejected and did not become a borough until 1884. The new councillors in the reformed corporations were elected by the householder ratepayers with three years residence, but the numbers of local voters were still fairly limited: Walsall now had 1,064 voters in the town and 839 in the Foreign, while Warwick had about 1,000 electors. It was by no means clear that the other large urban agglomerations would wish to proceed to incorporation.

At this stage the advantages, other than political, of obtaining a municipal charter were limited. It was only in the 1850s that new powers were granted to such town governments as saw fit to undertake them. Birmingham already had seven functioning commissions with considerable *ad hoc* powers over streets, markets, scavenging, the Poor Law, the highways and public order, paid for and administered by the properties townsfolk, some of whom saw little advantage in adding to their number. Despite considerable local opposition, the radicals pushed through the petition for incorporation, and the Birmingham Charter was issued in December 1838 (Gill 1952: 225). The other large midland towns showed no great anxiety to follow Birmingham's example. Although Wolverhampton had become a parliamentary borough in 1832, it did not seek incorporation until 1848, Hanley in 1856, Dudley in 1865 and Stoke on Trent not until 1874.

By the mid-century the major part of the political difficulties arising from the reform of 1835 had been resolved. In Birmingham, the Improvement Act of 1851 finally established the town council as the principal local authority absorbing the powers of the Town Commissioners (Gill 1952: 358; Smith 1967: 63). At Coventry the council consolidated its authority on its now more limited jurisdiction. However, the financial problems remained, and for the next decade the main object of most councils was to avoid expense, and economy was the watchword. In Birmingham the new council had sole responsibility for lighting streets and for sewers. The expense of proposed water and road works caused so much alarm that leading businessmen proved unwilling to serve on the new council, Birmingham banks refused to increase the corporation's overdraft and an 'economist party' led by Joseph Allday, and supported by the Ratepayers' Protection Society, was able to seize the reins (Briggs 1963: 214).

The financial problems were real, and almost all the new and the reformed corporations found themselves in difficulties. At Wolverhampton the corporation attempted to purchase the waterworks and incurred a debt of £6,500. They were unable to pay, the creditors put in the bailiffs who seized all the corporation property, including the mayor's robes and the police handcuffs. The town was only rescued by the personal credit and energy of the mayor, Edward Perry. Newcastle and Stafford were also in financial difficulties. Only Coventry was able to reform its financial procedure and go forward with some confidence to provide a waterworks, a public baths and a public cemetery, and to tackle the sewage problem and acquire a site for new markets (Searby 1964: 31–2).

Indeed it was the ever more insistent threat of disease which gradually forced the municipal governments of the nineteenth century to take on a wider role of public service. While the new corporations struggled to establish their legal and financial security a series of national royal commissions of enquiry were at work. They produced a mass of statistical and impressionistic evidence concerning the problems of housing, sanitation, water supply, lodging houses and public nuisances, much of it referring to the large towns and populous areas. These reports were for the most part written by enthusiasts and campaigners who brought to public attention the dirt, degradation, and appalling living conditions in Leamington Spa, and Stratford on Avon, as well as in industrial towns.

Public anxiety was even more effectively aroused by the typhus epidemics of 1837, 1839 and 1847, the smallpox epidemic of 1837 to 1840 and most of all by the outbreaks of cholera in 1832 and 1849. Cholera was especially feared and aroused wholesale panic. When Wolverhampton heard in November 1831 'that cholera morbus has extended to this Kingdom' a town meeting promptly set up a Board of Health, which divided the town into ten areas, each with its own committee to 'inspect minutely'. Cholera returned to Coventry and south Staffordshire in 1849. During the visitations of cholera an atmosphere of crisis prevailed, industry was stopped, and clergymen preached judgement and destruction. Birmingham escaped the cholera, a circumstance which the townspeople attributed to the 'good water'.

However, despite all the lessons of experience and the abundance of reports there was an underlying resistance to any form of compulsion. Whether it came from central government or from local government, compulsory legislation was regarded as dangerous and intrusive. Government intervention, it was felt, should be kept to a minimum and the work of providing services and ameliorating social problems should be left to private enterprise and to voluntary organisations; the legislation which resulted from the commissioners' reports was mostly permissive and enabling.

A number of midland towns took advantage of the Public Health Act of 1848 to establish Boards of Health, namely Coventry in 1849, Warwick in 1849, Stratford and Nuneaton in 1850, Leamington in 1852 and Wolverhampton in 1853. Rugby was not a municipal borough, but led by the school's headmaster, Dr Tait, it had already shown interest in public health and had petitioned in favour of the Bill. It was the first place to be granted a local Board of Health on 5 September 1849 and a selected council of nine was authorised to tackle water, sanitation and market problems. The new local newspaper, the *Rugby Advertiser*, took great interest in their proceedings and represented the town as divided between the 'Go aheads' and the 'Obstructives'. The provision of a water supply illustrates their difficulties. The Rugby Board had to engage engineers to undertake large public works, employ analytical chemists, make the choice of competing schemes, make surveys, collect statistics, calculate costs and predict demand. It was 1865 before a successful scheme was completed and 1874 before the town had a continuous supply of water by day and night. The successive schemes and undertakings were much debated in the town with a vigorous opposition constantly pointing out weaknesses and expense. An appeal to the Central Board for help involved them in greater difficulties. The Local Board elections fought on the water issue were bitterly contested and a special Act of Parliament had to be obtained before the way was clear (Simms 1949).

For a long time Birmingham convinced itself that it was a healthy town and ignored the Public Health Act, but in the 1860s it was forced out of its economist stance by a rising tide of sewage. From 1862 Thomas Avery, the new chairman of the finance committee, had sought to economise and to limit borrowing, but was now forced to recognise the urgency of the sewage problem and also to accept some limited degree of improvement, notably the founding of the municipal reference library (1865) and baths and wash-houses (1862) (Fraser 1979: 95–101).

The limits of what could be achieved by voluntary action and adoptive legislation were everywhere becoming painfully apparent. Increasingly, central government began to issue directives and guidelines and to require local action under the guidance of the Central Local Government Board. The Sanitary Act

Plate 5.3 The Dart Magazine, published in Birmingham, was famous for its cartoons satirising local politics. Here Joseph Chamberlain 'magically' produces £54,000, the profits of the first year of the operation of the municipal gas undertaking, 8 February 1875.

of 1866 made it a duty on local councils to suppress nuisances. In 1871 the appointment of medical officers of health was made compulsory and a new Local Government Board was established. For their part the local communities began to show a new enthusiasm for local 'progress' which was motivated by both political and ethical considerations.

The Municipal Franchise Act of 1869 had reorganised the franchise on a more systematic basis with the effect of increasing the numbers of electors. Ward boundaries in Birmingham and the larger towns were reorganised and municipal elections became a recognised field of political conflict and party organisation (Smith 1982: 226–7). At the same time the wealthier businessmen in Wolverhampton, Birmingham and other towns began to see the transformation of their town as a moral duty, a means of elevating both the community and themselves. Collectivism, with the individual finding fulfilment in the community, replaced laissez-faire as the fashionable principle of public behaviour among the self-appointed leaders. George Dawson, Robert Dale and other ministers in Birmingham presented as a primary religious duty the reforms of the living conditions of urban areas. William Harris, journalist, translated the religious message into lively criticism of the *status quo* in the *Town Crier*, while the Martineaux, the Chamberlains, the Rylands and other wealthy families shouldered the responsibility of urban reform. Joseph Chamberlain, at the age of forty and with twenty years' experience of large-scale business behind him, agreed to stand for election at the Birmingham Town Council in 1869 (Hennock 1973: 61–80). Popular versions of scientific evolution were promising a world in which effective, practical action could sweep away moral and social ills, and the fantasy of progress inspired many for the next fifty years.

Midland towns were by no means in the forefront of urban improvement. Glasgow, Liverpool and many other towns had begun to tackle the problems of health and amenities much earlier. Birmingham in particular had a great backlog of work to be done, but the council carried through the much needed changes with such a flair for advertisement and self-glorification that they convinced others besides themselves that they were 'in the van' and created the enduring legend of the 'best governed town'.

By 1875 the transformation of Birmingham Municipal Council was under way. Gas, water and improvement were tackled with the large-scale capitalisation and self-confidence of Victorian business methods. Two private gas companies were bought out at a cost of £2,500,000 and administration was handed over to a gas committee. This was immediately followed by the purchase of the waterworks at a cost of £1,350,000 and the municipality undertook to supply water to all parts of the town.

By 1875 the improvement scheme was introduced to restructure the business district of Birmingham between New Street and Snowhill railway stations on the model of the Champs Elysées in Paris. The primary objective was to enhance the status and attractions of Birmingham as a business centre.

289

The clearing and cleansing of the town centre was of secondary importance, but provided useful propaganda. Meanwhile, progress had been made in other spheres of municipal affairs. The provision of spaces for the poor to refresh themselves was made by a partnership between philanthropy and municipal action, and Highgate Park, Summerfield Park and Small Heath Park were laid out and opened. In 1874 Yeoville Thomas designed new council offices to provide a fitting grandiose background for the council. A borough hospital and borough cemetery were established, 1,000 trees were planted in the streets and £180,000 was spent on paving the footwalks with granite setts (Briggs 1952: 67–135). As the councillors sought to provide amenities and to improve the image of the town, they became correspondingly determined to raise the tone of the inhabitants. Dirt became synonymous with vice, and the temperance movement brought public houses under control.

For years Birmingham had been struggling to cope with the problem of providing sewage disposal for 400,000 people in a town far from the sea and with no large river. Matters had become indescribably difficult and the town had been made the subject of a Chancery injunction. Now a sewage-farm was established and gradually the 'biggest nuisance in the kingdom' was brought under control, the injunction was lifted in 1875 and the Tame and Rea District Drainage Board became responsible (Bunce 1885: 126–52).

Even when every qualification has been made it remains the case that an extraordinary amount had been achieved in a very short time. Capital was available, for the years from 1870 to 1873 were boom years in the Midlands and the businessmen who came into local councils were willing and able to promote their objectives with their own private fortunes. They were supported by an efficient machine of party electioneering and organisation and also by an effective local press. The impact of the articles and cartoons of the *Town Crier* can still be felt today.

The Pottery towns showed renewed interest in self-government and Hanley petitioned for incorporation in 1856. The new council took over the duties of the town commissioners, market trustees and highway commissioners, undertook the removal of nuisances and appointed and controlled a new police force, and borough magistrates were appointed to keep order and license public houses. The proposal was articulated by leading industrialists, notably E. J. Ridgway, and backed by the local newspaper, the *Sentinel*. In the main, the new councillors were those same individuals who had previously served as commissioners and on other bodies. The new town clerk was Edward Challinor, who had acted as solicitor for the incorporation process, and the first mayor was Mr E. J. Ridgway. Longton and Lane End were incorporated in 1865, Stoke in 1874 and Burslem in 1878. Tunstall and Fenton continued under their Boards of Health.

Thus, by 1882 almost all the urban and industrial areas had some form of elected government, which was publicly accountable and demonstrably active in providing amenities and leadership. However, it is easy to exaggerate the degree of real change which the changes in structure brought about. In New-castle under Lyme for example the municipal electorate in 1835 had been about one quarter of the adult males of the town and despite the Municipal Franchise Act (1869) the numbers of voters by 1910 was about half the total numbers of adult males, together with a small number of women. A higher proportion of these men voted and there was considerable activity at election time but the issues were entirely local and the main debate continued to be between 'the Improvers' who wanted to spend money on municipal development and the 'Economisers' who wished to save the ratepayers expense. In the 1870s Newcastle was still struggling unsuccessfully with the problem of disposing of their sewage, and the gas and water works were only purchased at the cost of a reduction of the expenditure on the baths and the public libraries (Bealey 1965: 64–72). In rural areas there was little change. The Poor Law unions became the vehicle of sanitary reform and from 1870 medical officers and sanitary inspectors were appointed. The impact of these new bodies in the countryside was often slight, and where improvements in education, water supply and housing standards were undertaken it was usually on the initiative of the local landowner and very much under his control. Wormleighton had to wait until after the Second World War for piped water and main drainage and at Flash in the Moorlands the villagers were still drawing water from the village well in 1984.

Throughout the nineteenth and early-twentieth century the Poor Law was separately administered. The 1834 Poor Law Amendment Act transferred responsibility from 15,000 parishes to 643 Poor Law unions. Warwickshire had 14 unions and 20 others in which Warwickshire parishes were combined with others across the county boundary. The Black Country parishes were gathered into five unions and two covered the Potteries. The responsible officials were the Guardians of the Poor, men of property to the value of at least £100 elected by landowners and ratepayers.

The permanent officials, including the relieving officers, the clerk and the union doctors, were employed by the central authority and clashes with the Guardians were not infrequent. The Guardians did, however, appoint the workhouse master and staff. The Wolverhampton workhouse master appointed in 1839 looked after 500 inmates for £70 a year and double the rations of the paupers. He continued in the job until 1891, by which time his income had increased to £253 and that of his wife to £172. Workhouses were built for the new unions and many were designed by well-known architects. In all the workhouses the paupers were expected to work breaking stones for the roads in the stoneyard, working as night soil men, scavenging, and picking oakum, despite the fact that many were old or mentally and physically handi-capped. The basic diet provided by the central poor law authorities for the able-bodied pauper, was oatmeal gruel, bread and cheese, and one or two meat meals a week. The practice of giving outdoor relief continued in spite of the intentions of the framers of the 1834 Act. However, the poor, the sick, the aged and the children comprised 95 per cent of all those who were relieved in their own homes. The maximum amount of out relief given to any individual was 3s. a week (Barnsby 1977: 100–46).

Coventry was not affected by the 1833 Act, and the Guardians there continued to operate under the 1801 local Act. The workhouse had been established in 1801; between 1812 and 1842 a silk mill was installed and the 18 Poor Directors contracted with the silk throwers for the paupers' labour. The pauper worker received 5d. a week. In 1843 the workhouse housed 70 silkworkers and a further 68 people who worked at handmills. The workhouse was clean, the food good, the clothing warm and the paupers were allowed out on Sundays. Outdoor relief was paid on a considerable scale. In 1832, 675 families were in receipt of regular weekly relief, a further 619 received casual relief and some had their wages supplemented. The average expenditure in the 1830s was £14,000. Criticism of the directors, both by the national commissioners and in the community, led in the 1840s to a harder line being taken and the cost of relief fell to about £7,000, despite the growing population. By an Act of 1873 the Coventry Union was formed with a Board of Guardians elected on the usual franchise, bringing Coventry into line with other Poor Law unions (Searby 1977e: 765–7).

Standards of sanitation, diet and medical treatment in the workhouses improved during the last twenty years of the century and a greater proportion of the physically and mentally ill were treated in specialist hospitals. Individuals were sent to Birmingham Eye Hospital, to the Birmingham Deaf and Dumb Institute and to the General Hospitals to which the Guardians subscribed annually, and the Lunacy Commissioners began to put pressure on local Guardians from the 1880s to make proper provision for the mentally sick. Progress was slow and any initiative on the part of the Guardians – for example, the provision of dental treatment at Wolverhampton cottage homes – aroused accusations of 'pampering the paupers'. There was in the early-twentieth century a great deal of ambivalence in responses to poverty, and much theorising about social change and progress co-existed with dismissive and judgemental attitudes towards the poor.

A general system of representative councils came into being between 1888 and 1894. Under the County Councils Act of 1888 the administrative responsibilities of Quarter Sessions were taken over by new county councils modelled on the municipal corporations. The justices of the peace retained their judicial functions and the county police forces were placed under the joint control of the JPs and the county councils. The Act excluded municipal corporations over 50,000 inhabitants, making them county boroughs, islands of independence surrounded by the county. Coventry and Birmingham were county boroughs in Warwickshire, Wolverhampton, West Bromwich, Walsall and Hanley in Staffordshire, and Dudley in north Worcestershire. The new county councils perpetuated to a remarkable degree the traditional patterns of county leadership, the same families as formerly occupied the new offices and the landed gentry continued to play a major role.

In 1894 the process of systematisation of local government was completed by the setting up of a series of subordinate councils responsible to the county councils, but with clearly defined areas of local responsibility. Municipal boroughs had the fullest powers. These included Leamington, Stratford, Sutton Coldfield and Warwick. Populous areas which did not qualify for municipal borough status were designated urban district councils and as such had powers to deal with public health and roads and to provide libraries and baths. Poor Law administration remained in the hands of the Poor Law Guardians. All of these bodies were elected by ratepayers and were both publicly accountable and closely controlled by the county and by central government. The Act also made provision for elected parish councils in the villages, but their powers were very limited, they were only allowed to raise a rate of 3*d.* in the pound and they had little significance at this period.

Seven years after becoming a county borough Birmingham's prestige was further enhanced when the status of the mayoralty was raised by letters patent and Sir James Smith became the first Lord Mayor of the City of Birmingham. In north Staffordshire, too, great designs were in preparation. The federation of the six towns of the Potteries had been under discussion since the 1830s and in 1888 the Local Government Board and the various councils discussed the possibility of a county of the Potteries or a county council of north Staffordshire. However, Hanley, having a population of over 50,000, claimed county borough status for itself. Longton then became the leader of the movement for federation and secured the services of the Duke of Sutherland as mayor and chief promoter of amalgamation. Even such weighty leadership was insufficient to overcome the combination of local loyalties, ancient boundaries and intertwining jurisdictions. In November 1908 a series of compromises was hammered out by a Local Government Board of enquiry and in December 1908 the Federation Act received the royal assent; it came into operation in March 1910, when the six communities surrendered their individual powers to the new County Borough of Stoke on Trent. The new council of 104 members soon occupied a 'gorgeously decorated and elaborately furnished chamber' in the town hall at Stoke on Trent (VCH Staffs VIII: 252–9).

In spite of the emphasis on household franchise, formal elections and public accountability, the personnel of the late Victorian county and town councils was still drawn from a fairly small segment of the communities they served. Candidates for election were not numerous and only a small percentage of the population actually voted. In the towns the councils continued to consist of the local industrial bourgeoisie. There was little change by 1914, though the movement by radical, liberal temperance reformers towards a control of public houses led to an increase in the number of men with interests in the trade seeking election from 1885 to 1897 (Hennock 1973: 144–7).

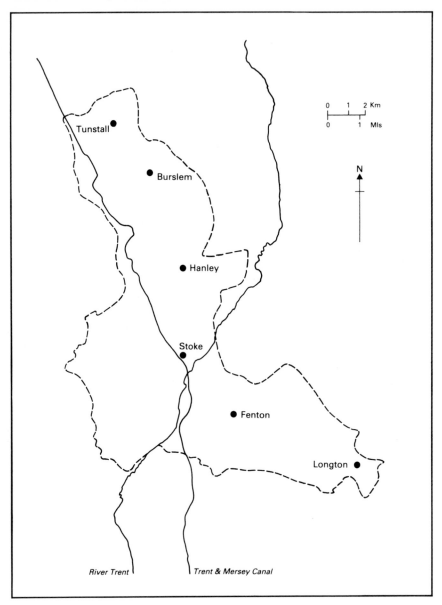

Figure 5.2　The Parliamentary borough of Stoke on Trent, 1900 (based on Morris Jones 1970).

Women began to take their places on county and borough councils from 1907, when the Qualification of Women Act enabled them to do so, but at first they were few in number, and very often those who did come forward came from the same families as the men and drew on traditional dynastic loyalties.

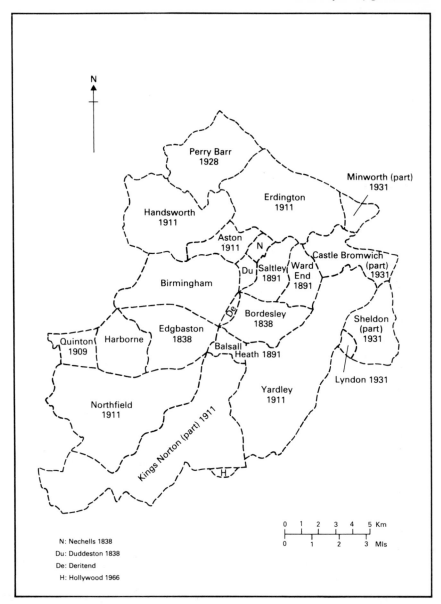

N

Perry Barr
1928

Minworth (part)
1931

Erdington
1911

Handsworth
1911

Aston
1911

N

Castle Bromwich
(part)
1931

Du Saltley Ward
1891 End
1891

Birmingham

De

Bordesley
1838

Sheldon
(part)
1931

Quinton Harborne Edgbaston
1909 1838

Balsall
Heath 1891

Lyndon 1931

Northfield
1911

Yardley
1911

Kings Norton (part) 1911

H

0 1 2 3 4 5 Km

0   1   2   3 Mls

N: Nechells 1838
Du: Duddeston 1838
De: Deritend
H: Hollywood 1966

Figure 5.3 The growth of the City of Birmingham to 1974 (based on Morris Jones 1970).

Few councillors were working class and those who were sat rather as individuals and independants than as part of the labour movement. Although local issues and the provision of local service formed the agenda of local councils, nevertheless the majority of councillors saw themselves as linked with the

Liberal or Conservative parties and local government was still seen as a preparation for national politics.

The period 1888 to 1914 was the heyday of local government, with councils exercising an ever wider influence over the day-to-day lives of the community. The traditional preoccupation with public health continued as medical officers struggled to get the death rate down. Notification of contagious diseases, sanitary measures and improved sewage systems gave hope of the control of disease, and isolation hospitals, cleansing stations and sanatoria were built on the outskirts of Coventry, Stoke on Trent, Birmingham, Stafford and most other large towns. Medical inspection in schools established the principle of preventive medicine, and the appointment of lady doctors and lady health visitors, together with the opening of the first infant welfare clinics, was seen as the remedy for the still obstinately high rate of infant mortality.

The continued growth of population necessitated ever larger and more expensive water undertakings. Birmingham Corporation Water Act in 1892 built the Elan Valley and Claerwent reservoirs in Wales and laid pipes to the Frankley reservoirs in the south-west of Birmingham.

Public libraries, baths, gymnasia, art galleries and museums were established with varying degrees of enthusiasm. In the Midlands many of these buildings were of encaustic yellow and red brick elaborately decorated and bearing on their frontage cumbersome and disproportionate carvings of the municipality's recently acquired coat of arms. 'Municipal Gothic' reached its apogee in the building of the Victoria Law Courts in Birmingham, decorated inside and outside with brilliant tiles, displaying in symbol and in illustration the achievements and responsibilities of the city.

The municipal buildings of the smaller authorities were, if possible, even more ostentatious and the urban landscape was further enhanced by a plethora of statues, drinking fountains, horse troughs and memorials. The respectable urban family took a well regulated and decent pride in the trees, pools and conservatories of the public parks. They dressed in their best to sit upon benches and listen to military bands playing popular classics, or cultivated prize blooms in their allotments to compete in the flower show.

It is perhaps to be expected that at the very time when central legislation and control was ironing out differences in the provision of services and in standards of accommodation, local government was ostentatious and self-conscious in establishing a local presence.

Chapter 32

The heroic age of Midland industry

In 1851 Britain was producing over 40 per cent of the total world output of manufactured goods and was trading throughout the world, especially to the Colonies and the United States. The investment of private capital reached a peak in 1845, government and public expenditure increased significantly, especially during the Crimean War, and industry was supported by the joint stock banks and the amalgamated family banks. Home demand for manufactured goods increased as the population grew and was strengthened by the growth of large-scale institutional customers, such as the armed services, schools, hospitals and above all the railway companies. The construction of private dwellings and public buildings was another important stimulus to growth, and trade was further encouraged by the proliferation of retail selling and by popular advertising.

The midland industries were in the forefront of this activity, both in the introduction of new products and the exploitation of new markets. They increased their output largely along traditional lines, but as always the great variety of midland trades renders generalisation more than usually superficial. The extractive industries, coal, ironstone and limestone mining, continued to expand without any marked discontinuities or changes of location. The south Staffordshire coalfield produced $7\frac{1}{2}$ million tons of coal a year by 1864. Development on the other midland coalfields was much less marked before 1854, but in the late 1850s and 1860s it accelerated. The north Staffordshire coalfield produced a million tons in the 1850s and 3 million tons ten years later. The Warwickshire coalfield had had a comparatively restricted market until the North Western Railway was opened in 1854, but coal output in Warwickshire subsequently rose by 10 per cent per annum and reached over 4 million tons by 1867. New pits were sunk on the edges of the exposed coalfield and on the concealed coalfield. The first deep mine was sunk on the Warwickshire coalfield at Baddesley in 1851, followed by Birchmoor (1860), Griff 4 (1850) and Griff 5 (1860), Amington (1870), Exhall (1870) and Charity (1874). The Wilnecote and Nuneaton mines on the exposed coalfield were also extended after a period of stagnation (Grant 1982: 337). New south Staffordshire mines were also deeper and sunk in new areas. West Bromwich had 65 collieries by 1865, where there had been 3 in 1825, Rowley Regis had 1 pit in 1827 and 13 by 1854. New mines were sunk to the north of the older areas at Wednesfield, and to the south at Halesowen. In the 1860s collieries were opened to a depth of 300 ft and more in the Cannock coalfield. In 1852 the Uxbridge colliery near Hednesford was opened by the Cannock Chase Company, then in 1866 the area around Norton Canes was exploited and deeper mines sunk at Aldridge and Coppy Hall. By 1880 Cannock Chase was producing some 4 million tons a year (Wise 1950: 279).

The ironstone mines which were so closely associated with the coal seams in north and south Staffordshire were still exploited. In the Black Country alone some 2,500 ironminers produced 786,000 tons in the 1860s, that is 10 per cent of national production. However, south Staffordshire ironstone was almost worked out, so now the Blackband ironstone of north Staffordshire was valued more highly. The northern field produced over 500,000 tons by the 1860s, almost half of which went to south Staffordshire ironworks, while the rest was consumed by north Staffordshire furnaces (VCH Staffs II: 130).

Much of the capital for the larger-scale collieries was invested by aristocratic landowners. The trustees of the Earls of Dudley made a determined effort to improve management. In 1836 they appointed an experienced and outstanding mining engineer, Richard Smith, at a salary of £1,200 a year plus $2\frac{1}{2}$ per cent of the profits. He reorganised the accounts, sought greater productivity, cut out much casual employment and closely supervised production through a middle management of permanent paid officials. He raised production to over a million tons of coal and 10,000 tons of ironstone. The net income from Lord Dudley's mines was $1\frac{1}{2}$ million pounds. Smith found it advisable to keep only the most profitable mines under direct management and from the 1850s the majority of the mines were leased out mainly on a basis of payments of royalties on sales (Fereday 1966).

In north Staffordshire, Ralph Sneyd opened mines at Finney Green and Silverdale and later at Leysett and by 1871 his royalties had increased from £7,000 to £29,000 per annum. Meanwhile, Lord Anglesey (Paget) received £91,000 per annum from his collieries, mainly in the Cannock area (Sturgess 1971: 176–85). Many lessees of coal mines were ironmasters, and numerous 'small capitalists', as the newspapers called them, leased a few pits and sold the coal to the ironmasters or to townspeople. A number of small pits remained, especially in the Gornal area, worked by a family burrowing into accessible seams.

The south Staffordshire iron industry reached its peak in 1859, when it produced a total of 752,000 tons, that is some 22 per cent of British production. By that date 190 furnaces owned by 55 firms were in blast. As south Staffordshire reached the limits of its potential, larger works were built in north Staffordshire in association with the new coal and ironstone mines. In 1830 north Staffordshire had 7 furnaces with an output of 18,200 tons, in

1852 21 furnaces and by 1870 30 furnaces, which produced 303,378 tons of pig iron a year (VCH Staffs II: 130).

Most of the new investment in iron production came from the same large landowners who were developing coal mines. The Sneyds of Keele established Silverdale before 1815 and the Earl of Granville opened Etruria Furnace (1839), Apedale (1840) and the Shelton Bar Company (1852). In south Staffordshire aristocratic landowners shared the leadership with family firms and partnerships of ironmasters. Victorian ironworks were great integrated concerns and their end product was not pig iron but highly specialised finished iron goods. Thus, at Wolverhampton Thorneycrofts produced about 700 tons of finished iron per week in the form of plates, angle iron, T iron, girders, sheets, hoops and bars from 74 puddling furnaces and 12 rolling mills. They owned mines as well as blast furnaces, made their own machinery and constructed their own canal boats. The Earl of Dudley's largest enterprise was the Round Oak Works, where he employed 600 men in 27 puddling furnaces and 5 rolling mills, making very high grade bar iron for sale to the Admiralty, to Japan and to China.

Many of the new firms achieved their initial success by responding to developments in civil engineering, as for example, the building of the railways, the Crystal Palace and the great London bridges. A notable case was the Patent

Plate 5.4   A Black Country rolling mill (no date).

Shaft and Axletree Company of Wednesbury, which prospered by supplying faggoted axles to both private and railway coach companies. By the 1860s the company had a workforce of 4,000, they mined coal and ironstone, manufactured pig iron, and had 86 puddling furnaces and a steel plant, foundries and engineering shops; they produced not only axles but wheels, turntables and structural work.

These large concerns were located throughout the coalfields, dominating the scene and transforming their environment. In the 'Iron District' the smoke from the works created a distinctive landscape and destroyed the terrain. The great integrated works were surrounded by a wide range of specialist firms which concentrated on one or the other stages of manufacture. One-third of all the puddling furnaces in the kingdom were concentrated in south Stafford-shire. Barrows and Sons (formerly Barrows and Hall) had 100 puddling furnaces, employed over 1,000 men, and produced more than 1,000 tons of very high quality iron a week. Woodside works was leased by Bramah and Cochrane from the Trustees of the Earl of Dudley in 1841 and secured the contract for manufacture of the iron frame for the Crystal Palace. In 1858 they produced 1,170 tons of iron and some cast steel to build railway bridges for the East India Railway Company (Gale 1966: 120–1).

The range and variety of manufactured articles made from iron was already very extensive in the 1830s, but further diversification took place in response to new markets and new needs. Within particular industries constant adaptions and improvement of old techniques, but comparatively few major innovations were made. The range of goods was particularly wide in the hollow-ware and plating trades. In the 1840s Clark's of Wolverhampton made hollow-ware more attractive by the introduction of enamelling, and the traditional japanning firms produced an ever wider range of flatware and found new uses for enamelled iron, as for example, enamelled advertising signs made in Bilston. In 1822 large-scale production of galvanised and corrugated iron was set on foot at the Vulcan Works, Spon Lane, West Bromwich, a trade which was soon taken up in Wolverhampton and Lye (Halesowen), and was encouraged by the demands of the Californian Gold Rush in 1849 and the Australian Gold Rush in 1851. Most of the pioneer firms were built up by men who had started as masters of small workshops, for example, Hills, Rhodes, Everson and Rounds at Lye (Hopkins 1974b: 423). Many firms benefited in the 1850s from the falling price of pig and bar iron and from the reduction during the period of the real costs of manufacture and distribution.

The building of the railways created an enormous appetite for the industrial products of Birmingham and the Black Country. Saltley railway carriage works were established in 1838, and by 1866 five companies there employed 3,000 persons in large-scale mechanised factories. Not only did they produce thousands of passenger carriages and goods waggons, but also maintained them on contract both for the railway companies and for the private firms, which ran their own rolling stock on the public railways. The laying of track led to a demand for screws as well as rails and chairs and the firm of Ryland attributed its speedy growth in the 1850s to the orders of the Great Western Company. Brass tubes, rails, knobs, taps, gauges, decorative features and many other items including station-masters' bells and the insignia of the porters' uniforms were required, all of which were made in the Midlands. The demand continued with the spread of railways overseas.

Tubes of many kinds were required by gas and water companies supplying the great towns, together with brass taps, connections, and fittings. The rapid development of shipping stimulated a demand for steam machinery, and brass fittings, chains and anchors were made in Cradley and Old Hill; tubes were made in Wednesbury and haulage machines, large lifting cranes, wire and rope hawsers, bridges and lighthouses were made in Dudley Port and in Smethwick.

Mid-Victorian England saw the growth of large public institutions – the army, workhouses, hospitals and boarding and day schools. These institutions gave large orders for a wide range of metal goods as well as pottery and sanitary ware, all made in the Midlands. The tube industry diversified to produce the iron and brass bedsteads with wire mattresses which replaced the earlier wooden bedsteads; by 1860 1,800 persons were employed in this trade. The steel pen nib was developed in place of the quill pen and millions of nibs were supplied from the two major works in Birmingham, namely Masons and Gillotts. In all this, brassworkers and ironworkers adapted old skills to new products; and, apart from the development of the seamless tube, there was little that the eighteenth-century workman would have found startling.

While development along traditional lines continued, some industrialists consciously sought out and employed men of experimental science and it was as the result of such a combination of talents that Elkingtons were able, in the 1840s, to replace traditional hand methods of silver plating by electroplating, using electric current in an acid bath to deposit a thin layer of silver upon a nickel base. Silver-plated spoons, knives, forks, plates, chandeliers, candelabra, and other objects could now be produced in quantity and the middle class and even the prosperous working-class housewives loaded down their dining tables with silver-plated ware. Elkingtons were soon employing 1,000 people (Timmins 1866, 1967: 474–95). Likewise, by the 1840s Askin and Evans had developed the refining of imported nickel at Selly Oak and later at Smethwick and Oldbury (Timmins 1866: 674–6).

Another great chemical manufacturing firm in the 1880s was Sturge and Albright, who made citric acid, phosphorus and other chemicals needed by the new industry. Red lead and powdered litharge was produced for glassmakers at several works at Smethwick and Tipton. By the 1860s Adkins and Company, Chance and Company and William Hunt produced 12,000 tons of soda crystals a year and 20,000 tons of oil of vitriol, also bleaching powder and muriatic acid. Adkins also produced household soap made from soda and tallow, boiling it up in great open vats, and using machines to cut and shape the soap tablets. 2,500 tons of soap a year were produced at Adkins and two other works in Smethwick and Birmingham. Manders at Wolverhampton produced varnishes, spirits and paints, originally for the japanning industry, but increasingly for house decoration. They also produced oil of vitriol, glauber and Epsom salts. By the 1860s midland industrialists were regularly supporting the British Association for the Advancement of Science and Industry. There was a conscious search for new applications of scientific and technical 'discoveries' and at least some of the leaders gloried in 'progress'.

The wars of the British Empire and the Crimea created a demand for weapons of war and in peacetime there was an increasing demand for sporting guns. The introduction of the cartridge led to the growth of ammunition and explosives companies, which after some very nasty accidents soon became subject to government control. As a result the Ammunition Company and later Kynochs Percussion Cap Works were sited at the edges of built-up areas and were large-scale enterprises from their beginnings.

In 1852 the brothers Tangye arrived in Birmingham from Cornwall and began supplying hydraulic machinery, lifting jacks, cranes and hoists for use in great engineering undertakings throughout the world. From the 1850s sewing machines, steam engines, draw benches, rolling mills, pumps, specialist scales and some agricultural machinery was made in the west Midlands. New products, including india rubber (1865), photographic chemicals (1860), and a form of plastic called Parkesine (1856), made their appearance on the market.

In 1830 the pottery industry exported 441,193 tons of crate ware and by 1845 twice that amount. Bone china ware was produced by Copelands, Mintons and Davenports to supply the middle classes with elaborate dinner services and other status symbols. The range of 'artistic' products, statuary, vases and table centres was constantly widened; the most successful being Parian porcelain ware, which was first introduced in 1845. Masons and Meakins and other firms continued to make their main business the mass production of durable, cheap, white and decorated earthenware. Stone, china and ironstone ware were introduced and sold not only to supply the family table, but also large-scale residential institutions such as orphanages, prisons, hospitals, barracks and boarding schools, and railway and steamship companies also became important customers. The toilet table, the conservatory, the hall and the fireplaces were all adorned, with umbrella stands, decorated tiles, door knobs and aspidestra pots. At the other end of the spectrum of human need, hot water bottles and chamber pots were needed in numbers more than commensurate with the growth of the population. From 1849 the widespread adoption of the earthenware water closet enabled Twyfords to take the lead in the mass production of sanitary ware.

By 1860 some 160,000 tons of clay were consumed annually, most of it coming from Devon, Dorset and Cornwall. The calcined bones and lime required in the china manufacture came from domestic sources, but also increasingly from South America. Chemicals for glazes, dyes and finishes, were introduced and cobalt, oxide, borax and boracic acid were used in quantity. The expanding ancillary trades included lithographers and transfer makers and specialist paper firms making the transfer paper.

The first successful machinery for forming pottery was introduced in 1863 when a Hanley potter installed machines for making cups. The extension of the Factory Acts to exclude children from the potteries in 1864 noticeably increased the enthusiasm of the potters for steam-powered jiggers to turn the wheels. The factory inspectors' insistence on minimum standards of hygiene and ventilation led to the rebuilding of many premises, and this rebuilding was often associated with the inclusion of steam power for a variety of tasks. The years 1863–5 were prosperous ones in the pottery industry, and this was a further incentive to acquire the status and satisfaction of 'modernisation'. By 1870 about one-third of the 300 or so firms had their own steam power. A range of steam jiggers, steam-powered wheels and steam lathes soon became available and by the 1870s had become sufficiently effective to gain general acceptance. Steam power was also applied to the making of slip, and in general, mechanisation was accepted as a legitimate alternative to human work.

Plate 5.5 Packing pottery in crates about 1840.

The duty on plate glass was reduced in 1835 and abolished in 1845. Almost immediately small glassworks spread along the Stour Valley, but it was the larger, established firms which benefited most from the abolition of the tax. From 1830 onwards sheet glass was made by forming a cylinder of glass which was then cut open while white hot, thus enabling glass makers to supply larger quantities and bigger sizes. They also introduced new methods of grinding and polishing sheet glass, which made it possible to use glass in the construction of large buildings. Chances' Glassworks supplied 1¾ million sq. ft of glass for the Crystal Palace. At first, small companies multiplied in response to the new opportunities, but subsequently the larger companies assimilated the smaller ones and controlled the trade, so that by 1866 there were only ten flint glassworks, one plate and crown works and two bottle works left in the Stour Valley, and the district increasingly specialised in high-class table ware and decorative work (Timmins 1866, 1967: 145–63).

The silk and other textile industries in the Midlands gradually adopted steam power and organised production in larger units. Between 1828 and 1848 the silk industry enjoyed a period of comparative stability, protected by a 30 per cent duty on imported manufactured silk goods. Although the trade was subject to considerable short-term fluctuations, in general it prospered. Even after the import duty had been halved in 1845 it was still able to enjoy something of a boom in the 1850s. Under these conditions the two silk-producing regions of the Midlands continued for a time along the lines already laid down. In 1840 Leek's 8 large mills employed about 750 persons, two-thirds of whom were women and girls; another 1,500 were employed mostly as domestic workers in Leek itself and in the immediate vicinity of the town. These included both the throwsters making thread and the weavers, a few of whom made ribbons, but who were mostly engaged in making silk handkerchiefs, scarves, borderings and trimmings. In 1830 Joshua Wardle founded the Leekbrook dyeing works, which produced the raven black dye used for mourning garments and ribbons. By 1854 four dyehouses had been built alongside the weaving mills on the river Churnett and other silk works had been established at Stafford, Alstonfield, Silverdale, Cheadle and Newcastle.

The small masters of the Coventry ribbon trade had little incentive to introduce new techniques. They enjoyed a double protection, both that of the tariff and that of the local press and town council. The fluctuations of demand could be met by taking on or putting off their outworkers and by renegotiation of price lists for piecework. In 1838 there were 129 single looms and 4,730 Dutch engine looms in the city. Twelve years later there were 700 steam powered looms but these were mainly in 'cottage factories'. The first of the cottage factories was built by Eli Green in East Street, and for a short time this intermediate type of organisation was characteristic. The size of each work unit remained small and several different producers shared the power of a single steam engine at the end of the row of cottages. From the 1850s the pace of technical and organisational change became more rapid. James Hart built a five-storey factory in 1857 with 250 power looms and he was soon followed by half a dozen other employers.

However, in 1860 the Coventry silk trade collapsed, when the Cobden Treaty with France repealed the silk duty, and the prolonged slump was intensified by a world shortage of raw silk. The domestic side of the industry suffered most. In Coventry 7,000 people were unemployed and half the population was living on doles and the charity of soup kitchens (Searby 1976–7: 65–7). In Leek, on the other hand, where steam-powered, large-scale weaving mills had been adopted earlier and more generally, there was less serious difficulty. The ten Staffordshire silk-spinning factories of 1850 had increased to eleven by 1862 and six others carried on both spinning and weaving. In 1861 Leek still had 244 workshops which did not rank as factories, but it was the factories which were able to weather the difficulties by concentrating increasingly on silk thread and embroidery materials.

By its nature, the Coventry watch industry was also resistant to large-scale organisation and the application of steam power. The city had 53 watchmakers in 1830 and the demand for their products increased with the growth of population, the coming of time-keeping in factories, offices and shops, and the growing need for instruments. Production was based on the ever greater subdivision of the processes (Searby 1976). An 1850 Directory of Coventry listed 60 watchmakers, 10 casemakers, 4 dial makers, 4 escapement makers, 8 gilders, 10 jewellers, 5 motion makers, 14 finishers and many others, all contributing to the making of large quantities of cheap watches for a mass market (Whites Directory 1850).

Among so many varied industries, exhibiting so many different methods of production, it is difficult to generalise about the hours and conditions of the workforce. The length and intensity of the work was conditioned by the demands of the process. Glassworkers could not work for more than six hours at a time, so the two shifts in the twenty-four hours were divided and the man alternated six hours on and six off for $4\frac{1}{2}$ consecutive days (Hopkins 1974b: 413). In the Potteries hours of work were rather longer than elsewhere in the Midlands, lasting from 6.00 a.m. to 9.00 p.m. in summer with meal breaks amounting to one and a half hours. Generally speaking, only the iron furnaces worked on Sundays, and most works had regular holidays for Christmas, Easter and Whitsun. The tradition that skilled workmen and outworkers, in particular, were independent sub-contractors rather than wage-paid employees persisted and was manifested in the freedom with which men absented themselves. The keeping of 'St Monday' was much commented on by contemporaries and persisted until modern times. The skilled and comparatively well-paid heavy chainmakers continued to determine their own hours, even during the Second World War, despite the Defence of the Realm Act and the blackout.

In many midland trades the 'day' or 'stint' for which a certain wage was quoted was a notional minimum based on a recognised output; moreover, the worker might do extra work when it was available. Thus, ironworkers were said to earn 2s. 6d. a day in 1842, but this 'day' consisted of a shift of about six hours' duration and many younger men worked 2 or even 2½ shifts per day, thus earning 5s. to 6s. 3d. (Worpell 1976: 35). On the other hand the week's real income was often based on four days' work. In the coal mines, where a stint was the time taken to cut 2 yds by 2 ft by 3 yds of coal from the face, the younger and stronger men could do 2 or even 2½ stints per day. There was, of course, no certainty from week to week that extra work would be available, nor even that a full week's work would be required. Given the prevalence of subcontracting, irregular hours, truck, short-term working and the 'day' or 'stint', all attempts to estimate weekly wages are liable to be misleading. It is certain, however, that take-home pay fluctuated widely both over a short period of time and between one worker and another. Puddlers, for example, were paid by the ton made and received additional piece rates and allowances. In the 1830s they usually earned about 9s. 9d. per ton and an average week's production was 5½ tons. The wage fell in 1840 to 1849 to 9s. 4d. per ton, rose in the 1850s to 9s. 6d. and then fell again in the 1860s to 8s. 7d. (Barnsby 1980: 212–13; Hopkins 1982: 229–31).

The aristocrats of the pottery trade were the throwers, who could re-putedly earn 40s. a week in 1841, and also the plate makers and painters. The lowest-paid groups were the women assistants, whose earnings were given as 9–15s., and the children who earned 2s. a week. In practice, the rates given were modified by counting the work good from oven with no allowance for waste, by allowances (the potteries version of the discount system), truck payments to assistants and, most important of all, short-time working.

Working conditions in the silk manufacture trade attracted favourable comment in the 1840s from the unlikely pen of Samuel Bamford, the reformer, who was 'very gratified' at the sight of well-fed and well-dressed women weavers, but recorded wages scarcely support a rosy view. In the period 1836–40 the wages paid by one firm of silk weavers for a 72-hour week varied between 2s. 6d. to 6s. A twister in a shade in 1842 reported that he earned 6d. a roll, his daily output being 7 rolls. Out of this 3s. 6d. he paid 1d. a roll to his boy helper, 2d. a day for shade hire, ½d. a day for fire, ½d. a day for candles and 1d. a day for oil and paper. This left him 15s. 6d. a week for himself, his wife and five children. Three of his children worked and between them contributed 12s. to the family income (VCH Staffs II: 210).

Coventry had a wide range of differentials, not only between men, women and children, but also between various types of loom used. A skilled first hand with a jacquard loom could earn 13s. 6d. a week, whereas a woman outworker on a hand loom could earn only 5s. a week, and two-thirds of the silk workers were women. With the help of his family a good man worker on the ala bar loom in the 1850s could earn up to £3 10s. a week in brisk times (Prest 1960: 74–6).

In many trades long pay or advances of wages ahead of work created a debt from the employee to the employer, which the employee could not pay off. As much as £5 might be advanced and then deducted from pay at the rate of 1s. or 2s. a week and it was claimed that offers to pay in a lump sum were refused. Between 1838 and 1840, 960 persons were jailed at Stafford for indebtedness to employers, of whom 584 were children and young persons. The piecework system of payment left a wide area of potential distrust and conflict. Truck shops continued throughout the period despite having been made illegal in 1831. Not only did truckshops offer poor stuff at high prices, but the hours of opening, the attitudes of shopkeepers and the lack of amenities added considerably to the irritation and sense of grievance they caused, and in small communities stories of exploitation and imposed misery circulated rapidly and deepened suspicion and anger (BPP 1843a). In the 1840s the potters tried to tackle the truck problem by bringing cases of evasion of the Truck Act to the courts and by a propaganda campaign, which included a letter to the Chief Constable and publicity for particularly hard cases, but their efforts met with little success.

By the mid-Victorian period most work was done on the employer's premises and under his control, yet the worker was still required in many cases to make payments or have deductions made for standings or for gaslight, paying, as it were, a rent for workspace. In some trades, examples of these residual practices of the domestic economy survived till the twentieth century. Meanwhile, a growing army of labourers, sweepers, warehousemen and other non-skilled workers were employed directly by the owners of the firms.

As the scale of enterprises grew and more machinery was used the number of industrial accidents, disasters and diseases increased and employment in many trades became more dangerous. As the mines became deeper the miners often penetrated old, unrecorded workings where carburetted hydrogen gas had gathered. Serious accidents became more and more common. Between 1837 and 1842 West Bromwich lost 83 men through pit accidents. In addition to miners crushed, burnt or killed in explosions, numerous cases were reported of men falling when being drawn up or down shafts or being drowned in flooded workings. Barnsby has calculated from the mining inspectors' reports that a major pit disaster occurred every 2½ years in south Staffordshire. This leaves out of account the constant toll of minor accidents, broken limbs, ruined eyesight and lungs. The safety lamp was introduced into Staffordshire in 1817, but was little used, partly because carbonic acid gas ('damp') was not the major problem (Barnsby 1977: 24–38). The inspection of mines and reporting of fatal accidents was compulsory from 1850 onwards, and by the 1860s the reports and public exhortations of the inspectors were making some impact. In 1867 a court decision made it clear that responsibility in law for safety in the mines lay with the coal owner and his agent, not the butties. From 1872 the employment of a qualified, certificated mining manager became compulsory.

Work in all branches of iron production was both dangerous and labor-

Black Country handworkers in the early twentieth century.
Plate 5.6 A Black Country nailmaker using the 'oliver'.

Plate 5.7 Brickmakers in the Black Country.

ious. Furnace men, puddlers, shinglers and rollers handled heavy weights and large masses of white hot and red-hot metal. Even with the assistance of steam cranes they were subject to great heat and exposed to constant danger. Reports of local doctors to commissions of enquiry, hospital records and the anecdotal evidence of newspaper reports reveal the horrific nature of major accidents at the furnaces and the daily toll of burns, eye injuries, embedded metal splinters and dislocations.

Women were employed to carry out simple repetitive processes for the mass production of standardised goods. They were extensively employed in penmaking, covered and linen button making, silk manufacture, nail making and pottery manufacture. In Staffordshire in 1871 one-sixth of all adults employed in the 'industrial class of occupations' were female and in Warwickshire more than one-quarter. In the industrial towns and villages the proportion was, of course, much higher. In the Potteries in 1861 12 per cent of all married and 38 per cent of all unmarried women worked in the pottery industry. They tended to leave at marriage or at least before the birth of the first child (Dupree 1977). On the coalfields women worked on the pit banks and their independent manners and speech attracted much comment from strangers. In 1871 nearly 10,000 females worked in nail manufacture in Staffordshire and Worcestershire, over 1,000 of them under the age of 15. Nearly 1,000 worked in making percussion caps and cartridges in and near Birmingham.

As the organisation of industry in the Midlands slowly shifted from home-based industry to workshop and factory units of production, the separation of men and women in the workplace became more usual. Women worked together in large groups often with a male supervisor making buttons, pens, percussion caps or decorating pottery. Much use was made of child labour in the Midlands. The child employment commission of 1833 found examples of children employed from the ages of five and six, particularly in the pin-heading trades. Many young people started work as assistants to an adult, who took them on and paid them a few pence in 'wages'. Boys worked in the ironworks, the brass casting shops, the rolling mills and as errand boys in the gun trades. Girls worked in the button shops, brick making, the japanning shops and pin making. The ironstone mines employed 70 boys to every 100 men and the collieries 30 boys to every 100 men. From 1842 boys under 10 were forbidden to work underground, but there was little real control (Barnsby 1971: 230).

In 1840 about 12 per cent of the workforce in the Potteries were boys and girls under 13; in 1862 4,500 children were employed in 180 pottery works. It was a feature of the children's work that they might be required to work longer hours than the adults, coming early to light fires and staying late to clear up. Boys assisted the men by wedging clay, running moulds, turning wheels and helping with plate making and cup and saucer making. Girls worked in the finishing department, painting earthenware, sitting at long tables, 10–30 in a room, supervised by an older woman.

The 1862 Child Employment Commission showed that children from 9

Plate 5.8 Chainmakers in Cradley, Worcestershire.

and 10 years of age were still employed in the Midlands, 2,000 of them in Birmingham alone. Machinery had replaced children in pin making and screw making, but children were still working 12 hours a day and more in the button shops and two-thirds of the brickyard workers were women and children under 12. In most trades boys under 14 usually earned between 1*s*. 6*d*. to 3*s*. a week.

The first extension of the Factory Acts to trades other than textiles took place in 1864 when the employment of children in the wax match trade and the percussion cap trade was controlled, immediately affecting several works in Birmingham. In 1867 the Factory Acts Extension Act and the Workshops Act brought many midland workplaces under regulation and inspection and places where more than 50 people were employed could take on children for only 30 hours a week.

After 1874 industrial Britain increasingly felt the cold wind of overseas competition. By the mid-1880s Belgian glass and Belgian iron had seriously undermined midland sales in Europe and were even imported into England. German competition caused anxiety from the mid-1870s and American competition from about 1879. The period 1870–1914 was one of very considerable readjustment in the Midlands. Some of the older trades decayed and even disappeared, others were only able to sustain a further development as a result of extensive reorganisation of their methods and structures. There was a shift from the production of hardware to engineering and to new composite metal products such as bicycles, motorcars and electrical machinery, and a transition from craft skills to precision engineering with a corresponding development of the machine-tool industry and the equipment for precise scientific measurement.

In 1855 Lord Dudley was building a great new iron furnace at Round Oak, but even then percipient observers could see that the south Staffordshire iron industry was in difficulties. The supplies of local ironstone were running out, freight rates were not competitive with other areas and new developments in the industry were overtaking their traditional methods. Staffordshire was not well placed to adopt the new Bessemer process for making mild steel, patented in 1857, for it required phosphorus free haematite ore not obtainable in the Midlands. Scarcely any of the Black Country ironmasters attempted to introduce the new technique, though later Lord Dudley (1893) at Round Oak and Hickmans at Bilston did convert their works to steelmaking by using the 'basic' open-hearth process of Gilchrist Thomas. They used imported ores and much scrap iron with which the district was all too abundantly supplied, and they lined their furnaces with local dolerite. Other ironmasters, namely the Thorneycrofts, the Baldwins, the Halls, the Onions, the Dawes and many others, avoided bankruptcy, closed their works and rebuilt their fortunes. In 1878 only 40 out of 160 blast furnaces were still working and 130 ironworks were at a standstill. In West Bromwich 6 firms closed in 5 years (Le Guillou 1972: 16–24). The puddling and rolling mills continued to operate, using pig iron imported from other areas. Steel could be rolled in mills designed to roll wrought iron and the rolling of sheet steel was developed in 1876 at Hattons and Company, Bilston. The Black Country still had 661 puddling furnaces in 1914 (Gale 1966: 118).

The north Staffordshire iron industry reached its fullest development in the 1870s with 36 blast furnaces and 400 puddling furnaces and 40 rolling mills, with associated wrought-iron works. Heaths, the largest single firm in Staffordshire, controlled 3 ironworks, 28 coal and ironstone mines, 8 blast furnaces, 144 puddling furnaces and 14 rolling mills. The north Staffordshire industry likewise suffered from the introduction of the acid steel process and many works closed so that by 1913 there were only 13 blast furnaces. Only Shelton had adopted the 'basic' open-hearth method of making steel and survived the crisis (Allen 1929: 233–47; Gale 1966: 102–19).

Meanwhile the south Staffordshire coalfield became more and more uneconomic. Drainage was the major problem; the Mines Drainage Commission achieved nothing, despite draining 56 million gallons every 24 hours. New mines opened after 1870 were deep and highly capitalised; Sandwell (1875), Hamstead (1877) and Baggeridge (1912) were all on the concealed coalfield. By the First World War output on the south Staffordshire coalfield had fallen from a peak of 9 million tons in 1865 to 3 million tons and the number of pits had fallen to about 200, only 11 of which employed more than 100 men

311

underground (Allen 1929: 281). Production in the Cannock Chase coalfield, on the other hand, increased rapidly, reaching 4 million tons by 1880 (VCH Staffs II: 82). The east Warwickshire coalfield also increased production and large-scale new mines were sunk to exploit the coal lying in the deeper concealed measures; for example, Kingsbury colliery was sunk in 1894 and Baddesley in 1896. The coal from these sources was sold mainly for domestic fuel, for industrial purposes and for public utilities, especially electricity generating stations (Grant 1982: 337–40).

Between 1870 and the First World War there were many innovations in the Potteries, including new and brilliant glazes, lustre decorations and the production of lithographed prints on back tissue, which could be easily applied to print curved as well as flat ware. The London firm of Doultons expanded into the Midlands by making pipes at Rowley Regis (1848) and sanitary ware at Burslem (1877). The first firm to develop the production of ceramic insulators for the electric telegraph was Bullers, whose product was soon in demand for electric railways, tramways, power companies and for domestic use both in Britain and the Empire. Other firms produced crucibles, bottles and mortars for the chemical industry and educational and industrial laboratories. Important advances were made in the design of kilns and the application of gas firing but diffusion of new techniques was slow and the old bottle kilns were still common in 1914. New machinery had been installed in most of the 300 firms by 1914, but it was the arrival of electric power which at last enabled small producers to use machinery and to reorganise the layout of their pot works to improve the flow of work (VCH Staffs II: 28–39).

The Burton brewing industry experienced its most rapid growth at this time. The rising population at home, the growth of overseas empire and the habits of urban life ensured ever growing demand. The opening of the Birmingham–Derby Railway in 1839 enabled Burton brewers to reach mass markets at home and abroad easily and cheaply. Between 1840 and 1880 the number of firms, the size and scope of individual firms and the output per employee all increased, so that production trebled every ten years. Expansion levelled off after 1880, but there was no serious decline. Steam power was introduced from the 1840s and both internal and market organisation became more sophisticated. The fermentation process was established in scientific terms in the 1860s and the principal Burton firms began to employ full-time chemists. The first such appointment was that of Böttinger to Alsopps in 1845 and by the 1870s Burton was foremost in the scientific study of brewing chemistry and its practical applications. One of the principal objectives, achieved by the 1880s, was to enable all-year-round brewing (Owen 1978: 86–9). By 1887 Birmingham and Aston had four large breweries and factories for the mass production of vinegar, mineral waters, sweets and custard powder.

Cadbury's chocolate firm moved from the centre of the town to rural King's Norton in 1879 and a large works was set up beside the railway and canal to produce cocoa and chocolate. All the big food-producing firms installed large-scale machinery, studied the science of their product and the psychology of their customers. They supported their trade with extensive advertising, the artistic and professional quality of which enriched the environment and gave status to their essentially humble products (Williams 1931: 57–100). HP Sauce, Bird's Custard, Branston Pickle, Cadbury's Drinking Chocolate became part of the collective experience.

Shoemaking, long established at Stafford, Stone and to a limited extent at Leek and Newcastle, reached its peak in the late-nineteenth century on the basis of rising home trade and the opportunities of selling in the colonies. In the early-twentieth century the numbers of firms declined, but the survivors introduced machinery and absorbed their competitors. Meanwhile, the midland textile industries survived by becoming more specialised. At Nuneaton, where three cotton mills remained in business, the ribbon workers turned to elastic web manufacture, woven address labels and the making of accoutrements and banners for Freemasons and Friendly Societies. There was no decline in the demand for building bricks and materials and in the 1880s a number of large terracotta firms were established in the district, supplying decorative tiles for houses, public houses, churches and later cinemas.

After 1870 the classic pattern of industry in the Midlands changed in the face of expanding world markets. Britain was now in competition with other industrialised nations, especially Germany, Belgium and the United States of America.

The older metalworking trades were adversely affected by the depression of 1876 to 1886, but not disastrously so. The brass trade continued to expand and diversify its products, concentrating increasingly on cheaper machine-made goods. The increasing demand for household and domestic appliances, the spread of sanitary equipment, the building of hospitals and the introduction of electric lighting, all ensured its continued prosperity as long as it could adapt old skills and equipment to new needs. The jewellery trade was regarded as one of the most depressed of the trades between 1885 and 1886, but the decline in demand for certain types of fashion goods was counterbalanced by the increase in demands for badges and insignia for the employees of railway and shipping companies, postmen and many others. The button trade failed to find new outlets and continued to decline. Germany captured the trade in vegetable ivory buttons (Allen 1929: 197–211).

The 700 or so watchmakers of Coventry and district survived the difficulties of the 1860s and 1870s better than most. In the 1890s, however, the challenge of factory-produced Swiss watches finally became too strong. The oldest watchmaking firm, Rotherams, turned its Spon Lane premises into the largest factory in Europe and produced 100 watches a day but most other firms went out of production, leaving only 5 in business by 1914. However, in 1863 the Coventry sewing machine company had begun manufacture of an American machine and in the same year commenced making an early type of bicycle

Plate 5.9   A Coventry watchmaker.

on behalf of the French, who held the monopoly. The French monopoly ceased in 1870 and several Coventry firms of bicycle makers were soon well-established in the home market, including James Starley, the Townsend brothers, George Singer and William Hillman, a firm which made both cycles and sewing machines. Skills were available for tube making, wire working, leather, stamping parts, making bearings, spokes, springs, enamelling, electro-plating and chrome plating. Villiers in Wolverhampton soon became the largest manufacturers of free wheels in the world. The cycling craze took possession of Britain's youth, both girls and young men, and the working man found bicycles an essential means of travel to work. By 1891 8,000 men were employed in making bicycles in England and Wales, 71 per cent of them in Coventry, Birmingham and Wolverhampton. By 1911 Birmingham was the largest of the three principal centres (Allen 1929: 291–314).

Many of the cycle and other manufacturers turned to making motorcars, parts and accessories, once the way was cleared by the removal of restrictions on the movement of 'light locomotives on highways' in 1896. Among the first was Lanchester who was quickly followed by Austin, Knight, Riley and Daimler. Soon there were twenty firms in Coventry and others in Birmingham,

Plate 5.10   The first Coventry to Birmingham motorcar run in 1897. The photograph was taken near Stonebridge.

Wolverhampton and Leamington. They made new demands on the local firms of founders, metalworkers and leatherworkers in the area. Sankey of Bilston, for example, a japanner, rescued his declining firm by pioneering the making of pressed steel bodies. Many smaller car firms sprang up out of an individual's skill and enthusiasm, but often disappeared just as quickly. The successful firms on the other hand expanded rapidly and erected large buildings for the assembly of standardised parts, often in green field sites. In 1906 Herbert Austin moved out of central Birmingham into Longbridge, eight miles from the city. The car trade provided new opportunities for small works and individuals, wayside blacksmiths at road junctions set up as garages, the first petrol pumps began to appear and the wealthy employed chauffeurs in place of coachmen. From about 1900 lorries and commercial vans and motor buses were produced by Guy, Maudsley and Daimler of Wolverhampton. By 1910, motor cycles were being produced at BSA Birmingham and at the Villiers and Sunbeam works in Wolverhampton. In the cycle and motorcar industries the machining of standardised and interchangeable parts quickly replaced hand labour.

New forms of power further facilitated mechanisation. Steam engines had been expensive and cumbersome to install and had to be kept constantly in work to be profitable. The introduction of the Otto gas engine from 1878 was

315

confined to larger firms until the patent expired, but the engine became available in a cheaper form after 1888. 20 per cent of the gas supplied by the Birmingham Municipal Gas Company was for manufacture and motive power. Already, however, electricity was competing with gas. Chamberlain and Hookham were making dynamos and electro-magnetic motors in 1886 with the particular needs of the electro-plating industry in mind, and a number of small firms installed electric power soon after 1900. The new source of power had the advantage for the small firm that it could be easily installed, was comparatively cheap and could be switched on and off at will.

By 1914 hand labour was largely superseded except in certain specialist areas such as the jewellery trades. From about 1900 the capstan lathe enabled many processes formerly carried out by skilled workers to be done by unskilled or female labour. Female employment increased, especially in the cycle and electrical trades.

The use of machinery gave rise in its turn to the emergence of a specialised machine-tool industry mainly concerned with supplying local needs. Herbert's of Coventry was founded in 1894 to make turret and capstan lathes, milling and grinding machines, drills and power saws. By 1903 they employed 930 men and supplied nearly every cycle manufacturer in Europe. By 1910 seven other firms of tool manufacturers had been established in Coventry and many more in Birmingham, Stoke on Trent, Wednesbury, Wolverhampton and the Black Country. In the rural area near Uttoxeter in north Staffordshire, a firm of ironmongers supplying local farmers was established by Henry Bamford in 1862. It soon became a major supplier of agricultural machinery, introducing new machines for mowing, harvesting and eventually diesel-powered tractors. All these machine-tool firms produced mainly for the home and imperial markets and their directors were vigorous in their support of imperial preference and fair trade. The introduction of the pneumatic tyre stimulated the growth of the new rubber industry and its location in the Midlands. By 1900 Birmingham had become the home of the main works of Dunlop, where 700 persons were employed. By 1914, 4,000 people were employed in the city on all sorts of rubber manufacture, including raincoats, wellingtons and tyres.

From 1888 onwards central electricity generating stations were established for public supply. At first the undertakings were local in character, but by the early-twentieth century they were much more ambitious. The Midland Electrical Corporation founded in 1897 provided power in an area ten miles around its generating station near Tipton. Similar companies at Stafford and Leek supplied the north, and Birmingham had its own undertaking from 1898. Stoke on Trent had four stations by the time of municipal amalgamation in 1902, when they were combined in a single undertaking. Wolverhampton had a municipal electric-light and power station from 1895, which from 1902 supplied the municipal trams and buses. These power stations not only generated power, but also created a demand for a new range of manufactured goods, namely, switchgear, light bulbs, wire, plugs and, as the potential began to be realised, of domestic labour-saving equipment. In 1891 the General Electric Company established a branch at Witton, and at Aston the firm of Lucas went from strength to strength (Tucker 1977: 8–22).

The quarter century before the First World War saw fundamental changes in management and organisation techniques. After the Companies Act of 1862 businesses run by public companies gradually replaced the old family firms. Birmingham had only 4 public companies in 1875, but there were 114 by 1900, and even the family firms began to professionalise management. Individual firms, having built up a dominant position in the market, combined with others producing related manufactures and with the suppliers of their raw materials to become large international integrated enterprises. A firm well launched on this path by 1911 was Kynochs, originally founded in 1870 by George Kynoch for the manufacture of percussion caps. By 1903 it had become an integrated firm with 6 factories in Birmingham, 1 in the Thames Valley, 2 in Ireland and 1 in Yorkshire. By this time they employed 6,000 people making soap, candles, glycerine, percussion caps, explosives, cupro-nickel, steel and copper. Kynochs had its own rolling mills, a printing works to manufacture the packing, three steamships to carry its goods, and from 1908 an explosives factory in South Africa. By 1914 18,000 people were employed at the Witton works alone (VCH Warks VIII: 104–209).

As firms became larger the stages of production were brought under more control. Management began to deal directly with the labour force, whether skilled or unskilled. The overlookers and subcontractors, who formerly bargained with management and then in turn paid their employees, were gradually replaced by foremen who merely supervised the work, and by workers who were paid a contracted wage directly by the management from its own office. Hours were enforced and continuity of work insisted on, many traditional breaks disappeared as national legislation and local initiative combined to reduce hours of work to a 50- or 54-hour week. It was on the whole a period of rising wages and improving conditions, but this made management all the more anxious to receive a full day's work. The precise regulation of hours was also encouraged by the spread of standard overtime and nightwork rates, and of a minimum wage; subcontracting became illegal in 1901. Management became concerned to control all stages of the work and, in a highly competitive market, costing of goods became much more critical. The composition and quality of materials became more significant with the increase of mechanisation, for faulty materials not only spoilt the work, but also damaged the machine tools. Direct selling of goods increasingly replaced merchanting through factors, especially as a greater amount of midland production was concentrated in the home and colonial markets as other foreign markets shrank behind high protective tariffs. Inevitably direct selling cost more com-

317

pared with factoring and required the employment of increased numbers of non-productive workers such as clerks, stockholders and messengers (Allen 1929: 373–80).

By 1914, although there were still many works where organisation of production was on traditional lines, there were far more large-scale works than was general nationally, and midland industrial organisation was for the most part complex and elaborate.

Chapter 33

Religion, education and leisure: 1830–1914

The evangelical impetus was sustained into the second generation and the Church of England continued to establish new parishes with the help of patronage and public subscription. In Birmingham alone five churches were built in ten years. From 1824 to 1836 the Bishop of Coventry and Lichfield was Henry Ryder, a man of manifest personal spirituality and an active administrator who sought to heighten awareness of spiritual matters. The diocese was divided in 1836 as part of a general reorganisation and north Warwickshire was transferred to Worcester diocese (VCH Warks II: 50). The first bishop of the reduced Lichfield diocese was Samuel Butler (1836–8), a reformer who, though sixty years old and occupying the see for only three years, nevertheless reduced pluralism, established rural deaneries and set up a diocesan board of education and a training college (VCH Staffs II: 69–71).

The clergy were still drawn mainly from the minor gentry and professional classes. In the large town parishes their financial position had greatly improved and some had salaries of £500–£1,000 a year (Smith 1982: 81).

In the face of secular reforms, secular ideologies and secular government, the Church of England was forced to re-examine its position and claims to a hearing. It now competed for attention with legal dissenting bodies and with utilitarian and liberal philosophies. It stood upon the authority of ancient Christian tradition rather than upon the state and legal settlement. It also sought to revitalise its liturgy, its moral teaching and its sense of mission. The Oxford movement had considerable impact in the Midlands and left a permanent memorial in architecture and in various colleges and organisations. Wealthy laymen, including some industrialists, provided funds and patronage and enabled enthusiastic young clerics to reform liturgy and parish life. A. J. Beresford Hope appointed Benjamin Webb to the living at Sheen and J. N. Bagnall presented Richard Twigg, 'the apostle of the Black Country', to St James's, Wednesbury. Whereas in 1849 only 3 Staffordshire churches had daily services, by 1854 there were 20. Sanctuaries were cleared of obstructions, choirs were trained in liturgical music and robed in surplices, and the

Lichfield Cathedral choir festivals attracted church choirs from all over the Midlands.

In both town and countryside church building continued apace, especially after the Act of 1843 simplified legal procedures. One-third of all the Church of England churches in Staffordshire in 1851 had been built since 1800, 82 of them since 1843. Industrialists and landowners headed the subscription lists in rebuilding and restoring parish churches on a grand scale; Sir George Gilbert Scott was employed at Temple Balsall, Enville and elsewhere. Miss Louisa Ryland provided the money for the rebuilding and decoration of Barford in 1844. The Allsop family paid for the new church of Holy Trinity at Burton on Trent, and Herbert Minton contributed largely to the rebuilding of Holy Trinity, Hanley.

There was, by the end of the nineteenth century, an urgent need to redraw diocesan boundaries to take account of changing distributions of population and wealth. The arrangement whereby all Warwickshire had been included in Worcester diocese had never been popular and proposals for reorganisation were frequently advanced but progress was inhibited by financial problems. These problems were overcome in part by Bishop Gore when he became Bishop of Worcester in 1902. A new diocese of Birmingham was created in 1905 and Gore became its first bishop and made St Philips, Birmingham, his pro cathedral. The diocese included the environs of the city in north-west Warwickshire but almost immediately work began to raise funds to make possible the creation of a second new diocese based on Coventry (Morrish 1980).

Meanwhile, the influence and cohesion of dissenting groups was increasingly evident. The number of Methodist chapels – Wesleyan, New Connexion and Primitive – increased notably in the towns and in some rural areas, and their preachers went out into the villages, public houses and workplaces, and onto street corners. The Wesleyan chapels at Bilston, Longton, Dudley and Hanley were grandiose buildings on elevated sites dominating the main streets, with pillared porticoes and flights of steps, and their Sunday schools, their social organisation and the secular prosperity of many of their leaders consolidated their distinctive moral stance. The Primitive Methodists grew in number among the poorer classes and were the major denomination in some parts of north Staffordshire.

In industrial and urban areas, Roman Catholic communities grew in confidence and in numbers, both by natural increase and by conversions. Under the leadership of Bishop Walsh, the headquarters of the midland district was transferred from Wolverhampton to St Chad's, Birmingham. Midland Catholics found themselves receiving from afar a number of exotic individuals, whose influence was to be far-reaching. John Henry Newman left Oxford University and the Church of England and became a Roman Catholic priest and eventually a cardinal. He lived for forty years in Birmingham where he founded and led the Oratory, a community of priests, and through his writings profoundly influenced the development of religious thought, and at the same time was known and remembered by the people of Birmingham as a familiar pastor. In Hanley an Italian Dominican, Dominic Barbieri, preached in broken English to the potters and colliers to great effect. The new young Earl John of Shrewsbury (1827–57) rebuilt Alton Towers and employed as his architect A. W. Pugin, a convert to Roman Catholicism intoxicated with his own particular vision of medieval architecture. Pugin applied his over-driven energies to the task of building churches, convents, almshouses and private homes for Catholic patrons and religious bodies in the Midlands. The most elaborate was St Giles', Cheadle (1841–6), decorated to the utmost within and without. His enthusiasm for rood screens, mural altars, side chapels and elaborate decoration conflicted even in his own day with the pastoral needs of the congregations who used his magnificent buildings.

A number of religious houses for both men and women were founded. The Dominicans were established at Stoke, Rugeley and later at Coventry; the Sisters of Mercy came to Handsworth, Birmingham, Cheadle, Wolverhampton and Coventry; Redemptorists were established at Hanley in Worcestershire; and the Sisters of Charity came to Birmingham (Kiernan 1950: 33–40). The clergy and lay leaders of all the denominations took a great interest in their parish Sunday and day schools and encouraged young middle-class people to spend much time giving lessons and visiting and erecting schools, and expected them to prepare teaching materials, pictures and booklets. Holy Trinity School at Coventry was built in 1853–4 with the aid of grants from the National Society, the State and from local contributions. It accommodated 863 children in boys, girls and mixed infants departments and was also used for evening classes.

Not all educational endeavour was concerned with children. The impetus derived from population growth, industrialisation and the extension of leisure encouraged a multiplicity of initiatives to provide classes, institutions and libraries for adult education. Some of these initiatives were ephemeral, inadequately resourced and badly planned, but others proved to be the starting point of permanent and influential institutions. They touched the lives of a large proportion of the middle and artisan classes in the towns and nurtured the skills and attitudes of industrial and urban society. The churches and many of the larger firms provided evening classes taught by volunteers from among the managers and their friends. The subjects studied often included Shakespeare, Tennyson and other uplifting poets, French, music and public affairs. The Birmingham Midland Institute, the West Bromwich Institution for the advancement of knowledge, the Longton Athenaeum and many other institutions sought to combine the interests of the middle classes in respectable and improving entertainment with a concern for the scientific enlightenment of artisans.

From 1826 onwards Mechanics' Institutes were founded in about fifty Staffordshire and Warwickshire towns. Lectures were held and libraries and study rooms provided for men of modest means, free from denominational associations. Subscriptions varied from 5*s*. a quarter to 1*s*. 6*d*. a quarter or 1*d*. a week.

For a few years Mechanics' Institutes attracted considerable support – Stratford had 270 members, Rugby had 2 institutions with 210 members between them and Coventry had 450 members. However, they failed to attract the 'mechanics' for whom they were founded. Classes and lectures did not provide skills but offered 'general intellectual pursuits'. Almost all depended heavily on the financial support of middle-class or aristocratic patrons, and they dwindled away in the 1850s. In the Potteries there was a short-lived attempt by the pottery workers themselves to set up an alternative organisation, which rejected patronage and gave opportunity for the discussion of Chartism, Owenism and general constitutional change as well as teaching literacy and numeracy. The potters saw education as a means of self-improvement both of their own social position and of society as a whole (Lowe 1970: 75–81).

In promoting education for both children and adults there was an intention, more or less explicit, to promote the virtues of hard work, orderly living and sober industry. Much of the social endeavour of the period, whether imposed from above by town councils, pursued with missionary zeal by the churches, or struggled for by the respectable artisan, was a battle against real dangers of chaos, violence and epidemic disease, all of which threatened urban society as a result of the unprecedented growth of population. In the Midlands educational endeavour brought together the interest of the governors, the respectable middle classes, the churches and those of the lower orders who aspired to social and professional enhancement. There was a considerable degree of real association between the different groups which did go some way to modify the conflicts and pressures of industrialisation and urbanisation (Smith 1982: 138–51).

The desire for self-help and improvement stimulated a demand for cheap literature and publishers, booksellers and newspapers multiplied. Warwickshire had 239 booksellers and bookbinders in 1841, half of them in Birmingham. Newspapers and weekly magazines became more numerous and enjoyed a wider readership. Subscription libraries circulated books through the post; there were railway bookstalls and most town booksellers provided a local loan service for those who could pay. The churches, mechanics' institutes and voluntary societies had for some years attempted to provide books for a wider social range – for example, workmen, schoolchildren and Wolverhampton, Coventry and Birmingham established public reference libraries under the Public Libraries Act of 1855, and one of the earliest in the Midlands was that of Walsall opened in 1859.

Nearly all these initiatives were promoted in the towns; corresponding efforts by squire and parson in the countryside were for the most part small-scale and short-lived. The result was to widen still further the cultural gap between the industrial town workers and the rural labourers. Literacy was

Plate 5.11 The Reverend Edward Girdlestone gives a tea party at Sedgley Vicarage for the Sunday School children, June 1837. The recently completed parish church of All Saints is in the background. Drawing by his sister.

associated with social and economic status and worldly success and its achievement led to promotion at work and the extension of the franchise rather than to bible reading and prayer.

During the last quarter of the nineteenth century the churches lost their monopoly of the provision of public education. The religious enthusiasm of the 1840s had given way to a new enthusiasm for popular science and rational efficiency. It is noteworthy that some of the leaders in the movement for a national, non-sectarian universal provision of schooling were men who had been prominent in supporting church schools but who now wished for a more systematic provision. Sir John Packington, a High Tory Anglican landowner, had been most active in the 1840s in the provision of Anglican schools, but by the 1860s he recognised the limitations of what the Church could do and was enthusiastic for state-aided education (Aldrich 1981: 10–14). By 1867 the Education League, a highly organised pressure group, was demanding prompt parliamentary action for the whole country. For the leaders, Jesse Collings, George Dixon and others, the need for secular education was far more imperative than the need for moral and religious formation. The Education League raised £60,000 in four months, started 113 town branches and circulated their leaflets to a quarter of a million supporters. Nevertheless, they took little part in the negotiations leading to the School Board Act of 1870 and were dissatisfied with it (Briggs 1952: 100–5). They would have preferred a totally secular system, wholly in the hands of local government. Instead the Act required the setting up of elected school boards to collect a special school rate only where the existing provision by the churches could be shown to be inadequate. Moreover, religious education of a minimal kind was permitted in board schools, so long as it was not denominational and subject to parents' right of withdrawal.

Birmingham School Board built schools at the rate of one a year, accommodating in each case over a thousand children. They took pride in allowing more generous space per child than the official minimum and using the best quality materials for buildings and furniture. By 1879 they employed 430 teachers and pupil teachers. Their schools symbolised the pride of the community in secular achievement and promoted the values of hard work, ambition, competition and public accountability (Briggs 1952: 101–10).

In Wolverhampton the church leaders maintained ascendancy and not only did the voluntary schools continue to command public esteem, but the School Boards included representatives of the churches, and the board schools kept religious education in their curriculum. At Stoke on Trent the rector was chairman of the School Board and the Board cooperated with the voluntary schools committee. By 1881 only one quarter of the school population was attending board schools, the majority attended church schools. In Sedgley, in contrast, four-fifths of the children were in board schools (Charlton 1975: 17–30). In Dudley the Board and its schools were the subject of constant partisan wrangling and the proportion of children in church schools actually rose by the end of the century (Hughes, L. 1980: 6–12). West Bromwich and Warwick were both in their different ways beneficiaries of aristocratic paternalism and they had little need for board schools.

There were also great differences between one board and another in enforcing compulsory schooling. West Bromwich was among the first to do so and had the highest school attendance record in the Midlands, but at neighbouring Walsall and Sedgley the Boards had to fight a long-drawn-out battle with parents who were unwilling to send to school children who could be profitably employed at home.

In rural areas the parish national school was still usually the only available school for the poor and was supported by both the squire and the parson. There was much absenteeism, girls were kept at home on washdays, and boys would absent themselves frequently, and some families still kept their children away on old country festival days such as Plough Monday and St Valentine's Day (Ashby 1961: 18–21).

Meanwhile there was rapid development in the provision of systematic adult education. Institutes of technical education and colleges of art and design were established on a permanent footing in almost every municipality in the

Midlands. Some of these had their origins in evening classes in public libraries, others were initiated by individual philanthropists or by particular trades. All were in some degree a response to the changing needs of industry and commerce. The experience of Coventry may stand for many. In 1883 a petition of masters and artisans led to the decision to establish a technical institute. The buildings were donated by a ribbon manufacturer and other wealthy individuals made substantial donations. The institute was opened in 1887 and from 1895 was receiving grants from the whisky money, and from 1890 from central government. For the rest it depended on the fees charged to students. In 1895 the institute was taken over by the corporation which also in 1902 became responsible for the schools of art. At first the institutes overlapped the work of the higher grade board schools and the pupil teacher centres. However, after 1902 they catered mainly for adults by offering as many evening as day classes. They attracted very large numbers of students to classes in engineering, metallurgy, building, electricity and kinetics linked to local industries and also to commercial subjects such as European languages, bookkeeping and accountancy, and the new skills of shorthand and typing.

The Balfour Act in 1902 brought the School Boards to an end and transferred their responsibilities to the new local education authorities, namely the municipal corporations and county councils. For the next ten years these authorities tended to concentrate on providing new secondary schools, especially in the towns. Schools like Wolverhampton Municipal secondary school, Bilston Girls Grammar School, Oldbury High School and many others deliberately copied the middle-class schools of the old foundations and Girls Public Day Schools Trust. They were usually single-sex schools, the children wore striped blazers, school ties and boaters. Cricket, tennis and football were played, French and Latin were taught and the patterns of behaviour, the structures of authority and the whole ethos and tone were deliberately middle class. Entry was by public examination, and even though there were free places many parents could not undertake the cost of uniform, books, travelling expenses and sports equipment. By 1914 the city of Coventry had 40 council schools with 15,300 children, 15 Church of England schools with 2,744 scholars, and 4 Roman Catholic schools with 724 scholars. Many of the new council schools, especially in the suburbs, were light, airy, single-storey buildings with large windows and some specialist rooms, but in central Birmingham, in many of the industrial villages of the Potteries and the Black Country and in most rural villages, the older national or board schools served without much improvement the needs of the children of the slums and the countryside. They were increasingly dilapidated, often overcrowded and lacked sanitary facilities and suitable heating systems.

Meanwhile the seventeen endowed schools in the Midlands had been required to submit to government commissions of enquiry, and under the Endowed Schools Act of 1870 schemes had been drawn up to remodel the foundations and constitutions of each of those which were to continue. Their trust deeds were overhauled, new schemes amalgamating various local charities were made which enabled them to put their affairs on a better footing, and in most cases to erect new buildings. Boys were entered for competitive examinations for the Civil Service and for the Indian Civil Service and for entrance to the universities, and successes were well publicised. Some of the schools were partly boarding and partly day schools. Others such as Walsall and Coventry were wholly for day boys. The numbers rarely exceeded 100 boys.

During the nineteenth century, Rugby was transformed from an endowed school catering for the local gentry to one of the foremost public schools, attracting the sons of the governing classes. Thomas Arnold, headmaster from 1828 to 1841, combined that post with the office of chaplain. He limited the numbers of boys to 260, developed the system of boarding the boys with undermasters, and the sixth form as a moral élite corps, cooperating with him in the moral training of the boys in the virtues of earnestness, integrity, honesty, loyalty and purity. He raised the academic standards and made admission to the universities the goal of achievement. Boys who could not or would not cooperate with his objectives were expelled. Between 1869 and 1875 the school was reorganised by the Public Schools Commission and the new trustees included representatives of the universities of Oxford and Cam-

---

Plate 5.12   The staff of the Sacred Heart School, Wolverhampton, about 1910. The sisters were members of a French congregation who had left France at the time of the secularisation legislation. They returned to France on the outbreak of the First World War.

bridge, the Royal Society, the Lord Chancellor and the masters of the school. In the late-nineteenth and early-twentieth century the headmasters and many of the undermasters were distinguished clergymen of outstanding brilliance, most of whom had either come from, or moved on to, high office in the Church of England. Christianity at Rugby was broad church and muscular, team games were introduced from 1870, and swimming, long-distance running, cricket and Rugby football were ritually cultivated.

Sunday schools, working-class day schools, and after 1870 Board Schools had always educated working-class girls as well as boys. In the larger towns in the 1880s girls were encouraged to continue to the higher grade schools and allowed to enter technical colleges, municipal art schools and adult education institutions. Their numbers in these courses remained small except in courses for typing and art but this was as much due to family responsibilities and lack of resources as lack of opportunity. Systematic education for middle-class girls was harder to come by. The King Edward VI Foundation established four girls' schools under its constitution of 1900 and a separate Girls' High School and from 1900 included two women among the governors. There were a number of initiatives by the Roman Catholic religious orders to found middle-class secondary schools for girls in Birmingham, Wolverhampton, Stoke on Trent and Coventry, to cater for the daughters of local Catholic families. In 1873 Canon Lowe extended the work of the Woodward Foundation to establish a High Anglican boarding school for girls at Abbots Bromley and by 1880 there were fifty girls being prepared for Cambridge local examinations. Between 1900 and 1910 such schools became more and more a girls' version of the public schools for boys; university entrance was an important objective, a wide range of subjects including mathematics and Latin were taught and team games, including basket ball, lacrosse and cricket, were played (VCH Staffs: 152–30).

In education as in every other sphere the emphasis was more and more secular. The governing bodies of the endowed schools by 1914 usually included representatives of the local municipal council or county council, and although the headmasters were still usually in holy orders assistant masters were frequently laymen.

The new secondary schools and also to some extent the new university college of Birmingham maintained the tradition of the pre-eminence of liberal and classical studies, stressing the all-round development of the individual. The technical colleges on the other hand provided courses very specifically directed to particular qualifications and opportunities in the world of work. There was no doubt in Edwardian England which commanded the greater public esteem, for, while the demands of technology and commerce became more and more imperative, a 'liberal education' was valued as the education of a gentleman (Smith 1982: 225–55).

The same distinctions between the amateur and the professional, between what was appropriate for gentlemen and for workers, were apparent in

327

leisure activities, especially sport. From 1870s there developed in the towns a large following for organised sport, especially football. Formal organised games on Sundays continued to be frowned upon as likely to interfere with keeping the day holy, but from the mid-century more firms began to close at 1.00 p.m. on Saturdays. One of the first to do so was probably Worsdells' engineering works and, in Birmingham, the half day movement was taken up widely in the Midlands in the 1860s. Football in an unorganised form was universal but from the mid-century the schools and the universities began to define the rules of the game and see it as part of the moral education of schoolboys and undergraduates. During the 1860s and 1870s the proponents of *'mens sana in corpore sano'* and of muscular Christianity were numerous and middle-class educators believed that for boys and young men playing team games encouraged virtues of honesty, modesty, self-control, continence, courage and leadership, all summed up in the phrase 'team spirit'. At the same time clubs and local leagues were formed among working people on their own initiative. Some 25 per cent of all the clubs known in Birmingham in the 1870s were based on public houses – the Unicorn, the Victoria Cross, the Grove for example and about 20 per cent on chapels or parishes (Mason 1980: 9–21). Others again were works teams – for example, Mitchells brewery and the Midland and Saltley railway companies. Competitions were organised and the teams were encouraged at matches by supporters who, with greater leisure and cheaper transport available, were willing to travel to away games. Football soon became the most popular organised sport both for participants and supporters. The Football Association was formed in 1863 and with some difficulty established an agreed set of rules; the Birmingham Football Association was set up in 1875 and the Staffordshire County Association two years later. Enthusiasm spread during the 1870s and the local newspapers were soon reporting matches and club news. Wednesbury had three strong teams in the early 1870s – the Strollers, the Old Athletic and Elwell's (a works team). In Walsall the young men of 'good social position' joined 'the Town', working men joined the 'Swift' and there was fierce rivalry between them. The Football League was founded in 1888 and Wolverhampton Wanderers and Aston Villa, West Bromwich Albion and Stoke were among its first members. The more prestigious clubs gradually ousted the lesser clubs from competition and by the 1880s were employing professionals, charging entry money to the public of 3*d.*–6*d.* a match and building permanent wooden 'stands' for the supporters. The clubs became fiercely competitive and their success in league and cup competitions became of paramount importance to the clubs and to their supporters. Working-class men prided themselves on an emotional and partisan support of 'their' team very different from the 'play the game' and 'good loser' ethic beloved of the middle classes. The post of club secretary became one of great local importance and secretaries such as H. H. Addenbrooke of Wolverhampton, or J. W. Thomas of Stoke City were soon gaining the financial patronage of local business men.

By 1914 the regular attendances at matches of leading midland clubs was well over 10,000 and the success or failure of the local team was the most important news in the local papers (Mason 1980: 138–75). Rugby football remained on the whole a middle-class sport in the Midlands, and clubs were often associated with old boys of the public schools. Old boys of King Edward's School Birmingham ran four rugby teams in 1908 and there were also famous teams at Leamington College and Trinity College School Stratford. Coventry Rugby Club was founded in 1871, probably as an extension of the activities of a cricket club, and a rugby club was founded at Moseley in 1879 which soon achieved a high reputation, winning the midland counties cup six times in the first eight years.

Cricket had long been part of the rural scene and matches were 'got up' on village greens and gentlemen's estates to mark special occasions. Teams of professional players visited the Midlands, playing exhibition matches against local teams as at Stoke in 1857 when George Parr of Nottingham brought his All-England eleven. He returned in 1865 to play at Trentham Park in the presence of the Duke of Sutherland, when despite ducal patronage and gentry subscriptions an entry fee was charged to defray the costs of the visit. Village and club matches were reported in the local press and the more ambitious clubs built up seasons of fixtures. In 1871 a county club was formed with the support of Lord Dartmouth, and A. H. Heath, ironmaster, colliery owner and MP for Hanley. Warwickshire formed a county club in 1883 and soon became a well-established 'first-class' team among the thirteen playing for the 'county championship'. They took on the MCC, other counties and even occasionally the gentlemen of Australia on their visits to England. The cricket teams were a mixture of amateurs and professionals and social distinctions remained very evident in cricket.

Golf and tennis were played mainly by the middle classes of the suburbs. The Coventry golf club was formed in 1887 and the first games played in the fields at Pinley until a nine-hole course was laid out on Whitley Common and other courses were provided by subscription clubs at Kenilworth, Sutton Coldfield, Rugby and Harborne and other middle-class residential areas. The new game of lawn tennis was also becoming popular in middle-class circles. Lawn tennis courts were laid out beside the homes of better-off families in town as well as country, and by the 1890s tennis had become one of the main forms of social gathering and contact among young people. For many young men and women of the turn of the century the most liberating influence was the bicycle which enabled people of modest means to travel, to explore the countryside and to associate with each other in one of the many cycling clubs which were formed. The opportunity for a holiday away from home was spreading down the social scale rapidly in the 1890s, and many Midlanders discovered the seaside and countryside of Wales. Aberystwyth, Llangollen, Barmouth and Rhyl were particularly favoured, and Fairbourne on the Mawddach estuary prospered as a new holiday settlement for English visitors mainly from the

Midlands. Many poorer industrial workers combined an opportunity for a change for the women and children with a chance to earn some money by going regularly to help in the market gardens and orchards of Warwickshire and Worcestershire, 'paypuckin' (pea picking), an activity which even the school board attendance officers were forced to legitimise.

In addition to organised sport, there was also a much wider range of indoor leisure activities available in midland towns by 1914. Choral societies flourished, for subscriptions were modest. People had more leisure and the music shops supplied sheet music at moderate prices. Birmingham triennial music festival was a major social and musical occasion and some local choirs achieved high standards and were able to employ soloists and conductors of note. Hanley choir received several visits from Delius as conductor and gave the first performances of his *Sea Drift* and also of Elgar's *King Offa*. Mendelssohn's *Elijah* and Elgar's *Dream of Gerontius* had their first performances at Birmingham. Church and chapel choirs provided an opportunity for the exercise of more modest talents and the 'anniversaries' continued to be major annual celebrations in the chapels of the industrial villages.

Coventry, Hanley, Warwick, Birmingham and Stratford on Avon and Wolverhampton all supported at least one commercial theatre throughout the nineteenth century but many of the ventures were shortlived: the theatres frequently changed names and management, and relied mainly upon visiting celebrities and companies, performing melodramas, pantomime and variety. The Theatre Royal, Aston, was one of the more successful and aimed from the first to appeal to the working-class family. By 1912 there were 7 theatres in Warwickshire, 12 in Birmingham and 22 in Staffordshire. The Shakespeare Memorial Theatre was founded at Stratford in 1879, providing regular performances of Shakespeare's plays, and in 1913 Barry Jackson founded the Birmingham Repertory Theatre in a determined attempt to champion the theatre as art as against the commercial theatre.

In 1901 Mr Edison's Animated Pictures were shown at the Coventry Corn Exchange, among them a film about the Boer War and another telling the story of Joan of Arc. By 1912 there were 11 cinemas in Warwickshire, 7 in Birmingham and 25 in Staffordshire, many of them in buildings adapted from other purposes (Clegg 1983).

By far the most important form of popular entertainment, however, was the public house. Drink had pervaded every aspect of both working and leisure life in the Victorian Midlands. Drink allowances were part of the wages of miners and of farm labourers; drink was essential in the high temperatures of furnaces and glass-works; new entrants to a trade got their 'footing' at public houses; and the public house was the scene of celebrations, benefit societies and social clubs. The Midlands suffered from widespread drunkenness and the Band of Hope and the temperance movements together with the chapels and churches tried to counteract the evil.

The flint-glass workers and other trade unions added their voices to those urging temperance. The watch committees and the police made determined efforts to punish those seen drunk and disorderly in public, and from 1869 magistrates became more and more unwilling to allow new licences and it became harder to evade the law. As licences became harder to get and easier to lose, publicans exercised a greater degree of control over their customers. Until the last quarter of the nineteenth century most midland publicans brewed their own beer and a very large staff of excisemen operated in the area. From 1880, however, the large-scale brewing companies took over the trade and the proportion of inns brewing their own beer in Birmingham dropped from 99 per cent in the 1870s to 15 per cent by 1890. The firms which could engage in large scale production, scientific management and advertising soon ousted the smaller brewers. At Burton Bass, Alsopp and Worthington drove out the lesser firms and competed fiercely with each other to obtain retail outlets. By 1915 Alsopps owned 461 tied houses mainly in northern England and south Wales, the Potteries and London. From 1890 onwards the large firms not only bought up retail houses but rebuilt them on a much grander scale, partly to associate drinking with respectability – even opulence, and partly to enable the public houses to handle larger numbers of customers. The new pubs were usually on corner sites, built of red brick and terra cotta with lights, clock-towers, stained-glass windows and conspicuous roof decorations which drew the potential customer from a distance. Inside they had magnificent oak or mahogany bars, large rooms and elaborate highly coloured terra-cotta tiling and moulded decorations. Social distinction was maintained within the building by separate public bars and more refined and well-furnished smoking rooms (Crawford and Thorne 1983).

The outdoor jug and bottle trade continued to be important but drinking at work declined rapidly, traditional allowances were replaced by new negotiated wage rates, many new kinds of work were introduced and the new management techniques eliminated many traditional breaks and rituals. Leisure activities were an increasingly important part of the lives of people of many social groups. The choice of activity was individual but reflected and reinforced the social groupings of class and of wealth.

Part six

The Midlands in the Twentieth Century

Chapter 34

Population, industry and social change in the Midlands: 1914–1939

The population of England increased from 33½ million in 1911 to 46 million by 1971, growing steadily if more slowly than in the nineteenth century. The decade of slowest growth was that of 1921–31 when the loss of some 34,000 young men killed in the war and the economic difficulties of the depression combined to retard the birth rate. Throughout the period death rates fell, reaching 11.7 per thousand by 1971, maternal mortality was almost eliminated and infant mortality was much reduced. The birth rate also fell throughout the period and the size of families was reduced.

The Midlands followed the same trend and broadly speaking were subject to the same influences. However, the rate of natural increase remained much higher than the national average and this continued to be the case until the 1960s. As a result the Midlands increased its share of the national population and had a higher proportion of people of working age (Rodgers 1972: 180–1). In the 1930s the birth rate in the industrial areas of the Midlands was higher than in any other part of the country and there were also high birth rates in the rural towns and in villages within travelling distance of the industrial areas. The population of rural mid-Staffordshire continued to decline until 1934 when it began to rise again as this area too began to attract young couples who worked in Stafford or the Black Country and travelled daily to work by bus, train or car. Similarly mid-Warwickshire began to attract an outflow of population from the older industrial areas. In contrast the city of Stoke on Trent had a declining population from 1931, for an increasing number of people who worked in the city lived in more pleasant residential environments outside the city boundaries.

Coventry grew rapidly between the wars. In 1931, just after the city's boundaries had been extended, the population numbered 168,900 people. In the following decade the number grew by 13 per cent, seven times more rapidly than the national average. During the war many workers were drafted into Coventry while many civilians were evacuated so that meaningful figures cannot be obtained, but in the decade 1946–51 Coventry grew by 33 per cent and in the following decade by a further 18 per cent. The rate of natural increase was about twice as high as the national average and in addition there was much immigration. In the 1950s many Poles and other displaced Europeans settled in Coventry, and the city also attracted many immigrants from Eire (Richardson 1972: 328–33).

Birmingham and the Black Country had also continued to maintain a high rate of natural increase between the wars and to continue to attract immigrants especially from the 1930s (Walker 1947: 168). After the war the population increased by 15.3 per cent in the decade 1951–61 and in the mid-1960s growth reached 1 per cent per annum. Four-fifths of this was due to natural increase, for the crude birth and death rates were both higher than the national average and the proportion of young people in the population was high. Only a small proportion of this increase was due to immigration and by the early 1960s there was an acute shortage of unskilled workers in the area. People from the Carribean, from India and Pakistan were encouraged to settle in the area, and although this movement was checked and the rate slowed down from 1962, by 1971 the population of the connurbation of Birmingham and the Black Country included 4.42 per cent of Irish origin, 2.5 per cent from the Carribean and 3.71 Asians. The largest concentration of new commonwealth immigrants were living in Handsworth where they comprised one-third of the population but this was quite exceptional (Sutcliffe 1974a: 363–99).

After the war new industries such as vehicle production and electrical engineering were established on new sites. As a result the population of Kenilworth rose five-fold between 1911 and 1971, and in the decade 1961–71 alone the growth was 39 per cent. Solihull grew twelve-fold between 1911 and 1971, Rugby more than three-fold. Stafford grew by 14 per cent during the 1960s and Cannock, Lichfield and Rugby all grew rapidly. Increasing numbers of people travelled to work as car ownership spread rapidly. Aldridge had been largely rural until the Second World War but by 1964 its population reached 58,900.

In the Potteries the trend already noticed before the war for the population to move out to the surrounding villages became even more marked and the population in the new areas of the old six towns declined very sharply indeed (Kivell 1975: 442–4). In some rural villages too the declining demand for agricultural labour led to a reduction of population and large-scale planning tended to close small schools, shops, post offices and to reduce local transport services. While fewer young families could live in the villages, there was much movement of car-owning retired couples into the more attractive villages, and much private money was spent improving and modernising village houses.

In September 1914 all over Britain men rushed to volunteer for service in the armed forces. By March 1916 the total number of volunteers had reached 2.5 million. Thereafter they were supplemented by conscripts until the total was 5.7 million. From Birmingham alone 150,000 men joined the armed forces, 54 per cent of all the men of military age. Of these 13,000 died and 35,000 came back disabled (Briggs 1952: 220). In every town and village in the Midlands the story was similar. Families of all classes sent fathers, husbands and sons to the front, and their sufferings, physical and mental, in the trenches were deeply impressed upon a whole generation, who were never to lose the sense of outrage and shock. Against this undoubted fact it would seem trivial to suggest that the four years of the First World War were not a great dividing line between eras of social change. Yet it must be said that in industry, agriculture, labour relations and the position of women, the war accelerated existing change rather than created new departures.

The war greatly stimulated development in the newer midland industries. The car and bicycle firms of Birmingham, Coventry and Wolverhampton supplied thousands of vehicles to the army and before the end of the war were also producing tanks, armoured vehicles and gun carriages. Lucas built a new seven-storey factory with government assistance and by 1916 were employing 4,000 (Nockolds 1976: 143–57).

There was already a shortage of some skilled workers by 1915 and many negotiations took place between unions and employers as, first, less skilled men and then women were brought in to replace the men who had joined the

Plate 6.1　The Royal Warwickshire Regiment leaving Sutton Coldfield for Yorkshire in July 1915. The regiment suffered terrible losses in France and Italy.

Plate 6.2   A munitions worker making Mills bombs in Birmingham, 1917.

forces. From January 1916 tribunals were appointed to adjudicate between the army and industry in cases where both wanted the same man and after the introduction of conscription in summer 1916 these tribunals heard thousands of cases a month in the Midlands (Briggs 1952). Plant was drastically reorganised and small firms were forced into co-operation with each other and with the larger firms. Discussions between management and workers took place on the shop floor, and labour representatives were appointed within the works and the local trades councils found themselves with a great increase of business.

The War Department made ever increasing demands upon Midlands industry. The overriding imperative of war production determined what should be produced, to what standards and how. Large firms were able to introduce new machinery, research and make new products and meet new standards, and consequently made great profits. On the other hand, conscription and the death of key personnel could be especially serious in the case of a small family firm, and it was harder for them to meet the demands of the War Department. Jewellery firms were especially hard hit, and it was not until 1917 that they were fully involved in war production and thus able to profit from war contracts (Brazier and Sandford 1921). The concentration on goods required by the War Department encouraged the trend away from hardware to light engineering, electrical goods and vehicle production. It also encouraged greater standardisation of product and the rapid circulation of information and adoption of technical innovation. These trends were to continue in the interwar period (Allen 1929: 373–80).

However, the great demand for munitions and goods ensured constant work and much overtime. Wages rose considerably and despite the sharp rise in food prices the working classes in general were not worse off in 1918 than they had been in 1914. Children's health and nutrition improved somewhat and the poorer families were able to obtain steady employment (Hopkins 1979: 214). The Birmingham Cooperative Society introduced a voluntary food rationing scheme and in March 1917 committees were set up to ensure equitable distribution of coal and of food. National food committees were set up in August 1917 on the model of the Birmingham committee and an experimental rationing system was tried out in that city (Briggs 1952: 200–20). A national rationing scheme was finally introduced in July 1918 for meat, bacon, fat, butter, margarine, lard and sugar, but rationing in the First World War was never severe nor rigidly enforced. War came home to the civilian population with the Zeppelin raids. The Chief Constable of Birmingham had issued a notice ordering the dimming of lights as early as November 1914 and in January 1915 arrangements were made for warning in case of attack. In January 1916 the first raid on the Midlands took place and Zeppelins were seen over Wednesbury, Walsall, Tipton, Dudley and Halesowen. The mayors of the Midlands met and agreed on lighting restrictions, the placing of four anti-aircraft guns, searchlight protection and signal intercommunication. A second Zeppelin raid took place in 1917 and a third in April 1918 but they did little damage.

The numbers of women working in offices, banks, local government, schools and nursing increased while others joined the WAAC or the Women's Land Army. Many working-class women were able to move from earning a living in the sweated trades or in domestic service to waged occupations with regular if long hours and a greater sense of personal independence. The top wage for the women was 32*s*. a week though many, especially those under 18 years of age, earned much less. Only single girls were employed, and married women seeking employment hid their wedding rings (Nockolds 1976: 151).

The war encouraged the development of mass-produced entertainment. The newspapers and the cinema became the most popular forms of cheap entertainment and information. Professional cricket and football were abandoned in 1915. Public houses prospered, but from 1915 alcohol was heavily taxed and licensed drinking hours were drastically reduced in order to encourage war work and reduce absenteeism.

Immediately after the war the demand for manufactured goods continued and even in the years of slump and recession people continued to buy cars, motorcycles, washing machines, film and cameras and electrical equipment. The Midlands profited from all the new opportunities, and as a result suffered much less severely from the depression than other old industrial districts. The Midlands formed part of a belt of territory stretching from Stafford to London which continued to prosper on the basis of rising demand for goods at home.

The production of small cars for a mass market was established in the twenties, and soon became the most important product of the Midlands. William Morris (Lord Nuffield) established a works in Coventry in 1921 and by 1926 was making a Morris car which sold for £125, while at Longbridge Herbert Austin rapidly recovered after near bankruptcy in 1922 by selling the Austin 12 for £168. The multiplicity of car firms which had sprung up before the war were now absorbed or replaced by a few larger firms: Morris, Austin, Humber, Rootes and Jensen. Whereas the early motorcar pioneers had been engineering enthusiasts developing the car for fellow enthusiasts, management after the war was concerned with mechanisation, marketing and the organisation of labour. However, the large firms continued to buy in many parts and accessories and many small firms prospered accordingly. In Birmingham and district by 1921 64,800 people were already employed in making cars and motorcycles and another 14,900 in making accessories. The development and production of aeroplanes had been rapid during 1916–18 and manufacturers such as Siddeley at Coventry found a ready market in supplying the new peacetime freight and passenger airlines which were being established throughout the world. In partnership with Armstrong both civil and fighting aircraft were manufactured at Whitley and later at Baginton. The manufacture of bicycles followed broadly the same line of development, with the multiplicity of small firms established before the war giving way to a few 'progressive' firms such as Sunbeam and Viking at Woverhampton (Allen 1929: 401–3).

All industries concerned with the supply of electric power and equipment had been growing rapidly since the beginning of the century but the establishment of the national electricity grid in 1926 made possible the orderly extension of supplies to every part of the country. The Central Electricity Board took over from the multiplicity of small electricity supply companies run by private enterprise and municipalities. Although it was to be many years before all the more remote rural areas had electricity supplies, the homes and industries of the towns, the residential suburbs and villages and the new and many old industries provided a huge home market for electricity (Henessy 1972: 51). By 1932 the Stafford works of the English Electric Company had four main departments producing machinery for power stations, switching equipment and fusegear, and very powerful electric engines. In Coventry the Peel-Conner works were completed in 1921 and the British Houston works became part of the American General Electric Company. Thomas Holcroft of Wolverhampton had manufactured hollow-ware in the nineteenth century but in the 1920s they were supplying castings, switchgear, fuseboxes and other electrical components. Many of the new firms and new branches were established on new sites and even in new areas to take advantage of road and rail transport to London. More and more use was made of aluminium and among the new aluminium firms was Birmetals which chose a high rural site just outside Birmingham, taking advantage both of clean air and low rates. Other firms such as Star Aluminium in Wolverhampton produced 'silver paper' wrappings, insulation for electric cables and strip and bottle tops.

A wider range of metals and alloys was used and bakelite was introduced at Tyseley in 1933, the first of a growing list of plastics. Coventry still had 30 manufacturers of silk ribbon in 1927 with 7,000 employees, but by 1935 there were only 13 firms with 5,000 workers. Long established firms were able to survive by specialist production of regalia, name tapes and badges. In addition Courtaulds rayon factory (founded in 1904) was by 1925 producing cellulose acetate yarn on a large scale and in 1927 opened a new works at Little Heath, Coventry, which was to become the headquarters of a wide empire. Man-made fibres were introduced for stockings and underwear and Courtaulds established branches at Branston near Burton in 1928 and Wolverhampton in 1929 and although the Burton branch was short-lived the Wolverhampton branch sited in open country to the north of the town employed large numbers of women producing both yarn and knitted fabrics. Just before the war ICI and Courtaulds combined to produce nylon yarn in Coventry (Richardson 1972: 153).

More and more firms amalgamated into great national and international companies. In 1927 Midland Tar Distilleries was formed from twelve midland companies, the oldest of which had been founded in 1857, processing the waste products of the gas companies to produce benzine, naphthalene and other chemicals as well as tar for roads and creosote. Kynoch's percussion cap works became part of Nobel industries and combined with seventy-eight other explosive firms throughout the world. This in turn became one of the four great companies which amalgamated in 1926 to become ICI.

341

Such works counted their employees in thousands. The great car firms were the largest employers: Massey-Ferguson at Coventry employed 10,000 and Humber 7,300. There were still many small family firms in the Midlands often making accessories or servicing the larger firms, but the small works was by no means the typical midland unit of production. In 1931 Birmingham had 5,856 factories but only 2,545 workshops.

Moreover, more of the persons employed were unskilled or semi-skilled workers using complex machine tools. Multiple boring drills which drilled 100 holes at a time, compound dies, hydraulic feeds, multispindle automatic lathes, all were doing the work formerly done by the skilled metal workers. Electric arc welding replaced hand welding, and hot press stamping took the place of casting and drop forging. Herberts in Coventry became the largest producer of machine tools in England, employing 2,000, but there were many similar firms in Coventry, in Wolverhampton, Tipton and Darlaston and also machine tool firms in the Potteries, Tamworth, Lichfield and Cannock, supplying the particular industries of those areas. To make the best use of sophisticated and complex machinery the large firms reorganised production. The automatic transfer of work from one machine to the next was introduced at the car and bicycle firms from the early 1920s. Already in 1913 at the Sunbeam works the chassis of cars had been mechanically moved from fitter to fitter. Reorganisation started at Longbridge in 1922–5 and by 1930 they had six miles of assembly line with 6,000 machines. Managers also introduced the 'scientific' measurement of the movements and output of the workers, trying to increase production by payment by results. Various systems were introduced, including that called after its inventor Charles Bedaux, which measured the work done by one worker in one minute and based remuneration on these 'units'.

Meanwhile the older industries on which the Midlands had been built were in decline. Pig iron production fell from 851,000 tons in 1913 to 440,000 tons in 1929 and even with the stimulus of rearmament only rose to 470,000 tons in 1939. Steel output on the other hand increased from a diminishing number of works from 365,000 in 1913 to 702,000 tons in 1939 since the availability of scrap and the local market enabled the works at Bilston and Shelton to continue (Wood 1976: 33).

Industries such as jewellery, tinplate and button manufacture, which had depended heavily upon hand and craft skills, declined in the face of mass production. A few families continued to make a living, usually by means of filling one particular niche in the market – as the Cradely hand chainmakers made chains for the lifeboats or the Wednesfield hand key makers worked for banks and the antique trade. Meanwhile, Birmingham jewellery became more and more a luxury trade, capitalising on skilled workmen and expensive materials.

Change in the pottery industry between the wars was more gradual. The demand for crockery for homes, hotels, institutions and schools kept up with the rising standard of living and there was a much greater demand for sanitary ware, electrical fittings and parts for fires, cookers and heaters. The switch bases for electrical gear were formerly imported from the Continent but the Potteries developed its own manufacture during the war. Between 1910 and 1919 the overseas export demand had expanded but thereafter the export for high quality bone china and manufacture collapsed and the Potteries depended more and more upon the production of earthenware for both the home and the overseas market, and the British Dominions.

From 1901 coalfiring of the kilns was gradually replaced by gas-fired kilns but there were still only 61 gas-fired kilns compared with 2,000 coal-fired kilns in 1938. The electric fired kiln was first introduced by Wedgwood in 1939 at their new works outside the Potteries area at Barlaston where continuous firing was introduced. In the older Potteries hours of labour were gradually curtailed from 54 to 47 and measures were imposed to reduce the incidence of industrial disease. However, management and outlook remained traditional. A minimum wage was introduced from 1920 but for all payments above this level the potters still depended on negotiations based on old price lists, and there was no uniformity of payment within the industry for similar work. The highest paid group were the throwers at 76s. a week. The majority of the workforce were women and, with a chronic excess of workers, wages remained low and correspondingly less impetus to vigorous management and mechanisation (VCH Staffs II: 38–45, 57–68).

Coalmining continued on all three coalfields of the Midlands but production was concentrated on the deeper mines of the concealed coalfields, and the capital costs of mining increased. The output was sold to domestic and industrial users, to the electricity generating stations and the gas works. In south Staffordshire, Baggeridge, on Lord Dudley's estate, and Sandwell Park and Hamstead on Lord Dartmouth's estate, deep mines continued to work but the mines drainage commission reported in 1921 that the greater part of the exposed coalfield was unworkable although some 43 million tons of coal were estimated to remain but the coalfield was one great 'waterfilled rabbit warren' and 61 tons of water were being moved for every ton of coal. Whereas in 1913 there had been 10,000 men employed, raising 2.6 million tons of coal, by 1919 there were only 5,000 men producing 1.6 million tons. Some very small scale mines still used family labour and served a wholly local market. The older parts of the Cannock coalfield were also being given up but new pits were opened further north, including Hilton Main in 1924, and production remained at about 4–5 million tons a year. In north Staffordshire new collieries were sunk at Wolstanton in 1920, Hem Heath in 1929 and Berry in 1932, all getting coal from more than 2,000 ft down. There were still about 500 miners in the Cheadle area in 1939 (VCH Staffs II: 87–105).

On the east Warwickshire coalfield, output also continued to expand to 5.8 million tons and the output was almost wholly sold within a twenty-mile radius. Binley colliery near Coventry began producing coal in the 1920s and

Dexter colliery in the 1930s. The modest increase in output was achieved mainly by reorganisation and the mechanisation of the older mines and while the costs of production were rising the numbers employed were declining (Wise 1950: 296–8).

The midland mines and miners were not isolated in separate mining communities and there continued to be a great demand for coal in the Midlands itself, so that neither the social nor the economic pressures were as acute as on other coalfields. Nevertheless some three-quarters of midland miners were already members of the Miners' Federation and participated in the national struggles between the miners' unions and the employers.

The growth of new industries, the increase of mechanisation and 'progressive' management created new tensions between employers and employed while the decline of older industries and rising unemployment contributed to the fears and anxieties of working people even while the Midlands prospered and the standard of living rose. After the war most of the skilled women who had been working in industry were quickly replaced by men but large numbers of unskilled women continued to work in the service sector, and in the newer trades – winding armatures by hand at Lucas, for example, or spinning rayon at Courtaulds. At the same time the high wages earned by men during the war were not maintained and with the slump in demand from 1919 the opportunities for overtime and bonuses were much reduced. Prices increased by 80 per cent but wages by only 60 per cent. Skilled steelworkers were earning at most £2 a week in 1926 and many men were earning about 30s. a week. In Coventry one-third of the engineers were unemployed, one of the highest figures in England. Already in 1922 the local newspapers were describing relief schemes and training schemes for the unemployed. Early in 1919 the national miners' federation had demanded shorter hours, a wage rise of 30 per cent and nationalisation and in 1921 midland miners like those elsewhere were on strike for four months in resistance to cuts in wages.

Increasingly, events in the Midlands were responses to national debates and conflicts, and political solutions to economic troubles seemed more urgent and more relevant to local conditions, than local particularism. In 1925 the coalowners terminated the 1921 agreement and attempted to return to district settlements, a longer day and a reduction in wages. Midland miners struck, as elsewhere, from July 1925 and remained out until the strike became a lockout in April 1926.

In the Midlands much of the workforce was still not organised in trade unions. Nevertheless the negotiations between central government and the large national unions influenced many among the non-union workmen and women as well as among their own members and there was considerable response in the Midlands when the call came for a General Strike in May 1926.

On 1 May there were public demonstrations in Coventry, Birmingham and Wolverhampton which attracted large crowds. On 3 May the transport workers, the printers, the building workers and the engineers were called out and there were no buses, trains, building work stopped and papers were produced by editors and journalists. On 4 May the iron and steel workers stopped production and on 5 May the journalists struck and all newspapers were suspended. At Coventry the AEU members were on strike but there was confusion concerning the car workers and it was not until 8 May that the car works closed. At Cadbury's, where unionism had been encouraged by management, there were 18 different unions in the works and only the engineers were on strike. Local leaders and workers found it difficult to obtain a clear plan of action as they received instructions from the general circulars of the TUC, from the national unions, from local union leaders and the local trades councils.

Emergency committees both of the Labour groups and of the local councils were in constant session and industrial areas received visits from Ellen Wilkinson and other leaders. On 6 May Justice Simon declared the strike illegal and on 8 May the trade unions who intended to strike were told that the TUC had countermanded the strike. On 9 May Oswald Mosley and other Labour leaders were declaring victory in sight and rallies were held in Coventry, Birmingham, Walsall and Wolverhampton. In Birmingham, Wolverhampton, Lichfield, Stafford and Stoke on Trent the strike was said to be supported '100 per cent' and only slightly less than 70 per cent in Coventry, Smethwick, Stourbridge, Walsall and Wednesbury. Meanwhile schools, shops and many workshops continued to work normally. Sport and other public entertainment continued unchecked and in the nine days supplies of food and coal remained sufficient. There were no reports of weakening of the strike, indeed more categories of workers were expecting to come out when, on 12 May, the general council of the TUC and the national unions called off the strike, a move that came as a surprise to local leadership and to the strikers themselves, who felt betrayed and confused (Large 1976: 1–43). Moreover, when the Midland Red bus drivers, the tram drivers and the men from Guy Motors, Averys, Tangyes and many other works went back they found that management would only take them back on conditions, and 'when work was available' and that they were required to apply for individual reinstatement. The miners remained on strike until the autumn when midland miners were among the first to return to work, declaring they had been starved into submission (Barnsby 1976b).

The Labour movement was weakened, especially after the Trades Disputes Act and the Trade Unions Act of 1927. The Birmingham Trades Council was bitterly divided between right and left and the withdrawal of Oswald Mosley in 1929 to found the New Party was a financial loss as well (Hastings 1980: 85) as a loss of leadership (Corbett 1966: 124–32). Membership of unions fell. The National Society of Pottery Workers lost half its membership, and the Coventry District Amalgamated Engineering Union, which in 1922 had been the leader of local unions with 11,000 members, had only 2,400 by 1931.

After the strike management was even more concerned to increase output, to sell more to a mass market and to reduce the costs of production by reducing the amount spent on wages. More and more men and women in the Midlands were becoming the servants of a machine and toolmakers were the only skilled men. Local factory inspectors and doctors occasionally voiced concern at the stresses imposed by these methods of working but there was little opposition from organised Labour. The TUC supported 'progressive' management in order to make British industry more competitive in a time of declining exports and the individual worker was constrained by the fear of unemployment and attracted by the hope of higher earnings. The great majority of assembly-line workers were not organised into unions in the 1920s and when spontaneous strikes broke out among unorganised workers they got little support from the unions. The girls of Lucas struck against the 'Bedaux system' in 1927, in 1932 and in 1934 but the *Town Crier*, the organ of the Birmingham Trades Council, was inclined to treat the affair with levity. Similarly the unorganised men of Hope window-frame manufactory at West Bromwich struck against the reorganisation of work but got very little support from organised Labour (Hastings 1980: 85). At Perry Barr in 1932, at a firm manufacturing carburettors, 300 women came out and then men struck at Austin and GKN, but without support. The Trades Council belatedly discussed the Bedaux system in 1936 and declared their opposition to it, but in practice most managements were able to introduce 'payment by results' without difficulty and more automatic machinery by judicious promises. Cadbury's doubled production by introducing an automatic chocolate-making machine and two years later dismissed the 'less efficient workers' (Williams 1931: 126–8), but were able to cheapen the product and increase sales.

Control of the processes of production passed from the shop floor to the manager's office and to the newly established process planning departments, where professional managers discussed policy with graduate engineers over the drawing board. Productivity increased every year but the demand for labour was reduced. Trade began to recover as rearmament got under way from 1934 and the number of unemployed began to decline sooner in the Midlands than elsewhere. Wages rose, though they fell as a percentage of the cost of living and in the Midlands hours remained long, twelve hours a day being quite common. Between 1934 and 1939 there was a great increase in trade union membership in the Midlands. The AEU in Birmingham increased its membership from 5,760 to 12,245, and in Coventry recovered to about 11,000 (Hastings 1980: 86–7).

Meanwhile, agriculture was suffering from the depression. During the First World War farmers had ploughed up grassland to grow food at rising prices, thus reversing the trend of the previous years. Government was forced to ration existing supplies, to control prices to the consumer, and to encourage corn production by subsidies. Price controls continued after the war until 1920, when the prices fell and the market was open to the competition of American wheat. Farmers, wherever possible, reverted to grassland farming. The Wheat Act of 1931 did something to improve the position but the growing of barley and oats was less and less profitable (Myers 1946: 594–6). Most of the soils of Staffordshire and Warwickshire were in any case more suitable to grassland farming, but on the light soils of south-west Staffordshire and in the Ashley area field crops of carrots and broccoli could be grown for the town markets. In central Staffordshire 10,000 acres were used to grow potatoes and around Tamworth and Lichfield the market gardeners grew more salads, spinach and small fruit.

Loss of heirs during the war, taxation and changing social habits made large estates a burden rather than an asset and many were sold up or drastically reduced. They were sometimes bought by men of small capital unable to invest in machinery or retain a large labour force. Farm buildings and fences were neglected and mechanisation was slow, and most farmers continued to use horses rather than tractors. Some of the better agricultural land was going out of use for farming and was being taken up for houses, roads and airfields. In the years immediately after the war there had been further attempts to create smallholdings. Near Canley, for example, 4,000 acres were divided into 150 holdings varying from 8 to 15 acres but it was difficult for anyone to make a living from the land in the 1930s and some at least of the occupiers were inexperienced and lacked capital.

During the war much timber had been felled and with the decline of great estates there was less interest in maintaining private woodlands. Public concern led to the creation of the Forestry Commission to buy up land not otherwise wanted for agricultural purposes for the planting of forests. Cannock Chase was the first such forest, composed of 5,000 acres of Scots and Corsican pine planted from 1920 on land acquired from the Marquis of Anglesey (Myers 1946: 603).

The countryside was coming to be used as a place of refreshment and recreation for the town-dweller. Cycling clubs were less fashionable than before the war but the overwhelming majority of young people owned and used cycles for recreation. Walking, rambling and hiking clubs proliferated and the 'open air life' became something of a cult. Charabancs and cars transported the less active in large numbers on day trips to beauty spots, families took a simple holiday in the country. Young men went camping and on walking tours. Many national organisations sought to protect and open up the countryside to the townsman. These included the National Trust, the Youth Hostels Association, the CPRE and RSPB and many more. In many villages of Warwickshire and Staffordshire cottagers and smallholders were glad to supplement their income by selling 'Teas'. The Lickey Hills, Penn Common and other well-loved places within reach by public transport attracted tens of thousands of visitors in the summer, while the older established tourist centres such as Stratford on Avon and Lichfield catered for a widening social range.

By 1939 85 per cent of the cultivated land of Warwickshire and 78 per cent of the cultivated land of Staffordshire was permanent grass, and some land had been allowed to revert to rough grazing. In general the grassland was used for pasture for dairy cattle. North Staffordshire supported some of the highest densities of dairy cattle in the country. The cattle were fed by grazing in the open in summer and in stalls on hay in the winter. More use was made of purchased foodstuffs and concentrates but although silage making had been introduced into the Midlands in the 1880s its use spread only slowly. After the war the prices of milk fell and farmers sought to cut marketing costs by selling to local towns or even selling retail from door to door themselves. Small producer retailers were especially numerous near Stoke on Trent and Wolverhampton. In 1933 the Milk Marketing Board was set up, with Thomas Baxter of Freeford, Staffordshire, as its first chairman and assured farmers of a minimum price for their product. As conditions improved in the 1930s farmers were building new cowhouses and calfhouses and more attention was being given to recording yields. Most milking was still done by hand for early milking machines proved cumbersome and unsatisfactory in use, and it was some time before all farmers had electricity supplies (Wise 1950: 303–23; VCH Staffs VI: 122–49).

From 1918 county councils and county boroughs found themselves taking on increased responsibilities, employing larger numbers of staff, performing an ever-growing volume of administrative work and duties of inspection, licensing and control. Municipal boroughs, urban district councils, also had more work to do and even rural district councils, in an uneasy and one-sided partnership with the county councils, were not exempt from an increased workload. Yet the real powers of local government were not increasing, for much of their work and policies were initiated and controlled by central government, by ministries of housing, transport, education and others. Birmingham, after several boundary extensions, was responsible for a million people, the largest municipality in the country, and Wolverhampton, West Bromwich, Smethwick and Stoke on Trent had all qualified as county boroughs. The county boroughs, like the counties themselves, provided all services, including hospitals, public health, roads, airports, primary, secondary and tertiary education and were responsible for the registration of births, marriages and deaths. Municipal boroughs, such as Stourbridge, Sutton, Sutton Coldfield and Wednesbury, carried a lesser but still substantial range of responsibilities including the provision of schools, police and magistrates.

The large county boroughs operated public utilities, such as gasworks and waterworks, and were able to make profits from trading and engage in large undertakings. Wolverhampton built new waterworks at Dimminsdale, a new £76,000 extensions scheme at the electricity generating station, and new sewage works at Barnhurst. In 1938 they built the Civic Hall with a fine concert hall and a small hall. One of the most important preoccupations of county and municipal boroughs between the wars was the provision of low cost rented housing to supplement the houses being erected by private developers. The principle of municipal housing had been established before the war but the numbers of houses built had been small. In 1919 under the Town

Plate 6.3   The Blitz in Birmingham, 16 August 1940. Families survey the destruction and the Anderson shelters which offered only limited protection.

Planning Act every county, county borough and municipal authority was required to submit its plans to the Ministry of Health and from 1923 and 1924 central government began to subsidise both municipal and private housing.

In the 1920s the building of municipal housing estates began in earnest. These estates were planned on the drawing board with repeating patterns of curving streets, cul de sacs and wide roads. Trees were planted, grass verges and open spaces provided and the tenants were required to cultivate their gardens or be in danger of losing their tenancy. The early estates consisted entirely of housing. Kingstanding estate became notorious as having a population larger than Shrewsbury but without a shop or a public house. Coventry municipal corporation built 2,500 houses at Radford in 1924, Newcastle under Lyme had built 660 houses by 1926 and Birmingham 13,485 houses by 1931. Council houses, though small and uniform, were well provided with water, electricity and gas and proved very attractive to young couples, who furnished them with the help of hire purchase agreements.

Private developers were building even more rapidly than the municipalities. In Birmingham for example they built 38,070 houses, nearly three times as many as the municipality. Many of these houses were built on the edges of

towns or around railway and bus routes out of town, creating 'ribbon developments'. The cheaper privately built houses were sold at about £400. Near
Wolverhampton three-bedroom houses with sitting room, living room and a
combined kitchen and bathroom, a large garden and space at the side for a
garage, cost £365; the deposit was £25 and mortgage repayments were 9s. 8d.
a week. Rates and water cost 2s. 7d. a week. Skilled workers at this time were
earning about £3 10s. a week, and could undertake such a purchase with the
help of one of the many building societies. By 1939 some 16 per cent of the
houses in Wolverhampton were new houses occupied by their owners. A
further 21 per cent were new council houses let at rents of about 10s. a week
(Barnsby 1966: 47–9).

However, the majority of the people continued to live in old houses. A
series of assessments of the housing stock were required from local authorities
by the Ministries of Health and Housing and it became evident that many
houses in the old industrial centres were substandard. Local authorities
attempted to improve sewage disposal and water supplies and considerable
progress was made in public health sanitation. Wednesbury, for example,
eliminated ash privies in the 1920s, reconstructed the sewers and set up a
sewage works between 1936 and 1939 and by 1930 had built 672 new council
houses. However, even the most energetic local authorities could do little to
buy out private landlords, demolish slum housing and remove and rehouse
their occupants until their powers were extended by the Housing Act of 1930.
Even then difficulties remained; local authorities were short of funds, central
government grants were inadequate, there were legal problems and there was a
shortage of building land for new houses. By 1939 most midland local
authorities had bought up large areas of slum property and had made elaborate
plans but little had been achieved when the war halted all building. Meanwhile
the slum properties continued to deteriorate, and the contrast between life in
the slums and in the suburbs became more marked and more painful.
Moreover, the new housing developments, whether municipal or privately
built, urgently needed schools, bus routes, libraries, clinics and other municipal
services, and most of the efforts of local government between the wars went
into providing amenities in the suburbs. In the town centres services continued
to be housed in well built but oppressive Victorian buildings with inadequate
facilities (MacMorran 1978: 69–73).

Between 1914 and 1934 local government spending on education greatly
increased. Birmingham was spending over £2 million a year by 1934, second
only to its expenditure on public works, and even a small borough such as
Wednesbury spent £59,000 in 1937. The increase in expenditure was caused
by the adoption of a national scale of salaries for teachers, the general price
rise, and the growth of the school population rather than by any improvements
in what was offered. Although education became increasingly standardised in
form and content under the directives of the Board of Education there were still
gross disparities of provision between various local authorities and between

the suburbs and the slums. A succession of national reports, Acts of Parliament and government initiatives sought to provide school education for the whole population between the ages of 5 and 14 but in terms of what was actually done performance lagged behind precept in the Midlands, especially in the sphere of secondary education.

After the First World War the authorities faced a great backlog of building and improvements and a serious shortage of school places. Coventry had 60 schools for 20,249 children but needed to build a further 40 schools on the new housing estates. In rural areas and industrial villages such as Brierley Hill, where they depended on the county to provide schools, there were still many one-room, two-teacher schools with primitive sanitation and obsolete heating.

The more intelligent and hardworking children could transfer to free secondary education in the new municipal grammar schools or in the older endowed schools by means of scholarships gained by competitive examinations. In Birmingham in 1939 there were only 6.9 secondary places all told for every thousand children, although the national average was 11 per thousand. The Hadow report of 1926 recommended the reorganisation of elementary all-age schools into infant, junior and senior schools with the object of improving the teaching of the 11–14 year olds. The larger authorities, with numerous schools, including Birmingham, Coventry and Wolverhampton, accomplished the transition in the 1930s with several junior schools feeding senior schools with two or three classes in each year. Even the large authorities found the reorganisation under Hadow difficult, and as at Stoke on Trent it was only partly achieved when building ceased in 1939. Church schools everywhere lagged behind council schools in the provision of new buildings, and in reorganisation, and a new disparity of provision became evident between the airy new council school and the old church school in dilapidated premises.

In rural areas and places such as Warwick, where population growth was slow, no new schools at all were built between 1914 and 1944 and reorganisation could scarcely even have been considered for a village where there was only one school and that a church school.

The majority of middle-class parents paid fees and sent their children to 'preparatory' or other private junior schools and thereafter to endowed, direct-grant or private secondary schools. The old endowed schools of the Midlands continued to provide courses aiming primarily at university entrance, and as the value of their endowments rose with the rising price of land, were able to support them with well qualified teachers, and resources of laboratories, libraries, gymnasia, dignified halls and comfortable staff rooms. The endowed church secondary schools, such as the St Philips, Birmingham or St Anne's at Abbots Bromley, followed the same pattern with the addition of religious formation of a particular denomination.

The University of Birmingham between the wars greatly enhanced its academic standing and public prestige. Student numbers increased to 1,600 by 1935, among them many more women than formerly. Many more of them were postgraduate students, scientists, medical students than before the war. The Faculty of Law and the Barber Institute of Fine Arts and thirteen new professorships were established. In the later 1930s a programme of research was initiated in the Physics Department in association with ICI, which was to lead to the development of the atomic bomb (Cheesewright 1975).

In midland towns most of the school leavers went directly into employment but there were opportunities for them to attend classes at the many and varied technical colleges, adult colleges, schools of design and industry and other institutions which by the 1930s were a feature of even the smaller municipal boroughs. These colleges, though making vigorous and important contributions to local industry and education, were often housed in late Victorian buildings. Coventry Technical College was in an old factory in Earl Street until 1937. They had very limited social facilities for either staff or students, and contributed to the prevailing impression that higher technical education was socially inferior to university education.

In other areas of life the municipal corporations and counties found themselves faced with more new tasks. To control what was seen at the time as 'an enormous increase in the volume of motor traffic' (Jones 1940 VI: 9) they provided pedestrian crossings, beacons, automatic changing lights for traffic control and introduced one-way traffic and limited speed to 30 mph in built-up areas. Driving licences were introduced in 1920, when local authorities became responsible for issuing them on behalf of the government (MacMorran 1978: 79–89). Wolverhampton, Coventry and Birmingham all established municipal airports but these had only a limited role before 1939.

In 1927 responsibility for the unions, Poor Law institutions and hospitals were handed over to the counties and county boroughs. Rates in the county boroughs soared to unheard of heights by the 1920s. In 1929 the system of rating of industrial property and government grants were overhauled at the request of the Treasury and in return General Exchequer block grants were introduced. In addition local authorities received grants from the Board of Education, the Ministry of Health, the Home Office, the Ministry of Labour, the Ministry of Transport and other government departments to assist in implementing particular policies and orders. While local authorities continued to speak with pride of the great expansion of their work, the large number of new enterprises and buildings, the growing numbers of their employees and widening sphere of their activities, in reality local authorities were becoming the agents of central control. When in 1931 the central government required economies to meet the national financial crisis, the local authorities had no choice but to stop programmes, and cut wages and salaries, and while the particular leadership or needs of a locality might influence policies, and encourage or delay action, the days of Victorian local 'self government' were over.

Chapter 35

The last chapter of regional history?

From 1939 the pressure of centralised policies upon the daily lives of people in the Midlands became dominant. During the war, industry, agriculture, leisure, movement and food supplies were all controlled by endless central directives, and advertisement propaganda and the BBC unified the experience of millions.

The Second World War was fought from the first by the local community as well as the armed forces. The Midlands was preparing for war as early as 1934 when the government began planning to increase the output of machine tools, vehicles, munitions and other essential materials of war. Midland industrial leaders were quietly contacted, 'contingency' plans drawn up, plant and storage space inventoried and the shadow factories prepared. Between 1932 and 1938 the production of vehicles including aircraft in Coventry had already doubled and employment in all branches of engineering had increased even more (Richardson 1972: 65–81).

Meanwhile, preparations were being made to protect the civilian population from attack from the air. All local councils looked to central government to finance preparations, but it was not until the Munich crisis of September 1938 that government money became available.

The Fire Services and the ARP were slowly organised and water supplies protected and in April 1939 emergency committees were appointed to control the day-to-day running of cities in wartime. The Earl of Dudley was appointed by the Home Office as regional commissioner for the Midlands, with headquarters in Birmingham, to co-ordinate civil defence throughout the region. Within a few days of the declaration of war the central government had been granted a wide range of powers to direct people, organise production, control movement and information, culminating in the Emergency Powers Act of 25 May 1940 (Sutcliffe 1974a: 15–23).

After the fall of France in May 1940 the Local Defence Volunteers (later the Home Guard) were recruited. Lieutenant-Colonel Heywood, Bart., of Rocester, was appointed commander of the Staffordshire force and within a few days 10,000 volunteers had registered in Staffordshire. Each volunteer was expected to be on duty one night in four over and above his normal working hours. Armbands and later uniforms were distributed and by 1941 the Volunteers were receiving weapons. The 24th Battalion at Tettenhall for example had 646 rifles, 2 Lewis guns and 391 carbine sten guns by the end of 1944, and much time was spent training the men to use them (Lewis 1970).

German bombers began to appear over the Midlands from June 1940, when a small force bombed the airfield at Anstey near Coventry. Over the south of England the Battle of Britain was fought during August and September and was followed by the London blitz from 7 September to 7 November. Meanwhile Birmingham was bombed in August 1940, the first of 63 raids. By the autumn, raids on the Midlands became frequent and children from Birmingham, Walsall and West Bromwich were evacuated to rural Staffordshire to join the much larger numbers sent from London, Kent and Essex.

On 14 November 1940 Coventry suffered the greatest raid so far directed against an English provincial city. Bombing began at 7.14 p.m. on the 14th and continued until 6.16 next morning, by which time 400 enemy aircraft had dropped 500 tons of bombs and 30,000 incendiaries. The fires were quite beyond the resources of the fire services, even though Coventry fire brigades were reinforced by those of Stoke on Trent and Nottingham. Many firemen were killed, including the whole of the Stoke brigade. The other services, the ARP and the WVS, were overwhelmed, 554 people were killed and 865 seriously injured. The cathedral was gutted; 46,000 houses were seriously damaged and 75 per cent of the city's factories and workshops suffered some damage; 180 shops were closed and the city lacked trams, buses, telephones, water, food and medical supplies. The railway station was immobilised and 20,000 people lost their ration books. Six hundred soldiers were drafted in immediately to clear the streets, keep order and set up army field kitchens to feed the people, while building workers were released from the army to go to Coventry to make the ruins safe and to provide temporary shelter (Richardson 1972: 82–7).

Birmingham's turn came on 19 November when 350 bombers attacked the city. Four hundred people were killed and there were 338 fires but the Birmingham fire brigade was able to maintain control. There were further raids on 20 November and again on the 22nd. This third raid caused more dislocation than either of the previous ones, for 600 fires were started and the water mains were destroyed. Three-fifths of the city was without water, and the fire brigades would have been helpless had there been a fourth attack. However, the Luftwaffe did not follow up the raid and shifted their attention to Southampton (Sutcliffe 1974: 27–9).

Raids continued throughout the winter but the next major attacks came in April 1941. Birmingham suffered very badly on 9 April, when 250 bombers released 650 high explosive bombs and 170 incendiaries, and 1,121 people were killed or injured. There was severe damage in Coventry from successive raids on the 8th, 9th and 10th April when Courtaulds, Armstrong-Siddeley,

Daimler and the GEC were damaged, and the Coventry and Warwickshire hospital was almost entirely destroyed. There was another major raid on Birmingham on 18 May 1941 but afterwards both the severity and the frequency of raids were much diminished. Other parts of the West Midlands escaped comparatively lightly. At Aldridge, for example, on 20 July 1942 300 incendiaries were dropped but only one person was killed and four injured since many fell in open ground (Lewis 1970). Wolverhampton, Burton and the Potteries all experienced raids but not on a scale to disrupt industry or seriously affect the civilian population. They did, however, keep the population on the alert and each night many people from the town centres went out to the suburbs to shelter with relations and friends, many others slept every night in damp shelters, and children's education was seriously disturbed. The winter of 1940–1 was exceptionally cold and there was an increase in deaths from pneumonia and similar illnesses. The loss of sleep, combined by the end of 1941 with very long working hours and limited transport facilities, placed the civilian population of the towns under real stress (Sutcliffe 1974a, 14–39).

By 1942 the danger of invasion had receded and the Midlands concentrated on the total mobilisation of all man and woman power. The farmers had found themselves 'in the front line' from September 1939 and subject to the authority of the War Agricultural Committees set up in each county. They were required to produce specified quotas of priority crops of wheat and potatoes and to plough up grass land for tillage. The committees did not only issue directives, but obtained tractors and teams of contractors to plough land for the farmers, and set up machinery departments to loan equipment, and the Warwickshire committee took over 13,000 acres of land themselves. Although quotas for crops had to be met, midland farmers continued to keep their large stocks of cattle. They were forced into a more intensive use of land and more intensive methods of rearing. Kale was grown for fodder and autumn calving was introduced to provide a winter milk supply, while many more poultry and pigs were kept on household scraps (Wise 1950: 312–14).

Despite mechanisation the shortage of labour became acute and the Women's Land Army, formed in June 1939, became an important and accepted part of the farmers' war effort. They often worked in mobile gangs employed by the county agricultural committee. In Staffordshire the initiative for the formation and leadership of the WLA came from Miss Harrison of Maer Hall 'who being then Master of Fox Hounds of the Staffordshire Hunt knew the country and farms well' (Lewis 1970: 30). When trained the girls received 28s. for a 48-hour week with overtime at 7d. an hour. Many of the Staffordshire volunteers were from the towns and training them presented problems.

The most important concern in the Midlands was to produce munitions, vehicles and materials for the forces. Government-owned machinery was installed in the works, all luxury trades were brought to a standstill and

Plate 6.4 A parade of the Women's Land Army in Leamington Spa during the Second World War.

workers in them were required to adapt themselves to new products 'for the duration'. The unions negotiated terms, making as much use as possible of the urgent demand for skilled men, and resisting dilution by unskilled and female workers. Many of the 'jobs' were in any case new and negotiations and adjudications were in any case inevitable, and there were numerous if short-lived strikes in the first two years. Strikes and lockouts were declared illegal and by 1942 even women were subject to direction of labour. Many workers were directed away from home and housed in hostels; Coventry had 16 such hostels each housing 500 workers. Government sought to make the transition easier by controlling profits, and insisting on canteens, medical aid and other improvements in the working environment. Skilled men, coalminers and other 'essential workers' were retained in the works and many more taken on. Gradually not only women but handicapped people, older workers and school leavers were mobilised. Chocolate makers made aeroplane parts, rayon workers made barrage balloons, button makers made military insignia, engravers made steel rulers and steel tube makers made shells.

Hours of work extended until most works were operating seven days a week by 1940 and twenty-four hours a day by May 1941. Wages, bonuses and overtime were correspondingly high, especially in the aero engine works. Regional Boards of Industry were set up in 1941 and joint production committees with representatives of management and of workers dealt with everyday adjustments of rates, processes and organisation within the works (Sutcliffe 1974a: 39–48). In all industries making for the war effort there was an army of inspectors to maintain centrally determined sizes, standards and qualities. At BSA 2 million components were being inspected a day by both managers and by the War Department. Air Ministry inspectors and War Department inspectors penetrated even the smallest family firms in the backstreets of Black Country villages, and their adventures there became legendary (Ward 1946: 162–4).

From 1942 onwards planning for reconstruction began to mean more than simply repairing bomb damage. The majority of people came to believe that 'after the war' it would be possible to reconstruct society, to improve the environment and to eliminate poverty by systematic and centralised planning. The Beveridge Report called for an attack on Want, Disease, Ignorance, Idleness and Squalor. The experience of war had for most people included an acceptance of discipline, whether in the armed or civilian services. It had also been an educational experience for they had been subject to five years of propaganda, instruction and information from the Ministry of Health, the

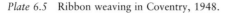

Plate 6.5   Ribbon weaving in Coventry, 1948.

Ministry of Food, and many other national bodies. In these and many other ways, the war undermined local particularism and modified local distinctions.

By 1944 the Home Guard and the Civil Defence were being run down and the hours of work began to be reduced. The plans for reconstruction began to take legislative shape with the Education Act 1944, the White Paper on Employment 1944, and the Town and Country Planning Act, and there was talk of a 'welfare state' and 'social engineering'. Local and regional development was to be subject to national planning to eliminate poverty and injustice. However, by the time peace was declared in May 1945 it was already evident that the grandiose plans for reconstruction and social reformation would be constrained by economic difficulties and disillusion even in the first years of peace. The thirty years after the war brought many changes but little fundamental transformation of society.

In the countryside after the war the continuation of subsidies prevented the reversion of the newly ploughed land to pasture and the proportion of arable to pasture continued to increase until it was again approaching the levels of the high farming era of the 1860s. By 1970 43 per cent of Warwickshire agricultural land was again arable. Farming was mechanised and agricultural machinery firms, such as Bamfords of Uttoxeter and Massey Ferguson of Coventry, supplied tractors which soon replaced horses to pull ploughs, planting, harvesting and spraying machines. Combine harvesters began to be used from the late 1950s. In 1965 a 400-acre farm near Stratford had a combine harvester, three tractors, ploughs, drills, harrows and rolls and the uncertainties of harvest were mitigated by a grain drier. Machinery was most effectively used in large fields, and so the hedges planted in the late-eighteenth century began to be grubbed up. Artificial fertilisers enabled farmers in south Warwickshire to introduce continuous growing on some arable land and the heavy clay lands of south-east Warwickshire were made to produce high yields of wheat and barley when worked with heavy tackle.

Although arable farming increased, cattle farming continued using more intensive rearing methods. Milk production was encouraged by the Milk Marketing Board and milk parlours and milking machines became general. Beef production increased and intensive rearing of pigs and of broiler fowl developed rapidly in Staffordshire and north Warwickshire, and some farmers undertook contract growing of soft fruit for the national soft drink and frozen food firms. At Welford on Avon, smallholdings which had flourished as market gardens were given up, since they could not continue to be competitive without heavy capital investment. Average farm sizes rose as farming required more capital, and small farmers, despite subsidies, found it difficult to survive. By 1971 there were 7,633 farmers in Staffordshire but they employed between them only 4,483 farm labourers. The smaller tenant farms used no hired labour at all and even farms of 400 acres employed only one or two men and a boy. The series of Town and Country Planning Acts introduced new controls into the countryside. An increasing body of legislation controlled crop spraying, ordered safety measures on the farm, determined the quality and nature of the product and marketing. The complicated system of subsidies and grants effectively influenced the policies of individual farmers.

The countryside continued to provide opportunities for amenities and recreation for the town dweller, although after the war he usually arrived by car. Conflict of use between farmer and townsman, disputes over commons and rights of way were no new thing but now tended to be decided by national commissions and legislation. More land went permanently out of use under roads, motorways, housing estates and airfields. By 1970 more than a quarter of Warwickshire was built up and unproductive.

After the war the dreariness of controls, shortages of raw materials, of food, of fuel and power continued for another five years – as long a period as the war itself, but without the sense of purpose and achievement which had then made them tolerable. Controls began to be eased from 1950, Cadbury's was again able to get cocoa beans, and metal and building materials were decontrolled. Those industries which had been relatively prosperous in the interwar years continued to supply the consumer markets at home and abroad. The range and variety of products continued to increase, especially in the period of national economic growth in the 1960s. Light pressing work and sheet metal working grew rapidly and many firms large and small produced semi-finished components which were passed onto sub-assembly and assembly firms. Herman Smith Ltd of Dudley, for example, founded in 1906 as manufacturers of hearth furniture, had by 1965 three factories in Dudley all making precision sheet metal fabrications and assemblies for aircraft aero engines, radios, and electronics industries, as well as oil heaters, electric fires and lighting fittings.

About one-fifth of the people employed in the West Midlands continued to earn their living in the motor trades. The vehicle industry reflected the cycle of booms and slumps of the national economy, though probably at a lower rate of overall growth than in the country as a whole. Great efforts were made by Austin and other firms to increase exports in the 1940s and 1950s and they achieved particular success with the Mini in 1960. Growth involved a great deal of capital investment in new buildings, and new machinery making greater use than ever before of automation and electronic control of assembly lines. During the 1950s and 1960s production was concentrated into the hands of a few large international companies, and firms tried to strengthen their control of the market by amalgamations. Austin merged with Nuffield to become the British Motor Company, and BMC in 1969 merged with Leyland to become British Leyland (Wood 1976: 156–8).

In 1948 the provision of electrical power was systematised under the British Electricity Board with area electricity boards to run the industry. The use of electricity replaced gas in the home and the workplace, and for public services. Public buildings and industry used more and more electricity for advertising, display and prestige. Midland electric companies found new outlets and produced new commodities, especially for the radio and television industries. The English Electrical Company at Kidsgrove near Stafford manufactured computers from 1954. New works were sited on the margins of earlier industrial areas or along the main road routes to the south-east or near the airfields. Leamington, Kenilworth, Warwick and Rugby were growing far more quickly than the Potteries or the Black Country, and Stratford on Avon attracted a large farm machinery works, a national insurance company, and light engineering and canning firms (Wood 1976: 151–5), while at Warwick there are firms making respectively meat pies, frozen foods, car door hinges and municipal vehicles.

In the post-war period all new individual ventures requiring more than 5,000 sq. ft of factory space had to apply for an Industrial Development Certificate and certificates were granted in accordance with national development policies. It seems probable that the IDCs did deflect some new industry away from the Midlands but so did the prevailing high wages, high rates, labour shortage, congested roads and high land prices (Rodgers 1972; Wood 1976: 237–60).

Producers aimed at mass production of standardised goods meeting a mass market generated by advertising and at holding prices as far as possible against a general background of inflation and rising labour costs. Those industries which were still able to make efficient use of large numbers of cheap women workers had a continuing advantage. Courtaulds had works at Wolverhampton, Nuneaton and Coventry where they employed thousands of women and Cash's had 1,000 workers. Small textile firms could exploit the same advantage and there were still 30 small ribbon works in Coventry, and textiles continued to be produced in small works in Leek and Rocester, and the hosiery industry had outliers in East Warwickshire. Shoes were made at Stafford, Atherstone, Nuneaton, Stone and Bilston. Lotus at Stafford was able to counterbalance its problems of isolation from the main centres of shoemaking by concentrating on high-quality products, vigorous advertising, mechanisation and economies of scale (Mountfield 1965). In contrast, in Walsall 17 wholesale and 70 small manufacturers of leather goods employed large numbers of women working sewing machines. In general the Midlands clothing firms survived better than those of the north of England (Wood 1976: 180–1, 204–13).

The coal industry was nationalised in 1946 and on 1 January 1947 the National Coal Board was established as a semi-autonomous authority under the Minister of Fuel and Power. The coal owners were compensated and the Coal Board bought Himley Hall from the Earl of Dudley as its headquarters. In the two decades after the war the policies were to increase productivity per man by a large programme of mechanisation concentrating on the more productive pits. The demand of the gasworks for coal was at first buoyant but in the 1960s the pottery industry and other local coal-using industries went over from gas to oil and electricity and there was a marked decline in the use of coal for a domestic fuel. In 1967–8 North Sea gas replaced gas made from coal and the gasworks closed. Between 1951 and 1971 the number of miners was reduced by 65 per cent. In north Staffordshire new mines were sunk at Florence, Wolstanton and Hem Head but the 20 mines of 1947 had been reduced to 13 by 1962. Wolstanton colliery is now the deepest mine in Britain. Output continued at about 6 million tons a year but with a considerably reduced labour force. Private small-scale open-cast mining continued under licence from the Coal Board in the 1950s but declined thereafter (Jones 1940: 74). On the Cannock coalfield by 1969 there were only four pits employing 5,050 men but output per man had increased 12 per cent since the war. A large new mine was sunk at Lea Hall in 1960 to supply the electricity generating station on the same site and in 1969 was linked directly to the NCB's national computer centre at Cannock. On the south Staffordshire coalfield Hamstead deep mine continued until 1966 and Baggeridge until 1968 and some smaller pits in Netherton and Bloxwich were still working in the 1950s but all mining had ceased by 1970. On the east Warwickshire coalfield the number of collieries declined sharply from 12 to 5 by 1969, although a new shaft was opened at Daw Mill in 1965. 5.1 million tons had been produced in 1956 but only 3.8 million tons in 1964, by which time only 8,955 men were employed (Wood 1976: 164–70; Moyes 1974: 111–20). Conditions favour modern machine mining, and productivity in this coalfield is very high.

Output in the British steel industry greatly increased in the post-war period and the midland works at Bilston, Brierley Hill and Shelton were substantially modernised. The Earl of Dudley's iron and steel works at Round Oak had been founded on the site of the Old Level furnace in 1857. In 1953 it was sold to Tube Investments and partly nationalised in 1967. It still employed 3,330 people and produced 500,000 ingot tons annually in the late 1960s. Shelton steel works in the Potteries underwent a massive reorganisation scheme in 1960 costing £19 million, to enable it to produce long bars of cast steel and to reduce production costs. It employed 2,500 in 1970. The Bilston steel works became British Steel in 1974, but by then the British steel industry was in difficulties and the midland works were all closed in the late 1970s. Their closure seemed to mark the passing of the distinctive and traditional midland industries. Meanwhile, at the other end of the scale, the last nail shops, small chain shops, key and lockmakers' shops were swept away and their tools and furniture taken to the new industrial museums. Glassmaking in the Stour Valley was declining, leaving only Stevens and Williams and Stuart Crystal to represent the older industries.

In the Potteries gas-fired and electric-fired kilns were introduced and coal firing and bottle kilns abandoned in the 1950s, the works often being remodelled on the existing sites in order to remain close to the specialist suppliers of materials, decorative finishes and equipment.

By the late 1950s the use of ceramics was being challenged by the introduction of plastic tableware and plastic sanitary ware while concrete was being used in the building industry instead of tiles and bricks. The pottery works remained small, 90 per cent of them employing less than 500 people in 1972. However, the small family firms were being taken over by large firms and holding companies who came to control 80 per cent of tableware production (Moyes 1972: 83–100).

The numbers employed in the construction and service industries in the Midlands was growing rapidly, although it still remained low compared with the national average. More and more men and women were employed in offices, in public services, and in the distributive trades. Only in transport were the numbers employed declining. The Potteries and the Black Country were especially slow to develop services and their town centres continued until the late 1960s to be composed of small shops, 'old fashioned' places of entertainment, narrow streets, hump-backed canal bridges and Victorian public buildings. There were fewer white-collar jobs and a higher proportion of skilled manual workers than elsewhere.

Many young people left school as early as possible to go straight into industry. In the 1950s and 1960s in Birmingham, the Black Country and Coventry, wages were well above the national average, there was a labour shortage and there was plenty of work for women to swell the family incomes. There were high rates of car and house ownership and money was spent on overseas holidays and domestic comfort. However, at the same period in rural Staffordshire and the Potteries the family income was no higher than the national average.

There were twelve midland Chambers of Commerce which sought to influence economic planning and industrial initiatives, and in 1964 a Midland Regional Group of Chambers was formed to facilitate cooperation with the west Midland planning structure. The Chambers of Commerce exercised face-to-face influence over local authorities but their influence on central government policies and broader issues was not great. They consisted mainly of the locally based firms while the large international combines tended to act independently. The Trades Councils of the west Midlands found themselves in a similar position. They continued to exercise a good deal of local influence but on larger issues they found it difficult to influence the ministries and economic planners (Sutcliffe 1974a: 110–19).

Management and workers were dealing with each other through representative and negotiators rather than as individuals. Union membership in the Midlands increased rapidly after the war and became normal among men and much more usual among women workers. The AEU had 80 branches and the Transport and General Workers Unions 118 branches in Birmingham. Although wages were high there was much industrial unrest, especially in the car firms in the 1950s. In Coventry, for example, there were major difficulties concerning the introduction of new machinery and the transfer of workers from aeroplane to car production (Richardson 1972: 112–17).

By the 1960s the economic advisers and planners were beginning to express concern about the economic future of the west Midlands. There was a decline in private investment, in new buildings and factories and the output per head in the area, despite automation and mechanisation, was not growing as rapidly as in other parts of the country. Long established businesses such as BSA were threatened with bankruptcy. Labour costs continued to be high and opportunities for work in many districts were dangerously dependent upon one or two sectors. Unemployment began to be of serious concern from 1966, and employment was soon declining more rapidly than the national average, especially in Coventry and Stoke on Trent. When the car and engineering industries began to make men redundant there was little alternative employment in the service sector or in new industries (Wood 1976: 80–7).

The Local Government Act 1929 had tried to encourage local authorities to combine in larger units of administration but they had proved reluctant and in the years after the war there was much public pressure for a reorganisation of local government to facilitate planning and reconstruction. Statistical reports and surveys proliferated and reports such as *Conurbation* by prestigious scientists, academics and industrialists adumbrated elaborate visions of a region transformed by good planning into an ideal setting for humans to dwell in. It was taken for granted that the means included a great increase in national control of initiative, of central government funding, and above all of the influence on decision-making of 'experts'.

Between 1944 and 1964 national and central governments attempted to realise these visions. Green belts were created around towns, derelict land was cleared and redeveloped with the help of earth movers and JCBs, conservation areas were listed, open spaces for recreation were protected and trees were planted. One of the most remarkable changes in the environment of the industrial areas was the transformation of the air and the atmosphere as smoke pollution was reduced. In 1945 the air over Bilston contained 85 tons of soluble matter and 192 tons of insoluble matter per square mile, and Coventry was worse with 90 tons of soluble matter and 153 tons of insoluble matter per square mile. The 1948 Clean Air Act and the declining use of coal at work and at home transformed the atmosphere of the Potteries, the Black Country and the Coventry region (West Midlands Group 1948).

The most urgent task which confronted county boroughs and counties after 1945 was to provide the people with decent homes. Local authorities were required to assess their needs under the Housing Act of 1944. There had been no private houses built during the war, and although demobilisation from the army was controlled, many who came out of the factories and mines as well as the services needed to be housed. By 1947 50,000 were awaiting housing in Birmingham and there was a massive need for slum clearance. Birmingham still had 29,000 back-to-back houses and many substandard houses in the city centre; 35,000 houses had no water-closets. Builders found it difficult to get permits and materials, so to ease the immediate problem prefabricated houses were built; Coventry, for example, built over 1,000 of them.

The local authorities were often forced to turn a blind eye to families of squatters in army huts and disused factory hostels and at Tile Hill, Coventry, 250 people were still living in huts in 1953. Building licences were abolished in 1954 and both private and municipal building proceeded apace. Government money was readily available for municipal housing. Coventry built 20 large estates, the largest at Tile Hill had 2,500 dwellings in houses and high rise flats. By 1965 a total of 16,000 dwellings had been built in Coventry. Walsall County Borough built 17,000 dwellings in houses and tower blocks and Wednesbury 5,500. One of the most ambitious schemes was at Dudley where in 1945 there were already 2,600 people on the housing list and 4,000 awaiting removal from slum dwellings. At Hillyfields, Dudley Housing Authority cleared derelict land using the new large earthmovers to shift soil banks, fill marl holes and open coalpits, and dealt with underground fires and flooded ground. Eventually 5,000 council houses and 1,000 private houses were built. In the older areas of the cities the planners undertook comprehensive development. Birmingham destroyed 30,000 houses in five areas and replaced them with tower blocks, shopping precincts, schools and services.

From the 1950s it proved increasingly difficult to contain new housing schemes within existing boundaries, and the principle of preserving a green belt around built-up areas was maintained with difficulty. Tamworth became an overspill area for Birmingham and the population grew from 23,000 in 1951 to 40,000 by 1971. Redditch, designated a New Town in 1964, was within the Green Belt, and only four miles from the Birmingham city boundary (Wood 1976: 223–4).

Meanwhile, the town and city centres had been drastically remodelled. The rebuilding of central Coventry began in 1947 despite shortages, in an atmosphere of post-war euphoria with the help of substantial funds from the Ministry of Works. The planned separation of shops and motorcars, the use of levels and the extensive use of the work of contemporary artists was seen as an exciting expression of what was new in town planning and architecture. The new cathedral, opened in 1962, was seen as a symbol of reconstruction and reconciliation. As the work developed, problems of access and new materials began to be apparent and car parking and road plans had to be revised to meet the great increase in traffic. By 1965 146 Coventry people out of every 1,000 were car owners (Richardson 1972: 300–6).

The remodelling of central Birmingham was on an even larger scale and was more or less complete by 1970. By then Herbert Manzoni, the city's chief engineer, had rebuilt extensive areas of the city centre. The largest development was the Bull Ring Shopping Centre, which cost £8 million and provided for 2 million shoppers. The city was surrounded by three concentric ring roads, and travel through the city was by urban clearway, much of it through tunnels under the city. The city skyline was dominated by tower blocks, the Rotunda of 24 storeys and the new municipal library (Sutcliffe 1974: 442–6).

Other towns followed the example of Coventry and Birmingham on a more modest scale and Wolverhampton, Stafford, Halesowen, Burton on Trent and even Lichfield and Newcastle under Lyme acquired their pedestrian shopping precincts, tower blocks and concrete underpasses. In the older towns zeal for modernisation was moderated by the countervailing pressures to preserve ancient monuments and buildings of architectural interest and to retain the attractions of the towns to tourists.

As the prices of building materials rose sharply in the 1960s the pressures encouraged local authorities and builders to use cheap materials and take short cuts. Three-quarters of new housing in Birmingham was in flats and 30 per cent of that was in tower blocks. One of the largest and latest developments in the Midlands was at Chelmsley Wood, where 10,000 dwellings were erected with multistorey flats, new primary and secondary schools, shops and services for Birmingham City Council. In the later 'comprehensive development areas' supermarkets and shopping precincts became a conspicuous feature and they were planned on the assumption that the majority of the families would be car users (Sutcliffe 1974: 432–42, 221–48).

By 1965 the housing lists had been reduced to manageable levels and with rising interest rates, inflation and growing unemployment, the pace slackened. Meanwhile, the inadequacies of the hastily built accommodation and the social problems of the high-rise dwellings were much canvassed, and disillusion with large-scale planning became fashionable.

The motorcar and the lorry had come to dominate the daily lives of the majority of the population and to take priority in the work of the planners. With the help of large subsidies from central government, the main highways were remodelled and the towns and cities were bypassed or surrounded by ringways. Birmingham's inner ring road cost £35 million, three-quarters of which came from government subsidies. The Midlands became the hub of the national network of motorways. The first Staffordshire section of the M6 was opened in 1962 and eventually the M1, M5 and the M6 were connected at the multilevel interchange at Gravelly Hill.

Railways were nationalised in 1948 and subsequent developments depended upon national decisions and planning. Passenger traffic continued to decline and in 1963 branch lines and local services were drastically reduced, especially in north Staffordshire. Stations were rebuilt and streamlined, and steam engines were replaced by diesel by 1965. Of the municipal airports only Elmdon developed international services, and its importance was further increased with the development in the 1960s of the National Exhibition Centre in the adjoining area.

The canals which had once been so important to the midland economy now mouldered and decayed. Even in 1947 only 10 per cent of the coal from the pits was taken by canal and this only for short hauls to the power stations. Soon commercial traffic ceased, many branch lines became unusable or were swept away in redevelopment schemes. There was some development of the

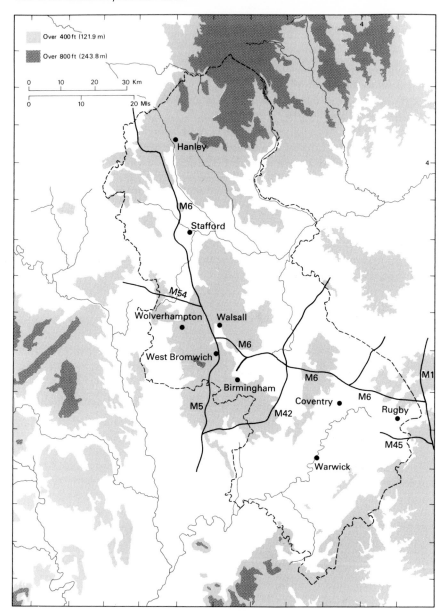

Figure 6.1 Motorways in the Midlands, 1986

leisure use of canals and voluntary groups preserved or even reopened stretches of canal for the use of part-time canal enthusiasts.

After the war the schools continued to face problems as shortages persisted but the school population grew rapidly, not only in the old industrial centres but also in country towns. Even Warwick experienced for the first time a shortage of school places and teachers. The 1944 Education Act implemented in 1947 was in the Midlands as elsewhere a real revolution in the provision of a national system of schooling for all children of 5–15. The smaller authorities relinquished their powers and responsibility for the provision of schools was placed in the hands of the counties and county boroughs. The principle of separate 'voluntary' schools was retained allowing Roman Catholics and Anglicans to provide schools which were subsequently maintained by the local authorities.

Between 1957 and 1965 there was a great programme of school building in the towns, housing estates and the industrial areas of the Midlands. Secondary schools were the most immediate priority as the babies born in the post-war period had by 1958 reached the secondary school age and the school population in the Midlands was even higher as a proportion of the whole population than the national average. There was an acute shortage of teachers and temporarily shortened training courses were hastily set up at Birmingham, Coventry, Wolverhampton and Madeley in north Staffordshire while the existing colleges were suddenly extended to meet the need. Many midland schools were habitually understaffed and three-quarters of the teachers had less than ten years' teaching experience.

By the mid-1950s both public opinion and the planners were rejecting the social evils believed to flow from the separation of secondary school pupils into three (or in most cases two) types of school, and comprehensive schools began to be preferred to the tripartite system. Revised plans had to be submitted by local authorities from 1953, and the issue became a political one. In Wolverhampton and Birmingham both the comprehensive and the tripartite system existed side by side for some time, but Coventry had eight comprehensive schools by 1964. By then the transfer from primary to secondary at the age of eleven was also coming under fire and yet another reorganisation took place with Staffordshire and Dudley changing to a three-tier system of first, middle and secondary schools.

Meanwhile, tertiary education had been expanding even more rapidly. Further education colleges in all the county and county borough authorities offered an ever-widening range of courses in association with industry and commerce and also extended their provision of academic courses. In 1966 technical colleges became polytechnics at Wolverhampton, Stafford, Coventry, Birmingham and north Staffordshire, offering degrees and other advanced courses.

After the war Birmingham University developed numerous new centres and departments, many of them providing advanced study related to industry and the public services. There were new departments of Materials, Science, Local Government and Urban Planning to educate experts and leaders, and the new departments of African and Russian studies reflected the changing horizons of the post-war world. Student numbers increased to nearly 8,000 and the numbers of staff to 1,100. The university budget expanded to £16 million, a quarter of which was raised by the university itself, while the contribution from local authorities fell from 50 per cent to less than 0.2 per cent (Sutcliffe 1974a: 355–6).

Keele University College was founded in 1949, making use of both disused army huts and of Keele Hall. It was envisaged as a bold attempt to move out of the traditional academic specialisms and to offer broad-based courses in close association with the outside world. It became a fully independent university in 1962 and expanded its curriculum, research and facilities, taking part in the general growth of universities in the sixties (VCH Staffs VI: 182–5). Warwick University was established in 1960 after some years of controversy on a large open site just outside Coventry with considerable support from local authorities and from midland industrialists (Richardson 1972: 266–9). Meanwhile the technical college at Aston in Birmingham became a College of Advanced Technology in 1964 and a University in 1966. It eschewed the traditional university setting and created a campus for 5,000 students on a 45-acre site in the city surrounded by the shops, works, and public services and buildings of the city (Sutcliffe 1974: 356).

In the post-war period, in the Midlands as elsewhere the adult individual was increasingly left to make moral choices for himself, and constraints upon personal behaviour and relationships whether exercised by the state, the churches or the local community did not merely lose force, but became in themselves socially unacceptable. How people behaved, how they spent their leisure time, and how they aspired to live were increasingly based on a looser and wider consensus. The particular place in which people lived became much less important in forming such attitudes and behaviour than such influences as the national or even international media of communication, radio, television and the press, and groups such as the trade unions, the political parties and the voluntary societies. Churchgoing continued to decline and the weekend became a time for family excursions by car and coach or of days spent in the peace of the countryside, in front of the television, or for the large numbers of working wives on household chores.

The Church of England made determined efforts to build new churches in the suburbs but depended increasingly upon middle-class support and voluntary fund-raising. The free churches too built new chapels in the suburbs, but often found that the city or town centre church was the most successful, drawing a congregation from a wide area by car. In general, churches were smaller and were often associated with the provision of community amenities, as they sought to cooperate with other agents of social amelioration such as the local social services and educational organisations. The new Coventry Cathedral embodied a vision of the Church of England as part of a total culture, artistic and social, and in unity both with other religions and with secular society (Richardson 1972: 172–3). For many, especially on the housing estates and in the factories, this vision simply did not exist and religion was regarded as optional and private.

The Roman Catholics made a major effort to provide suburban churches and even more to build their share of the new primary and secondary schools. They maintained a sense of achievement and security, at least until the 1960s when a period of reappraisal initiated within the church by the Second Vatican Council caused some loss of self confidence.

The Polish, Ukranian, Greek Orthodox, Serbian Orthodox and Latvian churches were established to form a focal point of cultural reinforcement and support for the groups unable or unwilling to return to Europe after the war. West Indians also tended to form their own churches rather than to join existing church communities and groups of Elim and Pentecostal Christians began to make their presence felt with an enthusiastic and extrovert mode of worship which attracted young Christians in a way which the older churches were finding difficult. In the 1960s when Hindus, Moslems and Sikhs arrived in the Midlands they quickly set up their own temples and mosques often at first in disused free church chapels and in private houses and by 1975 a purpose-built mosque in traditional style added yet another note to Birmingham's multicultural townscape. All these groups, Christian, Hindu, Sikh, and Moslem supported their churches with voluntary centres and services to assist their adherents to educate their children in their distinctive faiths, cultures and observances.

For the great majority of Midlanders the post-war period brought increased leisure and opportunities for entertainment and relaxation. Working hours gradually became shorter, though there was until the 1960s much overtime and shift work. The combination of high wages and increased leisure time led to a proliferation of every kind of commercial entertainment. The cinema continued to be popular in the Midlands throughout the war and cinemas increased their custom by opening in the mornings as well as afternoons and early evenings. This popularity continued immediately after the war. In 1950 there were 86 cinemas in Birmingham and even industrial villages such as Gornal had three or four. In December 1949 the BBC began to broadcast television programmes from Sutton Coldfield. The broadcasting of the Coronation in 1953 was for many Midlanders their first experience of television and thereafter the numbers of licences grew rapidly. Cinemas throughout the Midlands closed, and were turned into carpet warehouses and bingo halls, and only a few centrally placed cinemas retained their audiences. Professional football remained an important attraction although midland clubs had to provide better facilities, car parking and to advertise to keep up their attendances. Professional cricket clubs in the post-war period continued to attract considerable numbers and to be able to rely on the enthusiastic loyalty of their following. However, all the mass spectator sports were affected by television, by the spread of the family motor car, and the rising standard of home comfort. People preferred to enjoy entertainment in the comfortable environment of clubs, pubs and restaurants, and many commercial clubs were financed wholly or in part by the attractions of gambling, legalised since 1960. Meanwhile, very large numbers of midland men found escape and peace from the industrial and urban world in the popular sport of fishing, and the numbers setting out for the rivers at weekends soon exceeded those attending football matches.

By the 1960s both the theatre and classical music were in serious difficulties as costs rose rapidly. All the larger towns and cities maintained a wide range of voluntary societies which were largely self-financing but the numbers of people willing to support such activities on a commercial basis remained small and much talent and enterprise in this field tended to be creamed off by London. The Belgrade Theatre in Coventry was established in 1953 to be a non-profit-making Trust to encourage both professional and amateur theatre and theatre education. Like so many other initiatives of the period the original visions have been constrained by the rising costs of the 1960s and the recession of the 1970s, and success has depended upon civic and national patronage rather than local broad-based support (Richardson 1972: 318–23).

Another factor eroding local particularism was the growth of chain stores and supermarkets. With high wages and population growth in the

Plate 6.6   Brookfields Store, Stafford, an example of the development of the large department store in the early twentieth century.

Midlands in the 1950s and 1960s, there was a great extension of shopping facilities both in the new pedestrianised town centres and in suburbs. Between the wars department stores such as Beatties of Wolverhampton and Brookfields of Stafford had grown from local initiatives but now these were themselves taken over by large international companies, and in the High Street more and more shopping was done at Boots, Halfords and the local branches of W. H. Smith and Woolworth. Even bakers' and butchers' shops were part of large groupings and in the early 1960s the small grocer gave way to the supermarkets, not only in the town centres but also in the suburbs.

In the suburbs the large store with car-parking facilities and the minimum of service took over from the corner shop. In the villages shops closed and villagers like townspeople relied upon the car and the larger shopping centres. Off licences and licensed grocers multiplied in the days of affluence and Midlanders took to drinking wine and spirits as well as beer.

The numbers and variety of midland newspapers declined after the war. Birmingham was reduced to one morning, one evening and one Sunday paper all published by the same company. The Wolverhampton *Express and Star*, and the *Staffordshire Advertiser* continued to provide daily newspapers and the weekly *Dudley Herald* and *Stourbridge Express* and others survived, but many more closed. All the newspapers became more 'popular' in their layout and appeal, with much use of pictures and headlines, much less space given to council debates and official business, and much more to national news.

In choosing their representatives both for the local and the central government voters were influenced by national party political considerations. The Unionists and the Liberals lost much ground and the debate was mainly between the Labour and Conservative parties. The numbers of votes cast in the Midlands for each party fluctuated in line with the fluctuations of opinion in comparable areas elsewhere, and patterns were based on socio-economic divisions rather than regional considerations. In the post-war period almost all aspects of local government became subject to party politics. Before the war there had been a number of outstanding men who took part in both local and national government but whose power was based upon the loyalty of their local community. Such were J. C. Wedgwood at Newcastle under Lyme, and Patrick Collins, fairground proprietor, MP and Mayor of Walsall. So too in a rather different way were the Unionist party and the Chamberlain family in Birmingham. In the smaller authorities such as Walsall or Burton on Trent local issues, and the local applications of central policies continued to be of significance after the war (Steven 1968: 81–91) but in general the importance of local issues declined, and the number of councillors standing as independents or for minority parties was notably reduced.

The reorganisation of all local government into a two-tier system of counties and each with their subordinate authorities was the culmination of a considerable period of thinking about local government by academics and planners. They believed that too many authorities with too many powers and limited finance had led to disparities of provision between town and country and between one part of the country and another.

The Local Government Reorganisation Act of 1972 for the first time made a systematic revision of local government responsibilities for the whole country. The services and powers themselves were not altered but the counties and metropolitan districts were expected to provide for both town and country. The rural district councils, the boroughs and even the parishes remained as subordinate agencies of the counties. Local particularism was not merely seen as outdated, it was seen as divisive and harmful and those who questioned the value of the new large overriding bodies were urged to consider the needs and expectations of society 'as a whole' and to 'emphasise what is in common rather than what divides' (Pearce 1980: 252). The new organisation affected the Midlands as follows. 'Staffordshire' comprised the moorlands, Stoke on Trent, Newcastle, Stafford, south Staffordshire, Cannock Chase, Lichfield, Tamworth and east Staffordshire. The 'West Midlands' included Wolverhampton, Walsall, Dudley, Sandwell, Solihull, Birmingham and Coventry while 'Warwickshire' was subdivided into Nuneaton, Rugby, Stratford on Avon (which included all the southern rural area) and Warwick. The act became effective in 1974, but only twelve years later the metropolitan county was abolished.

The movement to centralisation and to large units of management left many people uneasy. They were disturbed by the concentration of power at the centre, and by a situation in which decisions appeared to be made by a faceless élite, industry to be controlled by impersonal economic forces and organised by international public companies, while politics were dominated by national rather than local imperatives. It was feared that such a society gave undue power to experts and to statisticians. It is perhaps a symptom of this anxiety that so many people wish to explore their own history. The study of local history, of regional history and of family history, genealogy and heraldry has become such a popular leisure-time pursuit that midland libraries and record offices have almost been overwhelmed by the demand for their services, and local history societies have sprung up in every village and town.

In tracing the history of West Midland people for a thousand years we have seen a transition from an agricultural society to a modern technological society. An agricultural society is by its nature particular to a specific environment of soil, climate, altitude and accessibility, and local resources are used to meet immediate needs. In the electronic age society reaches out into outer space, and man can create a total life-support system in almost any environment. It remains to be discovered whether the regional community has run its course. Time will show whether this survey is a valedictory exercise or whether there are further chapters of west Midlands history still to be written.

List of Abbreviations

BL   British Library
BRL   Birmingham Reference Library
BPP   British Parliamentary Papers. Collected papers published by the Irish Universities Press
CSP Dom   Calendars of State Papers (Domestic)
CRS   Catholic Record Society
DRO   Dudley Record Office
GPO   General Post Office Record Room
JRSS   Journal of the Royal Statistical Society
LJR   Lichfield Joint Record Office
PRO   Public Record Office
SHC   Staffordshire Historical Collections, formerly the transactions of the William Salt Archaeological Society from 1936 the Staffordshire Record Society
SRO   Staffordshire Record Office
VCH Staffs   Victoria County History of Staffordshire
VCH Warks   Victoria County History of Warwickshire
VCH Worcs   Victoria County History of Worcestershire
WCR   Warwickshire County Records
WLS   Wolverhampton Local Studies Library
WSL   William Salt Library
WRO   Worcester Record Office

List of unprinted sources *

* Indicated by (U) in the text.

Birmingham Reference Library Archives Department
   Birmingham Parish Register (St Martin's and St Philip's).
   Galton Mss: the papers of Galton and Farmer, gunmakers of Birmingham 1720–1770 (403 and 404).
   Gough Mss: Papers of Sir Richard Gough of Edgbaston.
   Hearth Tax Returns for Birmingham, Aston and Sutton Coldfield 1666–1683 (B.R.L. 660313 and 660535).

Report of the Committee on Orders in Council 1812, Report of Evidence, London.
Transcripts of Crown Pleas Relating to Birmingham 13 Edward I (transcribed by W. B. Bickley) (B.R.L. 379288).
Warwick Gift: the papers relating to James Sylvester of Birmingham, jeweller 1740–50 (unlisted).
Wyatt Mss: Papers relating to the Wyatt family of Birmingham and Lichfield.

Dudley Record Office
Earl of Dudley Mss: Sedgley Manor Court Rolls, Vol. IX.
Minutes and Records of Netherton Baptist Chapel 1654–1720.
Sedgley Survey 1614.

General Post Office Record Room
Pelover Mss 1660–1740.

Lichfield Joint Record Office
Probate of John Smith of Timore, Lichfield, April 1675.
Probate of John Wood of Leek 1673.
Probate of William Bourne of Wolstanton 1696.

Public Record Office
Privy Council uncalendared Mss of the reign of Charles II, PC/2/171 (1685).

Staffordshire Record Office
Aqualate Mss, D(W) 1788/56/7.
Bill Family Papers, D554/57.
Bolton Deeds, DS93 Account Book (1764).
Checkley Settlement Certificates, Checkley Parish Mss.
Hatherton Settlement Certificates, D260/M/PO/47.
Paget Mss, D(W) 1734/3/3/260.
Vernon Mss, D(W) 1790/133.

William Salt Library
Hand Morgan Collection, uncatalogued boxes 3 and 4.

Wolverhampton Local Studies Library
Churchwardens' Accounts, transcribed by N. Tildesley.

Worcester Record Office
Probate of William Hill of Oldswinford, May 1667.

Bibliography

Adey, K. (1974) 'Stafford in the sixteenth and seventeenth centuries', *Midland History*, ii, no. 3.

Aiken, J. (1795) *Description of the country thirty to forty miles around Manchester*, David & Charles, Reprint 1968.

Alcock, N. W. (1973) *A catalogue of cruck buildings*, Phillimore, London.

Alcock, N. W. (1975) *Stoneleigh Villagers 1597–1650*, The University of Warwick.

Alcock, N. W. (1977) 'Enclosure and depopulation on Burton Dasset', *Warwickshire History*, III no. 5 (Summer).

Alcock, N. W. (1981) *Warwickshire Grazier and London Skinner 1532–1555*, Oxford U.P., London.

Alcuin Society Vol. 26 and 27 (1924) Elizabethan episcopal administration Vol. ii. Visitation articles and injunctions 1575–1582, 1583–1603.

Aldrich, R. (1981) 'Sir John Packington and education in the west Midlands', *West Midlands Studies*, xvi (Winter).

Alexander, H. C. (1906) *Richard Cadbury of Birmingham by His Daughter*, Birmingham.

Allen, G. C. (1923) 'An eighteenth century combination in the copper mining industry', *Economic Journal*, xxxiii.

Allen, G. C. (1929) *The industrial development of Birmingham and the Black Country 1860–1927*, London, Reprint 1966.

Anderton, T. (1902) 'Birmingham Churches Now 1901–2', reprinted from the *Midland Counties Herald*, Birmingham.

Anstruther, G. (1968, 1975–7) *The Seminary Priests*, i, Ushaw, Durham, 1968; ii Mayhew McCrimmon Great Wakering, 1975; iii Mayhew McCrimmon, Great Wakering, 1976; iv Mayhew McCrimmon, Great Wakering, 1977.

Ardafyio, C. (1974) 'Warwickshire Canals', Birmingham M.A. *Aris's Birmingham Gazette 1741–1888*, Birmingham.

Ashby, A. W. (1912) 'One hundred years of Poor Law administration in a Warwickshire village', *Oxford Studies in Social and Legal History*, iii.

Ashby, M. K. (1961) 'Joseph Ashby of Tysoe, 1815–1919', *A Study of Old Village Life*, Cambridge.

Aston, M. (1960) 'Lollardy and sedition 1381–1431', *Past and Present*, **17**.

Awty, B. G. (1951) 'Charcoal ironmasters in Cheshire and North Staffordshire', *Transactions of the Historical Society of Lancashire and Cheshire*, **109**.

Bailey, J. R. (1982) 'The struggle for survival in the Coventry ribbon and watch trades 1865–1914', *Midland History*, vii.

Bailey, R. C. and Hardy, S. M. (1951) 'The downfall of the Gower interest', *Staffordshire Historical Collections*, New Series 48.

Baker, A. R. H. and Butlin, R. A. (1973) *Studies of Field Systems in the British Isles*, Cambridge.

Barley, M. W. (1961) *The English Farmhouse and Cottage*, London.

Barlow, F. (1979) *The English Church 1000–1066*, Longman, London.

Barnsby, G. J. (1965) *The Origins of Wolverhampton Trades Council*, Wolverhampton.

Barnsby, G. J. (1966) 'The Dudley working class movement 1750–1832', *Dudley Public Library Archive Department*, Transcript, Series 7, Dudley.

Barnsby, G. J. (1967) 'The Dudley working class movement 1832–1867, *Dudley Public Library Archive Department*, Transcript, Series 8, Dudley.

Barnsby, G. J. (1969) 'Social Conditions in the Black Country', Birmingham Ph.D.

Barnsby, G. J. (1971) 'The standard of living in the Black Country', *Economic History Review*, Second Series, xxiv.

Barnsby, G. J. (1975) *History of Housing in Wolverhampton 1750–1975* (n.d.), Wolverhampton.

Barnsby, G. J. (1976) *The General Strike in the Black Country*, Wolverhampton.

Barnsby, G. J. (1977) *The Working Class in the Black Country*, Wolverhampton.

Barnsby, G. (1980) *Social Conditions in the Black Country*, Wolverhampton.

Barratt, D. M. (1952) 'The inclosure of the manor of Wasperton 1664', *University of Birmingham Historical Journal*, iii, No. 2.

Barratt, D. M. (1955, 1971) *Ecclesiastical Terriers of Warwickshire Parishes*, 2 vols, Dugdale Society xxii and xxvii.

Bartley, A. J. (1967) 'Social and Economic Development of Wednesbury 1650–1750', M.A., London.

Bate, P. V. and Palliser, D. (1970–71) 'Suspected lost village sites in Staffordshire', *Transactions of the South Staffordshire Archaeological and Historical Society*, xii.

Bateman, J. (1971) *The Great Landowners of Great Britain and Ireland*, Leicester U.P. 1971 (Reprint of 1883, 4th edn).

Baxter, E. G. (1975–6) 'The social life of visitors to Leamington Spa', *Warwickshire History*, iii, nos 1 and 2 (Summer).

Beales, A. C. F. (1963) *Education under Penalty*, London.

Bealey, F. (1965) 'Municipal Politics in Newcastle under Lyme 1872–1914', *North Staffordshire Journal of Field Studies*, vi.

Bealey, F. (1971) 'Parish elections in Newcastle under Lyme Rural District in May 1961', *North Staffordshire Journal of Field Studies*, xi.

Bearman, R. (1972) 'The Gregorys of Stivichall in the sixteenth century', *Coventry & Warwickshire History Society pamphlets*, Coventry.

Beaver, S. H. (1964) 'The Potteries. A study in the evolution of a cultural landscape', *Transactions of the Institute of British Geographers*, xxiv.

Behagg, C. (1979) 'Custom, Class and Change; Trade Societies in Birmingham', *Social History*, iv. no. 3.

Beier, A. L. (1966) 'Poor relief in Warwickshire', *Past and Present*, 35.

Beier, A. L. (1969) 'Poverty and Poor Relief in Warwickshire 1540–1680', PhD, Princeton.

Beier, A. L. (1974) 'Vagrants and the social order in Elizabethan England', *Past and Present*, **64**.

Beier, A. L. (1980) 'Social problems of an Elizabethan country town', in P. Clarke (ed.), *County Towns in Pre-Industrial England*, Leicester.

Bell, C. and Bell, R. (1969) *City Fathers, The Early History of Town Planning in Britain*, London.

Bemrose, G. J. V. (1939–40) 'Notes on the early history of Staffordshire pottery', *Transactions of the North Staffordshire Field Club*, lxxiv.

Benson, J. (1979) 'Miners and their houses', *West Midland Studies*, xii.

Beresford, M. W. (1941–42) 'Economic individualism of Sutton Coldfield', *Transactions of the Birmingham Archaeological Society*, lxiv.

Beresford, M. W. (1959) 'The deserted villages of Warwickshire', *Transactions of the Birmingham Archaeological Society*, lxvi, 1945–6; lxvii.

Beresford, M. W. (1969) 'The origin of mediaeval boroughs in Warwickshire', *Warwickshire History*, 1, no. 2 (Autumn).

Berger, R. M. (1981–2) 'Mercantile careers in the early seventeenth century', *Warwickshire History*, v, no. 2 (Winter).

Berry, A. K. (1965) 'Henry Ferrers Antiquary', *Occasional Paper Dugdale Society*, xvi, Oxford.

Besse, J. (1733) An abstract *The sufferings of the people called Quakers*, 2 vols, London.

Best, R. D. (1940) *Brass Chandelier*, London.

Bickley, W. B. (1894) *Register of the Gild of Knowle in County of Warwick 1451–1535*, London.

Bickley, W. B. (ed) (1902) 'Lay Subsidy Roll for Warwickshire 1327', *Transactions of the Midland Record Society*, vi.

Bill, P. (1966) 'Five aspects of the mediaeval parochial clergy of Warwickshire', *University of Birmingham Historical Journal*, x, no. 2.

Bill, P. A. (1967) 'The Warwickshire parish clergy in the later Middle Ages', *Dugdale Society Occasional Paper*, xvii.

Bilston Parish Register 1684–1746 (1937) (transcribed Thomas, H. R.), Staffordshire Parish Register Society.

Birmingham Parish Registers (1889–1903) St Martin's Parish Birmingham (transcribed by Bickley, W. B.), Birmingham.

Birrell, J. R. (1961–2) 'The Forest economy of the Honour of Tutbury in the fourteenth and fifteenth centuries', *University of Birmingham Historical Journal*, viii.

Birrell, J. (1962) 'The Honour of Tutbury in the fourteenth and fifteenth centuries', Ph.D. thesis, Birmingham.

Birrell, J. R. (1969) 'Peasant Craftsmen in the Mediaeval Forest', *Agricultural History Review*, xvii, i.

Birrell, J. (1982) 'Who poached the King's deer?', *Midland History*, vii.

Bladen, V. W. (1926) 'The Potteries in the Industrial Revolution', *Economic History Review*, 1.

Bloom, J. H. (1865) *The Register Book of the Gild of Knowle*.

Board of Trade (1878–88) *Report as to the condition of nail makers and small chain makers in S. Staffs & E. Worcs.*, PP HC, 69, 1–iii.

Board of Trade (1907) *Enquiry into the cost of living of the working class in towns in the United Kingdom*, London.

Bond, W. G. (1927) *The Wanderings of Charles I and His Army in the Midlands 1642–1645*, Birmingham.

Bond, C. J. (1969) 'The deserted village of Billesley Trussell', *Warwickshire History*, 1, no. 2.

Bond, C. J. (1974) 'Deserted medieval villages in Warwickshire, a review of the evidence', *Birmingham and Warwickshire Archaeological Society Transactions*, lxxxvi.

Bond, C. J. (1982) 'Deserted medieval villages in Warwickshire and Worcestershire', Slater, T. & Jarvis, P. (eds) Norwich.

Bournville Village Trust (1941) *When We Build Again*, London.

Bournville Village Trust (1942) *Sixty Years of Planning. The Bournville Experiment*, Bournville.

BPP IUP (1818) Textiles. Committee upon the Silk Trade.

BPP (1822–3, 1834) 'Reports to the Children's Employment Commission', *Industrial Revolution Children's Employment*, 3 and 4 (1822–3), 5 (1834).

BPP (1841–3) 'Evidence of the Commission on the conditions of children's employment 1841–1843', *Industrial Revolution Children's Employment*, 10.

BPP (1842) 'Report on the conditions of children employed in the mines', South Staffordshire and Warwickshire, J. Mitchell 1842, *Industrial Revolution Children's Employment*, 7.

BPP (1843a) 'Midland Mining Commission first report 1843 XIII', *Mining Districts*, Vol. 1.

BPP (1843b) 'Report on the conditions of labour of women and children', *Industrial Revolution: Children's Employment*, xiii.

BPP (1843–5) 'Report on the conditions of the employment of children in Trades and Manufactures 1843–5', *Industrial Revolution: Children's Employment*, x.

BPP (1845a) 'Second report of the Commissioners to enquire into the state of large towns and populous districts 1845', *Health*, vi.

BPP (1845b) 'Second report of the Commission for the state of large towns and populous districts 1845', *Health*, vi.

BPP (1863–7) 'Reports to the children's employment commission', *Industrial Revolution: Children's Employment*, 13 (1863), 14 (1864), 15 (1865–7).

BPP (1875) *Report of the Inspector of Factories 30th April 1875* (The nail and chain district; Black Country).

Brazier, R. and Sandford, E. (1921) *Birmingham and the Great War 1914–1918*, Birmingham.

Briggs, A. (1948) 'Thomas Attwood and the Birmingham political union', *Historical Journal*, ix, 2.

Briggs, A. (1949) 'Press and public in nineteenth century Birmingham', *Dugdale Society Occasional Paper*, no. 8.

Briggs, A. (1952) *History of Birmingham. Volume II: Borough and City 1865–1938*, Oxford U.P.

Briggs, A. (1956) 'Middle class consciousness in Victorian politics', *Past and Present*, ix (February).

Briggs, A. (1963) *Victorian Cities*, London.

Briggs, J. H. Y. (1983) *A History of Longton*, Stoke on Trent.

Broadbridge, S. R. (1974) *The Birmingham Canal Navigations*, Vol. 1, 1768–1846, David & Charles, Newton Abbot.

Brown, C. M. (1979) 'The Schools of Chance Brothers at Smethwick', *West Midland Studies*, xii.

Brown, K. F. (1975–6) 'Two Walsall charters', *Transactions of the Lichfield and South Staffordshire Archaeological and Historical Society*, xvii.

Browne, A. L. (1939–40) 'James II's proposed Repeal', *SCH* (volume listed as 1939 but published in 1940).

Bryman, A. (1975) 'Religion in the Birmingham area', *Institute for the Study of Worship and Religious Architecture, Birmingham University*.

Buckley, F. (1927) 'Notes on the glasshouses of Stourbridge 1700–1830', *Transactions of the Society of Glass Technology*, ii.

Bunce, J. T. *et al.* (1878–1957). *History of the Corporation of Birmingham.* 1–3 Bunce, J. T.; 3–4 Vince, C. A. (Continuation); 5 Jones, J. T. (Continuation); 6 Black, H. J. (Continuation).

Bunker, R. C. (1952) Population growth of the Warwickshire coalfield since 1800, Birmingham M.A.

Buscot, W. (1940) *The History of Cotton College*, London.

Cadman, J. (1977) 'The social structure of Kingswinford village', *West Midlands Studies*, xiv (Winter).

Caird, J. (1852) *English Agriculture 1850–1*, London.

Calendar of Patent Rolls of Henry IV (1399–1400) 4 volumes (volume 1: 1399–1400), London, 1903–9.

Camden, W. (1586) *Britannia*, ed. R. Gough, London, 1789.

Camden, W. (1977) *Calender of State Papers Domestic*, London, 1661.

Cannadine, D. (1977) 'Victorian cities – how different?', *Social History* (January).

Cantor, L. M. (1962) 'Medieval deer parks in north Staffordshire', *North Staffordshire Journal of Field Studies*, ii.

Cantor, L. M. (1964) 'Medieval deer parks of Staffordshire', *North Staffordshire Journal of Field Studies*, iv, Keele.

Cantor, L. M. (1966) 'Medieval castles of Staffordshire', *North Staffordshire Journal of Field Studies*, vi.

Cantor, L. M. (1968) 'Medieval parks of earls of Stafford at Madeley', *North Staffordshire Journal of Field Studies*, viii.

Carpenter, M. (1980) 'The Beauchamp Affinity', *English Historical Review*, xcv.

Carter, W. F. (1965) Lay subsidy roll of 1332, Dugdale Society, vol. vi.

Carter, W. F. and Fry, E. A. (1899–1903) Lay subsidy roll of 1327, Midland record society, vols iii–vi.

Carus Wilson, E. M. (1965) 'The first half century of the Borough of Stratford-on-Avon', *Economic History Review*, 2nd series, xviii.

CRS (1921) 'Diocesan Returns of recusants, 1577', in *Miscellanea*, Vol. xxii, pp. 1–114.

Chadwick, E. (1837) *Report on the Sanitary Condition of England and Wales of the Working Class*, London.

Chalkin, C. W. (1974) *The Provincial Towns of Georgian England*, London.

Chalton, B. H. (1975) 'Education in Sedgley', *West Midlands Studies*, viii.

Chance & Co. (1919) *History of Chance Brothers and Co. Glass and Alkali Manufacturers*, Smethwick.

Chandler, G. and Hannah, G. (1949) *Dudley as it was and as it is today*, Dudley.

Chapman, S. D. (1965) 'Transition to the factory system in midland cotton spinning', *Economic History Review*, 2nd Series, ii, no. 3.

Chapman, S. D. (1967) *The Early Factory Masters*, David & Charles, Newton Abbot.

Chapman, S. D. (1971) *The History of Working Class Housing*, David & Charles, Newton Abbot.

Chatwyn, P. B. (ed.) (1924–63) 'Records of King Edward's School, Birmingham', 5 vols, *Dugdale Society*, iv, vii, xii, xx, xxv.

Chatwyn, P. B. (1951) *Old Warwick: a description of its old buildings*, London.

Cheesewright, M. (1975) *Mirror to a Mermaid*, Birmingham, University of Birmingham.

Cheney, M.. (1980) *Roger Bishop of Worcester 1164–1179*, Clarendon Press, Oxford.

Christiansen, R. (1973) *A regional history of the railways of Great Britain. Vol. VII The West Midlands*, David & Charles, 2nd edn, 1983.

Church, R. H. (1969) *Kendricks in Hardware. A Family Business 1791–1966*, David & Charles, Newton Abbot.

Church, R. H. (1977) 'Coffin furniture making', *Economic History Review*, 2nd Series, xxx, no. 3.

Clark, P. (1979) 'Migration in England during the late seventeenth and eighteenth centuries', *Past and Present*, 83.

Clarkson, L. A. (1966) 'The leather crafts in Tudor and Stuart England', *Agricultural History Review*, xiv.

Clegg, C. and R. (1983) *The Dream Palaces of Birmingham*, Birmingham.

Clinker, C. R. (1956) 'Birmingham and Derby Junction Railway', *Dugdale Society Occasional Paper No. 11*, Oxford.

Cobbett, W. (1809–20) *Cobbett's Complete Collection of State Trials*, 8 vols, London.

Coley, N. G. (1970–1) 'James Keir: soldier, chemist and gentleman', *West Midland Studies*, iv.

Collinson, P. (1967) *The Elizabethan Puritan Movement*, London.

Compton-Reeves, A. (1975) 'William Booth Bishop of Coventry and Lichfield 1447–1452', *Midland History*, iii (Spring).

Corbett, John (1966) *The Birmingham Trades Council 1866–1966*, London.

Congreve, T. (1917) *Scheme or Proposal for Making a Navigable Communication Between the Rivers of Trent and Severn*, London.

Coss, P. R. (1974) 'Coventry before incorporation', *Midland History*, ii.

Cossons, A. (1946) 'Warwickshire Turnpikes', *Birmingham Archaeological Society Transactions*, lxiv.

Court, W. H. B. (1937) 'A Warwickshire colliery in the eighteenth century', *Economic History Review*, vii.

Court, W. H. B. (1938) *The Rise of the Midland Industries 1600–1838*, London, Reprint 1953.

Crawford, A. and Thorne, R. (1983) *Birmingham Pubs 1890–1939*, Birmingham.

Cronne, H. A. (1951) 'The Borough of Warwick in the Middle Ages', *Dugdale Society Occasional Papers*, 10, Oxford.

Cross, C. (1976) *Church and People 1450–1660*, London.

Crossley, D. W. (1967) 'Glassmaking in Bagots Park', *Post-Medieval Archaeology*, 1.

Crossley, D. W. (1972) 'Performance of the glass industry in sixteenth century England', *Economic History Review*, Series 2, xxv, no. 3 (August).

Crouch, D. (1982) 'Geoffrey de Clinton and Roger Earl of Warwick', *Bulletin of the Institute of Historical Research*, 1v (November).

Dalley, W. A. (1914) *The Life Story of W. J. Davis*, Birmingham.

Darby, H. C. and Terrett, I. B. (1971) The Domesday Geography of Midland England (2nd edn), Cambridge.

Darby, H. C. (1971) *A New Historical Geography of England*, Cambridge.

Davies, G. L. and Hyde, H. (1970) *Dudley and the Black Country 1760–1860*, Dudley Library, Dudley.

Davies, M. G. (1977) 'County gentlemen and falling rents', *Midland History*, iv.

Davies, R. (1976–7) 'Railway development in Warwickshire', *Warwickshire History*, iii. no. 4.

Davis, R. H. C. (1976) 'The early history of Coventry', *Dugdale Society Occasional Paper*, 24.

Dean, K. (1972) *Town and Westminster 1906–45*, Walsall.

Defoe, D. (1724) *A Tour Through the Whole Island of Great Britain*, London; Penguin edn 1971.

Delieb, E. (1941) *The Great Silver Manufactory*, London.

Dickens, A. G. (1967) *The Reformation in England to the Accession of Elizabeth*, Arnold, London.

Dickinson, H. W. (1936) *James Watt Craftsman and Engineer*, Cambridge.

Dickinson, H. W. (1937) *Mathew Boulton*, Cambridge.

Dilworth, R. (1975) *The Tame Mills of Staffordshire*, David & Charles, Newton Abbot.

Dodgshon, R. A. and Butlin, R. A. (1978) *Historical Geography of England and Wales*, Academic Press, London.

Downes, R. L. (1930) 'The Stour Partnership in ironworks in 1726–30', *Economic History Review*, 2nd series, iii.

Doyle, P. J. (1969) 'Origins of recusancy; the Throckmortons of Coughton', *Worcestershire Recusant*, xiii (June).

Dugdale, W. (1730) *The Antiquities of Warwickshire*, ed. with additions by W. Thomas, 2 vols, T. Warren, London.

Duggan, E. P. (1975) 'Birmingham population', *The Local Historian*, xi, part 2.

Dunham, K. (1960) *The Gun Trade of Birmingham*, Birmingham Museum of Science and Industry, Birmingham.

Dupree, M. (1977) 'Family and the industrial revolution: a case study from the Potteries', Paper read to the Economic History Society.

Durst, P. (1970) *Intended Treason*, London.

Dyer, A. (1976–7) 'Warwickshire towns under the Tudors and Stuarts', *Warwickshire History*, iii, no. 4.

Dyer, A. (1981) 'The seasonality of baptism: an urban approach', *Local Population Studies*, xxvii (Autumn).

Dyer, C. (1968) 'Population and agriculture on a Warwickshire manor in the late Middle Ages', *University of Birmingham Historical Journal*, xi.

Dyer, C. (1972) 'A small landowner in the fifteenth century', *Midland History*, 1.

Dyer, C. (1980) *Lords and Peasants in a Changing Society*, Cambridge U.P.

Dyer, C. (1981) 'Warwickshire farming 1344–1520. Preparations for an Agricultural Revolution', Dugdale Society Occasional Paper 27, Oxford.

Dyer, C. (1982) 'Deserted medieval villages in the west Midlands', *Economic History Review*, 2nd Series, xxxv, no. 1. (February).

Ede, J. F. (1962) *History of Wednesbury*, Wednesbury.

Eden, F. M. (1797) *The State of the Poor*, 3 vols., London, Reprint, Carr, London, 1966.

Edwards, P. R. (1979) 'The horse trade of the Midlands', *Agricultural History Review*, xxvii.

Ellis, S. (1984) Stanley Ellis in correspondence with author (6.9.84).

Emery, F. V. (1962) 'Moated settlements in England', *Geography*, lxvii.

Evershed, H. (1856) 'The farming of Warwickshire', *Journal of the Royal Agricultural Society*, xvii.

Evershed, H. (1859) 'The farming of Staffordshire', *Journal of the Royal Society of Agriculture*, second series, v.

Fairclough, O. (1984) *The Grand Old Mansion. The Holtes and their Successors at Aston Hall*, Birmingham.

Farr, M. W. (1968) 'The Featherstones of Packwood', *Dugdale Society Occasional Paper*, cviii, Oxford.

Fereday, R. P. (1966) 'The career of Richard Smith 1783–1868', M.A., Keele.

Field, R. K. (1983) 'Migration in the later Middle Ages; the case of Hampton Lovett', *Midland History*, viii.

Finch, M. E. (1956) 'The wealth of five Northamptonshire families', *Northamptonshire Record Society*, xix.

Fines, J. (1963) 'Heresy in diocese of Lichfield and Coventry 1511–12', *Journal of Ecclesiastical History*, xiv, part i (April).

Finlayson, G. B. (1973) 'Joseph Parkes of Birmingham 1796–1865: a study in philosophical radicalism', *The Bulletin of the Institute of Historical Research*, xlvi.

Fisher, M. J. C. (1968) 'Churches of north Staffordshire moorlands', *North Staffordshire Journal of Field Studies*, viii.

Flick, C. (1978) *The Birmingham Political Union*, Hamden Connecticut Arc Books, Folkstone Dawson.

Flinn, M. W. (1961–2) 'William Wood and the coke smelting process', *Transactions of the Newcomen Society*, xxxiv.

Flinn, M. W. (1962) *Men of Iron*, Edinburgh.

Fogarty, M. (1979) 'Wolverhampton Athanaeum and Mechanics' Library', *West Midland Studies*, xii.

Fogg, U. (1981) *Chains and Chain Making*, London.

Foley, H. (ed) (1878) *Records of the English Province of the Society of Jesus 1877–1887*, London.

Ford, W. J. (1979) 'Some settlement patterns in the central region of the Warwickshire Avon', in Sawyer, P. H. (ed.), *English Medieval Settlement*, Arnold, London.

Fowler-Carter, W. and Wellstood, F. C. (1926) 'Lay subsidy rolls for Warwickshire 1332', *Dugdale Society*.

Fox, A. (1958) 'Industrial relations in Birmingham: the transition to organised wage labour 1890–1910', *Oxford Economic Papers*, New Series, vii.

Fox, L. (1953) *The Borough Town of Stratford upon Avon*, Stratford upon Avon.

Fox, L. (1984) 'The early history of King Edward VI school, Stratford upon Avon', *Dugdale Society Occasional Paper*, D. Stanford, Oxford.

Fraser, D. (1962) 'Weoley Castle', *Transactions of the Birmingham and Warwickshire Archaeological Society*, lxxviii.

Fraser, D. (1976) *Urban Politics in Victorian Cities*, Leicester University Press, Leicester.

Fraser, D. (1979) *Power and Authority in the Victorian City*, Blackwell, Oxford.

Fraser, P. (1966) *Joseph Chamberlain. Radicalism and Empire*, London.

Frost, P. M. (1973) 'The growth and localisation of rural industry in south Staffordshire 1560–1720', University of Birmingham PhD.

Frost, P. M. (1980) 'Yeomen, metal smiths and livestock in the dual economy of south Staffordshire 1560–1720', *Agricultural History Review*, xviii.

Gale, W. K. (1954) *The Coneygre Story*, Tipton.

Gale, W. K. (1966) *History of the Black Country Iron Industry*, London.

Garret, C. (1938) *The Marian Exiles*, Cambridge.

Gash, N. (1953) *Politics in the Age of Peel*, London.

Gault, R. C. (1939) *A History of Worcestershire Agriculture*, Worcester.

Gay, E. F. (1900, 1904) 'The Midland revolt', *Royal Historical Society Transactions*, New Series xiv (1900) and New Series xv (1904).

Gay, P. W. (1967) 'An economic survey of the British pottery industry', *North Staffordshire Journal of Field Studies*, vii.

Giles, B. D. (1976) 'High status neighbourhoods', *West Midlands Studies*, ix.

Giles, P. M. (1960) 'The felt hatting industry', *Transactions of the Lancashire and Cheshire Antiquarian Society*, 1959, lxix.

Gill, C. (1930) *Studies in Midland History*, Oxford.

Gill, C. (1952) *History of Birmingham*, 1, London.

Glover, J. (1978–9) 'Health and disease in Warwickshire', *Warwickshire History*, iv, no. 2.

Gooder, A. (1965) 'Plague and enclosure in a Warwickshire parish', *Coventry and Warwickshire History Pamphlets*, 2, Coventry.

Gooder, A. (1972) 'The population crisis of 1727–30 in Warwickshire', *Midland History*, 1, no. 4.

Gooder, A. and E. (1981) 'Coventry before 1355, unity or division?', *Midland History*, vi.

Gooder, E. (1967) *Coventry's Town Walls*, Coventry.

Gooder, E. (1970) 'The Knights Templar at Temple Balsall', *Warwickshire History*, 1, no. 3 (Spring).

Gordon, A. (1917) 'Freedom after ejection 1690–1692', *Manchester University Publication 114*, Manchester.

Gould, J. (1967) 'Food, foresters, fines and felons', *Lichfield and Staffordshire Archaeological Historical Society Transactions 1965/6*, vii.

Gould, J. (1971–2) 'The medieval burgesses of Tamworth, their liberties, courts and masters', *South Staffordshire Archaeological and Historical Society Transactions*, xiii.

Grant, A. (1977) 'The spatial development of the Coventry coalfield', Birmingham PhD.

Grant, E. G. (1978) 'The Warwickshire coalfield in the seventeenth century', *Dugdale Society Occasional Paper*, xxvi.

Grant, E. G. (1982) 'Changing perspectives in the Warwickshire coalfield' in Slater, T. R. (ed.), *Field and Forest*.

Green, C. (1973) 'Birmingham politics 1873–91', *Midland History*, ii. no. 2.

Green, M. A. (1908) 'Diary of John Rous', Camden Society, III Series, xv.

Greenslade, M. (1982) 'Staffordshire no-popery', *Staffordshire Catholic History*, 21.

Greenslade, M. and Stuart, D.(1965) *A History of Staffordshire*, Chichester.

Griffiths, P. (1976) 'Pressure groups in late Victorian England', *Midland History*, iii, no. 3.

Griffiths, R. A. (1979–80) 'The hazards of civil war the Mountford family and the Wars of the Roses', *Midland History*, v.

Gruenfelder, J. K. (1976) 'Two Midland parliamentary elections of 1604', *Midland History*, iii, no. 4 (Autumn).

Gullet, G. (1974) 'Changes in manufacture in Coventry', *West Midlands Studies*, iii.

Guttery, D. R. (1952–6) 'Stourbridge market in Tudor times', *Transactions of the Worcestershire Archaeological Society*, xxviii.

Guttery, D. R. (1956) *From Broad Glass to Cut Crystal*, London.

Guttery, D. R. (1969) *The Two Johns*, Dudley Library Transcript 13, Dudley.

Guttery, S. (1950) *The Civil War in the Midland Parishes*, Birmingham.

Haden, H. J. (1949) *Notes on the Stourbridge Glass Trade*, Brierley Hill.

Hadfield, C. (1966) *The Canals of the West Midlands*, Vol. VI Canals of the British Isles, David & Charles, Newton Abbot.

Haines, R. M. (1965) 'The administration of the diocese of Worcester in the first half of the fourteenth century', *Church Historical Society*, London.

Hamilton, H. (1827) *The English Brass and Copper Industries to 1800*, London, Reprint 1967.

Harding, S. M. and Bailey, R. C. (1951) 'The downfall of the Gower interest', *Staffordshire Historical Collection*.

Harley, J. B. (1958–9) 'Population trends and agricultural development from the Warwickshire hundred rolls of 1279', *Economic History Review*, 2nd Series, xi.

Harley, J. B. (1960) 'Population and land utilisation in the Warwickshire Hundreds of Stoneleigh and Kineton 1086–1300', Birmingham PhD.

Harley, J. B. (1964) 'The settlement geography of early medieval Warwickshire', *Transactions of the Institute of British Geographers*, xxxiv.

Harris, J. R. (1978) 'Attempts to transfer English steel techniques to France in the eighteenth century', *Business and Business Men*, Studies in Business Economic and Accounting History, Liverpool.

Harris, J. R. (1981) 'Birmingham hardware technologists in France before the French Revolution', Lecture given at Birmingham.

Harris, M. D. (1898) *Life in an Old English Town*, London.

Harris, M. D. (1907–13) 'The Coventry leet book 1420–1555', *Early English Text Society*, 4 parts.

Harris, M. D. (1924) 'The ancient records of Coventry', *Dugdale Society Occasional Paper*, Stratford.

Harris, M. D. (n.d.) *History of The Drapers' Company of Coventry*, TS in Coventry Library.

Harris, M. D. (1935) 'The register of the Guild of the Holy Trinity St Mary, St John the Baptist and St Katherine of Coventry', *Publications of the Dugdale Society*, xiii, London.

Harrison, C. J. (1967) 'The Willoughby ironworks', *Renaissance and Modern Studies*, xi.

Harrison, C. J. (1974) 'Social and Economic History of Rugeley and Cannock 1546–1597', PhD Keele.

Harrison, C. J. (1979) 'Elizabethan village surveys, a comment', *Agricultural History Review*, xxvii.

Harrison, C. J. (1979b) 'The Cannock Chase ironworks report of 1590', *North Staffordshire Journal of Field Studies*, xix.

Harrison, C. J. and Jones, A. C. (1978) 'A survey of Cannock Chase ironworks 1590', *English Historical Review*, xciii (October).

Harvey, B. F. (1979) *Westminster Abbey and its Estates in the West Midlands*, Oxford.

Harvey, W. (1906) *The Model Village and its Cottages*, Bournville.

Hastings, R. (1959) 'The Labour Movement in Birmingham', Birmingham MA.

Hastings, R. (1973) 'The general strike of 1926 in Birmingham', *Midland History*, ii, no. 4.

Hastings, R. P. (1980) 'The Birmingham Labour movement 1918–45', *Midland History*, v.

Hatcher, J. and Barker, T. (1974) *A History of Pewter*, London.

Hawkes-Smith, W. (1836) *Birmingham and its Vicinity 1836*, Birmingham.

Hay, D. and Linebaugh, T. (1975) *Albion's Fatal Tree*, London.

Heap, P. (1975) 'The politics of Warwickshire, an elite study', Yale PhD.

Heath, P. (1979) 'Staffordshire towns and the reformation', *North Staffordshire Journal of Field Studies*, xix.

Hebden, R. (1961–2) 'The development of the settlement patterns and family in Shenstone', *Lichfield and South Staffordshire Archaeological and History Society*, iii.

Henessy, R. A. S. (1972) *The Electrical Revolution*, Oriel Press.

Hennock, R. P. (1973) *Fit and Proper Persons*, London.

Henstock, A. (1969) 'Cheese manufacture and marketing in Derbyshire and north Staffordshire 1670–1870', *Derbyshire Archaeological Journal*, lxxxix.

Hibbert, T. (1910) *Dissolution of the Staffordshire Monasteries*, Pitman, London.

Higgs, W. (1962) 'Agriculture of Warwickshire', *Journal of the Royal Agricultural Society*.

Hilton, R. A. (ed.) (1952) 'Ministers' accounts of the Warwickshire estates of the Duke of Clarence 1479–80', *Dugdale Society*, xxi.

Hilton, R. H. (1949) 'Peasant movements in England before 1381', *Economic History Review*, 2nd Series, ii.

Hilton, R. H. (1950) 'Social structure of Warwickshire in the middle ages', *Dugdale Society Occasional Papers*, ix.

Hilton, R. H. (1960) 'Stoneleigh leger book', *Dugdale Society*, xxiv, Oxford.

Hilton, R. H. (1965) 'Freedom and villeinage in England', *Past and Present*, 31.

Hilton, R. H. (1966) *A Mediaeval Society*, London.

Hilton, R. H. (1969) *The Decline of Serfdom in Mediaeval England*.

Hilton, R. H. (1970) 'Lord and peasant in Staffordshire in the middle ages', *North Staffordshire Journal of Field Studies*, x.

Hilton, R. H. (1973) *Bond Men Made Free*, London.

Hilton, R. H. (1975) The English Peasantry in the later Middle Ages, London.

Hilton, R. H. (1982) 'The small town in the later middle ages, Evesham', *Midland History*, vii.

Hilton, R. H. and Fagan, H. (1950) *The English Rising of 1381*, London.

Hobday, E. (1910) *The Registers of Halesowen 1558–1643*, Parish Register Society.

Hodgetts, M. (1965–7, 1970–2) 'Elizabethan recusancy in Worcestershire', *Transactions of the Worcestershire Historical Society*, 3rd Series, 1 (1965–7), 3 (1970–2).

Homeshaw, E. M. (1955) *The Story of Bloxwich*, Bloxwich.

Homeshaw, E. M. (1960) *Corporation of Borough and Foreign of Walsall*, Walsall.

Hooke, D. (1981a) 'Open field agriculture. The evidence from pre-conquest charters of the west Midlands', in Rowley, T. (ed.) *The Origins of Open field Agriculture*, Croom Helm, London.

Hooke, D. (1981b) *The Anglo Saxon Landscape of the West Midlands*, British Archaeological Reports, British Series 95, Oxford.

Hooke, D. (1982) 'The Anglo Saxon landscape' in Slater, T. (ed.) *Field and Forest*, Norwich.

Hooke, D. (1983) *The Landscape of Anglo Saxon Staffordshire. The Charter Evidence*, Keele.

Hopkins, E. (1973) 'Anatomy of strikes in the glass industry', *Midland History*, ii, no. 1 (Spring).

Hopkins, E. (1974a) 'Working conditions in Victorian Stourbridge', *International Review of Social History*, xix, part 3.

Hopkins, E. (1974b) 'Changes in the size of the industrial unit 1815–1914', *West Midlands Studies*, vii.

Hopkins, E. (1975) 'Small town aristocrats and their standard of living', *Economic History Review*, xxviii. no. 2 (May).

Hopkins, E. (1977) 'Decline of family work in nailmaking', *International Review of Social History*, xxii, part 2.

Hopkins, E. (1978a) 'Small town aristocrats', *Economic History Review*, Series II, xxviii.

Hopkins, E. (1978b) 'Working class housing', *Midland History*, iv, no. 3.

Hopkins, E. (1979) *A Social History of the Working Classes*, London.

Hopkins, E. (1982) 'Working hours and conditions during the industrial revolution', *Economic History Review*, 2nd series, xxxv, no. 1 (February).

Hopkins, E. (1983) 'Religious dissent in the Black Country 1800–1850', *Journal of Ecclesiastical History*, xxiv, no. 3 (July).

Hopkins, E. (1984) 'Boulton before Watt: the earlier career reconsidered', *Midland History*, ix.

Horn, P. (1972) 'Warwickshire agricultural union', *Midland History*, i–iv (Autumn).

Hoskins, W. G. (1964) 'Harvest fluctuations in English economic history 1480–1619', *Agricultural History Review*, xii.

Hoskins, W. G. (1968) 'Harvest fluctuations in English economic history 1620–1759', *Agricultural History Review*, xvi.

Hoskins, W. G. (1950) *Provincial England. Essays in Social and Economic History*, Liverpool University Press, Liverpool.

Hoskins, W. G. (1953) 'The rebuilding of rural England 1570–1610', *Past and Present*, 4.

Hoskins, W. G. (1976) *The Age of Plunder. King Henry's England 1500–1547*, Longman, London.

Huffer, D. (1974) 'Wolverhampton to 1850', *West Midlands Studies*, vii.

Hughes, A. (1980) 'Politics, society and civil war in Warwickshire 1620–1650', Liverpool PhD.

Hughes, A. (1982) 'Warwickshire on the eve of the civil war. A county community?', *Midland History*, vii.

Hughes, L. (1980) 'Education in Dudley 1870–1890', *West Midlands Studies*, xiii.

Hurst, M. C. (1962) 'Joseph Chamberlain and west Midlands politics 1886–1895', *Dugdale Society Occasional Publication*, no. 15.

Hurwich, J. (1970) 'Nonconformity in Warwickshire', Princetown PhD.

Hurwich, J. (1977) 'A fanatical town: the politics of dissent in Coventry 1660–1760', *Midland History* Vol. iv. (Spring).

Husbands, C. (1980–1) 'Standards of living in north Warwickshire', *Warwickshire History*, iv, no. 6.

Hutton, T. (1952) *King Edward's School*, Birmingham.

Hutton, W. (1816) *The Life of William Hutton, Stationer of Birmingham*, London.

Hutton, W. (1976) *History of Birmingham 1783*.

Hyde, C. K. (1974) 'Technological change in British wrought iron industry 1750–1815', *Economic History Review*, 2nd series, xvii, no. 2 (May).

Ingram, R. W. (1981) *Records of Early English Drama*, Manchester University Press.

Jack, S. (1977) *Trade and industry in Tudor and Stuart England. Historical problems and documents*, Allen and Unwin, London.

Jay, R. (1981) *Joseph Chamberlain a Political Study*, Oxford University Press, Oxford.

Jeavons, S. A. (1962–3) 'The pattern of ecclesiastical building in Staffordshire during the Norman period', *Lichfield and South Staffordshire Archaeological and History Society Transactions*, iv.

John, E. L. T. (1970) 'The Warwickshire estates of the manor of Pipewell', *Warwickshire History*, 1, no. 3 (Spring).

Johnson, B. L. C. (1950) 'The Stour Valley iron industry in the late seventeenth century', *Transactions of the Worcestershire Archaeological Society*, NS, xxvii.

Johnson, B. L. C. (1951) 'The charcoal iron industry in the early eighteenth century', *Geophysical Journal*, cxvii, 2.

Johnson, B. L. C. (1952) 'The Foley partnerships. The iron industry at the end of the charcoal era', *Economic History Review*, Series 2, iv, no. 3.

Johnson, B. L. C. (1954) 'The iron industry of north Staffordshire', *Transactions of the North Staffordshire Field Club*, lxxxiii.

Johnson, B. L. C. (1960) 'The Midland iron industry', *Business History*, ii.

Johnson, D. A. (1968–9) 'The Dean's statutes for St. Edith's, Tamworth 1442', *Lichfield and South Staffordshire Archaeological and Historical Society*, x.

Johnson, D. A. (1964) *Staffordshire and the Great Rebellion*, Stoke on Trent.

Johnson, F. J. (1964) 'The settlement pattern of north east Staffordshire', University of Wales PhD.

Jones, E. J. T. and Collins, E. L. (1967) 'Sectoral advance in English Agriculture', *Agricultural History Review*, xv.

Jones, G. W. (1969) *Borough Politics 1881–1961*, Macmillan, London.

Jones, J. F. (1940) *History of the Corporation of Birmingham*, Vol. V, Part 1, Birmingham.

Jones, J. I. (1969) 'Licensed coalmining in north Staffordshire', *North Staffordshire Journal of Field Studies*, ix.

Jones, J. M. (1963) 'Local rivers as a source of power', *Birmingham Natural History Society*, xx, no. 2.

Jones, S. R. (1975–6) 'West Bromwich (Staffs) Manor House', *Lichfield and South Staffordshire Archaeological and Historical Society*, xvii.

Jones, S. R. H. (1978) 'The development of needle manufacturing in the west Midlands before 1750', *Economic History Review*, 2nd Series, xxxi, 3 (August).

Jones, W. H. (1903) *Story of the Municipal Life of Wolverhampton*, Wolverhampton.

Jones, Y. (1982) *Georgian and Victorian Japanned Ware of the West Midlands*.

Jordan, W. K. (1959) *Philanthropy in England 1480–1660*, London.

Josephs, Z. (1976–7) 'Mayer Oppenheimer, an eighteenth century Birmingham glass-maker', *Transactions of the Birmingham Archaeological Society*, 88.

Josephs, Z. (1980) *Birmingham Jewry*, Birmingham.

JRSS (1837) Survey of education in West Bromwich, vol. I.

JRSS (1840) Report of the Birmingham Statistical Society, vol. I (April).

Kellett, J. R. (1969) *The Impact of Railways on Victorian Cities*, Routledge Keegan & Paul, London.

Kemp, T. (n.d.) *The Book of John Fisher 1580–88*, Warwick Ms.

Kemp, T. (Trans. and ed.) (1898) *The Black Book of Warwick*, Warwick.

Kent, G. (1959) The Party Politics of Staffordshire 1830–1846, University of Birmingham MA.

Kent, J. R. (1981) 'Population mobility and alms giving', *Local Population Studies*, xxvii.

Kerridge, E. (1967) *The Agricultural Revolution*, Allen & Unwin, London.

Kidd, A. (1949) *History of The Tin Plate Working Society*, London.

Kiernan, R. H. (1950) *The Archdiocese of Birmingham*, Birmingham.

Kimball, E. and Plucknett, T. (1939) 'Warwickshire and Coventry county sessions of the peace 1377–1397', *Dugdale Society*, xvi.

Kingman, M. (1978) 'Marketing in sixteenth century Warwick', *Warwickshire History*, iv (Summer).

Kinvig, R. H. (1967) 'The west Midlands', in Mitchell, J. B. (ed.), *Great Britain: Geographical Essays*, Cambridge.

Kivell, P. T. (1972) 'The changing size and distribution of livestock markets', *North Staffordshire Journal of Field Studies*, xii.

Kivell, P. T. (1975) 'Post war urban residential growth in north Staffordshire', in A. D. M. Philips (ed.), *Environment, Man and Economic Change*, Keele.

Klingelhöfer, E. (1975) 'Evidence of town planning in late Saxon Warwickshire', *Midland History*, iii, no. 1. (Spring).

Kolbert, J. M. (1967) *The Sneyds and Keele Hall*, Keele.

Kolbert, J. M. (1976) *The Sneyds Squires of Keele*, Keele.

Knowles, D. M. (1948, 1955, 1959) *The Religious Orders in England*, 3 vols, Cambridge University Press, Cambridge.

Knowles, D. (1965) *The Monastic Order in England*, Cambridge University Press, Cambridge.

Lamb, A. (1979) 'Mechanisation and the application of steam power in the north Staffordshire pottery industry, 1793–1914', *North Staffordshire Journal of Field Studies*, xvii.

Lamont, W. (1979) *Richard Baxter and the Millennium*, London.

Lane, J. (1971) 'Farm and cottage inventories from Butlers Marston 1546–1755', *Warwickshire History*, 1, no. 5 (Autumn).

Lane, J. (1973) 'Administration of Butlers Marston parish', *Dugdale Society Occasional Paper*, xxi.

Lane, J. (1979) 'Apprenticeship in Warwickshire cotton mills 1790–1830', *Textile History*, x.

Large, M. (1976) *The Nine Days in Birmingham*, Birmingham.

Large, R. (1982) 'Urban growth and agricultural change in the west Midlands during the seventeenth and eighteenth centuries', in Clark, P. (ed.), *The Transformation of English Provincial Towns*, Leicester.

Larminie, V. M. (1980) A Seventeenth Century Gentleman, Newdegate of Arbury, Birmingham PhD.

Larminie, V. M. (1982) 'The godly magistrate', *Dugdale Society Occasional Papers*, 28.

Lawrence, Sister M. (1950) 'St. Mary's Abbey, Croxden', *Transactions of North Staffordshire Field Club*, lxxxv, lxxxviii.

Lawton, R. (1958) 'Population movements in the west Midlands 1841–1861', *Geography*, 42.

Lawton, R. (1967) 'Rural depopulation in nineteenth century England' in Steel, R. W. and Lawton, R. (eds.), *Liverpool Essays in Geography*, Liverpool.

Lead, P. (1977) 'North Staffordshire iron industry 1600–1800', *Journal of Historical Metallurgy Society*, 11/1.

Leadam, I. S. (1984–7) 'The inquest of 1517', *Transactions of the Royal Historical Society*, New Series, viii.

Leadam, I. S. (1899) 'The Domesday of enclosures', 2 vols, *Royal Historical Society*.

Leese, F. E. (n.d.) 'New draperies at Coventry', TS in Coventry Library.

Le Guillou, M. (1972, 1973) 'The south Staffordshire iron and steel industry and the growth of foreign competition 1855–1954', *West Midlands Studies*, pt I no. 5 (1972); pt II, no. 6 (1973).

Le Guillou, M. (1975) 'Freight rates and the Black Country iron trade 1850–1914', *Journal of Transport History*, New Series, iii.

Leland, J. (1911) *Leland's Itinerary*, ed. L. T. Smith, London.

Lewis, R. A. (1949) Two Partnerships of the Knight Family in the Eighteenth Century Charcoal Iron Industry, MA, Birmingham.

Lewis, R. A. (1970) *Staffordshire in Wartime*, Stafford.

Lewis, R. A. (1976) *The Home Guard in Staffordshire*, Stafford (August).

Lewis, R. A. (1983) *Staffordshire Farming*, 2 vols., Stafford (March and November).

Lloyd, H. (1975) *The Quaker Lloyds in The Industrial Revolution*, London.

Lloyd, S. (1907) *The Lloyds of Birmingham*, Birmingham.

Lloyd, T. H. (1961a) 'Stratford buildings, some aspects of the building industry in Stratford upon Avon', *Dugdale Society Occasional Paper*, xiv.

Lloyd, T. H. (1979–80) 'Chartism in Warwick and Leamington', *Warwickshire History*, iv, no. 1.

Lloyd, T. H. (1961b) 'Ploughing services on the demesnes of the Bishop of Worcester in the late thirteenth century', *University of Birmingham Historical Journal*, viii.

Lones, T. E. (1898) *A History of Mining in the Black Country*, Dudley.

Lowe, R. (1970) 'Mechanics institutions in north Staffordshire', *North Staffordshire Journal of Field Studies*, x.

McKendrick, N. (1960) 'Josiah Wedgwood: an eighteenth century entrepreneur in salesmanship and marketing techniques', *Economic History Review*, 2nd Series, xii.

McKendrick, N. (1961) 'Josiah Wedgwood and factory discipline', *The Historical Journal*, iv.

McKendrick, N. (1964) 'Josiah Wedgwood and Thomas Bentley. An inventor, entrepreneur partnership in the industrial revolution', *Transactions of the Royal Historical Society*, 5th Series, xiv.

McKendrick, N. (1970) 'Josiah Wedgwood and cost accounting in the industrial revolution', *Economic History Review*, 2nd Series, xxiii, no. 1 (April).

Mackney, D. and Burnham, L. P. (1964) *The Soils of the Midlands*, Harpenden.

McLeay, P. (1969) 'Wolverhampton Motor Car Industry 1896–1937', *West Midland Studies*, iii.

McLynn, F. J. (1979) 'The West Midlands and the Jacobite rising of 1745', *West Midlands Studies*, xii (Winter).

MacMorran, J. L. (1978) *Municipal Public Works and Planning in Birmingham, 1852–1972* Birmingham.

MacPherson, A. (1946) *Warwickshire: The Land of Britain Series, Part 62*, ed. Stamp, E. D., London.

Maddicott, J. R. (1979) *Thomas of Lancaster*, London.

Mallet, J. (1966, 1977) 'The Baddeleys of Shelton', *Transactions of the English Ceramic Circle*, vi, Part II (1966); Part III (1967).

Mander, G. (1923) *The Wolverhampton Antiquary Vol. 1*, Wolverhampton.

Mander, G. P. (1960) *A History of Wolverhampton*, Wolverhampton.

Mander, J. P. (1913) *History of Wolverhampton Grammar School*, Wolverhampton.

Marshall, W. (1796) *Rural Economy of the Midland Counties*, London, Reprint 1811.

Martin, J. E. (1979) Peasant and Landlord in the Development of Feudalism and the Transition to Capitalism in England, Lancaster PhD.

Martin, J. E. (1982) 'Enclosures and the inquisition of 1607', *Agricultural History Review*, xxx.

Martin, J. M. (1960) 'Social and Economic Trends in Warwickshire 1785–1875', M.Comm. (unpub. thesis), Birmingham.

Martin, J. M. (1967a) 'The cost of parliamentary enclosure in Warwickshire', *University of Birmingham Historical Journal*, ix; reprinted in Jones, E. L. (ed.), *Agricultural and Economic Growth in England 1650–1815*.

Martin, J. M. (1967b) 'The parliamentary enclosure movement and rural society in Warwickshire', *Agricultural History Review*, xv.

Martin, J. M. (1972) 'Marriage and population change in Tudor and Stuart Warwickshire', TS, Warwickshire Record Office.

Martin, J. M. (1973) 'Population and mortality in Tudor and Stuart Warwickshire', TS, Warwickshire Record Office.

Martin, J. M. (1976) 'The growth of population in Warwickshire in the eighteenth century', *Dugdale Society Occasional Paper*, no. 23.

Martin, J. M. (1977a) 'Marriage and economic stress in the felden', *Population Studies*, 31.

Martin, J. M. (1977b) 'Investigation into the small size of the household', *Stratford on Avon Local Population Studies*, xix.

Martin, J. M. (1978) 'The rich, the poor and the immigrant in eighteenth century Stratford', *Local Population Studies*, xx.

Martin, J. M. (1979) 'Parliamentary enclosure and members of Parliament', *Agricultural History Review*, 27.

Martin, J. M. (1981) 'Population, village trades and the emergence of a proletariat in southern Warwickshire', TS.

Martin, J. M. (1981–2) 'The family in the age of early industrialisation', unpublished TS.

Martin, J. M. (1982b) 'A Warwickshire town in adversity', *Stratford on Avon: Midland History*, vii.

Mason, E. (1975) 'The resources of the earldom of Warwick in the thirteenth century', *Midland History*, iii. no. 2 (Autumn).

Mason, F. (1976) *Wolverhampton: The Town Commissioners 1777–1848*, Wolverhampton Library TS.

Mason, F. (1979) *The Book of Wolverhampton. The Story of an Industrial Town*, Wolverhampton.

Mason, T. (1980) *Association Football and English Society*, London.

Mathews, A. G. (1924) *The Congregational Churches of Staffordshire*, London.

Mathews, A. G. (1948) *Walker Revised*, Oxford.

Mathias, P. (1959) *Brewing Industry in England 1700–1830*, London.

Mee, A. (1936–7) *The King's History of England Series* (Staffordshire and Warwickshire vols), London.

Milward, R. and Robinson, A. (1971) *The West Midlands*, London.

Mimardière, A. (1963) 'The Gentry of Warwickshire 1660–1720', Birmingham PhD.

Mimardière, A. (1964) 'A gentry family in Warwickshire', *University of Birmingham Historical Journal*, ix.

Mitchell, J. B. (ed.) (1967) *Great Britain. Geographical Essays*.

Moisley, H. A. (1951a) 'The industrial and urban development of the north Staffordshire conurbation', *Transactions of the Institute of British Geographers*, xvii.

Moisley, H. A. (1951b) 'The economic development of the Potteries coalfield', *Transactions of the Institute of British Geographers*, xvii.

Mole, D. (1979) 'Victorian towns', *Studies in Church History*, Ecclesiastical History Society, xvi.

Mole, O. E. (1976) 'Challenge to the Church, Birmingham 1815–1865', in *The Victorian City*, Vol. II, London.

Money, J. (1971) 'Birmingham politics and regional identity', *Midland History*, i, no. 1 (Spring).

Money, J. J. (1977) *Experience and Identity*, Manchester.

Morgan, P. (1970) 'South Warwickshire clergy in the late seventeenth century', *Warwickshire History*, i, no. 3 (Spring).

Morris, B. J. (1968) 'Catholics in the Diocese of Worcestershire 1676–1835', BA Dissertation, Birmingham.

Morris, G. M. (1969) 'The origins of primitive Methodism in Staffordshire 1800–1812', *North Staffordshire Journal of Field Studies*, ix.

Morris Jones, C. (1970) *Maps of Birmingham*, Birmingham.

Morrish, P. S. (1980) 'The struggle to create an Anglican diocese of Birmingham', *Journal of Ecclesiastical History*, xxxi, no. 1.

391

Morton, G. R. (1964–5) 'The Paget ironworks', *Transactions of the South Stafford-shire Archaeological and Historical Journal*, vi.

Morton, G. R. (1969) 'Alfred Hickman and Company', *West Midlands Studies*, iii.

Morton, G. R. (1972) 'The industrial history of Darlaston', *West Midlands Studies*, v.

Morton, G. R. (1973) 'Wrought iron trade of the West Midlands', *West Midlands Studies*, vi.

Morton, G. R. and Gould, D. J. (1967) 'Little Aston forge 1574–1798', *Journal of the Iron and Steel Institute*, 205.

Morton, G. R. and Mutton, N. (1967) 'The transition to Cort's puddling process', *Journal of the Iron and Steel Institutes*, 205 (July).

Morton, G. and Wanklyn, M. (1968) 'Dudley, a reappraisal', *West Midland Studies*, 1, Wolverhampton.

Moseley, A. F. (1970–1) 'Black Country chainmakers', *West Midlands Studies*, iv.

Mosler, D. F. (1974) A Social and Religious History of the English Civil War in Warwickshire, Stanford University PhD.

Mosler, D. F. (1981) 'The "other Civil War" internecine problems in the Warwickshire County: 1642–1659', *Midland History*, vi.

Moss, D. J. (1978) Thomas Attwood, Thesis PhD, Oxford.

Moss, D. J. (1982) 'The private banks of Birmingham 1800–1827', *Business History*, xxiv (March).

Moss, J. T. (1978) 'Attwood: a study in failure', *Cambridge Historical Journal*, 21, 3.

Moss, J. T. (1981) 'The Bank of England and the country banks', *Economic History Review*, 2nd series, xxiv.

Mountfield, P. R. (1965) 'The glove industry in Staffordshire 1767–1951', *North Staffordshire Journal of Field Studies*, 5.

Moyes, A. (1972) 'Employment change in the north Staffordshire conurbation 1951–1966', *North Staffordshire Journal of Field Studies*, xii.

Moyes, A. (1974) 'Postwar changes in coal mining in the west Midlands', *Geography*, 59.

Moyes, A. (1975) 'Second World War manufacturing and its significance for north Staffordshire', in Philips, A. D. M. (ed.), *Environment, Man and Economic Change*.

Moyes, A. (1979) 'The industrial economy of north Staffordshire in the Second World War', *North Staffordshire Journal of Field Studies*, xix.

Muirhead, J. (1909) *Nine Famous Birmingham Men*, Birmingham.

Muirhead, J. H. (1911) *Birmingham Institutions*, Birmingham.

Murray, A. (1813) *General View of the Agriculture of Warwickshire*, London.

Myers, J. (1946) *Staffordshire 1945, Part 61. Land of Britain Series*, Land Utilisation Survey of Britain, London.

Myers, J. (1952–3) 'Dr. Plot and land utilisation in Staffordshire', *Transactions of the North Staffordshire Field Club*, lxxxiii.

Neale, J. S. (1953, 1957) *Queen Elizabeth I and Her Parliaments*, Jonathan Cape, London.

Nef, J. U. (1932) *The Rise of the British Coal Industry 1540–1640*, London, Reprint 1966.

Nockolds, H. (1976) *Lucas: The First Hundred Years*, Newton Abbot.

Nokes, B. C. G. (1969) 'John English of Feckenham, needle manufacturer', *Business History*, xi, no. 1 (January).

Norris, J. (1957) 'Sam Garbett and political lobbying', *Economic History Review Series 2*, x.

O'Day, R. (1972) 'Thomas Bentham: A case study in the problems of the early Elizabethan episcopate', *Journal of Ecclesiastical History*, xxiii.

O'Day, R. (1975) 'Cumulative debt. The Bishops of Coventry and Lichfield and their economic problems', *Midland History*, iii, no. 2 (Autumn).

O'Day, R. (1979) *The English Clergy. The Emergence and Consolidation of a Profession 1558–1642*, Leicester University Press, Leicester.

O'Day, R. and Belatsky, J. (1979) 'The Letter Book of Thomas Bentham, Bishop of Coventry and Lichfield 1560–61', Camden Miscellany XXVII, *Camden Society 4th Series*, xxii.

Orpen, P. K. (1979) 'Recruitment patterns of the school master in seventeenth century Warwickshire', *Warwickshire History*, iv, no. 3 (Summer).

Owen, C. C. (1978) *The Development of Industry in Burton on Trent*, Phillimore, Chichester.

Owen, H. (1901) *The Staffordshire Potter*, Stafford, Reprint 1970.

Padley, R. (1951) 'The beginnings of the English alkali industry', *University of Birmingham Historical Journal*, iii.

Page, C. and Page, R. (1977) 'The enclosure of Snitterfields', *Warwickshire History*, iii, no. 6.

Palliser, D. (1963) 'The boroughs of medieval Staffordshire', *North Staffordshire Journal of Field Studies*, xii.

Palliser, D. M. (1973) 'Newcastle under Lyme and the alleged charter of 1173', *North Staffordshire Journal of Field Studies*, xiii.

Palliser, D. (1976) 'Dearth and disease in Staffordshire 1540–1670' in Chalkin and Havinden (eds.), *Rural Change and Urban Growth*.

Palliser, D. (1976) *Evolution of the Staffordshire Landscape*, Hodder and Stoughton, London.

Palliser, D. (1982) 'Brave new world or Malthusian trap?', *Economic History Review*, 2nd Series, xxv, no. 3 (August).

Palliser, D. M. (1983) *The Age of Elizabeth: England under the Later Tudors 1547–1603*, Longman, London.

Palliser, D. and Pinnock, A. C. (1970–1) 'Markets of medieval Staffordshire', *North Staffordshire Journal of Field Studies*, xi.

Pape, T. (1928) *Mediaeval Newcastle under Lyme*, Manchester.

Pape, T. (1938) *Newcastle under Lyme, Tudor and Stuart Times*, Manchester.

Pape, T. (1940) *Restoration Government and the Corporation of Newcastle under Lyme*, William Salt Library typescript.

Pearce, C. (1980) *The Machinery of Change in Local Government 1888–1974*, Allen and Unwin, for the Institute of Local Government Studies, Birmingham.

Pelham, R. A. (1937) 'The immigrant population of Birmingham 1686–1720', *Transactions of the Birmingham Archaeological Society*, Vol. lxi.

Pelham, R. A. (1939a) 'The early wool trade in Warwickshire and the rise of the merchant middle class', *Transactions of the Birmingham Archaeological Society*, lxiii.

Pelham, R. A. (1939b) 'The trade relations of Birmingham during the middle ages', *Transactions of the Birmingham Archaeological Society*, lxii.

Pelham, R. A. (1943) 'Migration of the iron industry towards Birmingham', *Transactions of the Birmingham Archaeological Society*, lxvi.

Pelham, R. A. (1945) 'Cloth markets of Warwickshire', *Transactions of the Birmingham and Warwickshire Archaeological Society*, 66.

Pelham, R. (1951) 'Crop returns for Staffordshire 1801', *Staffordshire Historical Collections*.

Pelham, R. (1952) 'Crop returns for Warwickshire', *Transactions of the Birmingham Archaeological Society*, lxviii.

Pelham, R. A. (1953) 'The establishment of the Willoughby ironworks in north Warwickshire in the sixteenth century', *University of Birmingham Historical Journal*, iv.

Pelham, R. A. (1963) 'The water power crisis of Birmingham in the eighteenth century', *University of Birmingham Historical Journal*, ix, i.

Pelling, H. (1967) *The Social Geography of British Elections 1855–1910*, Macmillan.

Penn, V. F. (1963–4) 'Lower Farm, Bloxwich, Staffordshire', *Lichfield and South Staffordshire Archaeological and Historical Society*, v.

Pennington, D. H. and Rootes, I. A. (1957) *The Committee at Stafford 1643–5*, SHC 4th Series, vol. I.

Pennington, D. H. (1966) 'Staffordshire in civil war politics', *North Staffordshire Journal of Field Studies*, vi.

Penny, R. I. (1971) 'Board of Health in Victorian Stratford', *Warwickshire History*, 1/6 (Autumn).

Perren, R. (1971) 'The land law and agricultural transformation 1870–1900', *Agricultural History Review*, xviii, i.

Pevsner, N. (1974) *Staffordshire. The Buildings of England*, Penguin, London.

Phillips, A. D. M. (1973) 'A study of farming practice and soil types in Staffordshire 1840', *North Staffordshire Journal of Field Studies*, xiii.

Phillips, A. D. M. (1975) 'Underdraining and agricultural investment' in A. D. M. Phillips (ed.), *Environment, Man and Economic Change*.

Phillips, A. D. M. (1979) 'A note on farm size and efficiency on the north Staffordshire estates of the Leveson Gowers 1914–1809', *North Staffordshire Journal of Field Studies*, xix.

Phillips, A. D. M. and Turton, B. (1975) *Environment and Economic Change*, London.

Philips, D. (1974) 'Riots and public order in the Black Country 1835–1860' in Quinalt, R. and Stevenson, J. (eds.) *Popular Protest and Public Order. Six Studies in British History 1790–1920*, Allen and Unwin, London.

Philips, D. (1975) 'Black Country magistracy', *Midland History*, iii, no. 3.

Philips, D. (1977) *Crime and Authority in Victorian England. The Black Country 1835–60*, Croom Helm, London.

Phythian-Adams, C. (1972) 'Ceremony and the citizen. The communal year at Coventry 1450–1550' in Clark, P. and Slack, P. (eds.) *Crisis and Order in English Towns*, Routledge and Kegan Paul, London.

Phythian-Adams, C. (1978) 'Urban decay in late medieval England' in Abrams, P. and Wrigley, E. (eds) *Towns in Societies*, Cambridge University Press, Cambridge.

Phythian-Adams, C. (1979) *Desolation of a City. Coventry and the Urban Crisis of the Late Middle Ages*, Cambridge.

Pinnock, A. C. (1971) Population and Property 1086–1539, unpublished MA Thesis, Keele.

Pinnock, A. C. (1974) 'Medieval population and prosperity of Staffordshire', *North Staffordshire Journal of Field Studies*, xiv.

Pitt, W. (1796) *Agriculture of Staffordshire*, Newcastle under Lyme.

Pitt, W. (1817) *A Topographical History of Staffordshire*, Newcastle under Lyme.

Plaister, J. (trans.) (1976) *Domesday Warwickshire*, Phillimore, Chichester.

Plot, R. (1686) *The Natural History of Staffordshire*, Oxford, Reprint (1973), Wakefield East Ardesley.

Pocock, T. (1888–9) *Travels Through England During 1750, 1751 and Later Years*, 2 vols, Camden Society, 42 (1888–9), (1889).

Poole, B. (1869) *Coventry, Its History and Antiquities*, Taunton.

Porter, S. (1976) 'Fires in Stratford on Avon in the sixteenth and seventeenth centuries', *Warwickshire History*, iii, no. 3 (Summer).

Pound, J. F. (1962) 'An Elizabethan census of the poor', *University of Birmingham Historical Journal*, viii, no. 2.

Prest, J. (1960) *The Industrial Revolution in Coventry*, Oxford University Press, Oxford.

Prosser, R. (1881) *Birmingham Inventors and Inventions*, Birmingham.

Prosser, R. (1951) Coventry: A Study in Urban Continuity, Birmingham MA.

Proudfoot, L. J. (1982) 'Parochial benefices in late medieval Warwickshire, 1291–1535' in Slater, T. R. (ed.), *Field and Forest*, Norwich.

Quinault, R. (1974) 'The Warwickshire County Magistracy and Public Order 1830–1870' in Stevenson, J. and Quinault, R. (eds) *Popular Protest and Public Order*, Allen & Unwin, London.

Radford, C. A. R. (1940) 'Dudley Priory', *Antiquaries Journal*, xx.

Rawcliffe, C. (1978) *The Staffords, Earls of Stafford and Dukes of Buckingham 1394–1521*, Cambridge.

Raybould, T. J. (1968a) 'The development and organisation of Lord Dudley's mineral estates', *Economic History Review*, 2nd Series, xxi.

Raybould, T. J. (1968b) 'System of management and administration on the Dudley estates 1774–1833', *Business History*, **10**.

Raybould, T. J. (1973a) *The Economic Emergence of the Black Country. A Study of the Dudley Estates*, Wolverhampton Polytechnic.

Raybould, T. J. (1973b) 'Charles Beaumont and the organisation of mineral enterprise on Lord Dudley's estate', *West Midlands Studies*, vi.

Raybould, T. J. (1984) 'Aristocratic landowners and the Industrial Revolution', *Midland History*, ix.

Razi, Z. (1980) *Life, Death and Marriage in a Medieval Parish*, Cambridge University Press, Cambridge.

Razi, Z. (1981) 'Family land and the village community', *Past and Present,* **93**.

Razi, Z. (1983) 'The struggles between the Abbot of Halesowen and his tenants', *Past and Present*, **95**.

Redmell, C. E. (1931) 'Population in the east Warwickshire coalfield', *Geography*, xvi.

Rhys, D. G. (1972) *The Motor Industry*, London.

Richards, E. (1964) 'Mathew Boulton and the art of political lobbying', *Historical Journal*, vii.

Richards, E. (1973) *The Leviathan of Wealth. The Sutherland Fortune in the Industrial Revolution*, London.

Richards, E. (1974a) 'The industrial face of a great estate', *Economic History Review*, xxvii, 2nd Series, no. 3.

Richards, E. (1974b) 'Leviathan of wealth: west Midlands agriculture 1800–1850', *Agricultural History Review*, **22.**

Richards, E. (1975a) 'The political interest of Trentham', *Midland History*, iii (Autumn).

Richards, E. (1975b) 'Social and electoral change on the Leveson Gower estates 1800–1860', *Midland History*, Vol. III, no. 2.

Richards, E. (1979) 'An anatomy of the Sutherland fortune. Income, consumption, investment and returns 1780–1880', *Business History*, xxi, no. 1.

Richardson, K. (1972) *Twentieth Century Coventry*, Macmillan, London.

Roberts, B. K. (1965) 'Settlement Land Use and Population 1086–1350', Birmingham PhD.

Roberts, B. K. (1968) 'A study of medieval colonisation on the Forest of Arden, Warwickshire', *Agricultural History Review*, xvi.

Roberts, B. K. (1975) 'The historical geography of moated homesteads in the Forest of Arden', *Birmingham and Warwickshire Archaeological Society*, lxxxviii.

Roberts, B. K. (1982) 'Village forms in Warwickshire' in Slater, T. R. and Jarvis, P. (eds), *Field and Forest*, Norwich.

Roberts, F. (1963) 'The Society of Jesus in Staffordshire', *Staffordshire Catholic History*, no. 3 (Spring).

Roberts, S. (1982) 'Politics and the Birmingham working class', *West Midlands Studies*, 15 (Winter).

Roberts, S. (1983) 'Independent Labour politics in Birmingham 1886–1914', *West Midlands Studies*, xvi (Winter).

Robey, J. A. and Porter, L. (1972) *The Copper and Lead Mines of Echon Hill*, Leek.

Robinson, E. (1959) 'The Boulton and Fothergill manufactory', *University of Birmingham Historical Journal*, vii, no. 1.

Robinson, E. (1965–6) 'Eighteenth century commerce and fashion', *Economic History Review*, 2nd Series, xvi.

Robinson, G. M. (1978) 'Components of Change in Agricultural Activity in the Midlands', M.Phil., Oxford.

Robinson, H. (1560) *Zurich Letters*, Parker Society 1842, 1st Series, ed. H. Robinson, Letter XXXV, 10 July.

Robson, G. (1978) 'Working class evangelists in early Victorian Birmingham', *Studies in Church History Ecclesiastical History Society*, xv, ed. D. Baker.

Robson, G. (1979a) 'Between town and countryside – contrasting patterns of churchgoing', *Studies in Church History*, xvi.

Robson, G. (1979b) 'The Victorian Black Country', *Studies in Church History Ecclesiastical History Society*, xvi.

Rodgers, A. *et al.* (1972) *Regional Development in Britain*, John Wiley, London.

Roll, E. (1930) *An Early Experiment in Industrial Organisation*, London.

Rolt, L. T. C. and Allen, J. (1977) *The Steam Engine of Thomas Newcomen*, Moorland, Hartington.

Roper, J. S. (1960a) 'Sedgley probate inventories 1614–1787', Sedgley TS.

Roper, J. S. (1960b) 'Wolverhampton Constables Accounts 1688–1714', *Wolverhampton TS*.

Roper, J. S. (1963) *Dudley. The Town in the Sixteenth Century*, Dudley.

Roper, J. S. (ed.) (1966a) *Dudley Probate Inventories*, 2nd Series, Dudley.

Roper, J. S. (1966b) *The Wolverhampton Town and Its Early History*, Wolverhampton.

Roper, J. S. (1962, 1968) *Dudley the Medieval Town*, Dudley.

Roper, J. S. (1969) 'Early north Worcestershire scythesmiths', *West Midlands Studies*, iii, Wolverhampton.

Roper, J. S. (1980) *The Churchwardens' Book of St Thomas, Dudley, Worcestershire 1618–1725*, Dudley.

Rose, R. B. (1965) 'Origins of working class radicalism in Birmingham', *Journal of Labour History*, iv (November), Canberra, Australia.

Rose, R. B. (1969) 'The Priestley riots', *Past and Present*, xviii.

Ross, C. D. (1951) 'The household accounts of Elizabeth Berkeley, Countess of Warwick 1420–1', *Transactions of the Bristol and Gloucestershire Archaeological Society*, lxx.

Ross, C. D. (1956) 'Estates and finances of Richard Beauchamp, Earl of Warwick', *Dugdale Society Occasional Paper*, 12.

Rowlands, M. B. (1965) 'Catholics in Staffordshire 1688–1791', MA, Birmingham.

Rowlands, M. B. (1965–7) 'Houses and people in Stafford in the seventeenth century', *The Stafford Historical and Civic Society, Transactions*.

Rowlands, M. B. (1967–8) 'Industry and social change in Staffordshire 1660–1760', *Lichfield and South Staffordshire Archaeological and Historical Society Transactions*, ix.

Rowlands, M. B. (1968–9) 'Stonier Parrott and the Newcomen engine', *Transactions of the Newcomen Society*, xli.

Rowlands, M. B. (1975) *Masters and Men in the Small Metalware Trades of the West Midlands*, Manchester University Press, Manchester.

Rowlands, M. (1977) 'Society and industry 1700', *Midland History*, iv, no. 1 (Spring).

Rowley, J. (1975) 'Adult education in Wolverhampton', *West Midlands Studies*, viii.

Rowney, I. (1983) 'Government and patronage in fifteenth century Staffordshire 1434–1459', *Midland History*, viii.

Rowney, I. (1984) 'The Hastings affinity in Staffordshire and the honour of Tutbury', *Bulletin of the Institute of Historical Research*.

Rowse, A. L. (1962) *Ralegh and the Throckmortons*, London.

Royal Commission on Historical Manuscripts (1974) *Papers of John Smythe of Bristol, Merchant 1538–1550*, London.

SHC (1880) Wrottesley, G. (ed.). Exchequer Subsidy Rolls for Staffordshire 1327, Vol. 1.

SHC (1884a) Wrottesley, G. (ed.). Hundred Rolls of Seisdon, 1255. The Staffordshire Hundred Rolls (Seisden 1255 and part of Totmanslow 1275), Vol. 1.

SHC (1884b) The Pleas of the Forest; Kings Henry III and Edward I. Vol. V, pt. I.

SHC (1886b) Wrottesley, G. (ed.). The Exchequer Subsidy Roll of 1327. Staffordshire Historical Collection, Vol. VII, pt. I.

SHC (1888) The Barons of Dudley Graisebrook H.S. Stafford, Vol. IX, pt. II.

SHC (1889) Wrottesley, G. (ed.). The Subsidy Roll of 6 Edward III, AD 1332–3, Vol. X, pt. I.

SHC (1896) Wrottesley, G. (ed.). Poll Tax 1379–81. Offlow and Cuttleshore, Vol. XVII.

SHC (1902) The Giffards from the Conquest to the present time, New series, Vol. V.

SHC (1903a) Extracts from the Plea Rolls of Edward IV, Edward V and Richard III. New series, Vol. VI, pt. I.

SHC (1903b) Wrottesley, G. (ed.). A history of the family of Wrottesley of Wrottesley Co. Stafford. New series, Vol. VI, pt. II.

SHC (1907a) Wrottesley, G. (ed.). The forest tenures of Staffordshire. New series 1907, pt. I.

SHC (1907b) Boyd, W. (ed.). Staffordshire suits in the court of Star Chamber, t. Henry VII and Henry VIII. New series, Vol. X, pt. I.

SHC (1908) Wrottesley, G. (ed.). A history of the Bagot family. New series, Vol. XI.

SHC (1913) Inquisitiones post mortem ad quod damuum etc., Staffordshire, ed. Wedgwood, J.C. 3rd Series, III, Stafford.

SHC (1915, 1916) Staffordshire incumbents and parochial records 1530–1680, London, W.S. Staffordshire Record Society, 3rd Series.

SHC (1917, 1920–2, 1933) Wedgwood, J. C. (ed.). Staffordshire Parliamentary History from Earliest Times to the Present Day, 3rd Series, Vol. I, 1213–1603 (1917); Vol. II, 1603–1780 (1920–2); Vol. III, 1780–1841 (1933).

SHC (1923, 1924) Gregan, E. (ed.). Lay Subsidy 256/31 Hearth Tax Returns for Seisdon and Offlow Hundreds 1666, 3rd Series.

SHC (1929–40) The Staffordshire Quarter Sessions Rolls, Burne, S. A. (1927) 1929, (1929) 1931, (1932) 1933, (1934 pt. 2) 1935, (1935) 1936, (1940) 1940.

SHC (1931, 1933) Thomas, H. R., 'Enclosure of the open fields of Staffordshire', Staffordshire Historical Collections.

SHC (1934, 1935) Thomas, A. L. 'Geographical aspects of the development of transport and communication affecting the pottery industry in north Staffordshire during the eighteenth century', Stafford.

SHC (1921–36) 1921 Lay Subsidy Hearth Tax Pirehill; 1923 Lay Subsidy Hearth Tax Seisdon; 1925 Lay Subsidy Totmanslow Offlow; 1927 Cuttlestone; 1936 Lichfield.

SHC (1936) Cutlack, S. A. (ed.). 'Gnosall Poor Law Records 1679–1837'. Staffordshire Historical Collection, 3rd Series.

SHC (1939) A. L. Browne (ed.). 'The Proposed Repeal of the Penal Laws and Test Acts', 3rd Series.

SHC (1957) Pennington, D. H. and Roots, I. A. (eds). The Committee at Stafford 1643–45, 4th Series, Vol. I.

SHC (1958) Kidson, R. M. (ed.). The Gentry of Staffordshire 1662–1663, 4th Series. Vol. II.

SHC (1960) Donaldson, B. (ed.). The Registrations of Dissenting Chapels 1689–1852, 4th Series, Vol. III.

SHC (1969) Vaisey, D. G. (ed.). Probate Inventories of Lichfield and District, 4th Series, Vol. V.

SHC (1970) Greenlade, M. (ed.). Poll Tax Returns, Lichfield 1377, 4th Series, Vol. VI.

SHC (1973) Heath, P. (ed.). Bishop Geoffrey Blythe's Visitation. Staffordshire Record Society, 4th Series, Vol. VII.

SHC (1979) Petti, A. (ed.). Roman Catholicism in Elizabethan and Jacobean Staffordshire. Staffordshire Historical Collections, 4th Series, Vol. IX.

SHC (1980) Robinson, D. Visitation of the Archdeaconry of Stafford 1829–1841, Staffordshire Record Society, 4th Series, Vol. X.

Salter, J. L. (1975) 'Warwickshire Clergy 1660–1714', Dissertation, MA, Birmingham.

Salter, J. (1977) 'Wills and inventories of the Warwickshire clergy 1660–1720', *Warwickshire History*, iii, No. 3.

Savage, D. and Fripp, T. (1924, 1926, 1929) 'Minutes of the borough of Stratford on Avon', *Dugdale Society*, i and ii (1924); iii (1926); iv (1929), Oxford University Press, Oxford.

Saville, G. E. (1973) *Kings Coughton*, Kineton.

Sawyer, P. (1979) *English Medieval Settlement*, Arnold, London.

Schafer, R. G. (1971) 'Genesis and structure of the Foley ironworks in partnership of 1692', *Business History*, xiii.

Schafer, R. G. (1978) 'Records of Philip Foley's Stour Valley ironworks 1668–1674', *Worcestershire Historical Society*, New series, ix.

Scholfield, R. (1963) *Lunar Society of Birmingham*, Oxford.

Schubert, H. R. (1957) *The History of the British Iron and Steel Industry 450 BC to 1775*, London.

Scrivenor, H. (1854) *History of the Iron Trade*, London.

Searby, P. (1964) *Coventry Politics in the Age of the Chartists*, Coventry.

Searby, P. (1976) 'Watchmaking in Coventry', *Warwickshire History*, Vol. III, no. 3. (Summer).

Searby, P. (1976–7) 'Local Government in Coventry. Progress and the parish pump', *Transactions of the Birmingham and Warwickshire Archaeological Society*, 88.

Searby, P. (1977a) *Coventry in Crisis, 1858–1863*, Coventry.

Searby, P. (1977b) 'Chartists and Freemen in Coventry', *Journal of Social History*.

Searby, P. (1977c) 'Relief of the poor in Coventry 1830–1863', *Historical Journal*, xx.

Searby, P. (1977d) 'Paternalism and Reform', *International Review of Social History*, xxii, pt. 2.

Sedgley Parish Register (1940) Transcribed by Thomas, H. R., *Staffordshire Parish Register Society*.

Shaw, M. (1979) 'Life in Wolverhampton 1841–71', *West Midland Studies*, xii.

Shaw, M. (1981) 'Individual behaviour and social change. The Irish in nineteenth century Wolverhampton', *West Midland Studies*, xiv (Winter).

Shaw, S. (1798, 1801) *The History and Antiquities of the County of Stafford*, 2 vols.

Shaw, S. (1829) *History of the Staffordshire Potteries*, Hanley, Reprint 1970.

Sheaill, J. D. B. (1968) The Regional Distribution of Wealth in England as Indicated by the 1524/5 Subsidy Roll, PhD, London.

Sheaill, J. D. B. (1972) 'The distribution of taxable population and wealth in England during the sixteenth century', *Transactions of the Institute of British Geographers*, iv.

Sherlock, R. (1976) *The Industrial Archaeology of Staffordshire*, David and Charles, Newton Abbot.

Sherwood, R. E. (1974) *Civil Strife in the Midlands*, London.

Sibree, J. and Caston, M. (1855) *Independency in Warwickshire*, Coventry.

Simms, T. H. (1949) *Rise of a Midland Town: Rugby 1800–1900*, Rugby.

Sketchley, J. (1767) *Directory of Trades*, Birmingham.

Sketchley, J. (1785) *Directory of Trades*, Birmingham.

Skipp, V. (1960) *Discovering Sheldon*, Birmingham.
Skipp, V. and Hastings, R. P. (1963) *Discovering Bickenhill, Birmingham.*
Skipp, V. H. T. (1970a) 'Economic and social change in the Forest of Arden 1530–1649', in Thirsk, J. (ed.), *Land, Church and People: Essays Presented to Professor H. P. R. Finberg, Agricultural History Review*, xviii, Supplement.
Skipp, V. (1970b) *Medieval Yardley*, Birmingham.
Skipp, V. (1978) *Crisis and Development. An Ecological Case Study of the Forest of Arden 1570–1674*, Cambridge.
Skipp, V. (1979) 'Smallpox at Solihull', TS, privately communicated (April).
Skipp, V. (1980) 'Chronological analysis of the 1727 demographic crisis at Solihull and Yardley', TS (August).
Skipp, V. (1981a) 'Epidemic and dearth mortality at Solihull 1680–1719', TS (April).
Skipp, V. (1981b) 'The evolution of settlement and Open Field Topography in North Arden down to 1300', in Rowley, T. (ed.), *The Origin of Open Field Agriculture*, Croom Helm, London.
Slater, T. R. (1977) 'Landscape parks and the farm of small towns in Great Britain', *Transactions of the Institute of British Geographers*, NS. 2.
Slater, T. R. (1978) 'Family, society and the ornamental villa', *The Journal of Historical Geography*, iv, no. II.
Slater, T. R. (1981) *A History of Warwickshire*, Phillimore, London and Chichester.
Slater, T. R. (1982a) *Preservation, Conservation and Planning in Historic Towns*, Birmingham University Working Paper Series no. 17.
Slater, T. R. (1982b) 'Urban genesis and medieval town plans in Warwickshire and Worcestershire', in Slater (ed.), *Field and Forest*, Norwich.
Slater, T. R. (1983) 'The origins of Warwick', *Midland History*, viii.
Slater, T. R. and Jarvis, P. (1982) *Field and Forest – An Historical Geography of Warwickshire and Worcestershire*, Norwich.
Slater, T. R. and Wilson, C. (1977) *Archaeology and Development in Stratford on Avon*, Birmingham.
Sleigh, J. (1883) *History of Leek,* Leek.
Smith, B. M. D. (1967) 'The Galtons of Birmingham', *Business History*, ix, no. 2.
Smith, C. J. (1951) 'Population movements 1851', *Geographical Journal*, **117**.
Smith, D. (1982) *Conflict and Compromise 1830–1914*, Routledge and Kegan Paul, London.
Smith, F. (1946) *Coventry 600 Years of Municipal Life*, Coventry.
Smith, K. (1975) 'Warwickshire apprentices and their masters 1710–1760', *Dugdale Society*, xxix, Oxford.
Smith, R. C. (1967) 'Sir Francis Willoughby's iron works 1570–1610', *Renaissance and Modern Studies*, xi.
Smith, T. (1846) *A Miners Guide*, London.
Smith, T. S. (1979) 'The persecution of Staffordshire Roman Catholic recusants 1625–40', *Journal of Ecclesiastical History*, xxx.
Smith, W. A. (1967) 'The town commissioners in Wolverhampton 1777–1848', *West Midlands Studies*, i (December).
Smith, W. A. (1970–1) 'The contribution of the Gibbons family to technical development in the iron and coal industries', *West Midlands Studies*, iv.
Smith, W. A. J. (1972) 'John Wilkinson and the industrial revolution in south Staffordshire', *West Midlands Studies*, v. (Summer).

Smith, W. A. (1978) 'Combinations of ironmasters in the west Midlands during the industrial revolution', *West Midlands Studies*, xi.

Speake, R. (1971) 'The historical demography of the ancient parish of Audley 1538–1800', *North Staffordshire Journal of Field Studies*, XI, ii.

Spufford, P. and M. (1964) *Eccleshall*, Keele.

Stanley, M. J. (1982) 'Medieval tax returns as source material', in Slater, T. R. (ed.), *Field and Forest*, Norwich.

Stapleton, A. C. (1892) *The Chetwynds of Ingestre*, Stafford.

Steven, M. (1968) 'Political parties and local government in Burton on Trent 1966', *North Staffordshire Journal of Field Studies*, viii.

Stevenson, J. and Quinalt, R. (eds) (1982) *Popular Protest and Public Order. Six Studies in British History 1790–1920*, Allen & Unwin.

Stroud, D. (1950) *Capability Brown*, Faber, Reprint 1975.

Strype, J. (1709) *Annals of the Reformation*, London.

Sturgess, R. W. (1960) 'Agricultural change in Staffordshire 1780–1850', *North Staffordshire Journal of Field Studies*.

Sturgess, R. W. (1965) The Response of Agriculture in Staffordshire to the Price Changes of the Nineteenth Century, PhD, Manchester.

Sturgess, R. W. (1966) 'Revolution on the clays', *Agricultural History Review*, xiv, pt. II.

Sturgess, R. W. (1971) 'Land ownership and mining in nineteenth century Staffordshire', in Ward, J. T. and Wilson, R. G. (eds), *Land and Industry*, David & Charles, Newton Abbot.

Styles, D. (1969) 'St. Mary's Warwick', *Dugdale Society*, xxvi.

Styles, P. (1934) 'The development of county administration in the late eighteenth and early nineteenth centuries illustrated by records of the Warwickshire court of quarter sessions 1773–1837', *Dugdale Society Occasional Papers*, no. 4, Warwick.

Styles, P. (1936) 'The corporation of Warwick 1660–1835', *Transactions of the Birmingham Archaeological Society*, lix.

Styles, P. M. (1949) 'A seventeenth century Warwickshire clergyman, Thomas Pilkington, Vicar of Claverdon', *Transactions of the Birmingham Archaeological Society*, lxv, Reprint 1978.

Styles, P. (1951) 'A census of a Warwickshire village in 1698', *University of Birmingham Historical Journal*, iii.

Styles, P. M. (1962) 'The social structure of Kineton Hundred', *Birmingham Archaeological Society Transactions*, lxxviii.

Styles, P. M. (1963) 'The evolution of the law of settlement', *University of Birmingham Historical Journal*, ix, pp. 33–63.

Sutcliffe, A. (1974a) *History of Birmingham, Vol. III*, Birmingham.

Sutcliffe, A. (1974b) *Multistorey Living. The British Working Class.*

Sutton, J. (1967) *The Battle of Hapton Heath*, Stafford.

Sutcliffe, A. (1974b) *Multistorey Living. The British Working Class Experience*, Croom Helm, London.

Sutton, J. (1967) *The Battle of Hapton Heath*, Stafford.

Swift, R. E. (1980) 'Crime and ethnicity. The Irish in Wolverhampton', *West Midland Studies*, xiii.

Tann, J. (1974) 'Suppliers of parts for the Boulton and Watt steam engines 1775–1795', *Transactions of the Birmingham Archaeological Society*, **86**.

Tann, J. (1976) *The Development of the Factory*, Cronmarket, London.

Tann, J. (1978a) 'Boulton and Watt's organisation of steam engine production before the opening of Soho Foundry', *Transactions of the Newcomen Society*.

Tann, J. (1978b) 'Marketing methods in the international market', *Journal of Economic History*, xxxviii.

Tann, J. (1980) 'Makers of improved Newcomen engines', *Transactions of the Newcomen Society*, **1**.

Tann, J. (1981a) 'Mr. Hornblower and his crew', *Transactions of the Newcomen Society*, li.

Tann, J. (1981b) *Papers of Boulton and Watt. Vol. I. The Steam Engine Partnership 1775–1825*, Diploma Press.

Tann, J. and Breckin, M. J. (1978) 'The international diffusion of the Watt engine', *Economic History Review*, 2nd series, **31**.

Tate, W. E. (1949) 'Enclosure acts and awards relating to Warwickshire', *Transactions of the Birmingham Archaeological Society*, lxv (1943–4).

Tate, W. E. (1967) *The English Village Community and the Enclosure Movement*, Gollancz, London.

Taylor, A. F. (1955) Birmingham School Board 1870–1903, Birmingham MA.

Taylor, A. T. (1960) 'Subcontracting system in the British coal industry', in Presnell, L. S. (ed.), *Essays presented to T. S. Ashton. The Industrial Revolution*, London.

Taylor, C. C. (1968–9) 'The origins of Lichfield', *Lichfield and South Staffordshire Archaeological and Historical Society*, x.

Taylor, E. (1972a) 'A craft society in the age of general unions', *West Midland Studies*, v.

Taylor, E. (1972b) 'Midland County Trades Federation', *Midland History*, i, no. 3.

Taylor, E. (1974) 'Working class merchants in the Black Country 1863–1914', Keele PhD.

Templeman, G. (1948) 'The sheriffs of Warwickshire in the thirteenth century', *Dugdale Society Occasional Paper*, 7, Oxford.

Tennant, A. J. (1977) Brailes. A Feldon Community, Leicester MPhil.

Thirsk, J. (1964) 'The Common Fields', *Past and Present*, **29**.

Thirsk, J. (ed.) (1967) *Agrarian History of England and Wales, Vol. IV 1500–1640*, Cambridge University Press, Cambridge.

Thirsk, J. (1969) 'Horn and thorn in Staffordshire: the economy of a pastoral county, *North Staffordshire Journal of Field Studies*, ix, 1–16.

Thirsk, J. (1970) 'Seventeenth century agricultural and social change', in Thirsk, J., *Land, Church and People*, Reading Museum of English Rural Life.

Thirsk, J. (1978) *Economic Policies and Projects*, Oxford.

Thirsk, J. (1984) *Agrarian History of England and Wales*, Vol. V, Cambridge University Press.

Tholfsenn, T. (1953–4) 'Artisans in Victorian Birmingham', *University of Birmingham Historical Journal*, iv.

Thomas, J. (1936–7) 'Josiah Wedgwood as a pioneer of steam power', *Transactions of the Newcomen Society*, **17**.

Thomas, J. (1937) 'The pottery industry and the industrial revolution', *Economic History*, vii.

Thomas, J. (1971) *The Rise of the Staffordshire Potteries*, Adams and Dart, Bath.

Thompson, F. L. M. (1963) *English Landed Society in the Nineteenth Century*, London.

Thorpe, H. (1954) 'Lichfield: a study of its growth and function', *Collections for a History of Staffordshire 1950 & 1951*, Kendal.

Thorpe, H. (1965) 'The lord and the landscape', *Transactions of the Birmingham Archaeological Society*, lxxx.

Thorpe, H. (1971) 'The evolution of settlement and land use in Warwickshire', in Cadbury, D., Hawkes, J. and Radlett, R. (eds), *A Computer Mapped Flora: A Study of the County of Warwickshire*, London.

Timmins, S. (1865) *The Resources, Products and Industrial History of Birmingham and the Midland Hardware District*, Birmingham, Reprint Cass, 1967.

Titow, J. Z. (1969) *English Rural Society*, Allen & Unwin, London.

Tonks, J. (1978) The Lyttletons of Frankley 1540–1640, MLitt.

Torrington, J. B. (5th Viscount) (1934–8) *The Torrington Diaries Containing Tours Through England and Wales 1781 and 1794*, 4 vols, Andrews, C. B. (ed.), London.

Toulmin-Smith, L. (1871) 'Men and names of Birmingham in 1482', *Transactions of the Birmingham Archaeological Society*, Vol. 1, 1870, Birmingham.

Trainor, R. (1982) 'Peers on an industrial frontier' in Cannadine, D. (ed.), *Patricians, Power and Politics in Nineteenth Century Towns*, Leicester.

Treadwell, J. M. (1974) 'William Wood and the company of ironmasters', *Business History*, xvi, no. 2 (July).

Tucker, D. G. (1977) 'Electricity generating stations for public supply in the west Midlands 1880 (1977', *West Midlands Studies*, x (Winter).

Tunsiri, V. (1964) Party Politics of the Black Country and Neighbourhood, 1832–1867, MA Thesis, Birmingham.

Tyack, G. C. (1970) Country Houses in Warwickshire, 1650–1800, BLitt, Oxford.

Underhill, E. A. (1941) *The Ancient Manor of Sedgley*, Sedgley.

Vance, J. E. (1967) 'Housing the worker', *Economic Geographer*, xliii.

Valor Ecclesiasticus (1810–34) A valuation of all ecclesiastical preferments in England and Wales, 6 vols (Commission on the Public Records of the Kingdom), London. Originally drawn up in 1535.

Varnom, M. S. (1980) 'The Crown and local government under Richard II', *Warwickshire History*, iv, no. 5 (Summer).

VCH Staffordshire. I (1908) ed. Page, J.; II (1967) ed. Greenslade, M.; III (1970) ed. Greenslade, M.; IV (1958) ed. Midgley, M.; V (1959) ed. Midgley, M.; VI (1979) ed. Greenslade, M.; XVIII (1976) ed. Greenslade, M.; VIII (1963) ed. Jenkins, J. G.

VCH Warwickshire. I (1904) ed. Page, W.; II (1908) ed. Page, W.; III (1945) ed. Salzmann, E. F.; IV (1947) ed. Salzmann, E. F.; V (1949) ed. Salzmann, L. F.; VI (1951) ed. Salzmann, L. F.; VII (1967) ed. Stephens, W. B.; VIII (1969) ed. Stephens, W. B.

VCH Worcestershire. I (1901) ed. Doubleday, H. A.; II (1906) ed. Page, W.; III (1913) ed. Willis Bund, J.; IV (1924) ed. Willis Bund, J.

Wagstaffe, J. M. (1970) 'The economy of Dieulacres Abbey, 1214–1539', *North Staffordshire Journal of Field Studies*, x.

Walker, G. (1949) 'Population in Birmingham Black Country between the wars', *University of Birmingham Historical Journal*, 1, no. 1.

Walker, J. (1714) *An Attempt Towards Recovering an Account of the Numbers and Sufferings of the Clergy of the Church of England*, London.

Walmsley, J. F. R. (1968) 'The censorii of Burton Abbey and the Domesday population', *North Staffs. Journal of Field Studies*, viii, Keele.

Walmsley, J. F. R. (1972) 'The estate of Burton Abbey eleventh to fourteenth centuries', Birmingham PhD.

Warburton, W. H. (1931) *A History of Trades Unions Organisation in North Staffordshire Potteries*, Stoke on Trent.

Ward, D. M. (1946) *The Other Battle*, BSA.

Ward, J. (1843) *The Borough of Stoke on Trent*, Stoke on Trent.

Warrilow, E. J. D. (1960) *Sociological History of Stoke on Trent*, Stoke on Trent.

Watkins, A. (1981) 'The development of Coleshill in the Middle Ages', Warwickshire History, v, no. 6.

Watson, T. H. (1957) Reform Elections in Staffordshire 1831–2, BA Thesis, Birmingham University.

Watts, L. (1979–80) 'Birmingham Moat: its history, topography and destruction', *Transactions of the Birmingham Archaeological Society*, lxxxix.

WCR (1935–53) Calendar of the Quarter Sessions Order Books and Papers of Warwickshire 1625–1640. 8 vols, Johnson, H. E. (ed.) for the Warwickshire County Council.

WCR Hearth Tax, Vol. 1, Kineton Hundred.

Weatherill, L. (1971) *The Pottery Trade*, Manchester.

Wedge, J. (1794) *A General View of the Agriculture of Warwickshire*, London.

West Bromwich Library (17th and 18th centuries) Lissiemore Transcripts of papers relating to West Bromwich in the Public Record Office.

West Midlands Group (1948) *Conurbation*, Birmingham.

West Midlands Planning Authorities Conference (1972) *A Developing Strategy for the West Midlands*.

Wheatley, P. (1971) 'Staffordshire' in H. C. Darby and I. B. Ternels (eds), *Domesday Geography of Midland England*, Cambridge.

White, A. W. A. (1970) *Men and Mining in Warwickshire*, Coventry and North Warwickshire History Pamphlets, 7, Warwick.

White, A. W. A. (1971) 'Condition of mining labour on a Warwickshire estate before the industrial revolution', *Transactions of the Birmingham Archaeological Society*, lxxxiv.

White, A. W. A. (1972) Economic Growth of the Warwickshire Coalfield, PhD Birmingham.

White, W. (1850) *Directory of Coventry*, Sheffield.

White, W. (1873) *Friends in Warwickshire in the Seventeenth and Eighteenth Centuries*, Birmingham, Reprint London, 1894.

WHS (1893) 'Lay subsidy roll for the County of Worcester, circa 1280', Willis-Bund, J. W. and Amphlett, J. (eds), *Journal of Worcestershire Historical Society*, Oxford.

WHS (1893–7) 'The register of the diocese of Worcester during the vacancy of the see usually called *sede vacante* 1301–1435', Willis-Bund, J. W., 2 vols, Vol. 1.

WHS (1895) 'Lay subsidy roll for the County of Worcester, I. Edward III', Eld, J. F. (ed.), *Worcester Historical Society*, Oxford.

WHS (1898–1902) 'Episcopal registers diocese of Worcester register of Bishop Godfrey Giffard 1268–1301', 2 vols.

WHS (1899) 'Lay subsidy roll A.D. 1332–3', Amphlett, J. (ed.), *Worcestershire Historical Society*, Oxford.

WHS (1907) 'Register of the Gild of the Holy Cross Stratford on Avon', Bloom, J. H. (ed.), *Worcestershire Historical Society*, London.

WHS (1927) 'Register of Walter Reynolds – Bishop of Worcester 1308–1313', R. A. Wilson (ed.), *Worcestershire Historical Society*.

WHS (1907–29a) 'The register of William de Geynsborough Bishop of Worcester 1302–7', Willis Bird, J. W.

WHS (1907–29b) 'Register of William de Geynsborough Bishop of Worcester 1302–7', Willis Bird, Wilson, J. & R. A. (eds), *Worcestershire Historical Society*.

WHS (1930) 'Register of Thomas de Cobham', Pearce, E. H. (ed.) *Worcestershire Historical Society*, London.

WHS (1910–12) 'Court rolls of the manor of Hales 1230–1307', Amphlett, J. and Hamilton, S. G., *Worcestershire Historical Society*, 3 parts in 1 vol., Oxford, Reprint London, 1933.

WHS (1952) 'Halesowen Churchwardens' Accounts', F. Somers (ed.) *Worcestershire Historical Society, London*.

WHS (1963) 'The Court rolls of the manor of Bromsgrove and King's Norton', A. F. C. Baber (ed.), *Worcestershire Historical Society*, New series.

WHS (1966) 'A calendar of the register of Wolstan de Bransford', *Worcestershire Historical Society*, New series, iv, London.

WHS (1972) 'A calendar of the register of Henry Wakefield', W. P. Mareth (ed.), *Worcestershire Historical Society*, New series, vii.

WHS (1976) 'Register of Clifford Bishop of Worcester 1401–7', W. E. L. Smith (ed.), Toronto.

Wilde, P. D. (1975) 'Location problem of the English silk industry in the mid nineteenth century', in A. D. M. Phillips (ed.), *Environment Man and Economic Change*.

Wilde, P. D. (1979) 'Power supplies and the development of the silk industry', *North Staffordshire Journal of Field Studies*, xix.

Willan, T. S. (1951) 'The navigation of the river Weaver', *Transactions of the Chetham Society*, 3rd series, iii.

Williams, D. W. (1976) 'Midland hunger riots of 1766', *Midland History*, iii (Autumn).

Williams, I. A. (1931) *The Firm of Cadburys 1831–1931*, London.

Williams, S. (1967) *Farming in the Midlands*, London.

Willmore, F. (1887) *A History of Walsall and its Neighbourhood*, Walsall.

Wilson, P. R. (1979–80) 'Depopulation in Long Itchington Parish', *Warwickshire History*, iv, no. 4.

Wise, M. (1948) 'Factors in the growth of Birmingham', *Geography*, xxxiii.

Wise, M. J. (ed.) (1950) *Birmingham and its Regional Setting. A Scientific Survey*, Birmingham.

Wolverhampton Library (1512–1603) Churchwardens Accounts, transcribed by Tildesley, N. J.

Wood, A. C. (1950) 'A history of trade and transport on the River Trent', *Transactions of the Thoroton Society*, liv.

Wood, H. (1958) *Borough by Prescription*, Tamworth.

Wood, P. (1976) *Industrial Britain: The West Midlands*, David & Charles, Newton Abbot.

Woods, D. C. (1973) 'Borough magistracy of the Black Country', *Midland History*, iii, no. 3.

Woods, D. C. (1979) 'Borough magistracy of Black Country towns', *West Midland Studies*, xii.

Woods, D. C. (1982) 'Operation of the master and servants act in the Black Country 1858–1875', *Midland History*, vii.

Woods, R. (1978) 'Mortality and sanitary conditions in Birmingham 1870–1910', *Journal of Historical Geography*, iv.

Worcester Record Office (1671) Probate Records, William Hill of Oldswinford (May).

Wordie, J. R. (1974) 'Social change on the Levison Gower estates 1714–1832', *Economic History Review*, 2nd Series, xxvii, no. 3 (August).

Wordie, J. R. (1982) *Estate Management in Eighteenth Century England*, Royal Historical Society.

Worpell, J. G. (1976) 'The iron and coal trade of the south Staffordshire area 1843–1853', *West Midland Studies*, ix (Winter).

Wrightson, T. (1965) *New Triennial Directory of Birmingham 1818*, Reprint.

Wrigley, E. A. and Schofield, R. S. (1981), *The Population History of England 1541–1871*, A Reconstruction, London.

Yates, E. M. (1955) 'A contribution to the historical geography of north west Staffordshire', *Geographical Studies*, ii.

Yates, E. M. (1974) 'Enclosure and the rise of grass land farming in Staffordshire', *North Staffordshire Journal of Field Studies*, xiv.

Yates, E. M. (1975a) 'Aspects of Staffordshire farming in the seventeenth and eighteenth centuries', *North Staffordshire Journal of Field Studies*, xv.

Yates, E. M. (1975b) 'Aspects of open field agriculture in Staffordshire', in Philips, A. D. M. and Turton, B. J. (eds) *Environment Man and Economic Change*, London.

Index

Numbers in italics indicate a reference to a plate, figure or table.